Amarna Diplomacy

Amarna Diplomacy

The Beginnings of International Relations

EDITED BY

RAYMOND COHEN AND RAYMOND WESTBROOK

The Johns Hopkins University Press

Baltimore and London

Johns Hopkins Paperbacks edition, 2002
9 8 7 6 5 4 3 2 1

The Johns Hopkins University Press
2715 North Charles Street
Baltimore, Maryland 21218-4363
www.press.jhu.edu

Library of Congress Cataloging-in-Publication Data will be found
at the end of this book.
A catalog record for this book is available from the British Library.

ISBN 0-8018-7103-4 (pbk.)

To William L. Moran,
whose monumental contribution to Amarna studies
provided the inspiration for this project.

Contents

Preface

The chapters in this volume began life as contributions to a conference held September 17–19, 1996, at the Rockefeller conference center, Villa Serbelloni, Bellagio, Italy. We would like to thank the Rockefeller Foundation for making the conference possible by putting the center and its facilities at our disposal. The gracious hospitality of the director and staff of the Villa Serbelloni were instrumental in ensuring the success of our deliberations. We would also like to thank the Littauer Foundation and the Johns Hopkins University for their generous financial support toward the costs of conference travel and of publishing this volume. We incurred a further debt of gratitude to the Charles F. Singleton Center for Italian Studies of the Johns Hopkins University, whose director, Elizabeth Carter, made available to us the Villa Spelman, Florence, for the work of editing the conference papers. It is an especial pleasure to acknowledge the efforts of a number of individuals whose help was invaluable in realizing the project: Gilbert Bonnan of the Hebrew University of Jerusalem; Jane Dryer, secretary of the department of Near Eastern Studies, the Johns Hopkins University; and Dorothee Puccini, secretary of the Villa Spelman.

Abbreviations

AHW	*Akkadisches Handwörterbuch*
ANET	J. Pritchard, ed., *Ancient Near Eastern Texts Relating to the Old Testament*
ARE	J. Breasted, *Ancient Records of Egypt*
ARM	Archives royales de Mari
CAD	*Chicago Assyrian Dictionary*
EA	*Siglum* of Amarna texts following the edition of J. Knudtzon, *Die El-Amarna Tafeln,* Leipzig 1914. In this volume also applies to the translations in Moran, *The Amarna Letters*
KBo	Keilschrifttexte aus Boghazköi
KUB	Keilschrifturkunde aus Boghazköi
PM	B. Porter and R. Moss, *Topographical Bibliography*
PRU	Palais royal d'Ugarit, C. Schaeffer, Mission de Ras Shamara
TT	Theban Tomb
Urk. IV	K. Sethe and W. Helck, *Urkunden der 18. Dynastie*
YOS	Yale Oriental Series, Babylonian Texts

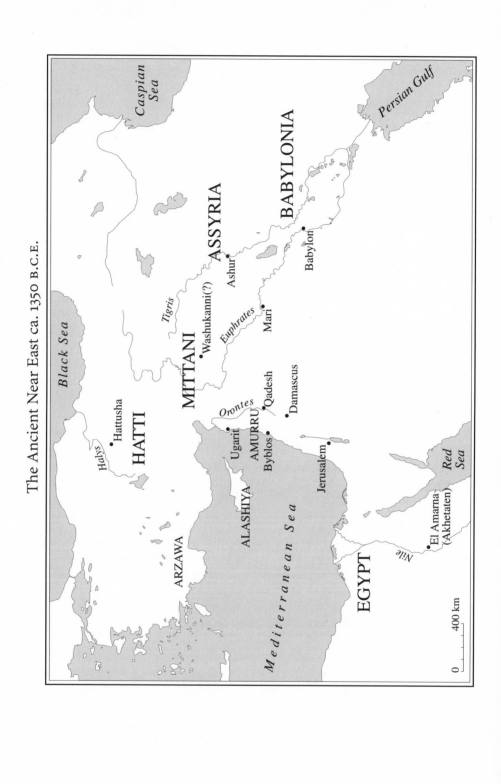

The Ancient Near East ca. 1350 B.C.E.

Table of Events

Ancient Near Eastern historians use a confusing variety of archaeological, linguistic, and historiographic terms to refer to chronological periods. Those of relevance here are:

1. The *Middle Bronze Age,* ca. 2000–1550 B.C.E. In Mesopotamia, the same period is also called the *Old Babylonian* (OB) Period. Its best-known figure is king Hammurabi of Babylon. In Egypt, it is roughly equivalent to the *Middle Kingdom* and the *Second Intermediate Period.*
2. The *Late Bronze Age,* ca. 1500–1100 B.C.E. The *Amarna Age* (fourteenth century) falls within this period. In Mesopotamia, it is known as the *Middle Babylonian* (/*Middle Assyrian*) Period. In Egypt, it is the period of the *New Kingdom,* which comprised Dynasties 18-20. The kings of the Amarna correspondence are among the later kings of the Eighteenth Dynasty. Dynasties 19-20 were known as the Ramesside era.

Although the broad sequence of events in the Late Bronze Age is clear, there is considerable uncertainty not only about details but about chronology (relative as well as absolute). This table uses the dating adopted in J. Sasson, ed., *Civilizations of the Ancient Near East,* 4 vols. (New York: Charles Scribner's Sons, 1995). Events that occur at an uncertain time within the period are marked by an asterisk.

ca. 1580	Kassite Dynasty takes control of Babylonia
1539–1514	Ahmose, king in Egypt. Eighteenth Dynasty begins
	*Consolidation of Hurrian kingdom called Mittani
1514–1493	Amenhotep I, king in Egypt. Egyptians acquire empire in Nubia
	*Assyria becomes vassal of Mittani

Egypt's sphere of interest in Western Asia

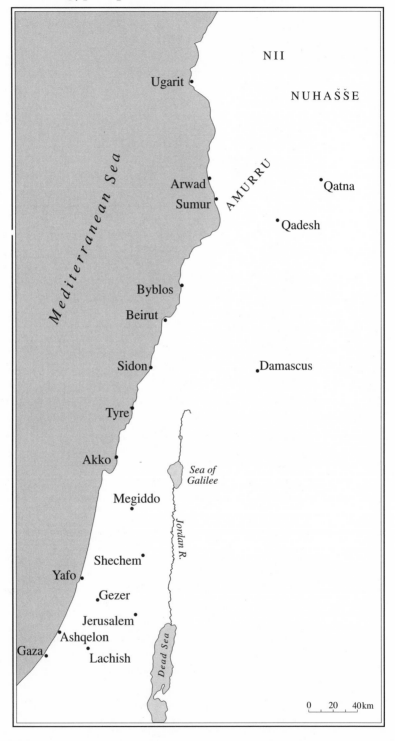

NII

NUHAŠŠE

Ugarit

AMURRU

Qatna

Arwad
Sumur

Qadesh

Mediterranean Sea

Byblos
Beirut

Sidon

Damascus

Tyre

Akko

*Sea of
Galilee*

Megiddo

Jordan R.

Shechem

Yafo

Gezer

Jerusalem
Ashqelon

Gaza
Lachish

Dead Sea

0   20   40km

1493–1483	Thutmose I, king in Egypt. Campaign in Western Asia: first hostile encounter with Mittani
1479–1425	Thutmose III, king in Egypt. Egyptians defeat Canaanite coalition at Megiddo: beginning of Egyptian empire in western Asia. Regency of Hatshepsut (until 1458) *Assyria frees itself from Mittanian rule
1425–1400	Amenhotep II, king in Egypt. *Artatama I, king in Mittani
1400–1390	Thutmose IV, king in Egypt. Peace between Egypt and Mittani. Thutmose IV marries daughter of Artatama I
1390–1353	Amenhotep III, king in Egypt *Shuttarna II, king in Mittani. Amenhotep III marries his daughter Gilu-Hepa (1380) *Tushratta, king in Mittani *Suppiluliuma I, king in Hatti *Kurigalzu I, king in Babylonia. Amenhotep III marries his daughter **Beginning of Amarna Archive** *Kadashman-Enlil I king in Babylonia (to 1376?) *'Abdi-Ashirta consolidates Amurru under his rule *Hittite foray into north Syria *'Abdi-Ashirta is killed *Amenhotep III marries daughter of Tushratta
ca. 1375–1347	Burnaburiash II, king in Babylonia
1353–1336	Amenhotep IV (Akhenaten), king in Egypt.
1349	Amenhotep IV changes his name to Akhenaten and establishes the Aten's cult center in a new city at el-Amarna *Aziru and other "sons of 'Abdi-Ashirta" reestablish their father's kingdom *Suppiluliuma I campaigns in Syria *Assyria under Assur-Uballit I (1366–1322) enters into diplomatic relations with Egypt *Rib-Hadda of Byblos is exiled
1336–1322	Ephemeral rule in Egypt of Nefernefruaten and Smenkhkare
1332–1322	Tutankhamun, king in Egypt **Amarna archive ends** *Tushratta is assassinated; civil war in Mittani; end of Mittani as a great power
1322–1319	Ay, king in Egypt. Tutankhamun's widow asks Suppiluliuma

Amarna Diplomacy

CHAPTER ONE

Introduction: The Amarna System

RAYMOND COHEN AND RAYMOND WESTBROOK

The Amarna Project

In 1887, a remarkable cache of documents was found at Tell el-Amarna in
Egypt, the ancient site of the palace of King Amenhotep IV (better known
as Akhenaten) in Akhetaten, his abandoned capital. It consisted of 350 or so
letters from the mid-fourteenth century B.C.E. between the Egyptian court
of the Eighteenth Dynasty and other states of the ancient Near East. The letters were edited in 1907 by J. A. Knudtzon, who attempted to place them
in chronological and geographical order. His numbering system is still used
(with the siglum "EA") and accepted as a reasonably accurate guide to the sequence of letters. In 1992 W. L. Moran, of Harvard University, published the
letters in English, drawing on almost a century of scholarship. In so doing he
made the archive available to the general reader and provided the key stimu-
lus to the present project.

The letters themselves can be grouped under three headings: The *international* correspondence consists of about fifty diplomatic documents mostly
sent to Pharaoh by the rulers of other Great Powers and lesser independent
states. A wide variety of subjects are dealt with: dynastic questions, particularly marriage, the exchange of gifts, alliance and strategic matters, trade,
legal problems, the mechanics of diplomacy. Although the files are very incomplete, taken together they provide a rare insight into the international
relations of the time. The second batch of more than three hundred *imperial* documents consists of administrative correspondence mainly sent to
the Egyptian court from Egypt's Canaanite (western Asian) empire. Many of
the letters deal with the vassals' domestic problems, quarrels between vas-

sals, trade and tribute, and internal security. The wider strategic question of Egypt's relations with its neighbors is also touched upon, providing a common thread between the international and imperial correspondence. A third batch of documents, not included in Moran's compilation, were intended for training purposes in school and are beyond the scope of this book.

This volume of essays arises out of a workshop on the Amarna Letters that was held at the Bellagio Study and Conference Center of the Rockefeller Foundation from September 17 to 19, 1996. The participants were eight historians of the ancient Near East, eight scholars from the social sciences specializing in contemporary international relations, and two working diplomats. Over several days of intensive discussion we attempted to shed new light on the documents themselves and on the system of diplomacy they depict, to reconstruct the international relations of the ancient Near East, and to identify universal features of international politics.

The sixteen essays in this volume have been revised and edited in light of the discussions that took place at the conference. Although the diplomats, Ambassador Robbie Sabel and Mr. Avi Binyamin, were unable to participate in this stage of the project, the other members of the workshop benefited greatly from their presentations, comments, and anecdotes from practical experience, the influence of which are discernible in the written contributions.

In what follows, we have tried to retain the spirit of dialogue that prevailed at the original conference and deliberately avoided segregating "ancient" from "modern" approaches. Our starting point is the international system, the set of (in this case) states in regular interaction and contact. It is the system that provides the context and structure within which component entities are constrained to act. From the whole, we move on to a study of the part: Egyptian foreign and imperial policies, reflecting the goals and needs generated by Egypt's involvement in the wider system. At a third and final level of analysis, we examine the pragmatic aspects of diplomacy between the Great Powers: the system of mutually beneficial exchanges of goods, gods, and persons; negotiating tactics; and the diplomatic mechanisms that were called upon to implement policy and manage relationships.

The volume is thus an interdisciplinary effort, which will, it is hoped, be of inherent interest to scholars and students in many fields. The results must, however, be justified also in terms of the contributory disciplines individually.

From the point of view of the ancient Near Eastern specialist, this project is an opportunity to apply to the Amarna Letters concepts and tools of analysis drawn from the social sciences in general and international relations in particular. A century of intensive work by specialists has resulted in considerable advances in our understanding of the script and language of the Letters. Where not broken, the text can be deciphered and translated at least literally with reasonable confidence. Progress on the understanding of the content of the Letters has been considerably less satisfactory. Little correlation has been made between the seemingly trivial issues, the disingenuous or hysterical rhetoric, and the repetitive arguments of the ancient rulers, on the one hand, and the system of international relations that forms the context for their discourse, on the other. It remains unclear how these elements fit into and form the system.

The reason is not hard to find: most specialized scholars, being essentially trained in philology, are ill-equipped to examine the Letters as political documents. Yet it is as political documents that they are most important. The Amarna Letters represent the culmination of a tradition, developed over centuries, through which states might communicate with one another in a common language, might pursue their interests and resolve their differences by reference to common standards and conventions, and might inform themselves of and accept or resist the moves of their neighbors without necessarily resorting to war. An accurate translation of the Letters' content, still less an analysis of their implications, is not possible unless the concepts that underlie them are properly appreciated.

In recent years, more sophisticated techniques adopted from the social sciences have been used by historians of the period. A further step is needed, however, if this approach is to be fully exploited, namely, the inclusion of experts from the social sciences, in particular from political science, in the process of analysis. On the one hand, enormous cultural and material differences exist between the community of the ancient Near Eastern Great Kings and the present global community represented by the United Nations. On the other, it is often assumed that there are certain constants in the conduct of international actors that are predicated on the logic of international interaction and the structure of the international community. Through cooperation across disciplines, culturally grounded forms of expression can be interpreted in terms of responses to invariable problems. Rational choice and decision-making theory, strategic and geopolitical analysis, anthropology and psychology, intelligence and diplomatic theory, and the tool kit of ideas drawn upon by political scientists can all shed light on the Amarna material.

The advantage for ancient historians in interpreting the Letters is that they gain a context within which to place apparently meaningless or pointless statements. The *political* context is provided to essentially *political* communications, inadequately understood because dressed in the discourse of ancient cultures that did not have at their disposal the vocabulary of modern analytical thought. Through this medium, the text can be analyzed in terms of our own culture and indeed translated into its language(s).

For the international relations scholar, this exercise presents a fascinating challenge. Although incomplete, the Amarna correspondence contains sufficient material to permit concerted study in reasonable depth of the first *international system* known to us. It is in the Amarna period that we observe for the first time the Great Powers of the entire Near East, from the Mediterranean to the Persian Gulf, interacting among themselves, engaged in regular dynastic, commercial, and strategic relations. The mechanism for the political management of this interconnected set of relationships was Amarna diplomacy, a diplomatic regime consisting of rules, conventions, procedures, and institutions governing the representation of and the communication and negotiation between Great Kings.

The more elaborate justification for this project is as an exercise in broadening horizons. Since its inception after the First World War as a discipline in its own right, international relations has in effect sought to achieve two complementary goals: theoretical understanding of the abiding nature of relations across sovereign collectivities and greater insight into contemporary international affairs. Often, preoccupation with current issues — the United Nations, the Cold War, regional integration, globalization — has determined the theoretical agenda. With some distinguished exceptions, this has meant that generalizations about international relations are derived from a narrow database drawn, at best, from the nineteenth and twentieth centuries. If we assume that sovereign collectivities have engaged in more or less regular international contact for at least 4,500 years, it can be seen that modern scholars have tended to restrict their attention to about 200 of those years, or only 4 percent of this immense span of time.

While there is every justification for the policy analyst or current affairs specialist concentrating on the present and recent past, there is no reason for the theorist concerned to interpret the deeper forces at work to ignore 96 percent of international history. For many of the international phenomena we investigate, the number of cases in the contemporary period is quite small, hindering meaningful comparative analysis. Preoccupation with a few well-known events of the twentieth century, the Sarajevo–Munich–Suez–Cuba syndrome, is particularly restrictive and misleading. Obviously, adequate data are not available for the entire four millennia; but where they are, there is surely a good case to be made for reflecting on and comparing as broad a range of variations of these phenomena as possible.

Consideration of remote periods certainly has its difficulties and drawbacks. Making sense of the Amarna Letters, even in translation, is harder than reading *Foreign Relations of the United States*. It requires substantial background knowledge and interdisciplinary dialogue. But it is worth the effort. Most hypotheses about international behavior are based on the received truths of the age or the experience of the observer. Testing those hypotheses *synchronically* against recent events risks circular reasoning, or "proving" something with the same evidence used to generate it in the first place. It is more suggestive and methodologically sound to work *diachronically,* deriving hypotheses from one period and testing them against another. Thus, the Amarna Letters enable us to investigate the validity or explanatory utility of controversial modern assumptions, concepts, and theories in a totally unfamiliar setting.

To put it another way, comparison of the working of international systems thousands of years apart enables us to put things in their historical context, to think beyond the short term. Students of the present never really know how things work out; they have difficulty enough identifying salient trends. When we study ancient periods, we acquire limitless hindsight; we can determine consequences over the long run in a way that is impossible for the student of contemporary affairs.

True, ancient history lacks immediate "relevance," narrowly defined. But this remoteness from contemporary concerns is educative about such fundamental features of the contemporary international system as states, national identities, borders, sovereignty, government, international law, the balance of power, diplomacy, and so on. Are these permanent or transitory features of international life? How have these concepts been understood in times past? Have functional equivalents to them existed?

Remoteness can also aid objectivity. Many writers in the West care very much if democratic government and economic interdependence promote peace, if alliances and armaments are conducive to stability or its opposite, or if diplomacy and international law are essential to conflict resolution. Since we live in the present, we are concerned with and involved in consequences. Even ostensibly theoretical research may serve, consciously or not, some policy agenda. The debate over the validity of the democratic-peace theory is a case in point. Such commitment may contaminate data and bias analysis. All the more reason for investigating, whenever we can, such subjects far away and long ago. Who cares if the Hittites or Hurrians prevailed?

Despite the seeming irrelevance of ancient history, we would also argue that some contemporary issues are amenable to investigation in the context of Amarna (and other historical periods). An example is the sources of international stability. The Amarna system existed for at least two hundred years, with few major wars between the Great Powers. Are there possible lessons here? How did Great Kings avoid war? What mechanisms of conflict resolution, if at all, did they resort to?

The Amarna Correspondents

The Amarna Letters span the reigns of the Egyptian Eighteenth Dynasty rulers Amenhotep III (called Mimmureya/Nimu'wareya/Nibmureya in the Letters) and Akhenaten (=Amenhotep IV, called Naphurureya in the Letters), and possibly another king, Smenkhkare or Tutankhamun. Akhenaten is famous for his religious revolution, in which he concentrated official worship on the sun god, Aten. His accession to the throne is recorded in the Letters and provides a major chronological reference point. It appears to have had unsettling effects on Egypt's neighbors.

All but about ten of the documents are letters received by the Egyptian court. The correspondents may be divided into three categories: fellow Great Powers, independent states, and Egypt's vassals in Canaan.

Great Powers

The period from the late sixteenth to the twelfth century B.C.E. is referred to by Near Eastern archaeologists as the Late Bronze Age. In political terms, it has been called the "Great Powers' Club," because the area was divided up among a few major powers who regarded themselves as members of an exclusive group. Their rulers were entitled to call themselves "Great King" and to use the term "brotherhood" to describe their relationship. *Egypt* had joined the club in the fifteenth century, after the campaigns of Thutmose III had taken Egyptian arms as far as the Euphrates and won for Egypt an empire in Canaan. The other members, and correspondents with Egypt in the Amarna Letters, were Mittani, Babylonia, Hatti, and Assyria.

Mittani (EA 17–30), also known as Hanigalbat and as Nahrin, was centered in northern Syria, between the Tigris and the Euphrates, with its capital at Washukanni (exact location as yet undiscovered). It was often referred to as the land of the Hurrians, after its main ethnic component, which had coalesced in the fifteenth century to form a major empire. Egyptian expansion had led to war between the two kingdoms, which had been resolved by a truce and later by a marriage alliance. By the time of the Letters, it was an old ally. The sole correspondent in the Letters is King Tushratta. Later, Tushratta was assassinated and his kingdom destroyed by internecine warfare. His son Shattiwaza fled to the Hittites, who reinstalled him on the throne of a much-reduced kingdom as a vassal.

Babylonia (EA 1–11) is also called Karaduniyash or Shanhar in the Letters. At the end of the sixteenth century, it had been taken over by a foreign dynasty, the Kassites, who had, however, quickly assimilated. Its correspondents in the Letters were the Kassite king Kadashman-Enlil I and his successor Burra(/Burna)-Buriyash II.

Hatti (EA 41–44) was a kingdom in eastern Anatolia that had been founded by the Hittites in the early second millennium B.C.E. It is sometimes called after its capital, Hattusha. After decline in the early fifteenth century, its fortunes were revived by King Suppiluliuma, who invaded Syria, taking vassals from Mittani and eventually from Egypt. He is the sole correspondent with Egypt, Mittani being the victim of Hittite expansion at the time of the Letters, and Egypt's turn coming only shortly thereafter.

After the death of Tutankhamun, to whom one letter (EA 41) may be addressed, an agreement with his widow to marry Suppiluliuma's son failed when the Hittite prince died on the way to Egypt, possibly murdered by the widow's opponents. This led to armed reprisals by the Hittites. By their own account, Egyptian prisoners brought back to Hatti carried with them an epidemic that ravaged the kingdom for some years, killing Suppiluliuma himself. Intermittent warfare with Egypt followed for the next fifty years, culminating in the battle of Qadesh, a direct clash between the imperial armies under Suppiluliama's grandson Muwatalli and Ramesses II, respectively. No decisive victory was won, but the Hittites appear to have had the upper hand. Sixteen years later, Muwatalli's successor, Hattusili III, concluded a peace treaty with Ramesses II.

Assyria (EA 15–16) had been a vassal of Mittani but, by the time of the Letters, had not only broken free but was asserting itself as a Great Power. Its king, Assur-uballit, was an energetic monarch responsible for a major expansion of territory. His establishing diplomatic relations with Egypt led to protests by the Babylonian king Burra-Buriyash (EA 9), but apparently he later made his peace with Babylonia, marrying his daughter to Burra-Buriyash's son. Relations with Hatti were troubled, as the two states vied for control of the former territory of Mittani, with Hatti reluctant to admit Assyria into the Great Powers' club.

Independent States

The two independent states that appear in the Amarna Letters are Arzawa and Alashiya. *Arzawa* (EA 31–2) was a medium-size power on the south Anatolian coast west of the Hittite sphere of influence. It was courted by Egypt with the proposition of a diplomatic marriage. *Alashiya* (EA 33–40) was a kingdom located on Cyprus. Known as a source of copper, it conducted extensive trade with Egypt.

Vassal States

By far the largest component of the archive is the letters from some forty vassals of Egypt in Syria-Palestine (EA 45-339, 362-67, 369-71, 378, 382). Of course, they are by no means equally represented, nor does the quantity of correspondence bear any relation to their size or importance. Important buffer states in the north, such as Ugarit and Damascus, are represented by a mere handful of letters, while the bulk of the letters are from a single hand, that of Rib-Hadda of Byblos. The most noteworthy Egyptian vassals in the Amarna Letters were the following:

Amurru (EA 60-67,156-71). One of the northernmost vassals of Egypt and a gateway to Syria, it flourished under the charismatic leadership of 'Abdi-Ashirta, who expanded its territory at the expense of the neighboring kingdoms. 'Abdi-Ashirta constantly claimed to be a loyal vassal of Egypt (EA 60-65), which appears initially to have tolerated his actions, in spite of the constant warnings of Rib-Hadda, ruler of Byblos. However, his expansion must have reached a point where it threatened Egyptian interests, perhaps after he had occupied the Egyptian garrison at Sumur, claiming to have rescued it from another set of raiders. The Egyptians sent an expedition; 'Abdi-Ashirta was captured and taken to Egypt (EA 108, 117), where he apparently was executed (EA 101).

'Abdi-Ashirta was succeeded by his numerous sons, headed by Aziru, who set about restoring the fortunes of their kingdom. Again, they pursued a policy of local expansion while at the same time placating the Egyptians and seeking to be accepted as a loyal vassal (EA 156-71). Aziru was summoned to Egypt and managed to persuade the Egyptian king of his good intentions. He was permitted to return home, ostensibly to face the new menace of Hittite forces on the northern border. Aziru, however, was playing a double game: while pretending to protect Egyptian interests, he was negotiating with the Hittites. The Egyptians became suspicious when they discovered that Aziru was in consort with Aitukama of Qadesh, at that point a Hittite ally (EA 162; cf. EA 59, from the citizens of Tunip). Aziru eventually went over to the Hittites and remained their loyal vassal for the rest of his reign.

Byblos (Gubla) (EA 68-138, 362, + 139-40). Its ruler, Rib-Hadda, was the most prolific of all the Amarna correspondents. He tirelessly complained of the dangers to his kingdom and his own position caused by the expansion of 'Abdi-Ashirta and later of Aziru. He had the satisfaction of seeing 'Abdi-

Ashirta fall but was then deposed himself by his brother and sent into exile (EA 137–38).

Shechem (Šakmu) (EA 252–54). Its ruler, Lab'ayu, had a career similar to that of 'Abdi-Ashirta of Amurru. Lab'ayu expanded at the expense of his neighbors, provoking their complaints to Pharaoh (e.g., Biridiya of Megiddo, EA 244), while he continued to protest his loyalty and good intentions. He was eventually captured, apparently by the Egyptians or at their order, but his sons replaced him and continued his policy.

Qadesh (Qidšu/Qinsa) (EA 189–90). This city represented the northern-most edge of Egyptian influence. At the time of the Letters, it was ruled by Aitukama, who went over to the Hittites and consorted with Aziru of Amurru in attacking other Egyptian vassals on the Hittites' behalf (cf. EA 151, 162, 175–76, 363). The city and its territory became a bone of contention between Egypt and Hatti and changed hands several times in the decades leading up to their peace treaty. It was also noteworthy as the site of the greatest battle of the Egyptian-Hittite war.

Damascus (EA 194–97). Like Amurru and Qadesh, this was an important northern buffer state. It suffered for its loyalty to Egypt by being attacked by the latter two (EA 151; cf. EA 189). It was ruled by Biryawaza, who was note-worthy for being the subject of a protest to Pharaoh by the Babylonian king for robbing a Babylonian caravan (EA 7).

Ugarit (EA 45–49). Although it does not figure prominently in the Letters, Ugarit was a wealthy and very important port city on the Syrian coast. Shortly after the period of the Letters, it was absorbed by the Hittites into their empire and became a loyal Hittite vassal.

A word of explanation is necessary about the *'Apiru (/ḫabiru/ḫapiru),* who receive frequent mention in the vassal correspondence. There is much dispute as to their identity, but they were apparently landless elements or fugitives who, as brigands, attacked the settled areas or hired themselves out as mercenaries. In the Letters, the word is also used as a general term of abuse in denouncing one's opponents.

Script and Language

Although the archive was located in Egypt, the Letters are written on clay tablets in cuneiform script, the writing system used throughout western Asia at the time. The language of most of the Letters is Akkadian (Babylonian), which was the lingua franca of international relations. In their correspondence with the Egyptian overlord, the vassals relied on a local version of Akkadian containing many words and grammatical forms from their own regional dialect. In corresponding with Arzawa, which evidently did not have the facilities to make translations into Akkadian, the Egyptians used Hittite. One letter from Mittani (EA 24) is in Hurrian, for reasons that are not clear. The Egyptian language does not appear to have been used at all in international correspondence.

The reason why the powers, great and small, preferred to use Akkadian, a language utterly foreign to most of them, was that it served as a lingua franca through which they could conduct their relations. In attempting to define *lingua franca* Professor Moran has drawn our attention to the concept of an *interlanguage,* an artificial development designed to serve as a neutral intermediary between different cultures.[1] In social science, this would be called a medium for constructing intersubjective reality in a world of many cultures.

It is in its *polycultural* nature that the Amarna system may have the most to teach us. By polycultural, we mean a society in which different cultures coexist on equal terms. *Multiculturalism* refers usually to the tolerance of minority cultures by a dominant culture.[2] Since the Renaissance, the international system has been dominated by European culture and values. Until very recently, great civilizations such as China, Egypt, India, and Iran were not admitted as full-fledged members of the diplomatic club. The great challenge facing the contemporary international system in the future will be to accommodate non-Western civilizations not as tolerated minority cultures but as equal cultures in their own right. The only precedent for a viable polycultural system is Amarna. Speaking totally unrelated languages, worshipping an assortment of gods, possessing widely divergent cosmologies, the rulers of the Amarna Age were nevertheless able to sustain a viable international system over a long period.

Amarna and Its Antecedents

The Amarna system does not mark the absolute beginning of international relations in history. The first decipherable written records from the early third millennium B.C.E. already reveal a world composed of organized polities in the form of city-states, which exchanged envoys; negotiated, formed, and broke alliances; and made treaties in solemn form. From mid-third millennium Syria we have preserved a treaty, apparently on equal terms, between Ebla and the neighboring kingdom of Abar-SAL, and from Mesopotamia of the same period another treaty, possibly of vassalage, between King Naram-Sin of Akkad and an Elamite ruler.

The forms, conventions, and rules of international relations had been developing for hundreds, perhaps thousands, of years in Mesopotamia, based on necessity (in the absence of a hegemon), trial and error, and that silent form of diplomacy, international trade. But they did not yet amount to an international system. The early second millennium saw further development, as the whole of Mesopotamia and Syria was divided among rival city-states striving for hegemony, a situation that led to a frenetic pace of diplomatic activity, with alliances made and broken, and mini-empires won and lost, as reflected in the correspondence of the Mari archive. The success of the best-known figure of the Mari Age, King Hammurabi of Babylon, in forging most of Mesopotamia into a single if ephemeral empire, was due as much to his diplomatic as to his military skills. At the same time, this too was not yet a full-fledged *international* system: it was confined to the city-states of Meso-potamia/Syria, with their close cultural, linguistic, and religious ties, and to kingdoms on the periphery such as Elam, which historically had been part of the same cuneiform civilization, and it was characterized by almost constant warfare, diplomacy being an ad hoc tool in the process of empire building. It was only in the Amarna Age that the horizons of diplomacy expanded to the whole of the ancient Near East and acquired the concept of a group of equal powers, a "club," membership in which gave responsibilities as well as privileges.

It was a system that, although not static, gave a modicum of stability and peace to the region for more than two centuries. Mittani, "the sick man of the Near East," lost its empire and was reduced to a vassal state, but this was as much due to civil war as to external pressure. There were minor skir-mishes and clashes with vassals as surrogates, but major battles, such as that between Hatti and Egypt at Qadesh or between Assyria and Hatti at Nih-riya, were rare and exceptional events. The Hittite archive from Boghazköi, the other point of reference for the extended Amarna Age, records the sys-tem still functioning a hundred years after the letters in the Amarna archive were written. When the system finally collapsed, bringing about a period of turmoil that was marked in particular by the disappearance of Hatti from history, it was not from reasons inherent in the system, such as institutional decay or warfare between the Great Powers, but from the intrusion of outside forces. When civilization reasserted itself, it was in the form of hegemonic empires, which gave less scope for diplomacy, although they continued to use the concepts and instruments refined during the Amarna Age, many of which passed into the Greek and Hebrew spheres and thus came to form part of the heritage of modern international relations.

The Amarna system was, therefore, not the beginning of international re-lations nor was it a dead end, but to borrow a Churchillian phrase, it was the end of the beginning. It was the culmination of an organic development that drew together the elements of native Mesopotamian statecraft into a machinery for truly managing international relations. Not until the Amarna Age, in the circumstances of a multipolar, polycultural system encompassing the Great Powers of the ancient Near East, could the machinery of statecraft achieve its full potential, traversing immense barriers of distance, language, culture, and political tradition. In the following pages we explore how and why it did so, and what were the consequences.

PART I

The International System

CHAPTER TWO

'The Great Powers' Club

MARIO LIVERANI

International Relations in the Amarna Age: Some Interpretive Trends

Since the discovery of the Amarna Letters in 1887, it has become clear that the ancient Near Eastern polities maintained intensive and sophisticated relations among themselves, and that such relations were formalized according to standard procedures. Not by chance, the first presentation of those documents to the English-speaking world bore the title "Oriental Diplomacy," and the obvious similarity of ancient and modern procedures was emphasized.[1]

At the end of the nineteenth century, nothing similar was known for other periods of ancient Oriental history. When additional documents were recovered — in the Hittite capital of Boghazköi[2] and in the Syrian city-states of Ugarit[3] and Alalakh[4] — the label "Amarna Age," besides referring to its precise chronological limits, was also used in a wider sense, in order to define the entire Late Bronze period (ca. 1550–1200 B.C.E.), especially when dealing with international relations.

In the meantime, however, other international networks, especially from earlier periods, happened to be brought to light by the discovery of rich archives, so that scholars started speaking about a "Mari Age" in the eighteenth century[5] and, more recently, of an "Ebla Age" in the twenty-fourth century.[6] The Amarna Letters cannot any longer be considered exceptional: a formalized system of international relations existed through the entire course of ancient Near Eastern history, while the quality and amount of the extant data varies, due to the obvious vagaries in the archaeological recovery of cuneiform tablets.

While the interpretation of the Amarna Letters as diplomatic documents has always been current among ancient Near Eastern historians, scholars in the field of international relations, dealing basically with our contemporary world, had and still have obvious problems with awareness of the existence of such remote material and with acceptance of its relevance to their own discipline. Nevertheless, use of the Amarna (and similar) texts in the framework of general histories of ancient diplomacy has been an established fact at least since Numelin's *Beginnings of Diplomacy.*

The problem has become more relevant after World War II and the subsequent process of decolonization. As a side effect of major political and economic changes, the historical and social sciences had to change their paradigms, transforming themselves from Eurocentric to multicentric. This is true both of ancient history and of international relations: the emergence of different traditions, the enlargement of data in space and backward in time, require a complete rethinking of the very bases of those disciplines. The study of international relations in the framework of political sciences had been founded on contemporary data and a strictly Eurocentric tradition — both presuppositions now about to be put in doubt. The study of the Amarna Letters is just one contribution (and a minor one at that) that can help us to generate an enlarged and historically deepened view of interstate relations.

In such a transformation, it might be useful to make reference to a well-known historiographical debate about the interpretation of ancient economies in terms that have been labeled "modernist" and "primitivist," a dilemma that can be applied to the study of ancient political relations as well.[7] The modernist approach, largely predominant in the first half of our century, presumed that the "laws" regulating economic (or in our case, political) relations, and reconstructed on the sole basis of modern (or even strictly contemporary) evidence, are valid for the history of mankind. The primitivist approach, on the other hand, presumes that every society, or at least every evolutionary stage, has its own laws, so that an analysis of ancient economy in terms of modern market would be largely deceptive.

To some extent, this is also true for our topic: an implicitly modernist approach, especially by scholars with juridical training, considered the legal documents, including international documents like treaties and letters, in the framework of a juridical terminology and conceptualization that had been built on a tradition continuing from Roman law to modern laws and procedures.[8] Oriental diplomacy received rather poor treatment in such a context, as characterized by a prevalent despotic (and therefore selfish) form of rule and by an endemic bent for bargaining and deception.

It was during the 1960s, in connection with already mentioned trend toward decolonization and multipolarity, that new vistas were transferred from disciplines such as semiotics, political anthropology, and economic anthropology to the study of ancient Near Eastern texts, including the Amarna Letters. A part of those studies, however, were produced by our "Rome school" and published in Italian, so that they remained partly unknown or undervalued in the English-speaking world.[9] Only recently have they been more widely accepted and used.

The previously mentioned dilemma between a modernist and a primitivist reading of our data, is also related to the literary form of the texts. A strictly juridical analysis has obviously been privileged in the case of international treaties, whereas letters would appear better suited to a kind of decoding that takes due account of their embeddedness in the social setting of their time. The discussion below shows that the Amarna Letters are basically built on a small-scale model, are of a rather primitive outlook and of a social rather than a properly political nature, so their interpretation can reach a deeper level by taking into account such an anthropological approach. However, recourse to ethnographic parallels, while certainly useful for enlarging the set of possible scenarios and for understanding alien behavior,[10] should not be used to lower the level, scale, and formalization of the ancient Near Eastern states so as to assimilate them to much simpler and smaller tribal communities or embryonic polities. Comparison must be a tool for understanding, not a rationale for leveling.

The peculiar character of the epistolary documents is more easily understood by contrasting it with other kinds of texts.[11] On the one hand, the concepts of border, tribute, alliance, political dependence, etc., are defined in the properly juridical texts (especially the international treaties) in precise and unequivocal terms and with the evident aim of establishing fixed reference points for possible litigation. On the other hand, different kinds of texts have different purposes, different semiological configurations, and deserve a different kind of analysis. Royal inscriptions, as is well known, deal with the very same subjects of war and peace, border and tribute, but with the aim of getting political acceptance. Therefore, they are best analyzed in terms of propaganda or, more generally, of persuasive messages.

As for letters, they also belong to the class of persuasive messages (although quite distinct from the royal inscriptions), and their statements cannot be taken at face value, as statements of fact.[12] In decoding a letter, especially a diplomatic letter, the logic and procedures of bargaining, of rhetorical argument, of emotional metaphors, are much more apposite than a strictly juridical logic.

Family Metaphors and the "Enlarged Village"

It is immediately evident, even on a cursory reading of the Amarna Letters exchanged between "Great Kings,"[13] that international relations were shaped on the model of interpersonal relations currently obtaining at the level of face-to-face communities: family or village or neighborhood.[14] Since time immemorial, we presume, relations with external groups had taken place in forms like hospitality, intermarriage, and exchange of services and goods, whereby the procedures of inner relationships in daily life were reused, in a slightly modified form, in order to fulfill a new and rarer purpose.

The family metaphor is immediately evident in the pervasive use of the term "my brother" (*aḫī*) to address the partner (the "my father" (*abī*) metaphor being reserved for a more aged partner). Yet the most suitable model for external relations could not be the nuclear family or the self-sufficient household but rather the small community, the village or neighborhood or clan within which the individual families would interact. From the most trivial but socially meaningful usage, to "ask (news of) the health" (*šulma ša'ālu*) of the partner (plus his wife, children, belongings, etc.),[15] to the most demanding negotiations for interdynastic marriages, the interpersonal level is the only one in use. No other "code" has been introduced to regulate interstate, strictly political relations.

Such a state of affairs is only too obvious in the case (the only one attested in antiquity) of patrimonial states, belonging to the person and family of the king and identified with him. It is also true that the actual practice of intermarriage among the royal houses made the "brotherhood" terminology something more than an abstract metaphor.[16] Yet sometimes we get the impression that the "enlarged village" syndrome was conditioning the relationships well beyond its expressive use.

EA 7, from the Babylonian king Burna-Buriash to Akhenaten, is representative of such a syndrome. The usual exchange of greetings (the above-mentioned *šulma ša'ālu* formula), which was normally perceived as a pure formality, is here enlarged and elaborated as if Pharaoh should in fact know that the Babylonian king had been sick.[17] The distance (more than 2,000 km) is eliminated in order to address the partner with a complaint (for not sending any message wishing him a quick recovery) that would be perfectly appropriate for social interrelationships in the limited environment of village or neighborhood but is only paradoxical in a long-distance epistolary exchange.

Exactly the same oddity is to be found in EA 3, the protest by the Babylonian king Kadashman-Enlil at not having been invited to a feast in the

Egyptian residency at Amarna, and in his demonstrative counterinvitation of Pharaoh to a feast at Babylon.[18] This kind of failure of reciprocity, impoliteness, and lack of regard is a constant problem in a small-scale society but is odd when transferred to relations between such distant courts.

The same could apply to the refusal by the Babylonian king in still another letter (EA 11:21–22) to send the bride with too small an escort: "My neighboring kings [would say], 'They have transported the daughter of a Great King to Egypt in five chariots (only)!'" It is as if the other kings were looking out of their windows at the wedding party passing by and judging its economic and social relevance.

Did Burna-Buriash really think that Pharaoh lived in the next block? The problem of real distance is in fact raised in the same letter, and "specialists," that is, messengers (both Egyptian and Babylonian) have to confirm to the apparently ignorant Babylonian king that Egypt is indeed a distant country, and that it takes months to send news and receive answers. Burna-Buriash officially accepts the messengers' testimony and consequently decides to pardon Pharaoh's lack of regard. Of course, he must have been well aware beforehand that the messengers' trip took months and that Egypt was quite a distant country. And of course the whole mise-en-scène is aimed at the usual business of bargaining, arguing, and so on. All this is quite obvious, but the small-scale model was so pervasive as to make people imagine that such unbelievable doubts were, if not true, at least likely.

Theoretical Outline

Whatever expressive level is adopted, ranging from strictly juridical formulations to common-life metaphors, the existence of a theoretical reference system seems evident. Since I have dealt at length with such a system elsewhere, I provide here only an essential outline.

Time

The basic pattern "from good — through evil — to good" is present, even pervasive. This means in practice relegating the positive model of behavior to a past that is largely atemporal, even when apparently set in historical events.[19] Possible negative incidents are set in the intermediate phase of a recent past and must now be quickly surmounted. Present (and future) relationships must be better than before (e.g., gifts must be multiplied, love must be increased).[20] This becomes particularly evident when a new partnership was established or renewed, following the enthronement of a new king—a case especially well documented in the Amarna archive, whose time span includes the enthronement of Akhenaten.[21]

Space

The border, both in its technical definition and in its "cosmological" implications, has a paramount relevance in treaties and royal inscriptions.[22] But in letters dealing with the normal conduct of affairs, the most evident spatial feature is territoriality. The practical principles of territoriality, in a multi-centered world, are monopoly of taxation and monopoly of responsibilities.[23] The latter is especially represented in the Amarna Letters, in connection with international lawsuits (EA 7:73–82; EA 8; EA 16:37–42; EA 38).

Protagonists

The two-level arrangement of polities (great vs. small kingdoms), which is clearly reflected in the procedures regulating the above-mentioned lawsuits,[24] sets the stage for a limited membership of the so-called Great Powers' Club.[25] Problems of diachronic change (especially the decline of Mittani and the rise of Assyria) and of marginality (e.g., the Mycenean world) receive considerable attention in other documents from the Late Bronze Age, in its wider sense, but are present only incidentally in the Amarna Letters because of the restricted time span of that archive.

Content of Relationships

Lévi-Strauss's trio of items of exchange in human relationships — messages, gifts, and women — is well represented in the Amarna Letters. In a sense, it might seem that the exchange of messages is instrumental in the conduct of the other two; goods are also exchanged especially in connection with marriage. Yet every kind of exchange has a worth of its own; moreover, all are ultimately pursued as part of the supreme purpose (see below).

The Basic Principle

The exchange makes pervasive even obsessive reference to the basic principle of reciprocity.[26] The very obsessive insistence on the reciprocal nature of relationships has probably something to do with doubts about its effective observance. The evident existence of mental reservations (by the Egyptian side; see below), however, does not affect too much its theoretical acceptance as the only possible starting point for the functioning of an international community.

The Purpose

We could rationalize that the supreme purpose is to avoid wars, but this is not evidenced by the Letters. These point to keeping in contact as the final end of diplomatic relations, as an end endowed with a value of its own.[27] In the definition of the supreme purpose, some theoretical contradictions appear between self-sufficiency and exchange, between centralism and multipolarity, and between prestige and interest.[28]

Sanctions

Divine sanctions are in the fore in the treaties and other normative texts; and a military sanction is attested in royal inscriptions as the obvious outcome for major disagreements. Note that the "trial by battle" theory of war as a divine judgement strictly connects the two kinds of sanctions.[29] Yet in the Letters, divine and military sanctions do not feature. The only apparent sanction is the end of relationships themselves (EA 8:30–33). This is due, first, to the letters being related to the normal conduct of affairs and, second, to a conceptual inability to deepen consciousness beyond the simple ascertainment of the existence of the system itself (see above).

Operative Procedures

The enlargement of the village perspective to include the entire Near East — the entire *oikumene* as conceived in the Late Bronze age — brings about the solution of practical problems. First is the pace of diplomatic contacts.

In comparison with the strictly seasonal structure of Pharaoh's relations with the Syro-Palestinian vassals,[30] the exchange of letters among Great Kings is more flexible, both because the distance is longer and because matters are less essential. However, a basically seasonal pace is necessarily in use, because travel has to avoid the bad season of winter rains. Covering the distance between Amarna (or Thebes) and the Asiatic capital cities cannot take less than a month (to Washukanni) or a month and a half (to Hattusha or Babylon) for a fast courier, and around twice that (two to three months) for a caravan of loaded donkeys. So it is evident that a two-way trip, including time for nego-tiating and for preparing the return caravan, took an entire year, unless there was a particular reason for pressure.[31]

Flexibility is mostly related to an even slower pace of journeys, with mes-sengers/ambassadors detained for an entire year or even for several years.[32] The rules of hospitality that protect the messenger during his stay abroad also prevent him from leaving without the host's consent: "What are messen-gers? Unless they are birds, are they going to fly and go away?" (EA 28:2). Should detention be protracted, however, contacts were pursued by different persons.

The objective slowness of the journeys, basically for technological reasons, and the possible additional delay for political reasons, are exacerbated by the practice of repeated bargaining, which makes it almost impossible to resolve a transaction in only two "moves," request and acceptance. Such a problem is in fact perceived as dramatic by those partners of Egypt who were interested in the commercial aspects, namely, Assyria and Alashia. (The Assyrian king explicitly protests against a system so overelaborate that "it does not even cover the cost of the journeys.")[33] The other partners, however, seem happy enough with the current slow pace, being interested rather in the political aspects of the relationship, aspects that are better satisfied by endless nego-tiations than by efficient and fast arrangements.

An economy of journeys is also evident in the occasional habit of entrust-ing merchants with official state letters, a use attested for Babylonia (Salmu is a "merchant" in EA 11:Rs. 8, but a "messenger" in EA 7:73) and for Cyprus (EA 39–40). The precise status of the personnel entrusted with carrying let-ters seems variable but generally proportionate to the matter in hand: dynas-tic marriages are discussed by high-ranking "ambassadors" (like the famous Keliya and Mane who negotiated the Mittanian marriage), whereas trivial problems can be entrusted to merchants. Routine letters are delivered by anonymous professional couriers.[34] A mismatch between the rank of the mes-senger and the relevance of the subject matter gives rise to open disputes.[35]

Messengers and ambassadors, when leaving the territory of their own community and traveling through a hostile or at least ambiguous space, were to a reasonable extent protected by the laws of hospitality (especially at their final destination) but nevertheless subject to claims of interception and tolls by local potentates (especially during the journey). Petty kings and tribal chieftains would want to profit from the international trade passing through their lands, and we have explicit attestations of similar attempts (cf. esp. EA 7:73–82; EA 8:13–29). But the Great Kings were generally able to reaffirm their higher authority by granting the messengers a protection that was the practical outcome of their "monopoly of responsibility." Safe conducts and letters of warning are the customary tools for preventing problems with the local chiefs (EA 30; EA 255).

Similar "normal" tools were not always enough, however. Even the local kings were not (or not always) in full control of their respective territories. Remote villages, pastoral tribes, and bands of outcasts were not infrequently responsible for robberies and murders — and the merchants' caravans were, of course, an especially tempting prey. These incidents were dealt with by the principle of objective responsibility (according to whose territory is in question) and of a hierarchical pyramid of judicial competence. In the Amarna Letters, we have hints at this system, which is more extensively documented in the texts from Ugarit.[36]

In the practical running of the entire system, written documents, ranging from formal treaties to letters, also play a role. That role does not contradict the customary nature of rules, nor their family or neighborhood models, nor the mostly oral channels of negotiation. The material aspect of a written document provides an additional feature for validation and use. Texts are stored in archives, to be retrieved, checked, and even quoted in case of need, to enforce the burden of tradition with a more precise apparatus of quotations. The frequent recourse in written replies to literal quotations from the original message, on the one hand, emphasizes the oral (dialogue-like) model of negotiation but, on the other, makes the relevance (in terms of juridical validation) of the written words evident.

Without doubt, recourse to written documents and to a "third" language of common acceptance (Babylonian) singles out the inner core of the civilized *oikumene* from its looser periphery, where barbarian peoples do not write, do not keep archives, and practically do not speak (because they speak incomprehensible languages), so that the most convenient pattern for interaction is the extreme model of "silent trade" — the exact opposite of the verbose negotiations of the Amarna letters.

Coping with Contentiousness

In the framework of the theoretical principles and practical procedures outlined above, the Amarna Letters are largely concerned with the management of disputes between partners. Contentiousness of this nature is partly ceremonial, if intended to establish one's superior role in the negotiation, and partly utilitarian, if intended to obtain major economic benefits.[37] In any case, it is so pervasive that it must be considered not simply a deviation from the norm but a feature (and a characteristic one at that) of the system itself.

We can distinguish between a "micro-contentiousness" within a single negotiation and a "macro-contentiousness" that is the result of a confrontation between major traditions and different ideologies. Micro-contentiousness is best evidenced by comparing the norms of hospitality and gift exchange (and of human interaction in general) with their practical application — or, rather, inversion — in the Amarna Letters.[38] The fundamental norms are that gifts, like hospitality, cannot be asked for, must be given, must be accepted and appreciated, and must be reciprocated, in an increased amount.

Gifts Cannot Be Asked For

In the Amarna Letters there is an insistent recourse to direct requests for gifts. A "guilty conscience" is evident in the alleging (or fabrication) of excuses, which in a sense allow the disqualifying act of asking to be bypassed.[39] The extreme point is reached by stating that the requested item will be refused if delivered too late to be used for the alleged purpose (EA 4:36–50). The fictional character of the alleged purposes is apparent from their long use through time, even their inheritance from king to king.

Gifts Must Be Given (in a disinterested way)

In the Letters and related documents, besides and in contrast to general statements of a disinterested attitude in gift-giving, a true and proper stereotyped procedure is in use for not giving, or at least for postponing giving.[40] Also, in this case, a guilty conscience is made apparent by the use of obvious "diplomatic" excuses, excuses so obvious that the addressee must have been fully aware of their falsity.[41] The procedure is evidently used in order to match the official model of gift-giving with the real matter of commercial transactions. Delay is, in fact, used to negotiate more favorable terms of exchange.

Gifts Must Be Accepted and Appreciated

In the Letters, gifts obviously are accepted but are rarely appreciated. The quality and amount of the items received are frequently disputed, especially Egyptian shipments of gold or golden objects, the Egyptian gold being dismissed by the Asiatic kings from the outset as "common as dust," "to be simply gathered up from the ground" (EA 3:15; EA 7:69–72; EA 10:19–20; EA 20:46–59; EA 29:70–75). Also, in this case, it is evident that a strictly commercial evaluation interferes with a gift-exchange fiction: the Egyptian gold objects smelted into ingots and weighed on their arrival in Babylon or

Washukanni are the clearest cases of a much-debased ceremoniality. Yet the gift-giving ideology is perceived in the fact that the dispute is not framed in terms of financial value but of pride and renown.[42]

Gifts Must Be Reciprocated

The utopian norm of increased returns is well known and explicitly enunciated as a statement of purpose (EA 35:50–53; EA 19:68–69); in practice, however, the countergifts seem to be carefully balanced and are postponed in time by slowing down the messengers' journeys. It has been noted that in pre-monetary societies, delay in countergifts (or counterprestations) fulfills a function analogous in financial terms to interest on capital.[43] Of course, in a long chain of reciprocated gifts and countergifts, both partners try to get quickly and reciprocate slowly, so that their opposed strategies cancel each other out.

Macro-contentiousness is especially apparent between Egypt on the one side and all the Asiatic kingdoms on the other. This is partly because the Amarna archive, by its very nature and location, polarizes the position of Egypt vs. the rest of the world. If we had letters exchanged between Hatti and Assyria (as we do in the thirteenth century B.C.E.) or between Mittani and Babylonia, we could perhaps point out other motifs of ideological conflict. But it is also true that a basic difference between Egypt and Asia is the real result of long-established different traditions and of unbalanced demographic, military, and economic weight.

The Egyptian refusal to grant its Asiatic partners complete parity in rank is quite evident and is, in fact, a central feature of the entire system. I have already noted that its application to the exchange of women emphasizes its properly ideological character—because women are, of course, available everywhere and do not share the possible ecological idiosyncrasies of other items.[44] In the discussions among the concerned parties, we notice at this point a progressive clarification of the social and ideological reasons, from the Amarna correspondence to the Egyptian-Hittite correspondence at the time of Ramesses II.

In the Amarna Letters the reasons are rather grossly stated. On the one hand, Pharaoh states in absolute terms that "an Egyptian princess has never been given to anybody" (EA 4:6–7) and accuses his Babylonian partner of selling his daughters off for money (EA 1:61). On the other hand, the Babylonian king has recourse to the disqualifying suggestion of disguising a commoner "as if she were a princess" (EA 4:12–13). Both sides seem far from a real understanding of each other's reasons. A century later, in the negotiations between Ramesses and Hattusili (and especially the latter's wife Pudu-Hepa), the Egyptian refusal of matrimonial reciprocity is duly explained as a symptom of a refusal of parity in rank ("brotherhood," in the terminology of the time). The purpose of an interdynastic marriage, on the other hand, is duly explained by political and social values.[45]

Although the movement of princesses from Egypt to Asia always constituted a problem, the movement of princesses from Asia to Egypt was current practice. But also in this case, two distant ideologies gave rise to misunderstandings and conflicts. The Asiatic princesses, sent to Egypt in order to become first-rank wives and queens (as was usual in inter-Asian dynastic marriages), were added to the pharaonic harem once they arrived and were mixed with a variety of nonroyal wives and concubines. The discussion between Amenhotep and Kadashman-Enlil (EA 1:10–52) about the fate and status of the Babylonian princess raises a central problem — although in practice the discussion is on a rather banal level, the one side raising the question of the "visibility" of the princess, while the other side raises the question of the adequacy of the messengers.

The very same problem of visibility as an expression of correct political relations (i.e., parity) is evident in the parallel discussion about the Babylonian chariots (loaded with gifts) having been mixed with the vassals' chariots (loaded with tribute) in a parade at the Egyptian capital (EA 1:89–92).[46] Here, there is no doubt a problem of audience and media, with a sharp distinction between internal and external messages that is quite revealing as to the aims and implications of the various political texts of the time. But there is also the problem of an ideology (namely, the Egyptian one) that is so deeply rooted in a centralized worldview that it is practically incapable of fully accepting real parity in rank and a real reciprocity in the exchange of goods.

Conclusions

In summary, apart from possible terminological problems (whereby "interstate relations" might perhaps be less anachronistic than "international relations"), it is quite evident that the Amarna Letters are the product of an international community of mutually independent polities, whose long-lasting and rather intensive contacts generated precise norms regulating their interactions.

The procedures in use — with a twofold level of formalization, to be used in the juridical and epistolary documents, respectively — are perfectly suited to the level of complexity and the pace of interaction. In particular, the "family" or "neighborhood" metaphors are perfectly suited not only to the personalized nature of relationships but also, and more significant, to the mix of friendship and rivalry, concord and competition, that is characteristic of similar situations.

The frequent quarrels function as a way of discharging hidden aggressiveness. This is especially connected with a difficult compromise between the motives of prestige regulating the relations of every king with the inner public of his own kingdom and the motives of interest regulating interstate relations. As compared with the purely utilitarian model of barter (or its extreme form, silent trade), the model of "endless quarrel" is better suited to keeping alive sociopolitical relations than to the efficient conduct of affairs.

Recourse to ceremoniality, to a conventional (and more or less explicitly accepted) code of stereotyped behavior, is effective in singling out a civilized center from a barbarian periphery. A correct way to do things is clearly regulating peace and war, trade and marriages, border disputes and exchange of messages. Such a code of behavior cuts across different cultural traditions, and is the result of a time-honored selection of adjustments and compromises.

CHAPTER THREE

International Law
in the Amarna Age

RAYMOND WESTBROOK

Where an international society exists, relations between its members will be governed not only by common political conventions but also by agreed rules of law. In the ancient Near East, international law had a venerable tradition, being attested virtually from the beginning of written records.[1] Formal treaties were a frequent instrument of foreign policy, and customary international law was appealed to in diplomatic protests and negotiations. Thus, although the Amarna Letters are not legal documents, international law is important to understanding them. This chapter provides a background to the worldview of the correspondents, by sketching in outline some of the fundamental legal conceptions upon which their diplomatic démarches were based.

The State

International law in modern theory is the system of law that governs relations between states (as opposed to domestic law, which is the ordinary law governing relations between individuals within a state or other political entity). It is therefore necessary first to establish whether, in the ancient Near East, states existed in a form to which we can meaningfully attribute a role in international law and, if so, what was meant by a state.

The modern concept of the state as a legal entity is based on the model of the corporation: an artificial person recognized by law, whose "acts" are the result of imputation to it of the acts of its officials. It is this existence separate from its members, albeit fictive, that gives the state capacity to be a subject of international law.[2]

Ancient law had not developed the concept of the corporation and could not therefore rely on it as a model. The usual form of government was monarchy, and all acts of the monarch were apparently personal; they were not attributed to his country acting as a separate person.[3] Ancient law could not conceive of the state as a legal entity.

The modern model, however, is not the only possible paradigm for a state. Ancient Near Eastern law achieved the same role for its political societies as states in modern international law but by a different route: the application of a model based on the particular structure of its own societies and their domestic law.[4] Other contributors to this volume have shown the importance of the family metaphor in international politics.[5] For international law, the operative metaphor was that of the household.

Ancient Near Eastern society was strongly hierarchical. It was based not on the individual but on the household. The household, called the "house," was a socioeconomic unit headed by a "father," whose extended, multigenerational family lived under his authority. It was normally a geographical unit also, in the sense that "house" also meant land—a dwelling at least, if not agricultural land. Subordinate members of the household consisted not only of obvious family members such as wives, sons, daughters, daughters-in-law, and grandchildren, but also dependents in a client status, and slaves.[6] A typical society consisted of a coalition of household units. The word "man" often referred not to any male individual, but to a head of household.

Within this structure, the king was regarded as no more than a householder on a larger scale, his household being the aggregation of households that made up a political society. The population of the state was his household and the territory within its borders the household land. In this regard he was often referred to simply as a "man," for example, "Aziru, the man of Amurru."[7] The constitutional relationship between king and citizens relied on a metaphor drawn from the hierarchy within a household: he was their master; they were his slaves. The metaphor of slavery would more accurately be regarded as a metonym, since it was only certain aspects of slavery, such as obedience and loyalty, that were regarded as applicable. In domestic law, there was a sharp distinction between free citizens and slaves.

The king was by no means the apex of the hierarchy. Above him stood the emperor, if he were a vassal king. He and his household, that is, the population of his country, were all slaves of the emperor. Again, the term was used metaphorically, to denote subordinate members of a household. Above the emperor was yet another stratum, that of the gods, to whom all owed obedience, and even the pantheon itself could contain a hierarchy of households.

The state may be identified as a household at a median hierarchical level,

at the point where the head of household, a king, came under the direct jurisdiction of the gods with regard to his own and his subordinates' actions.[8] It
would be a distortion to speak of the king's actions being "imputed" to his
household, as in the corporate model, but as we shall see below, other legal
doctrines unknown to modern law provided channels through which the
same result might be achieved.

The Amarna Letters provide evidence of the conscious use of this legal
model. The greeting formulae of the Great Power correspondence follow a
stereotyped pattern, a typical example of which is (EA 1:1–9):

> Say to Kadashman-Enlil, the king of Karadunishe, my brother: Thus
> Nibmuarea, Great King, the king of Egypt, your brother. For me all
> goes well. For you may all go well. For your household, for your wives,
> for your sons, for your magnates, your horses, your chariots, for your
> countries, may all go very well. For me all goes well. For my household,
> for my wives, for my sons, for my magnates, my horses, the numerous
> troops, all goes well, and in my countries all goes very well.

The apparently personal greeting is, in fact, an assertion of legal status. Para-
doxically, its "personal touch" establishes that the correspondence between
the writer and the addressee is not personal but is carried on in their official capacity. Not only are the official titles of both given but the salutation
also moves from the personal household to those features identifying it as a
median household in the hierarchy and, therefore, a state, namely officials,
armed forces, and territory. Even as between suzerain and vassal, the legal
model was alluded to: the Egyptian king was careful to address his vassals as
"X, ruler (lit.: 'man') of the city Y."[9]

International Law

Jurisdiction

International law was a system of rules regulating relations between kings,
as heads of median-level households. The system was under the jurisdiction
of the gods, who constituted its court or courts. Enforcement was by the gods
or by legitimate self-help, sanctioned by the gods. Three problems arise in
this regard.

First, if jurisdiction is divine, then its rules might be considered as being
in the realm of religion rather than of law. Kestemont regards them as extra-
juridical norms, on a level with norms of honor, honesty, and conscience,
which demonstrate the impotence of international law rather than its pres-

ence.[10] I would argue that there was no such separation in the ancient world. Everyone, without exception, believed in the gods: the gods were part of the real world as they saw it, just as they saw the Earth as being flat. The divine legal system governed human behavior no less than human courts, and its sanctions, if less certain in their application (but not by much), were equally feared. Notwithstanding the occasional breach and the rationalization of misconduct, the behavior of states was conditioned by what they saw as an effective legal system. Natural calamities such as plague, drought, flood, and defeat in war were attributed to divine justice, and steps were taken to make legal reparation in light of them. In his Plague Prayers, the Hittite king Mursili identifies the cause of a plague afflicting Hatti as the breach of a treaty with Egypt by his father, Suppiluliuma. He seeks to assuage the gods by making reparations to Egypt and returning Egyptian prisoners.[11] A similar action was taken by David regarding a breach of treaty by his predecessor Saul, which was identified as the cause of a drought (2 Sam. 21:1–11). From this perspective, one might even argue that ancient international law was more genuinely law than is its modern counterpart.

Second, the subjects of modern international law being essentially states, individuals have no standing before its tribunals. Not so the ancient divine courts. The gods judged everyone, whether king or commoner, emperor or slave, and every individual within a state could seek direct recourse to divine justice through prayer. Ancient international law was distinguished from domestic law in the degree rather than in the total absence of accessibility. For the individual, the gods were a residual court, a tribunal that would punish those offenses that escaped human courts (for lack of evidence), and the ultimate court of appeal where human courts could not or would not provide justice.[12] In disputes between kings, in contrast, the divine tribunals were courts of first instance. There was no other authority to which they might have recourse.

Third, the system is further complicated by the existence of vassal kings. Such kings were subject to the jurisdiction of their emperor and thus one step removed from the jurisdiction of the gods. Two factors, however, need to be taken into consideration. One is that empires in the Amarna Age were not administrative units, but each contained a core state where the emperor would be a mere king, answerable to the gods and his peers, and ruling his subjects directly, in the manner of all other kings. The second factor is that domestic sovereignty could be distinguished from suzerainty by what I will call the "doctrine of impermeability." An ordinary head of household had a certain jurisdiction over the subordinate members of his house, subject to the rules of law and custom. His control, however, was not impermeable. The king's court regularly adjudicated inner-household disputes, between husband and wife, between two wives or wife and concubine, between father and son, and even between master and slave. For an emperor, however, the affairs of his vassals' subjects were beyond his reach. Litigants from within a vassal state could presumably petition the gods if unsatisfied with royal justice, but there is no evidence that they could ever go over the head of their own king by appealing his decision to the emperor. The suzerain did not interfere in the internal jurisdiction of his vassals; he only adjudicated disputes between vassal kings or between his own nationals and nationals of vassal states. Vassal kings therefore had an independent domestic legal system, which is one of the essential characteristics of a modern state, and they occupied a place in the hierarchy above that of domestic households. As between themselves, they could conduct an active foreign policy, make alliances, and even acquire their own vassals, depending on the policy of the imperial power.[13] The Amarna Letters attest to alliances between vassals within the Egyptian empire against fellow vassals (EA 74, 149) and to the building of mini-empires such as those of Lab'ayu of Shechem and 'Abdi-Ashirta of Amurru (EA 244, 253, 254, 280; EA 83, 90). Only where they impinged directly on their interests would the Egyptians intervene. Accordingly, it is unwise to be too dogmatic: just as international law was not a hermetically sealed system but one characterized by degree, so the capacity of vassals to be the subjects of international law must be recognized as limited, but real. The juridical role of the gods, which became more direct as households rose in the hierarchical ladder, took on a qualitative difference at the level of kings, including vassal kings.

Doctrine

Certain doctrines of domestic law unfamiliar to modern systems enabled the household model to function effectively at the level of international law, endowing the actions of kings with the same effects as does the fiction of legal personality for the modern state. I would point to three in particular that are illustrated below:

1. The head of household had legal authority vis-à-vis outsiders: he could enter into legal obligations that bound his whole household or individual subordinates.
2. The head of household's own obligations could be enforced against his subordinates. Of particular importance for international law are the possibilities of vicarious or collective punishment. In the first instance, a subordinate member could be put to death for an offense that the head of

household had committed, it being regarded as punishment of the head of household himself.[14] In the second, the whole household could be destroyed, together with its head, where the latter had committed a serious offense against a hierarchical superior.[15]

3. The head of household in principle owned all family property, and on his death the members of his household who constituted his primary heirs became his automatic, universal successors. In this way, a juridical continuity of the household was ensured.

Customary International Law

The two most important sources for international law are custom and treaty. Customary international law is difficult to identify in the ancient sources, since it does not derive from legal instruments. It is also difficult sometimes to distinguish a legal rule from a rule of etiquette, since the response to both, barring a serious legal infraction, was generally the same: a diplomatic protest.[16] In three areas, concerning envoys, foreign nationals, and extradition, there appear to have been customary rules.

Envoys

EA 30 is a passport or letter of credentials of a Mittanian envoy.[17] In EA 15, the envoy's credentials are included in the Assyrian king's message of introduction. Although it was an obvious diplomatic necessity, there is no evidence that such a letter was legally required in every case to establish an envoy's credentials. The envoy of a friendly state was regarded as a guest of the host monarch, who was responsible for his housing and maintenance. The length of stay was entirely at the discretion of the host, whose permission was necessary before the envoy could depart.[18] Inordinate retention of an envoy would lead to protests, but as it was, strictly speaking, legal, the reaction was muted. The Mittanian king retaliated in kind (retorsion) or sent a lower-level envoy (EA 29:155–61) but, at the same time, appealed for Egyptian cooperation (EA 28).

The modern doctrine of diplomatic immunity, whereby a diplomat is not liable in the courts of the host country for his illegal acts, is not attested in ancient Near Eastern records. Indeed, the Amarna Letters suggest that at the very least, the host country could demand that the offending diplomat be tried and punished by his own country. In EA 29:173–81, Pharaoh demands that the Mittanian king impose the death penalty on two of his own diplomats (cf. EA 24:IV 35–39 = para. 28), whom Pharaoh claims committed (unspecified) crimes while in Egypt but who had since returned to Mittani. The Mittanian king points out that he has already conducted a judicial investigation in the presence of Mane, the Egyptian ambassador, apparently on the basis of an earlier demand, and has put them in chains and transported them to the border (in anticipation of extradition?). Nonetheless, he readily agrees to Pharaoh's new demand, on condition that proof be given of a capital offense: "Now, may my brother establish the nature of their crime, and I will treat them as my brother wants them treated."

There is evidence, however, of a doctrine of diplomatic inviolability, in that a serious attaint to the person or dignity of a diplomat by the host country would be regarded as an attack on the diplomat's country and, hence, casus belli.[19] In EA 16, the Assyrian king was in a delicate position. His envoys had complained to him about being made to stand for hours in the sun (along with the rest of the Egyptian court) at one of Akhenaten's interminable religious devotions.[20] He could not protest their treatment directly, for the envoys were treated no differently from the Egyptian courtiers and no diplomatic slight was intended. Instead, he argued: "If staying out in the sun means profit for the king, then let him (a messenger) stay out and let him die right there in the sun, (but) for the king himself there must be a profit" (43–49).

The suggestion that the Egyptian king was entitled to kill envoys for his own profit must be taken as rhetorical; in practice, it would have been regarded as a serious breach of international law. At the same time, the appeal to self-interest is a telltale sign of the absence of firm legal grounds.

Foreign Nationals

There is substantial evidence of a rule of customary law imposing liability on the host government to compensate foreign nationals who had been the victim of serious crimes on their territory. The starting point is a doctrine of domestic law, recorded in the Laws of Hammurabi 22–24:

> If a man commits robbery and is caught, that man shall be killed. If the robber is not caught, the person robbed shall declare his losses before the god, and the city and mayor in whose district the robbery was committed shall compensate him for his lost property. If it is life (i.e., murder), the city and mayor shall pay his family one mina of silver.

The local authority had a responsibility toward the victim akin to that of an insurer. It has been pointed out by Green that the same doctrine was applied to foreign victims, who were entitled to look to the local ruler for compensation, pending apprehension of the culprit.[21] In an Egyptian story set in the twelfth century, Wen-Amun, an Egyptian passing through the Phoenician port of Dor, had some valuables stolen from his ship by a member of his crew. He at once notified the prince of Dor, claiming that the losses were his responsibility. The prince admitted in principle an obligation to compensate Wen-Amun from his own treasury but found a legal loophole in the fact that the thief was from Wen-Amun's crew (a member of his own foreign household, so to speak). As Green points out, it is improbable that there was a treaty between Dor and Egypt at the time, so the basis of the prince's liability must have been customary law (p. 117).

Several treaties from Ugarit almost contemporaneous with the Amarna correspondence stipulate compensation from the public purse for the robbery and murder of nationals of Ugarit in the territory of Karkemish, and vice versa. A curious feature of one of these treaties, in which the victims (significantly) are merchants, is that the public authority is liable to make a fixed payment of three minas of silver for murder victims, whether the murderers are caught or not, but are liable to pay simple compensation for goods stolen *only if the robbers are caught*.[22] I conclude that the purpose of the treaty was not to establish liability, but to *limit* existing liability under customary law. The authorities were prepared to act as paymaster of first resort, but were not prepared to accept open-ended liability for plundered caravans where there was no hope of recouping their expenditure from the actual culprits. In this light, the fixed payment for murder may also be seen as a limitation of liability. The normal system of retribution for murder in the ancient Near East was a dual right of the victim's relatives: to execute revenge or to accept ransom payment from the culprit in lieu of revenge.[23] Since the ransom demanded for the culprit's life could theoretically be considerably higher, the fixed sum of three minas represented a limit on the primary payment of compensation by the public authority, which it might not be able to recoup from the culprit, even if he was caught.

I have discussed these sources in detail because they are necessary to understanding the full legal significance of EA 313 and EA 8. In EA 313, the murder of Egyptian merchants by brigands on the territory of a vassal is dealt with by the vassal paying the local Egyptian commissioner "400 shekels of silver, plus 1000." Moran notes that it is a strange way to write 1,400 shekels (n. 4). The point is that there are *two* payments for two separate matters: compensation in lieu of ransom and compensation for goods stolen, in that order. The normal customary law is followed, unaffected by the vassal-suzerain relationship.

In EA 8, the Babylonian king informs the Egyptian king that some Babylonian merchants were robbed and murdered by Egyptian vassals in Canaan, and continues: "In your country I have been robbed. Bring them to account and make compensation for the money that they took away. Put to death the men who put my servants to death, and so avenge their blood" (26-29).

The Babylonian king's identification with his merchants is the other side of the coin of vicarious punishment: an offense against a subordinate member of the household is an offense against the head of household. His demand for compensation directly from the Egyptian king fits in perfectly with the rule of customary law. But his demand that the Egyptian king execute vengeance on the killers, rather than pay compensation and exact ransom from them, was probably more than was required in strict law. For this reason, as we have seen in EA 16, the Babylonian king appeals to his counterpart's self-interest: "If you do not put these men to death, they are going to kill again, be it a caravan of mine or your own messengers, and so messengers between us will thereby be cut off" (30-33).

We thus see the difference in this letter between a legal and a political argument: a legal claim needed no elaboration, since the relevant rule of customary international law was accepted by the parties as binding on them; a political demand needed support, by threat of sanction, offer of advantage, or appeal to self-interest.

Extradition

Kings had a traditional discretion to grant or refuse asylum to fugitives. As between kings of equal status, they were under no legal obligation to return fugitives upon demand, unless it was specifically provided for by treaty, which was frequently the case.[24] Of course, it might be considered an unfriendly act to harbor a fugitive, in which case a request for extradition would be granted as a favor.

As between suzerain and vassal, the former had no duty to extradite, but the latter did.[25] The Egyptian king in EA 162 exercised his right with regard to various political refugees who had fled to Amurru, and the ruler of Amurru, so recalcitrant in other matters, showed no reluctance to comply.

Treaties

Legal Basis

In the domestic legal systems of the ancient Near East, a contract between heads of household would bind their respective households. It is no accident that *rikiltu,* the term for "contract" in Akkadian, the international lingua franca of the Amarna Age, was used without discrimination for international treaties. A treaty between kings was simply a contract that would bind their "households" in the same way.

In a domestic contract, it was often the practice to secure ancillary obligations by means of a promissory oath, for example, provisions against future revendication. The oath took the form of a curse that the speaker called down upon himself should he break his promise. In doing so, he invoked the name of the king or specific gods, who were expected to execute the curse. Where the obligations of the contract were entirely future or contingent, as in a contract of betrothal, it was possible for the contract to consist solely of an oath.[26] This was precisely the case with treaties, which only involved future or contingent obligations.

In some aspects, however, international treaties differed significantly from domestic contracts. Since kings were under the direct jurisdiction of the gods, treaty oaths were in the name of the gods alone. Domestic contracts were witnessed by the parties' peers, and disputes over breach could be brought before a variety of courts but ultimately before the king, as fountainhead of justice. Domestic courts had the power to punish a party for breach of the divine oath.[27] In treaties, however, the role of witnesses was played by the gods, their names (and seals) being appended as witnesses to the treaty tablet. (The presence of human witnesses is rarely even mentioned.) In consequence, the gods had a dual role: as witnesses to the treaty and as "gods of the oath," in which capacity they were responsible for punishing any breach. As a treaty between Mursili II of Hatti and Tuppi-Teshup of Amurru pithily prescribes:[28] "If Tuppi-Teshup does not observe the terms of the treaty . . . then these oath gods will destroy Tuppi-Teshup, together with his person, his wife, his son, his grandsons, his house, his city, his land, and his possessions."

Although they were personal agreements between kings, treaties bound the populations of their respective countries by reason of the doctrine of householder responsibility. If there were a breach of the treaty, the gods could respond by destroying either the king himself (personal punishment), his subjects (vicarious punishment), or both (collective punishment). They bound the parties' successors under the doctrine of universal inheritance, although it was politically more prudent to gain a fresh, direct commitment from the new monarch.

In summary, treaties were contracts on the domestic model but gained their international character from two factors: the position of the contracting parties on the hierarchical scale, and their being purely within divine jurisdiction.[29]

Formation

In contrast to modern law, treaties did not have to be in written form.[30] They were frequently committed to writing, especially when concluded through the agency of envoys, but the legal core of a treaty was an oral agreement, the written version being a record thereof and of evidentiary value only. The legally binding element was the promissory oath that the parties swore by the gods. The oath in fact achieved much the same purpose as writing in modern law: it was a ceremonial formality that emphasized the seriousness and durability of the undertakings. Hence, it is not surprising that references to treaties in the Amarna Letters sometimes simply use the word "oath." In EA 74, Rib-Hadda warns the Egyptian king that ʿAbdi-Ashirta of Amurru has made an alliance against him with the revolutionary leaders of Ammiya. As Moran points out, the literal phrase is "placed an oath" (145, n. 13). In the same way, in EA 149, Abi-Milku of Tyre reports that Zimredda of Sidon exchanged oaths with the rulers of Arwada in preparation for a joint attack on Tyre.

In addition, there could be ceremonies attending the oath, which, if not legally necessary, further emphasized the formality of the agreement. For the oath-swearing reported in EA 74, ʿAbdi-Ashirta assembled the parties in a temple, although the oath procedure did not strictly require it. Where the parties met face to face, there were various customary ceremonies, such as slaughtering an animal or sharing a meal or drink. Two Mesopotamian kings from the Old Babylonian period are reported to have sworn the oath, slaughtered an ass, sat down to drink together from the same cup, and finally exchanged presents.[31] In Gen. 31:44–54, after Jacob and Laban had made a treaty in solemn form, the two sides ate bread together. In light of these sources, the Egyptian king's complaint to his vassal Aziru in EA 162 takes on new significance:

> Now the king (of Egypt) has heard as follows: "You are at peace with the ruler of Qadesh. The two of you take food and strong drink together. And it is true. Why do you act so? Why are you at peace with a ruler with whom the king is fighting? And even if you did act loyally, you considered your own judgment, and his judgment did not count."

The reference is not to mere conviviality; it is an unmistakable allusion to the celebration of a treaty.

Where the parties were separated, envoys had to be used to conclude the treaty. The envoy would present the king with a list of stipulations (usually on a tablet), to which the latter had to swear. The procedure is well documented in Old Babylonian diplomatic records,[32] and it was still in use in the preparing of the Egypt-Hatti peace treaty.[33] It was evidently used by the Hittite king in the vassal treaty that he offered Addu-nirari of Nuhašše, reported in EA 51,[34] and by Aziru of Amurru in demanding a special oath of safe conduct from the Egyptian king and his high officials (EA 164:27–42).

Typology

Scholars normally divide ancient Near Eastern treaties into two categories: parity treaties and vassal treaties.[35] In the former, two independent rulers enter into an agreement on terms of reciprocity, usually with substantially identical obligations. Korošec wondered how an independent ruler could have an obligation imposed upon him by another ruler without compromising his sovereignty.[36] The answer is that the ruler was submitting not to the other party but to the higher authority of the gods, recognized by both parties.

A vassal treaty in its purest form was unilateral: the vassal made a series of promises under oath to the suzerain. Promises under oath by the suzerain on specific issues were not excluded, however; even if not under oath, they were still binding insofar as their breach would release the vassal from his oath.[37] The balance of obligations depended on the relative bargaining power of the parties. Indeed, as Liverani has pointed out, a Hittite treaty with Kizzuwatna is presented as if it were a parity treaty, even with mutual oaths, but was in substance a vassal treaty.[38]

Serious doubts have been expressed as to the legal status of vassal treaties. Korošec regarded them as only partly creatures of international law: "halbvölkerrechtlich" (35–36). Other commentators have pointed to lack of consent or lack of sovereignty in the vassals as flaws in their status as instruments of international law.[39] We cannot go into these difficult questions at length here, but I will make two points that are of particular relevance to the Amarna correspondence.

First, in legal theory, if not in political reality, vassals entered voluntarily into a treaty with their overlords. Given a choice between death and vassalage, a threatened ruler would not unnaturally choose the latter. According to an Egyptian account, Canaanite rulers besieged in Megiddo begged mercy from Thutmose III, and in return for sparing their lives, he imposed upon them an oath.[40] Furthermore, the initiative might come from the greater power, if political circumstances made it expedient to court smaller states. In EA 51, Addu-nirari of Nuhašše proudly reported to his Egyptian suzerain his rejection of a Hittite offer of a vassal treaty.[41]

Second, a formal treaty was not a prerequisite for vassalage. Returning to the model of the hierarchical society, the political relationship between hierarchical superior and subordinate was characterized by membership of the former's household. This in itself gave rise to mutual obligations: loyalty and obedience by the subordinate on the one hand, and responsibility of the superior for actions by and wrongs to the subordinate on the other, using the metaphor "slave/master" or "father/son." Accordingly, the superior was entitled to punish the inferior for breach of the customarily expected duties.[42]

Nonetheless, a superior might regard his own authority as insufficient to ensure obedience and seek to strengthen his hold on the subordinate by adding a divine guarantor. For example, the Egyptian ruler Ramesses III used the oath to get one of his artisans to report misconduct among government workers.[43]

The same rationale applied to vassals. The emperor could not maintain an army permanently on vassal territory. A treaty provided a supplementary mechanism for enforcing loyalty, through the oath and its divine sanctions.

For both these reasons, therefore, it is better to think of vassal treaties in terms of negotiated settlements (in a political market that could favor buyers or sellers) than of imposed edicts.[44] After all, all that a treaty added was the divine sanctions promised by the vassal's oath. If the overlord could impose his will by brute force, he would have no need of them.

The Egyptian and Hittite Systems

It has been argued that the Hittite and Egyptian conceptions of international treaties during the Amarna period were different in kind. The Hittite system was formalized through treaties because it was based on agreement, whereas agreement with an inferior was excluded a priori for Pharaoh, who, in truth, regarded even equal powers as inferiors. Instead, the Egyptian model was the correct behavior expected of an official within the administration.[45]

I would qualify that view by arguing that any differences between the Egyptians and the Hittites were of political choice, not legal system. First, as we have seen, treaties are not necessary to a vassal relationship, so that the Egyptians' failure to use them would not necessarily be evidence of a different legal regime.

Second, the oath was by no means unthinkable to the Egyptians. We have seen its use in internal administration after the Amarna period. The Egyptians had indeed procured loyalty oaths from vassals at the logical time for such oaths, when they had been in an expansionist phase more than half a century earlier.[46] Although presented through the absolutist perspective of

Egyptian propaganda, their very acceptance of oaths by the gods was an admission that they could not rely entirely on their own power in their relations with their vassals. Whether the practice of taking oaths continued with each successor to the vassal throne is not clear; there are certainly references in the Amarna Letters to oaths by the vassals (EA 148, 209).

Third, it was not unthinkable for the oath to be taken by the Egyptian king himself. The peace treaty with the Hittites required an oath, which Ramesses II had no hesitation in mentioning approvingly in a letter.[47] In EA 164, as we have seen, Aziru of Amurru, faced with an Egyptian demand that he present himself at the Egyptian court to explain his actions, insisted that the king and his senior officials first swear an oath guaranteeing him safe conduct. It is reasonable to suppose that Aziru's condition was met, since he subsequently traveled to Egypt and returned safely.

For all these reasons, I consider that in spite of Egypt's reticence on the subject, treaties — parity and vassal — formed as much a part of the Egyptian conception of international law as they did for the Asiatic states. In this light, the proposal of a treaty by Alashiya in EA 35:42–43 should be considered a serious offer to which a positive reply could be expected from Egypt. In EA 24 III:109–19, the Mittanian king quotes a standard military assistance clause from a treaty that is similar to the mutual clauses found in the Egypt-Hatti peace treaty.[48] Whether it refers to an existing treaty or a proposed one, it assumes that whatever political difficulties stood in its way, such a treaty with Egypt had no legal impediment.

Conclusions

In this brief sketch, I have only been able to touch upon some of the many aspects of international law revealed by sources from the ancient Near East. I hope, however, that enough has been covered to demonstrate the importance of law in the thinking of the correspondents to the Amarna Letters. In negotiations between both equal and unequal powers, all parties carried with them and deployed the common conceptions and long-standing traditions of a functioning system of international law.

CHAPTER FOUR

The Amarna Age:
An International Society in the Making

RODOLFO RAGIONIERI

The Amarna Age represents an exciting challenge for the scholar of international relations (IR) because it opens a window on the formation of the first significant, extended international society in the history of humankind.[1] This process took place in a political, ideological, and economic environment totally different from that which favored the expansion of the states of Christian Europe into our present global international society. This poses two major questions. The first is whether we can apply modern research concepts to the international politics of other ages and cultural milieus. Specifically, how should a political scientist approach the diplomatic correspondence of the second millennium B.C.E.?[2] Second, there is no consensus among IR theorists either on the idea of an international society or on its process of formation.

I draw on two distinct schools of thought, which can nevertheless be fruitfully combined to investigate this process of societal formation: the English school of international relations and Constructivism. Then I move on to the main subject of this chapter, the international society of the Amarna Age. I highlight its process of development, paying special attention to its rules and institutions.

Theoretical Framework

What is an international society? An *international system,* not at all the same thing, exists when a set of states interact in such a way that each of them has to take into account the capabilities and possible actions of at least one of the others. However, an *international society* comes into being when "a group of states, conscious of certain common interests and common values, form a society in the sense that they conceive themselves to be bound by a common set of rules in their relations with one another, and share in the working of common institutions."[3] A sharper distinction sees a system as defined only by its interactions, a society by the sharing of fundamental values: Wight maintains that "a states-system will not come into being without a degree of cultural unity among its members."[4] International societies can be either anarchical or hierarchical. Anarchy is to be understood here in its IR sense: an international society is anarchical if there is no legitimate power over and above that of the constituent states. It is hierarchical if a supreme, overarching authority is accepted as legitimate by the other members. A special case is found when these two ideal types combine. Wight defined this case as a secondary states-system, a structure whose "members are not unitary actors but complex empires or suzerain states-systems."[5]

A much-debated question is whether an effective distinction can in fact be made between system and society. For example, James claims that it is almost impossible to make this distinction because "interaction requires both rules and communication, and reflects some common interests."[6] Use of the criterion of shared culture is unsatisfactory, however, because it would admit only a limited number of states. Nevertheless, James argues that the word "society" is better suited to characterize the set of states interacting at a certain historical period.

When considering the process of formation of an international society, the transformation of a system of interacting parts into a community underpinned by common interests, values, rules, and institutions, a key issue arises: whether the behavior of actors can be explained on the basis of rational choice or in terms of the idiosyncratic motives of the agents. In the jargon of IR theory, the choice is between rationalism and Constructivism.[7] Both varieties of rationalism, Neorealism and Neoliberal Institutionalism, assume that the preferences of states (or the utility functions of the actors) are externally (exogenously) given.[8] According to this school of thought, the result is either a permanent situation of conflict or one of cooperation fuelled by common interests. But no real change in the structure of preferences is brought about by interactions, common practices, or shared or conflicting identities.

The concept of international society is considered with suspicion by Neorealists. Nevertheless, some authors defining themselves as Neorealists have shown interest in the idea. For example, Buzan maintains that society is the natural result of the logic of anarchy: the need to survive and adapt impels social relations.[9] Buzan's attempt to bridge Neorealism and the English school is dealt with further below.

The second school of thought I draw on is usually labeled in contemporary IR theory as Constructivism. The main idea behind this approach is that agents are engaged in permanently constructing structures that, in turn, condition their actions. Moreover, agents' interests and actions are molded not by supposedly objective factors like power and security but rather by subjective factors, such as identities and visions of the social (and nonsocial) world. According to Wendt, Constructivism agrees with Realism that states are central units of analysis in international political theory. It differs from both kinds of structural rationalism in that it considers the key structures in the state system as intersubjective rather than objective, and it considers identities and interests as socially constructed, not exogenously given.[10]

Classical Realism, it should be emphasized, in the form put forward by Hans Morgenthau, is not diametrically opposed to Constructivism.[11] This is apparent in Morgenthau's analysis of the balance of power. Morgenthau concludes that the balance of power as such is not sufficient to maintain equilibrium. Rather, the latter must be underpinned by cultural homogeneity; to use Raymond Aron's terminology, by "a number of elements, intellectual and moral in nature, upon which both the balance of power and the stability of the modern state system repose."[12] These elements are intersubjective rather than given, more like issues of identity and mutual expectation, than the rational maximization of utility.[13]

Whether one or the other approach is better does not concern me here, and no single school of thought should be drawn on exclusively in considering the formation of an international society. Buzan maintains that he uses a Neorealist approach but then writes that "through the interactive operation of trade, war and the balance of power, the transfer of technologies (both mechanical and social), intermarriage, travel, and the homogenizing effect of periods of hegemony, suzerainty, dominion, or imperial rule, units will tend to become more similar to each other. This is Waltz's logic of anarchy generating like units."[14] Buzan's peculiar version of Neorealism becomes clear when he refers to "the desire for a degree of international order" and the "acceptance of a shared identity."[15]

It is a matter of semantics whether you conclude that Waltz's logic of anarchy or the construction of an intersubjective social reality by practice and adjustment is in operation. The ambiguity found here is simply the ambiguity of real life, in this case, of social and political interaction. It is indeed extremely difficult to distinguish definitively between what is dictated by sheer power and "objective" interest, and what is conditioned by subjective factors. The further we move beyond pure survival, the more security is influenced by subjective factors, and the more interaction becomes intersubjective rather than objective.

There are two further grounds for drawing on Constructivism in tandem with the English school: the distinction between inside and outside dimensions of politics, and the fact that we are interested in a process of societal formation.

First, any theory whose premise is that states are unitary actors characterized by rationally optimizing behavior assumes, explicitly or implicitly, the existence of two closely related—but not equivalent—institutions: sovereignty and a system of self-help under anarchy.[16] Both Neorealism and Constructivism take as the implicit starting point of their discourse the sharp distinction between inside and outside, between domestic and international politics.[17] In contrast, the Amarna Age was marked by an overlapping and mingling of domestic and interstate levels that cannot be equated with our views of the political world. One even wonders whether there was any idea of politics as an autonomous activity.

As far as the second point is concerned, international society in the Amarna Age was not yet fully developed: general principles of interaction seem to have been agreed, but actors were still adjusting to each other. Even if preferences are considered to be imposed from without, in the Amarna Age the players were for the first time interacting in an environment that went well beyond their familiar domestic milieu. A further conundrum is whether they were consciously and purposefully building a diplomatic system or simply accommodating to a new situation in an unplanned way according to their different perspectives.

The Amarna International Society

Before considering the formation of Amarna society, its institutions, rules, and roles, three points should be stressed:

1. The states of the Ancient Near East formed an international society, at least during the last centuries of the Late Bronze Age.
2. The Amarna Age was an international society in the making, the first of its kind.
3. Amarna society was structurally different from other international societies.

My central contention is that Amarna was a society in the making. This implies that before the Amarna Age there was an interstate *system,* but not an international *society,* as described above. Greater Mesopotamia was already a system at the end of the third millennium. During the first half of the second millennium, the whole ancient Near East, and possibly beyond, could be considered a system.[18] But it is not until the Mari Age (first half of the eighteenth century) that a possible candidate for an international society in the making presents itself. Nevertheless, it was short-lived and included much less territory and fewer states than did Amarna.[19] In earlier periods, then, the oscillation between unification and fragmentation points to very weak integrative social elements.

Also important is that closer diplomatic and economic interactions, labeled by Zaccagnini in this volume as "interdependence," brought about significant changes for all actors, especially the major ones. The Great Kings had to learn to live within the limits of their power. Moreover, two necessities had to be kept in harmony: on the one hand, domestic stability and consensus, often based on an ideology of superiority with respect to foreign rulers; on the other hand, the existence of outside powers and the need to conduct external relations. Actors had to adapt, to some extent consciously, to a new environment in a period of transition and change.

Who, though, were these actors, the members of the Amarna society? The Amarna archive falls into two parts: the correspondence between Great Kings, and that between Pharaoh and his Canaanite vassals. This conforms to our view of a purely anarchic international system in the second half of the second millennium B.C.E. From the Letters we observe quite different types of relations between actors of distinct rank, each of which has some control over territory. Thus, members of the society included not only the major powers (Egypt, Mittani, Hatti, Babylonia, Alashiya, and later, Assyria) whose rulers called each other brothers, but also the minor states that came under the suzerainty of the Great Kings. These minor rulers, appearing in the second part of the correspondence, were linked to their suzerain in a state of submission, the metaphor for which is the servant-master relationship.

The Amarna states-system reflects the characteristics — common interests, values, rules, and institutions — regarded as defining an international society and is examined in detail below. First, however, it is worth observing that contemporary actors tended to picture the unit of politics in terms of domestic society. States were not conceptualized abstractly but were thought of as synonymous with the person of the ruler, or at most with his household, wives, magnates, troops, horses, and chariots, in line with the formula repeated at the beginning of every letter. Hence, the various metaphors used in the correspondence, such as brotherhood and the master-slave relationship, correspond to the vision of a structured society. These metaphors reflected the paradigms of relationships available to the rulers either in their extended family or in their own area of direct control. Their use suggests the difficulty in thinking of external relations as an autonomous area of activity and, indeed, the overall difficulty of thinking "theoretically," as we might anachronistically put it. Use of these metaphors was not accidental; the structure of interstate society was probably thought to reflect that found in domestic society — lords bound to each other by ties of brotherhood, their servants in a position of total subordination.

The common interests of the Amarna Great Kings were much the same as at many other periods of history: the maintenance of domestic stability, in the sense both of internal social harmony and the preservation of suzerain-vassal relations. For the suzerain, it was important to keep a hold over his vassals, who in turn had an interest in emphasizing the exchange of dependence for protection.[20]

Rules are the third element defining an international society. They are patterns of behavior that are considered desirable or normative in given situations.[21] Kratochwil adds that their function is "dealing with the recurrent issues of social life: conflict and co-operation."[22] They can be either fixed by interstate agreement, derived from a moral standard, or simply accepted by dint of established practice. The theoretical question, which is differently answered by the various paradigms of IR, concerns the origins and causes of rules. According to Realists, rules and norms are just the formal expression of power relations. For their part, Liberal Institutionalists hail their emergence as proof that states' rationality is not so bounded and shortsighted as most Realists claim. A third position is taken by Constructivism: rules are certainly constrained by power relations, but other important factors contribute to their development, like shared practices and the need for stable identities. Moreover, interests and identities are not determined by the structure of the system but by a continuous process of structuration: agents constantly erect structures, which in turn modify agents' preferences.

What rules can be recognized, how were they formed, and how did they affect the identities of members of Amarna society? In the correspondence we detect several rules, mainly revealed by complaints about their violation (EA 9, EA 28) or unsatisfactory fulfillment (EA 1, EA 2, EA 4, EA 29). There are two main types of rules: rules of reciprocity and rules of submission. Relationships of submission had always existed in the history of the ancient Near East; it is the rules governing diplomatic relations between notionally equal Great Kings that were just taking shape.

The first rule of reciprocity is more a general principle than a specific rule: mutual trust, asserted forthrightly by Amenhotep III in EA 1. It is nevertheless interesting that Egyptian kings seem to interpret this rule in a self-serving way; they are allowed to mistrust the kings of Babylonia, but the latter are granted no such right. Here is an interesting case of tension between the rules of Amarna society and the self-perception and ideology of the most powerful ruler in the region. Reciprocity is not unconditionally guaranteed. If the Egyptian king marries a Babylonian princess, then the king of Babylonia, argues Kadashman-Enlil, can surely marry a daughter of Pharaoh (EA 2, EA 4). Often, reciprocity took the form of a trade-off between equal status, represented by the exchange of princesses, and compensation in the form of gifts when, in fact, there was no reciprocal marriage (see, e.g., EA 13 and EA 14). Pharaoh never misses an opportunity to demonstrate some kind of superiority, for example, in his treatment of messengers. Moreover, brotherhood and reciprocity did not necessarily imply mutual help in difficult situations, as claimed by Tushratta (EA 24 and 29), who was seriously exercised by a perceived Hittite threat.

The rules of submission were very clear: a vassal could not maintain relations with Great Kings other than his suzerain. Conversely, the suzerain had to protect the vassal. This rule is mostly evident in the vassals' complaints. Nevertheless, as Liverani explains, the issue of protection was complicated by misunderstandings arising from the use of two native languages, Egyptian and West Semitic, mediated by a third common language, Akkadian.[23] The contrasting needs of the vassal princelings and of the Great Kings also complicated matters.

In the Amarna international society there were two main roles: major power and vassal. Nevertheless, there were ambiguous cases. When the Assyrian king Assur-uballit sent messengers to Egypt, Burna-Buriash complained to the Egyptian king, either Akhenaten or Tutankhamun.[24] The crisis resulting from this event can be viewed from two different perspectives: either as a violation of rules, or as a change of roles. Assyria's unclear position, its transitional status in terms of power, prestige, and commercial relevance, allowed Burna-Buriash of Babylonia, Assur-uballit of Assyria, and the Egyptian king respectively to interpret Assyria's role differently. Burna-Buriash eventually accepted the change, however, and we know that he married a daughter of the Assyrian king, Muballitat-Sherua, thus stabilizing and further legitimizing the Assyrian role.[25] From the point of view of Assur-uballit, it was a successful attempt to assert his role as a Great King in international politics.

From the different rules setting standards for diplomatic behavior, it is clear that this international society had a double character. On one level, it was an anarchical society from the perspective of relations among the major powers. Great Kings did not acknowledge any of their number as possessing legitimate hegemonic power, and no country was recognized as enjoying special status. This is true even though Egypt's kings never considered themselves on an equal footing with the others, as is clear from EA 1, for example, and as demonstrated by Egyptian royal marriage practices. Nevertheless, this ideological pretension was never acknowledged.

The structuring of relations between the Great Kings can be interpreted as follows: at first, Great Kings shaped their relations according to the ideology of brotherhood. But power relations were decisive in determining who could enter the Great Powers' Club. Thus, we have a double aspect: naked power on the one hand, and an intersubjective, constructed, fraternal identity on the other. Afterward, as we see from the exchange of letters between Egypt and Babylonia, the principle of reciprocity was applied less strictly than the ideology of brotherhood would require. When Babylonia's request for an Egyptian princess is refused, departure from the principle of reciprocity has its source in the clash between the internal and external identities of Pharaoh. At home in Egypt, he was considered and considered himself as a god, at least from the point of view of his public image. Abroad, in his external relations with other Great Kings, he was supposedly on an equal footing. Thus, the rules of the game were the product of an interplay between different factors: power, the domestic identity of the king, and the adjustment of the ideology of brotherhood, a basic element of interstate relations, to the different exigencies of the rulers.

Anarchy was not the only feature of international politics in the Late Bronze Age in the Near East. At the same time, there was an equally important hierarchical dimension, the relations between Great Kings and their vassals. One could argue that vassals were not first-rank actors in international society because the significant relations were those conducted among major powers. Nevertheless, they were second-rank members of international society because they could play a role by shifting their allegiance from one suzerain to another. Moreover, the main rule of the society directly concerned the relations between vassals and suzerain. The actor/member distinction distinguishes Amarna both from the modern world, which is anarchical in the absence of a superordinate authority, and also from the international societies to be found in the *oikoumene* of Byzantium, Europe in the Middle Ages, and classical Islam. The latter were hierarchically organized international societies whose legitimacy was grounded in religion.

There were also minor kings, like 'Abdi-Ashirta, who tried to gain advantage or increase their power, in part by violating the rule of submission or by attacking other vassal princelings. This behavior weakened neither the hierarchical character of society nor the legitimacy of the generally accepted order, just as the existence of brigands or of organized crime does not, in principle, annul the legitimacy of the territorial state.

The Institutions of the Amarna International Society

As we have seen, the workings of international society are made possible by institutions. If Amarna was an international society in the making then the nature and evolution of its institutions become a key issue.

Institutions are variously defined in IR. The Merriam-Webster *Collegiate Dictionary* defines an institution as "a significant practice, relationship, or organization in a society or culture." Within the IR discipline, Keohane defines institutions as "related complexes of rules and norms, identifiable in space and time." [26] Bull's definition is more general and closer to the dictionary definition: "By institution we do not necessarily imply an organization or administrative machinery, but rather a set of habits and practices shaped toward the realization of common goals." [27]

I adhere here to the notion of institution in the broader sense. In the Amarna correspondence it is possible to find traces of assorted practices constitutive of a diplomatic regime, such as dynastic marriage, the exchange of gifts, the correspondence itself, and the regular exchange of messengers. An initial interesting question is whether war and the balance of power can be considered, in this context, as institutions, as was the case during the golden age of the balance of power in Europe (1713–89 and 1814–1914), or as war was during the age of the warring states in classical China (475–221 B.C.E.).[28]

The balance of power was not, strictly speaking, an institution of Amarna society. Surprisingly, in modern terms, the major powers did not try to balance each other by means of alliances. Egypt, for instance, did not appear to use Arzawa to block the rise of Hatti. Moran has argued that the Egyptian interest in a diplomatic marriage with Arzawa was to pave the way for some form of implicit anti-Hatti alliance, but Arzawa was later conquered by Hatti, with no evidence for Egyptian intervention.[29] Moreover, during the Hittite and Assyrian takeover and the destruction of Mittani/Hanigalbat (see EA 29), Egypt remained more or less passive. According to the "old paradigm," this behavior was to be explained by Akhenaten's relative lack of interest in foreign policy.[30] If this is not so, as Liverani insists, Egyptian inactivity seems to have been linked to a low level of interest in events occurring outside its sphere of influence. Ancient Greeks, Romans, and modern European statesmen would have been concerned at the disruption of the system of security on the edge of their spheres of influence. Egypt seemed more inclined to maintain contact with all her peers — to manage, by diplomatic means, the society of Great Kings rather than engage in a complex regulation of the balance of power.

In the various tripolar or multipolar situations that arose, like the last stage in the Mittanian drama or the Babylonian–Assyrian–Egyptian triangle, there is no attempt on anyone's part to use force or the threat of force, as balance of power logic entails. Two reasons, technological and ideological, can be adduced for this — to us — remarkable lacuna. First, balancing implies the continuous flow of information between the various Great Kings, something not possible at this time. Moreover, the actual implementation of the mechanism of the balance of power implies the concerted use of military force. To this end, not only is communication vital but also the capability of moving armed might to the theater of operations at the right moment. It seems that, at the time, the ability to deploy military forces over a long distance at the time was far lower than that needed for conducting an effective balance of power policy. It is also doubtful whether the very idea of maintaining *equilibrium* by means of shifting alliances between Great Kings had yet formed in the minds of diplomats and rulers. To conclude, it may be that a rough balance of power existed in practice, but that is insufficient to interpret it as an institution.[31]

A strict balance of power probably only emerged for the first time as an institution of international society in the Hellenic subsystem of city-states.[32] A rudimentary balance did exist in the post-Assyrian system (from the fall of Assyria and Nineveh to the Achemenid expansion). It was not managed, however, by the complex web of alliances, diplomacy, and wars we can observe in preclassical and classical Greece, or in late medieval and Renaissance Italy, but rather by a rough standoff resulting from great battles like those fought at Karkemish or on the river Halys. In fact, the Hellenistic kingdoms imported the complex and subtle practice of the balance of power, as we know, it into the Near East.[33]

Nevertheless, Egyptian power had its limits. These were not only military and technological but also ideological in character. Egypt, a militarily and economically prevailing power, entered a system of interstate relations shaped by Akkadian culture and was thus in the curious situation of having to adapt to a foreign culture instead of making its own cultural imprint. The Egyptian ruling elite had to accept this situation while continuing to display a certain degree of contempt for other cultures.

What of the institution of war? It is noteworthy that the incidence of war decreased during the Amarna Age, even though, on the basis of estimates of probability, it should have increased. War was certainly fought in conformity with certain conventions and understood in terms of a definite ideology.[34] Resort to war was not excluded, but it did not play the role that it performed in the European balance of power or in the ancient Chinese system. Force and war were used on an ad hoc basis in bilateral relations, not as a mechanism to preserve the balance.

Martin Wight defined diplomacy as the "master institution" of international society.[35] This is particularly appropriate in our case, since war and the balance of power, for technical and ideological reasons, did not perform the function they possessed later. Diplomacy in the Amarna Age cannot be compared to the system of resident embassies but should be understood in the context of the effective means, requirements, and assumptions of the time. Diplomacy and its methods, the envoy and the cuneiform tablet, were the means by which kings and vassals could establish contact and give shape to a permanent web of formal relations. It performed political and ideological functions, transforming existing ties of dependency into the more complex web of an international society possessing anarchical and hierarchical aspects. Moreover, diplomacy permitted the reconciliation of the various self-centered ideologies and identities.

Clearly, diplomacy mainly took the form of correspondence, with all its protocol and formal expressions. The safety of messengers was an important aspect of this institution, even though, as usual, we observe this rule in its infringement and when messengers are not permitted to report home. In EA 3, the messenger sent by Kadashman-Enlil of Babylonia to Amenhotep III is detained for six years; the Babylonian king protests that this would not have occurred in his father's day. Similar complaints are made by Tushratta (EA 28). Customary international law, as Westbrook argues in this volume, underpins the normative expectations of Great Kings and must be considered a central institution of Amarna society. Dynastic marriage and exchanges of gifts are other institutions strikingly reflected in the Letters.

Two aspects of the correspondence between the Great Kings must be taken into account. First, the bargaining over gold, gifts, marriages, an escort for a princess, and so on, was authentic. Kassite-Babylonian kings attached importance both to status and to gold, and they were accused of selling their daughters for Egyptian gold. For their part, the Assyrians had long been engaged in international trade. At the same time, the negotiation is more than routine; the kings act as though they were purposefully setting standards. Obviously, they were not consciously building an international society. But they perhaps did realize that "the first time is often considered a constitutive experience in human relations, setting the pattern for future encounters."[36] Although these exchanges of letters and messengers were not a novelty, the intensity of exchanges and the development of often implicit rules of the game marked a difference from previous ages.

Acceptance of brotherhood contradicted Egypt's hegemonic ideology, with its concomitant organization of space into center and periphery.[37] On the Assyrian side, Assur-uballit seemed to be aware that he was setting new standards when he wrote in his first letter to the king of Egypt (EA 15): "Up to now, my predecessors have not written; today I write to you."

Conclusions

Wendt lists four basic interests generated by the corporate identity of the state, which usefully encapsulate the motives underlying the behavior of Amarna actors considered in this chapter:

1. physical security, including the state's differentiation from other states;
2. ontological security or predictability in relationships with the world, implying a desire for stable social identities;
3. recognition by other actors, over and above survival through brute force;
4. development, in the sense of realizing human aspirations for a better life, for which states are repositories at the collective level.[38]

Albeit in varying degrees, the first three points help to circumscribe the role of Amarna actors. In its literal sense, the fourth point is important only for modern states. But in terms of the exchange of gifts, to be understood in relation to the metaphors of the extended family and the "enlarged village," it also has relevance to Amarna rulers.[39] The formation of Amarna society, then, did not merely reflect calculations of power, nor is the balance of power sufficient to explain the working of this Late Bronze Age system. To understand how the rules, institutions, and roles of Amarna society emerged, we must also look at processes of mutual adjustment and modification, diplomatic interactions, and the intersubjective play of shared ideas, mutual perceptions, and joint expectations.

CHAPTER FIVE

Realism, Constructivism, and the Amarna Letters

STEVEN R. DAVID

As someone unfamiliar with ancient Near Eastern studies, I approached the Amarna Letters with the question of what it can teach me about my own field, contemporary international relations. I was pleased to conclude that the Amarna Letters were an ideal source to help resolve an ongoing debate between Realists and Constructivists that is at the center of much that is being written about contemporary international relations. The debate concerns what determines the behavior of states and other actors in the international system. Constructivists argue that how we think and talk about politics determines how we behave. A discourse of conflict, for example, will lead to war, one of cooperation will lead to peace. Realists, in contrast, argue that the world is an independent reality that imposes itself on us regardless of our subjective understanding of it. It does not matter how we express ourselves or how we perceive our surroundings, because the reality of the material world will determine our actions.

The Amarna Letters can play a critical role in settling this debate on how discourse affects behavior. Because the Letters were written before many of the contemporary ideas of political science were developed and well before the principles of Realism were put forth, they are a good indication as to the impact of discourse on behavior. If those living during the Amarna period behaved in a manner consistent with Realism, despite not being familiar with Realist ideas, it would be a powerful argument against Constructivism. Conversely, if the ancients behaved in ways that did not conform to Realism but instead reflected the prevailing ethos of the times, the Constructivist position would be enhanced.

This chapter is in three parts. First, I briefly discuss the major assumptions of Realism and Constructivism. Second, I argue why Realism better explains the politics of the Amarna period than does Constructivism. Finally, I consider some objections to using Realism for the Amarna period and explain why they are ultimately not persuasive.

Realism and Constructivism

Although Realism means different things to different people, there is a rough consensus as to what it entails.[1] Realism is a view of the way the world works. It does not dictate how people and states must behave. Instead, Realism says in effect, this is the way the world is. If you wish to survive and prosper, you must acknowledge its essential reality and act accordingly. Realists also emphasize continuity in international relations. The persistence of war, the fear of other countries, the rise and fall of Great Powers, competition among states, and the formation and dissolution of alliances are seen as permanent features of world politics.[2] The reasons the world has remained as it is and will not change derive from several assumptions maintained by most Realists.

The Realist paradigm is framed by two underlying assumptions. First, Realists see human nature as fixed and flawed. People are aggressive, acquisitive, hateful, and violent. Even if a given individual is "good," he or she cannot assume the same is true for their neighbors, forcing one to be constantly vigilant to the evil machinations of others. The best we can hope for is to mitigate the harmful impulses of others by convincing them they have more to lose than gain by acting wrongly. The second fundamental assumption of Realism is that we live in a world of international anarchy. Anarchy does not necessarily mean chaos. Rather, it simply means that there is no central authority that makes and enforces rules of behavior. Each unit is free to determine what its interests are and how best to realize them. Because of the absence of a regulating authority, competition among states, sometimes leading to war, is an ever-present feature of international politics.

In addition to these two fundamental assumptions, several other beliefs are held by most Realists.[3] First, states are able to hurt one another. Because they possess offensive military capability and there is no world government to provide security, states rightly see other states as threatening. Second, this threat is made worse by the fact that states can never be certain about the intentions of other states. Third, states seek to survive, to maintain their independence and autonomy. Finally, the leaders of states behave rationally to achieve their ends. Although they lack perfect information and may make bad decisions, leaders will seek to develop policies that will provide them with the best possible outcomes.

As a result of these assumptions, we can expect states to behave in certain ways. First, states will seek to increase their power. Power is sought to increase the survivability of states (strong states will be better able to deal with adversaries) and as an end in itself. Second, states will align in ways to ensure that no one state or group of states emerges preponderant. In an environment of anarchy, overwhelming power cannot help but be a threat to others. Since states seek to survive, they will form balances of power to prevent other states from becoming too dominant. Third, a Realist world is one of self-help. Alliances may be sought and international law invoked, but in the final analysis, states recognize that they are responsible for their own security and will distrust means to protect them that are not under their complete control. Fourth, efforts by states to take steps to defend themselves will be seen by other states as threatening. Since there is no clear distinction between offensive and defensive weaponry, any efforts by a state to improve its security will be perceived as endangering the security of others. (Realists refer to this situation as the "security dilemma.") Fifth, war is not to be taken lightly, but it is a legitimate means to ensure one's independence. Preserving one's survival and autonomy are preferable to peace. Sixth, conventional morality has little or no place in a Realist world. The greatest immorality is to behave in such a manner as to endanger the existence of your state. Finally, cooperation can occur in a Realist world, but it will always be limited and temporary. Concerns about cheating and bestowing a relative advantage on a potential adversary will severely limit the extent and frequency of cooperative behavior.

The Constructivist view of the world differs sharply from the Realist vision.[4] For Constructivists, the world is not some independent reality that imposes itself on all who live in it. Rather, shared discourse, or how communities of individuals think and talk about the world, determines behavior. The fundamental structures of the world are social rather than material. Everything we see is mediated by our existing theories, making it impossible to have a clear distinction between subject and object. The interests of states are socially constructed and not to be assumed a priori.

The expectations states have for one another is the key to how they will interact. If states expect other states to be friendly and cooperative, if they define their interests in a communitarian way (as is the case with the democracies of Western Europe), war and the threat of violence will be absent. Conversely, if states expect others to take advantage of them at every turn, as the Realists would have us believe, cooperation and peace will not prevail. International anarchy is not the "cause" of anything and certainly not the cause of international conflict. As Alexander Wendt argues, anarchy is what states make of it.[5] Although entrenched patterns of behavior and thought make rapid changes difficult, the discourse and prevailing culture of the international system will ultimately determine how states act and whether peace or war will characterize international politics. Thus, fundamental change in the behavior of states — not continuity — is both possible and likely, in the Constructivist view.

Realists are doubly guilty in the eyes of many Constructivists. They are guilty for mistakenly arguing that the world is an independent reality that forces itself on the observer rather than a creation of that observer. They are also guilty for producing a discourse that creates a world where the threat of war or its occurrence are the dominant features of international politics. Realists counter that they are simply describing the world as it is. Discourse reflects the material reality of the world and is not an independent cause of behavior. We may wish things to be different, but ultimately states and people have to confront the reality of their surroundings, which induces them to behave in ways that Realists predict.

The Amarna Letters and the Realist-Constructivist Debate

A good place to start with the role of the Amarna Letters in the Constructivist-Realist debate is the essay in this volume by Cohen. Although it is not clear that he would call himself a Constructivist, Cohen presents a Constructivist argument in his analysis of the Amarna Letters, "All in the Family: Ancient Near Eastern Diplomacy."[6] Cohen makes the case that the Amarna Letters revealed an international system perceived as an extended family. Instead of leaders focusing on state interest, as Realists would have it, the major powers acted in ways dictated by familial obligation and brotherhood. As Cohen explains:

> Strangers to the philosophical thinking later invented by the Greeks, these kings were incapable of conceiving of international relations in terms of the sort of political abstractions we now take for granted, such as the national interest, the balance of power, or justice. In the Ancient Near East, tangible attachments — love, family ties, filial piety, and marriage — were the only bases for obligation that made sense. Foreign policy was accordingly preoccupied with relationship issues (25).

I disagree. My interpretation of the Amarna Letters reveals a world where leaders sought to achieve the national interest as they understood it and were experts at playing balance of power politics. Although Cohen is correct to point out the familial tone of much of the Amarna correspondence, the actions of the leaders were fully consistent with Realist thinking. The states of the Amarna period lived in a world characterized by international anarchy, in which constant struggles for power ensued. Individuals lied, cheated, and stole in a manner all too reminiscent of contemporary times. Leaders expanded at the expense of their neighbors; balances of powers formed to check hegemonic states; Great Powers established spheres of influences that were constantly encroached upon by other states; the strong preyed upon the weak; and the weak did their best to survive. War, or the threat of war, was the primary means of resolving conflicts. In short, the states of the Amarna period behaved much like the states of today and much like Realists would predict. That they did so without the concepts of Realism to influence their actions is a strong argument in favor of the universal logic of the Realist model.[7]

My case for the Amarna period fitting the Realist model rests both on secondary sources that describe politics during this time and the Amarna Letters themselves.[8] Drawing from the above discussion, I identify several key concepts of Realism. I then show how each concept was consistent with the dealings of states and leaders during the Amarna era.

Anarchy

The defining context in which politics took place in the Amarna period was one of international anarchy. There was no overarching authority beyond that of the states to impose order. What order existed came through the power of the major states and their vassals. A consistent theme running through the Amarna Letters is the need of weaker states to secure help from the stronger in order to preserve their security. Leaders recognized that in a world without any overarching authority, only help from the powerful could protect them from aggression by others. The leader of Byblos, Rib-Hadda, for example, constantly begged Pharaoh for help in dealing with the expansionist Aziru (see, e.g., EA 104). Appeals to gods might be useful and were often invoked, but no head of state relied on such appeals alone. The leaders of the Amarna period recognized, as do leaders today, that efforts to achieve security in an environment of anarchy require either self-help or the assistance of other states.

If anything, anarchy was an even more important factor in the time of Amarna than in the modern world. In the contemporary era, anarchy is said to exist between states; in the Amarna period, anarchy existed not only between states, but also within the vast unsettled lands beyond states. As such, a constant preoccupation of states was to prevent the spread of anarchy (in the form of savage tribes) from overwhelming the state. States repeatedly sent military expeditions beyond their borders to push back the forces of chaos and thus preserve order within their own boundaries.

Ironically, the concern with spreading anarchy that characterized the Amarna period is making a comeback in the post–Cold War world of today. As Robert Kaplan has argued, the threats many states currently face are not so much from other states, as was the case for much of modern history, but rather from disorder that spills over state boundaries.[9] Just as Egypt had more to fear from warring tribes than it did from any rival country, so today do the leaders of such countries as Nigeria and Zaire worry more about chaos seeping through their frontiers than they do about organized invasions from neighboring states. Perhaps if chaos continues to spread in what used to be called the Third World, the leaders of the West will have even more in common with the Pharaohs of the Amarna period as they attempt to isolate themselves from the forces of disorder in an increasingly tumultuous world.

Uncertainty of Intentions and Offensive Capability

A key observation of Realism is that you can never be certain about the intentions of others. They may speak in peaceful, reassuring terms, but that tells you nothing about what they really intend to do. Because there is no government beyond that of the states to protect you if you guess wrong, leaders are forever trying to determine the true aims of their fellow heads of state.

This description certainly holds for the leaders of states of the Amarna period. Many of the Amarna Letters were written to persuade leaders of the good intentions of the sender. Lesser princes seeking Egyptian support took pains to reassure Egypt that they were in fact acting in Pharaoh's interests (see, e.g., the letters of 'Abdi-Ashirta, leader of Amurru, reassuring Pharaoh that he was a loyal and valuable ally; EA 60–65). Egypt, for its part, was frequently concerned that allies were saying one thing but doing something else. In some cases, such as with 'Abdi-Ashirta, they were correct. The desire to understand the intentions of states comes up very clearly in Assyria's efforts to "see" Egypt, that is, to get a sense of its intentions as it tries to take its place among the Great Powers of the international system (EA 15).[10] For the states of the Amarna Age, no less than today, there was no certainty in what your neighbors were up to, whatever their declared intentions might be.

The inability to predict what other states might do was so important because then (as now), states retained the capability to hurt and even destroy each other. The Amarna Letters are a litany of aggression, conquests, and urgent pleas for assistance. Chariots, infantry, and archers may have been replaced by modern armies and nuclear weapons, but the threat they posed to neighboring states was as intense as exists today.

States Seek to Survive

A principal aim of states during the Amarna period was to survive. As Realists would predict, an anarchic international system made up of states with the capability of hurting one another places a high premium on the struggle of those states to do what they can to preserve their existence. Egypt, as the major power in the region, was critical to that survival. Pharaoh's ability to ensure that his subjects were protected (*naṣru*) was central to Egypt's attractiveness as a patron.[11] Pharaoh not only protected the security of his vassals from external attack through the stationing of Egyptian garrisons, he also on occasion provided security details to protect individual leaders from internal unrest. In later times, the Praetorian Guard of the Roman Empire and the security forces of East Germany in the Third World, during the Cold War, would provide similar functions of protection and control. In one respect, the security provided by Pharaoh was even more important than that of modern times. As Mario Liverani notes, Pharaoh not only ensured the physical survival of his subjects, he also held out the promise of life after death.[12]

Great powers not only protected friendly leaders, they also threatened the survival of those who would leave the fold. When 'Abdi-Ashirta's expansion became a threat to Egypt, Pharaoh apparently had him assassinated (EA 101). When 'Abdi-Ashirta's son, Aziru, apparently aligned with an enemy of Egypt, Pharaoh threatened his survival and that of his family: "If for any reason whatsoever you prefer to do evil, and if you plot evil, treacherous things, than you, together with your entire family, shall die by the axe of the king" (EA 162). Then as now, appealing to the need to survive in a dangerous world was a powerful weapon of states.

Struggle for Power

Realists predict that a struggle for survival in an anarchic realm will inexorably lead to a struggle for power. Such was certainly the case during the Amarna period. Major powers sought to increase their power as much as they could to advance their own interests. They built city walls and sent out troops to suppress potential threats. Egypt in particular amassed a great empire in large measure to preserve its domestic security. Relying chiefly on native city rulers under the control of Egyptian political officers, Pharaoh was able to project his power far from the center of Egypt at a minimal cost to himself.

Expansion not only provided a margin of security for Egypt, it also played a key role in legitimizing Pharaoh's rule. Expansion of his power demonstrated that Pharaoh was acting with the blessing of the gods while securing the tribute he needed to justify his position with the nobility. The struggle for power was also a hallmark of the vassal states, who were constantly at war with one another. Indeed, their fervent requests for Egyptian assistance stemmed from either their desire to expand at the expense of their neighbors or from fear that their neighbors' expansion would victimize them.

The struggle for power is clearly indicated in the emergence of Assyria as a great power, as documented in EA 15. In this letter, Assyria seeks to send an emissary to Egypt for the first time: "Do not delay the messenger whom I sent to you for a visit. He should visit and then leave for here [Assyria]. He should see what you are like and what your country is like, and then leave for here." As Pinhas Artzi argues, this letter is an effort by Assyria both to achieve recognition as a great power and to "see" Egypt.[13] The most dangerous time in international relations is when a rising Great Power seeks to supplant an existing one. The harsh tone of this letter and the tense feeling it invokes reflects the jockeying for power that characterized relations between the great states more than any concept of brotherhood.

Alliances and Balances of Power

The origins of alliances during the Amarna period are familiar to students of contemporary international relations. States concluded alliances to achieve interests that they were unable to realize on their own. Through the vassal states, Egypt obtained protection of its major caravan routes, ensured a steady flow of tribute to Egypt, received intelligence about potentially threatening developments, and acquired bases for Egyptian forces. The vassal states enabled Pharaoh to project power far from the center of Egypt and thus helped keep away the forces of disorder.[14] For their part, the vassals received the military support of Egypt, which enabled them to achieve a measure of political autonomy and helped with their own plans of expansion. Although the vassals pledged an oath of loyalty to Pharaoh, their allegiance was temporary; they maintained the option to realign should interests dictate. In addition to the vassal states, Egypt also maintained alliances with Great Powers, notably Mittani and Babylonia.

As is true today, weaker states sought to attract more powerful allies by highlighting (and perhaps exaggerating) the function they performed for their stronger neighbors in supporting their material interests. In letters to Egyptian officials, for example, 'Abdi-Ashirta explains the benefits of his aligning with Pharaoh based on Amurru's role in protecting Egypt's security, economic well-being, and its expatriate citizens (EA 62, 60, 371).[15] These same interests lie at the origins of contemporary alliances.

The Amarna period also demonstrated the relevance of balance of power politics. Balances of power regularly formed, dissipated, and reformed during the Amarna era. Egypt controlled its vassal states through policies following basic balance of power logic, such as divide and rule. Some allies, like 'Abdi-Ashirta, became too powerful and thus threatened the balance of power. Egypt responded by intervening against 'Abdi-Ashirta, thus employing a basic tool for maintaining a balance of power system (EA 101). When Egypt became too powerful, it drove allies away, as was the case when Aziru went over to the Hittites. Perhaps one of Aziru's goals in realigning was to counter Egyptian power, which threatened Amurru, especially as Amurru sought to expand. Egypt's forceful efforts to dissuade Aziru from realigning (EA 162) demonstrated its concern that upsetting the balance of power would present an unacceptable threat to its security. Egypt's own expansion was halted in pure balance of power fashion when its efforts to project its influence in the north were stymied by the major powers of Mittani and the Hittites. Thereafter, much of Egyptian effort was designed to confront the resurgent threat posed by the Hittites. (This explains the Egyptian alliance with Arzawa in an effort to outflank the Hittite threat.) The ancients may not have known the term "balance of power," but they acted as if they did.

War

At the heart of the Realist vision is the view that war or the threat of force is the ultimate arbiter of conflicts of interest. If anything, war was even more central to the politics of the Amarna period than it has been in modern times. The major powers and the vassal states were constantly at war or preparing for war. Despite all the talk of brotherhood, war was seen as a perfectly natural tool to advance a state or a leader's interests. By being victorious in war, the leader of a state kept the forces of disorder far from his frontiers and reassured his subjects that he was governing effectively. As best as I can determine, war presented no moral difficulties. It was an acceptable and regular policy for the advancement of interests.

Other Examples of Realist Behavior

In the Amarna period other types of behavior that are consistent with Realism were displayed. Security dilemmas were a constant source of concern.

For example, the efforts of Amurru to expand may well have been undertaken for defensive reasons. Nevertheless, those efforts could not help but raise concerns in Egypt and other powers for their own security, leading to conflict. Spheres of interest, a common feature of international politics in the Realist conception, characterized the Amarna Age. Babylonia's demands that Assyria not be allowed to establish foreign relations independent of it is basic sphere-of-influence politics. Political assassination, fomenting insurgency, and rampant corruption characterized the Amarna states, just as they have characterized much of modern politics.

Finally, human nature emerges in familiar ways in the Amarna period. We recognize the haughtiness of Pharaoh, the seemingly limitless ambition of 'Abdi-Ashirta and his sons, and the desperation of Rib-Hadda as he sought Egyptian assistance. We understand the efforts of vassal states to couch their self-interest in terms of the interests of the states from whom they seek help. The need for prestige played as central a role then as it does today. It would be difficult to come up with a stronger case for the continuity of human nature than is presented by the all-too-familiar behavior described in the Amarna Letters.

Why the Constructivist Case Is Not Persuasive

Despite the many examples of Realist behavior during the Amarna period, objections have been raised to the Realist case. The counterargument rests on four pillars. First, it is claimed that actions in the Amarna period, rather than relying on brute power politics, were influenced heavily by belief in brotherhood and the ultimate power of the gods. Second, the leaders of the Amarna period were incapable of thinking structurally, that is, they could not think in terms of balance of power and so were unable to establish one, at least for any extended period. Third, although Realism may have predominated between the Great Powers and their vassals, this was not the case among the Great Powers themselves. Here peace and cooperation were the norm. Finally, since we know little about the politics and especially the personalities of the leaders during the Amarna period, it is impossible to state with confidence that any approach, be it Realist or Constructivist, is superior in explaining what occurred so long ago.

Although seemingly persuasive, these objections either singly or taken together do not negate the Realist case. There is no question that the theme of brotherhood and family permeates the Amarna correspondence. The Great Kings routinely address each other as "brothers." The state is seen as a household in which the king is the father and the subjects are the members of his family. What is less clear is what this all means in terms of actual behavior that would contradict the Realist viewpoint. That leaders of countries would refer to one another as "brother" did not prevent them from fearing one another, subverting the power of potential rivals, and occasionally going to war with one another. Precisely because the discourse of brotherhood and family did not cause the leaders to behave in ways inconsistent with Realism, the Constructivist view is found wanting.

The role of the gods is also invoked in order to demonstrate that the actors of the Amarna period behaved in ways antithetical to Realism. This argument has merit. From all available evidence, it does appear that leaders genuinely believed in the power of the gods. As Westbrook argues in this volume, the enforcement of treaties in part depended on the belief that to break a treaty would bring punishment by the gods in the form of natural calamities, such as drought or plague. These punishments would only be alleviated after due reparations were paid. Moreover, victory in war depended on being on the right side of the gods. If you did not have justice on your side, the gods would ensure that you would lose. Rather than living in a world of international anarchy in which states were free to chart their own course, Constructivists emphasize that the shared belief in the power of the gods brought a measure of order and justice to the Amarna system.

Belief in the power of the gods may have mitigated the anarchy of the Amarna period but did little to challenge it. Undoubtedly, some treaties were not breached because of fear of the gods' wrath. Perhaps some wars were not fought because one side felt it did not have justice—and therefore the gods—on its side. But treaties were, nevertheless, constantly infringed, and wars continually erupted. Moreover, when treaties were not adhered to, the aggrieved parties did not wait for the gods to act but, in true Realist fashion, took matters into their own hands. Self-help was not regarded in any way as incompatible with the divine authority that figured so prominently in the making of treaties. It is also not clear how the need to believe in a justification for war served as a deterrent to battle. In modern times, tyrants from Adolph Hitler to Saddam Hussein presented elaborate justifications for war that objective observers would dismiss as blatant aggression. Despite belief in the power of the gods, a world in which treaties are constantly broken, and wars or their threat continually arising, is very much a Realist world.

The notion that warfare predominated among the vassal states and not among the Great Powers may be empirically true, but even so, it does not undermine the Realist view. The "long peace" in Europe and among the major powers from World War II to the present is seen by many as a tribute to such basic Realist concepts as deterrence and the balance of power. There is no reason why the same could not be true of the Amarna period. Great powers do their best to avoid wars with one another because they recognize the costs. Realists argue that peace among the Great Powers can never be permanent, but there is little in the Amarna period to contradict this assumption. Even among the Great Powers of the Amarna era, the threat of war was a constant preoccupation. Egypt was at the threshold of a hundred-year war with Hatti; Assyria aggressively forced its way into the Great Powers' rank; Babylonia was constantly fearful of barbarian invasion; and Mittani was soon to be destroyed by the Hittites and Assyrians. Instead of a static peace informed by brotherhood and family, the Great Powers of the Amarna period were either at war with their neighbors or were vigilant for any sign that war would soon erupt.

The view that Realists could not think structurally and thus made balance of power mistakes is indeed a challenge to Realism. This argument acknowledges the classical Realist assumption of flawed human nature but takes issue with the more modern conception of Realism (at times referred to as Neorealism) that emphasizes anarchy as the root cause of international war and alignment. According to Realists, in an environment of anarchy, states will form balances of power to protect themselves. If so, why did Egypt attempt to ally with Arzawa, which was far away and subject to control by its enemy, Hatti? Once Hatti moved to make it a vassal, why then did Egypt do nothing, thus demonstrating its inability to project power in remote lands? Even more perplexing is Egypt's abandonment of Mittani and easy acquiescence to Assyria's bid for great power status despite strong Babylonian objections. Why would Egypt alienate two key allies, especially since it should have recognized its need for them to counter Hittite power?

There are two Realist responses to why Egypt acted in ways that apparently contradicted balance of power logic. First, Realism does not dictate behavior; it simply tells states what they face and expects that over the long term, they will act in ways (such as pursuing a balance of power) that will ensure their long-term survival. That states at times act in ways contrary to balance of power logic does not invalidate Realism as an approach. Prior to World War II, why did Britain and France guarantee the security of Poland in 1939, when they were in no position to come to its defense? Why did Britain and France not ally with the Soviet Union to counter the rising threat of Nazi Germany during the 1930s? States in a Realist world do not always follow Realist dictates. Nevertheless, the costs incurred by such non-Realist actions, over time, convince states not to go down that path again.

Second, we cannot be sure that the examples cited above are true violations of Realist logic. Because the information we have on the Amarna period is so scarce, compelling reasons that conform to Realism may be latent. Thus, Egypt may have cultivated Arzawa as a means to outflank the Hittites in the hopes that its intentions alone would deter the expansion of Hittite power. Pharaoh may have had good reason to ignore Babylonian objections (perhaps Babylonia was engaged in a double game against Egypt) and may not have sought to strengthen Mittani because he recognized it as a power on the decline that no Egyptian assistance could reverse. All of this is pure speculation, but in the absence of detailed, reliable history, it is misleading to discredit Realism based on actions that just appear to be inconsistent with balance of power logic.

Constructivists assert that the absence of good information on the Amarna period can, of course, just as easily discredit Realism as support it. We know little about the personalities of the leaders, the domestic situations they faced, and even the specific actions they undertook. Critics of Realism are justified in asserting that in such an indeterminate context, it is easy to find what you are looking for. Just as Realists can build on vague hints and vast gaps in knowledge to assert that their approach is reinforced by the Amarna period, so too can others with different approaches find support for their views. Rather than a real test of theories, the Amarna period becomes a kind of Rorschach test for scholars to project their own pet beliefs.

There is much to this argument. A great deal of the politics of the Amarna period can be interpreted to support views differing from Realism, including Constructivism. As we have seen, placing greater emphasis on brotherhood, the gods, or behavior that seemingly contradicts Realist beliefs leads to conclusions antithetical to Realism. In this sense, the Amarna period lends itself to a Constructivist view, even if that construction turns out, for some, to be Realism.

Nevertheless, even if not all the Amarna Letters support Realism, the essence of the correspondence is still very much in accord with the Realist view. Professions of brotherhood, belief in the gods, and ignorance of contemporary concepts of political life did not prevent the leaders of the Amarna period from acting in ways familiar to Realists. Yes, Constructivist elements were also present, but they were marginal. In the final analysis, the Amarna period, like contemporary times, confirms the eternal truths of the Realist approach.

Conclusion

The world of the Amarna Letters differed greatly from our own. The state had not yet emerged as a coherent entity, nationalism had yet to surface, interdependence among peoples was limited, communications were slow and difficult, and wars were waged with primitive weaponry. Moreover, as Cohen correctly pointed out, concepts such as the national interest or balance of power would not be articulated for centuries, placing the leaders of the Amarna period in a very different mind-set than our own.

But it is precisely because the Amarna Age was so different from our own that its similarities are all the more striking. Then as now, states threatened one another with no overarching authority to resolve disputes. Alliances formed and dissolved, struggles over power were commonplace, and war or its threat remained a prime means of resolving disputes. None of this "proves" that Realism is correct and Constructivism misguided. Nevertheless, that states acted according to Realist precepts millennia ago is persuasive evidence that the world does indeed impose its own logic on its inhabitants, and that logic is consistent with the Realist view.

PART II

Foreign Policy

CHAPTER SIX

The Egyptian Perspective on Mittani

BETSY M. BRYAN

When Akhenaten came to the throne, he inherited a long and complicated history of relations with Mittani. The Syrian kings were long-time foes who had become diplomatic allies, and, as such, surely represented a great deal to Akhenaten. An understanding of how the Egyptians portrayed Mittani (more often termed "Nahrin" by the Egyptians) throughout the Eighteenth Dynasty can aid our understanding of Amenhotep III and Akhenaten's perceptions of their Mittani contemporary, Tushratta.

Early Contacts: Thutmose I

Egypt most probably sent its first military expedition into the Syrian regions held by Mittani during the reign of Thutmose I, although no contemporary reference to "Nahrin" or "Mittani" (*Mtn*) remains to us for this earliest campaign.[1] The clearly established accounts of Thutmose I's Syrian expedition derive from the monumental rock-carved tomb inscriptions of Ahmose, son of Ebana, and Ahmose Pennekhbet, both of whom hailed from the city of Nekheb (Elkab) in Upper Egypt. Although these specifically refer to Thutmose I's campaign in Nahrin, the inscriptions were the work of the soldiers' descendants in the mid-Eighteenth Dynasty. The accounts, therefore, were formulated in the wake of Thutmose III's startling victories in Syria.

The only certain contemporary monument that has seemed to make reference to the Mittani expedition of Thutmose I is the Victory Stela of Year 2 left at the Third Cataract in northern Sudan: "His southern boundary is as far as the frontier of this land, the northern as far as that inverted water (*mw ḳd*) which goes downstream (northward) in going upstream (southward)" (*Urk.* IV, 82–86).

For decades, this text has been interpreted to contain a reference to the Euphrates, which flows from north to south—a direction opposite to that of the Nile. The "inverted water" was later interpreted by scholars to mean also the Persian Gulf, into which the Euphrates emptied.[2] Further research into the meaning of *mw kd* led to Louise Bradbury's argument that the region described in the Tombos inscription is rather that of the Fourth Cataract in the northern Sudan, where the Nile flows from north to south, rather than along its normal route.[3] In light of Bradbury's and others' discussions, it must be concluded for now that an implied reference to the Euphrates cannot be confirmed. Direct references to Nahrin and Mittani, both commonly applied in Egyptian documents to the Hurrian state, occur with certainty only in the reign of Thutmose III, although the soldiers buried at Elkab claimed to have fought there under Thutmose I. The account of Ahmose, son of Ebana, probably inscribed late in the reign of Thutmose III, informs us that Thutmose I first reached Retenu (an unspecific designation for the southern Levant) and then relates that "his majesty arrived at Naharina; his majesty (life, prosperity, health) found that foe martialing the battle troops (*ts.f skw*). Then his majesty made a great slaughter among them; numberless were the living prisoners which his majesty brought away from his victories" (*Urk.* IV, 9–10). Both Ahmoses claimed to have captured a chariot and horses, the son of Ebana having been rewarded doubly because he also delivered the Mittani elite alive, on the chariot. Neither soldier described the region in any way, nor is it clear from the context to whom Ahmose son of Ebana referred as "that foe" of Naharina.

Only when read with Thutmose III's Annals for the Eighth Campaign in Year 33 does the meaning of the inscription by Ahmose, son of Ebana, become slightly clearer. In the report of the Eighth Campaign, Thutmose III recalled his grandfather's accomplishment in Nahrin (*Urk.* IV 697). He stated that "he set up another ⟨stela⟩ beside the stela of his father, the King of Upper and Lower Egypt, Aakheperkare ⟨Thutmose I⟩." This was in a region that required the crossing of a river, which Thutmose III then used to transport troops. (The claim that it was the Euphrates cannot be confirmed.[4]) Again, the phrase "that foe of Nahrin, the defeated," occurs, but here it is specified that it was his towns and villages that Thutmose III conquered somewhere to the north of Nii, itself specified as being in Nahrin (*Urk.* IV 698). The booty list from this foray includes three rulers (*wrw*), implying the vassals of the Mittani king (*Urk.* IV 698). Therefore, "that foe of Nahrin," as used in the Thutmose III Annals, may well have referred to the Mittani ruler in Washukanni and, given the nearly contemporary composition of the Elkab "autobiographies," to Thutmose I as well. We must conclude, however, that

Egyptian engagement with Nahrin/Mittani was extremely limited in the beginning of the Eighteenth Dynasty. Skirmishes with Mittani vassals in Nahrin first occurred during Thutmose I's reign, but the conquest of northeastern regions did not occur for another thirty-six or more years, when Thutmose III began his Syrian expeditions. Rather, the consolidation of a Nubian empire occupied the interests of Thutmose II and Hatshepsut, bringing as it did enlarged amounts of unworked gold to Egypt and consequent fame for the rulers throughout the Near East.

Perhaps Thutmose I, on his brief expedition to Syria, encountered enemies and war technology beyond the capability of Egypt's armies, which almost certainly had fewer chariots than Mittani at the time. Had there been substantive territorial or material acquisitions made, it is difficult to believe the mention of Nahrin would not have appeared prominently in the preserved monuments of Thutmose I, Thutmose II, or Hatshepsut. Far more likely is the supposition that Thutmose I found the Mittani vassals to be superior military powers and that he departed after leaving an inscription and perhaps conducting an elephant hunt in Nii to the south.

It was left to Thutmose III to develop an army capable of conquering the Mittani vassals. Having done so, through his references to the carving of stelae in Syria, Thutmose III may well have recast Thutmose I's activity in Syria into a context similar to his own description of empire building. This had the benefit of underlining how much more the third Thutmose had accomplished than the first, while at the same time promoting the connection between the two sovereigns. Since Hatshepsut had relied heavily on her position as Thutmose I's daughter, it would have been advantageous at home for Thutmose III to develop his own association with the founder of the reigning Thutmoside line.

From Conflict to Coexistence: Thutmose III to Amenhotep II

If we may conclude from the absence of texts that Mittani was, until Year 33 of Thutmose III, a rival too powerful to be mentioned in Egyptian monumental inscriptions, then the king's conquest of the Syrian vassals was a truly significant achievement. The hitherto poorly attested state of Nahrin suddenly appears in every type of hieroglyphic inscription: in addition to the Annals of Thutmose III inscribed in stone within Karnak temple, the king's apparent crossing of the Euphrates *(Pḥr wr)*[5] appears in the Gebel Barkal Stela (*Urk.* IV 1232) from the Fourth Cataract in Nubia, on a Karnak obelisk (now in Istanbul, *Urk.* IV 587), on the Poetical Stela from Karnak (*Urk.* IV 613), and on the Armant stela (*Urk.* IV 1245–46). References to Nahrin also occur among the numerous toponym lists from the reign.[6] At the same time, the king's contemporaries composed autobiographies for their own tomb chapels and there related their involvement in the Nahrin expeditions. Among the most famous of these texts is TT 85 (*Urk.* IV 890–95), by Amenemheb, called Mahu, who described his experiences in several campaigns in Syria: he mentioned Nahrin, a toponym called *Wˁnˁ*, west of *Ḥȝ-r-bw*, probably Aleppo, and Karkemish (*Kȝrykȝ-myš*). Amenemheb specified that he saw the victories of Thutmose III in *Snḏȝr*, Zinzar on the Orontes, and he boasted of taking two men, *mariannu,* as captives at Qadesh. He continued to echo the Years 33–42 campaigns by then referring to Thutmose III's elephant hunt in Nii and, finally, to the Qadesh siege mentioned for Year 42 in the Annals.

The amount of booty taken during the Syrian campaigns was impressive, both for the ruler and for his soldiers. With the exception of the aftermath of the Year 33 Eighth Campaign, throughout the Annals revenue from Naharin — either the plunder of the army or what the king captured (*ḥȝḳ* or *kfˁ*) — was listed as booty. Apparently, Naharin did not at this time offer yearly deliveries (*inw*), as the Annals clearly indicate by contrasting its one-time delivery after the Year 33 campaign with that of other areas designated as "from this year" *m rnpt tn* (*Urk.* IV 699–703).[7] This might be interpreted to mean that the defeated Mittani vassals alone were the source of Egypt's revenues, not the Mittani ruler in Washukanni. Thutmose III claimed in the Eighth Campaign Annals entry that he brought as living captives 3 vassal chiefs (*wrw*) along with their 30 wives, 80 men, or *mariannu,* and 606 male and female slaves. He also listed revenues of 513 male and female slaves, 45 deben 1/9 kite of gold (some 11 pounds), along with 260 horses, chariots worked in silver and equipped with weapons, nearly 600 cattle, 5,504 livestock animals, 728 vessels of incense, and *bȝḳ* oil (*Urk.* IV 698–99). From other expeditions and revenues, the king mentioned acquiring specifically from Nahrin (excluding Djahy and Retenu), suits of armor, horses, chariots, including some worked with gold and silver; bronze helmets, bows, and other weapons (*Urk.* IV 711–712, Year 35); as well as captives and horses taken near Qadesh in Year 40 (*Urk.* IV 730). Although the listed objects and people are sizable, the yearly deliveries from Retenu and Djahy included far more items of precious materials. Clearly, Thutmose III was still in the process of warfare with Mittani.

Among his campaign awards, Amenemheb claimed to have received the gold of honor at least four times under Thutmose III: twice he mentioned receiving a gold lion, in addition to flies, armbands, and collars of gold rings.[8] The gold lions appear to have been a specially designed award for combatants in the Syrian campaigns, and they are pictured, coupled with the flies, in two Theban tombs, those of Dedi (TT 200) and the Royal Butler Suemniwet (TT 92).[9] In the latter's tomb are also two scenes showing war matériel, including Syrian-style helmets, armor, chariots, and weapons, as described in the Annals.[10] One of these scenes was part of a presentation before Amenhotep II, newly ruling alone following the death of Thutmose III; the other formed part of an accounting scene that included horses and piles of precious metal rings, as well as captives.

The participation in the conquest of Syria, including Nahrin, by a newly formed Egyptian military elite is memorialized in at least eleven Theban tombs from the reign of Thutmose III and early in that of Amenhotep II, in addition to numerous private statue and stela inscriptions.[11] In these tomb chapels, the emphasis was on the captives of military expeditions and on the wars or soldiers themselves, as much as it was upon luxury items acquired from foreign deliveries. The military aspect of Egyptian-Mittani encounters was to be short-lived, however. Rather, the prestige of things Syrian began to soar. Tombs decorated after the first decade of Amenhotep II's rule celebrated the revenues as foreign impost, particularly of an exotic nature, the elements of conquest being formalized within celebratory processions. For example, in the tomb of Kenamun (TT 93), decorated late in the reign of Amenhotep II, there is no text describing the Syrian wars, no accounting of booty as in Suemniwet's chapel (TT 92), and no presentation of the foreign chiefs' children, as in Amenemhab's (TT 85). Instead, one wall shows the New Year's presents for the king. Among them are numerous weapons and coats of armor, as well as two chariots.[12] The label for the chariot in the higher register boasts of the wood being brought from the foreign country of Naharin, while a chariot below it is labeled to suggest its use in warfare against the southerners and the northerners. A pile of Syrian-style helmets is beneath the upper chariot, and a pile of ivory is beneath the lower one — clearly a suggestion of booty from the two regions.

Also among the New Year's gifts in Kenamun's tomb is a group of glass vessels imitating marbelized stone.[13] This type of glass was particularly characteristic of northeast Syria and northern Iraq. Indeed, the large-scale introduction of core-formed glass into Egypt was probably a result of the Mittani wars. Quite possibly first developed in Mittani centers, such as Tell Brak and Tell Rimah, glass vessels were quickly among the prized objects copied (and frankly improved upon) in Egypt.[14] Silver and gold vessels (often described in the booty lists as "flat bottomed") associated with the Mediterranean littoral (referred to as the "workmanship of Djahy") also came as revenue from Naharin (Year 33), and as with glass, Egyptian-styled copies of these Syrian vessels quickly became the fashion.[15]

Along with Syrian-styled luxury items came the gods of the region, and it is in the reign of Amenhotep II that cults of the Syrian deities Reshep and Astarte were heavily promoted in Egypt.[16] It is significant that the fashion for Mittani-style items far outlasted the fashion for military decoration. The gold-lion awards referred to above were never displayed after the early reign of Amenhotep II, but Syrian-type metal and glass vessels continued to be status objects throughout the Eighteenth Dynasty and were copied in a variety of forms within Egypt. Likewise, the scenes of presentation of Mittanian war captives and booty gave way after the early reign of Amenhotep II to the preferred scene of foreign representatives offering their prized luxury objects in obeisance to Pharaoh.[17]

In the iconographical transformation of Mittani from archenemy to a compliant source for prestige luxury goods we can track Egypt's path toward an alliance with Nahrin. Although their identification as Syrian is uncertain, the burial of three wives of Thutmose III, whose names are certainly Asiatic and whose wealth in gold was profound, weighs in favor of the changing Egyptian view toward the East. The same king who campaigned to conquer Retenu and Nahrin for twenty years then married women from the region and showered them with riches. Despite the battles of Amenhotep II yet to be fought in Syria, Egypt's interest in peace was imminent at the close of Thutmose III's reign.[18]

Amenhotep II carried out two (not three) campaigns in Syria, the first probably in Year 7, the latter in Year 9.[19] The expeditions were reported in several versions. The first campaign concentrated on the defeat of unaligned chiefs and rebellions among recently acquired vassals. Among the latter, the region of Takhsy, mentioned by Amenemheb (TT 85), was a primary and successful target. The seven defeated chiefs of that region were taken back to Thebes, head down on the royal barge, where six were hanged upon the temple wall. One was carried all the way to Napata, in the Sudan, where his body was hanged, no doubt as an example to the local population (*Urk.* IV 1287–99). The plunder claimed from Amenhotep's first campaign contained a staggering 6,800 deben of gold and 500,000 deben of copper (1,643 and 120,833 pounds, respectively), along with 550 *mariannu* captives, 210 horses, and 300 chariots.[20] The second campaign in Year 9 was largely carried out in Palestine.

It is probably intentional that *none* of the monumental texts of Amenhotep II contains a hostile reference to Mittani or Nahrin, even though the inscriptions narrated the Syrian campaigns of the king! Gone is the designation "that foe of Nahrin," and in its place several times is the archaic Egyptian generic term *Sttyw,* or *"Asiatics."* The language of the stelae, composed after the conflicts had ended, in Year 9 or later, reflects that peace with Mittani was at hand. Indeed, the Memphis stela of Amenhotep II contains an addition at the end, reporting that the chiefs of Nahrin, Hatti, and Sangar (*Urk.* IV 1309) arrived before the king with gifts to request offering gifts (*ḥtpw*) in exchange, and the breath of life: "Then the ruler of Naharin, the ruler of Hatti, and the ruler of Sangar acknowledged (*sḏm n*) the great victory which I had performed, everyone one imitating his neighbor with every present of every foreign country. They spoke from their hearts on behalf of their ancestors, in order to request gifts from his Majesty and in quest of giving the breath of life to them."[21]

Diplomatic Relations and the Language of Egyptian Inscriptions

The report on the Memphis stela was certainly the first official announcement of the creation of a Mittani alliance, although good relations with Babylonia and others existed in the reign of Thutmose III, for the Annal's Eighth Campaign entry provides the booty and deliveries (*inw*) of Nahrin, followed by the deliveries of *Sngr* (where lapis of Babylonia, *Bbr3,* is mentioned) and *Ḥt3 ʿ3*. Although it is true that no written treaties are attested between Egypt and these Near Eastern states for the Eighteenth Dynasty (and we might not expect them, except from Hatti), the exchange of gifts and envoys between rulers approximated a formal statement of "friendly diplomatic relations," as we can see in the numerous Amarna Letters requesting the establishment or renewal of such exchanges. Perhaps Amenhotep II's inscription mentions that the rulers spoke of their ancestors because of the common Near Eastern practice of reciting the history of relations at the time of their renewal.

The importance of Amenhotep II's new alliance with Nahrin was underlined by its exposition in a column inscription from the Thutmoside columned hall (*w3ḏyt*), between Pylons IV and V at Karnak temple in Thebes, the home of the great god Amun-Re. This location was significant, because the hall was at that time already venerated as the place where Thutmose III received a divine oracle proclaiming his future kingship (*Urk.* IV 156–62). In addition, the association of the hall with the Thutmoside line going back to Thutmose I made it a logical place to boast of the Mittani relationship. The inscription singles out Syria: "The chiefs (*wrw*) of Mittani (*My-tn*) come to him, their deliveries (*inw*) upon their backs, to request **peace** (*ḥtp*) from his majesty in quest of the breath of life" (*Urk.* IV 1326). The meaning of the term *ḥtp* has been discussed by Lorton and Liverani, but there is more that can be said.[22] The language used had a specific political force with regard to trade or diplomatic status. At the same time, it had a religious/ideological one, like all hieroglyphic texts, relating as it did by definition to the divine world, for the word for hieroglyphic script was *mdw-ntr*, or "divine utterance." In the text cited above, *htp* refers to the exchange gift given to open diplomatic relations. In perhaps the earliest inscription referring to such associations, the Autobiography of Harkhuf, dating to the Sixth Dynasty, the causative form of this word, *shtp*, describes what the Egyptian envoy did for the ruler of the African state of Yam in order that he in return might facilitate and protect Egyptian trade in the region.[23] The result of Harkhuf's gift giving to the ruler of Yam was the acquisition of African goods, a military escort from the army of Yam, and a secondary diplomatic association. Harkhuf's description of his dealings with the ruler of Yam did not hide the fact that it was the Egyptian who approached the African ruler.

The common translation of *htp* is "to be at peace" or "to be at rest"; as a noun, it means "satisfaction" or "offering," but from the religious sector its true meaning is "to be propitiated," whereas *shtp* means "to propitiate." Temple reliefs often show personifications of the regions of Egypt carrying alternatively piles of offerings or simply the *htp* sign to demonstrate the king's constant propitiation of the gods.[24] The effect of propitiation is a balance where order rules, and one may expect a quid pro quo in exchange for the "offering." Thus the inscription of Amenhotep II meant that the deliveries (*inw*) brought by the Mittani chiefs were their *htp*, "propitiation," and they hoped to receive *htp* (reciprocity) in return, indicating a peaceful balance between the two powers that would then lead to stable relations. The continuing relations were indicated by Pharaoh's "giving the breath of life," and it was a request for this ongoing association that the Egyptian inscriptions ascribe so emphatically to foreign rulers. It is interesting to point out, in addition, that such a request by the ruler of Yam to Merenre, king of Egypt, does not appear to have been present in Harkhuf's text. His gift exchange facilitated an immediate rather than a long-term trade association.

Because this relationship with Mittani was both new and prestigious, Amenhotep II's inscription amplified the announcement: "It is a mighty occurrence that has never been heard since the times of men and gods, that this country, which did not recognize Egypt, (now) comes to (make) request of the Good God" (*Urk.* IV 1326). The Egyptian king boasted that Mittani made the overture,[25] even though precious few Egyptians were ever able to read the inscription in situ (due both to limited access and limited literacy). However, the king's audience, which comprised the gods and the elites of Amenhotep II's own court, some of whom may even have participated in composing such a text, needed no persuasion. By the close of Amenhotep II's reign the portrayal of Mittani was brought into line with that of Egypt's other close allies. To the home audience, these brother kings of Babylonia, Hatti, and Nahrin were always presented in the guise of suppliants who requested life from the Egyptian king. The hard-won peace with Syria is betrayed, however, by Amenhotep II's enthusiasm for it. Clearly, Amenhotep II considered this alliance to be a boon at home as well as abroad, and we may suppose that his reference to Syria's former ignorance of Egypt deliberately underlined the trade benefits of this diplomatic coup.

Consolidation and Alliance: Thutmose IV to Amenhotep III

Amenhotep's successor, Thutmose IV, did leave record of a brief campaign in the east, but most of his activities regarding Syria proper are known to us from the Amarna Letters.[26] EA 51 credited him with installing a king in Nuhašše, and EA 59 referred to his control of Tunip. EA 85 noted that Thutmose IV visited Sidon, where arrangements for lumber from the Lebanon were made. Nahrin itself figured only on the king's two extant toponym lists, along with Sangar, Tunip, Shasu, Qadesh, and Takhsy. The stability of Egypt's Syrian holdings in the reign of Thutmose IV is certainly implied both by the contemporary documents and by the later letters. If there were minor hostilities, they were obviously settled when the king married Artatama I's daughter, thus sealing a treaty of brotherhood (EA 29:16–20). It may have been the renewal by Thutmose IV of Amenhotep II's "brotherhood," and the arrival of the Mittani emissary with the Syrian princess, that inspired scenes such as that in TT 91, where Mittani chiefs are shown requesting the "breath of life" from the ruler. Similar scenes appeared in TT 63 of the treasurer Sobekhotep, TT 78 of the military scribe Horemhab, and TT 90 of the police chief Nebamun.[27] The marriage of the king to the princess of Nahrin is not confirmed from Egyptian documents, as was the marriage of Amenhotep III to Gilu-Hepa. Nonetheless, it is safe to say that Egyptian interest in things Mittanian continued to increase in Thutmose IV's reign, as witness private and royal representations of Syrian-styled objects, such as those in the tombs mentioned above and depicted in relief on the king's Karnak Fourth Pylon court.[28]

Although with the later reign of Amenhotep III we are in the time of the Amarna Letters, that king showed a strong interest in Mittani relations much earlier than the time represented by the cuneiform archives. The Mittani Marriage Scarab (*Urk.* IV 1738) commemorated with obvious enthusiasm the king's union with Gilu-Hepa, his first Mittani bride, and bears a Year 10 date.[29] It carried the following inscription after the complete royal titulary:

> The King of Upper and Lower Egypt, lord of the cult act, Nebmaatre, chosen of Re, the son of Re Amenhotep, ruler of Thebes, given life; the

great royal wife Tiye, may she live. The name of her father is Yuya; the name of her mother is Tuya. Marvels which were brought to his majesty, (life, prosperity, health), the daughter of the Chief (*wr*) of Nahrin, *S3tyrn3* [Shuttarna], *Kyr-gy-p3* [Gilu-Hepa], and the choicest of her female entertainers (*ḥnrw*): 317 women.

The Egyptian Context of Diplomatic Marriages

Diplomatic marriage was, of course, already a well-known practice in Mesopotamia, occurring in both Ur III and Mari texts, in addition to the Amarna Letters. It appears from the Amarna archives that these unions were the primary substantive return the Egyptian rulers expected from all their brotherhood relations during the Amarna era. Despite the valuable goods acquired from dowries, the Letters betray that Amenhotep III was motivated by the acquisition of the royal women and not by their movable wealth alone. Indeed, his tone is quite deprecating in a letter to Kadashman-Enlil, where he says that his brother appears to give his daughters away for "a little gold" and sarcastically states that "should your sister acquire any wealth here I'll send (it) to you!" (EA 1:52–62).

The Egyptian rulers viewed their marriage alliances as something more valuable even than gold, silver, copper, cedar, or other valued commodities. EA 1, 17, 19, 20, 23, 26, 27, 28, 29 reveal the perspectives of the Babylonian and Mittani rulers, as well as the Egyptian view on the position of both Egyptian and foreign wives of Pharaoh. The Babylonian kings did not include salutations to their sisters or daughters in extant letters, but they showed obvious concern that their prestige vis-à-vis Egypt was affected by giving and not receiving wives. EA 1 also indicates that Kadashman-Enlil questioned the court position of his sister as queen. The Mittani ruler Tushratta's first letters addressed his sister Gilu-Hepa and ignored Tiye, the actual Great Royal Wife; upon the Mittanian queen's death, Tushratta attempted to insist upon his daughter Tadu-Hepa's becoming "mistress of Egypt," while still ignoring Tiye. Only upon Amenhotep III's death was the de facto position of Tiye acknowledged, and in the last extant missive from Tushratta, she was referred to as "the principal [and favorite] wife of Nimmureya." Some of the misunderstandings between rulers with regard to foreign queens are clarified by reference to Egyptian culture and history, for diplomatic marriage may be traced all the way back to earliest Egyptian history, and its significance within Egyptian culture may have been in some ways deeper than in nearby Asian countries.

The Egyptian rulers' view of their marriages surfaces to some degree in the hieroglyphic text of the Marriage Scarab. For example, it was an obvious slight to the Mittanian princess that no title was applied there to Gilu-Hepa as royal wife. Even more significant is the positioning of Tiye as Great Royal Wife, with respected (though nonroyal) parentage, as prologue to the Mittani marriage announcement. Tiye, according to this inscription, may be said to have participated with Amenhotep III in the diplomatic alliance. Indeed, the reality of her primacy following Amenhotep III's death is seen in EA 26, from Tushratta to Tiye, to whom he wrote to resume and effect diplomatic relations.

However, the scarab inscription betrays a fundamental difference between the meaning of marriage in Egypt and elsewhere. Here Tiye's claim as Great Royal Wife was asserted not only to protect her heirs' inheritances but also to identify her separate claim to affluence—her own and that of the marital union. Egyptian women of the New Kingdom brought independent wealth into a marriage, could will it to whom they wished, and should dissolution take place, could withdraw intact what they brought into the alliance.[30] During the marriage, however, the husband controlled the use of this wealth. In addition, women, and thus their spouses, received inheritances from their parents; this might mean anything from a small addition to the dowry to the entire estate, including titles, benefices, etc. During the marriage, the man was required to provide a maintenance allowance—later clearly identified in marriage contracts as *s'nḫ*, "that which causes to live." This may have derived from the wife's family as well.[31] Finally, women had claim to one third of the acquired marital estate upon the man's repudiation of the marriage, and probably upon his death as well.[32] The allusion to Tiye and her parents by name on the scarabs thus refers to her economic position as spouse.[33]

The status associated with the *potential* holdings in a marriage was great[34] and was commonly boasted of in tomb inscriptions. In practice, the independent wealth of women, in particular elite women, encouraged arranged marriages to join assets. During the Old Kingdom (ca. 2700–2100 B.C.E.) and Second Intermediate Periods (ca. 1700–1550 B.C.E.), kings' daughters married officials or local governors.[35] Queen Khasnebu of the Second Intermediate Period (Thirteenth Dynasty) was the daughter of powerful southern aristocrats married to a king so powerless he is unnamed on her monuments. Spalinger summed up the historical situation in this way: "The monarch had to rely upon his alliances with the powerful houses of his day and they in turn relied upon their king for the maintenance of their power. . . . It is significant that the name of the husband of queen *Ḥ'.s-nbw* [Khasnebu] is nowhere mentioned, almost as if he were a non-person. No doubt the monarch was quite weak at the close of Dynasty XIII."[36] Only slightly later, following the probable example of the Middle Kingdom, and no doubt to protect themselves from claims of families outside the dynastic line, the Eighteenth Dynasty rulers barred the marriage of king's daughters outside the court, and this equally extended to unions with rulers from other Near Eastern countries.[37]

To return to royal diplomatic unions,[38] there is evidence for them in Egypt as early as the First Dynasty (ca. 3000 B.C.E.), when a certain Neith-hotep, a royal female from an Egyptian polity north of Abydos (perhaps Lower Egypt itself), was married to a king, most likely Aha. Since Neith-hotep and, slightly later in the First Dynasty, Queen Merneith, both became regent rulers of Egypt's First Dynasty and built royal funerary monuments that they endowed from the state treasury, the seriousness of the royal female claim to marital wealth cannot be overemphasized. Hatshepsut's regency to Thutmose III in the mid-Eighteenth Dynasty, following the death of her husband and half-brother Thutmose II, similarly recognized the major queen's right to control the marital assets, including the heir's inheritance, despite his birth from another woman. In addition, as wife of the last king and daughter of the last but one, Hatshepsut embodied the ultimate female rights to the royal fortune, such that she was able not only to place the child Thutmose III under her agency but also to take over the kingship itself. Like Sobeknofru in the Twelfth Dynasty, who, as the daughter of Amenemhet III, became first co-regent with and then sole successor to Amenemhet IV (probably not of the royal family), Hatshepsut's purity of lineage in the absence of a grown heir focussed the wealth in a woman's hands. Indeed, had the Hittite prince sent to marry an Egyptian queen, either Ankhesenamun or Meretaten, not been (apparently) murdered, a Hittite prince as king would no doubt have been as nameless as Queen Khasnebu's husband in the Thirteenth Dynasty![39]

It is in light of this overall economic and political view of marital alliances that we must cast Amenhotep III's great passion for marrying Babylonian, Arzawan, and Mittani princesses. These unions did not allow the wives, once widowed, to claim a third of the ruler's wealth, but rather required their marriage to the royal successor. This was, in that sense, more profitable to the king than the typical elite Egyptian marriage. Nevertheless, while there is no indication that the Egyptian king could make claim to any real property in the Near Eastern states, the king could certainly boast to a home audience of a potential claim to the thrones of the Near East. As we have seen, the dowries, although considered the independent wealth of the foreign princesses, could have been used by the Egyptian ruler during the marriage, perhaps even partly to finance the upkeep on the queens' households in Egypt. If, like Gilu-Hepa, each woman brought several hundred retainers, the maintenance was certainly oppressive. In light of how the king could have benefited at court from the suggestion of his claim to the great thrones of the world, Amenhotep III apparently found these marriage arrangements satisfying, at least for a while.

Amenhotep III's Mittani Policy

Late in Amenhotep III's reign and despite continued involvement with his Mittani counterpart, Nahrin figures several times in royal inscriptions from Egypt. A Luxor Temple open-court architrave, west facing, west side, states: "He made a valiant name in every foreign country, his war shouts having circulated through Nahrin, when he placed fear in their hearts, as their bellies split open" (*Urk.* IV 1693, 17–19). Nearby, on a hypostyle hall architrave deriving from the same period late in Amenhotep III's rule, the king was described as "he whose mace smote Nahrin" (*Urk.* IV 1696). These strong negative images were probably composed in the last decade of the reign, when the open court and hypostyle were added to the temple. A nearly contemporary stela from the king's funerary temple has a similar pungency. There the king is represented upon his chariot besieging Asiatics with the accompanying legend: "He who tramples Nahrin with his valiant strong arm" (i.e., army). Beneath the scene appears a further label: "Nahrin, Kush, defeated, Upper Retenu, and Lower Retenu are under the feet of this Good God like Re forever" (*Urk.* IV 1658, CG 34026).

These three portrayals are more hostile than any formal Egyptian representation of Mittani since the early reign of Amenhotep II. Compare the marriage scarab inscription for the king and Tiye composed earlier in the reign. Referring to Tiye, the scarab states, "She is the wife of a victorious king, whose southern boundary is at Karoy (Napatan region of Sudan), the northern at Nahrin" (*Urk.* IV 1741). This merely confirms the joint border of the two great states.

The motivation for re-demonizing Mittani late in the reign of Amenhotep III is uncertain, but hints remain to us. At exactly the same moment, Pharaoh was in negotiation with Tushratta to marry his daughter Tadu-Hepa, following the death of Gilu-Hepa, perhaps of plague. Certainly, it could be argued that Nahrin was randomly chosen in these inscriptions to serve as the king's whipping boy, but the choice would have controverted a nonaggressive attitude toward Mittani in the public portrayals for the sixty years dating back to the establishment of brotherhood. Furthermore, there are indications that Amenhotep III could have been able to see the coming eclipse of the Hurrian state (EA 17's reference to warfare with Hatti; EA 24's proposal of mutual defense). Perhaps he was preparing to take advantage of the situation. At nearly the same time, he worked out an alliance with Ugarit (EA 45), which appears for the first time on a toponym list at Soleb temple decorated in the last decade of the reign.[40] The trade provided by a vassal Ugarit may have seemed, in the shadow of a growing Hittite influence on western Syria, a less costly means to Syrian products.

Amenhotep III may have continued his negotiation to marry Tadu-Hepa with less enthusiasm than he exhibited for the union with Gilu-Hepa. (The likelihood that his health was failing at the time may have contributed here as well.) EA 24, the Hurrian letter, in my opinion, contains indications of a troubled brotherhood. First, Amenhotep III had not provided as much for the bride price as Tushratta would have wished, and the Mittani king made the request for gold statues (molten gold) as if in compensation and reassurance of the Egyptian ruler's good intentions (III 66–71, 108–118). This was perhaps not a sound diplomatic tactic, but it is there nonetheless. He then warned Pharaoh not to listen to bad things about Tushratta or Hanigalbat [Mittani] (IV 1–29), unless spoken by his approved messengers, Mane and Keliya. By the time the ruler in Egypt had heard this much of the letter, warm enthusiasm for marrying Tadu-Hepa might have cooled considerably, though he went ahead with the union. Tushratta's later attempts to beseech Akhenaten to send him the solid gold statues requested first in the Hurrian letter were almost certainly in vain from the beginning. Seen from this vantage point, when Akhenaten inherited the brotherhood with Tushratta and potential claim through marriage to the throne of Mittani, he did not gain the prestige that his predecessors had over the preceding seventy years. Perhaps it should not then be surprising that there is nothing at all about Nahrin from the monumental Egyptian documentation of Akhenaten's reign. Tushratta's demise came soon enough that hostile references to Mittani, such as those left by Amenhotep III, were probably unnecessary. The Egyptian king's attitude toward Mittani had thus completed a gamut that ran from respect, even awe, for its might in the early days of the dynasty, to hostility toward an archenemy in the middle years, then to public appreciation of Mittani as new-found ally or suppliant of Egypt, to contempt for a weakened foe, and, finally, to silence.

CHAPTER SEVEN

Intelligence in the Amarna Letters

RAYMOND COHEN

Among the many topics that the Amarna correspondence touches on is that of political intelligence.[1] A number of the letters, particularly from Egypt's Canaanite vassals, are intelligence reports, contain intelligence items, or refer to intelligence issues. There are also intelligence references in the Great King correspondence.

Until not long ago, the subject of intelligence was very much the "missing dimension" of diplomatic and military history, rarely written about and little appreciated. Key episodes of modern history—Munich 1938, D-Day 1944, Cuba 1962—only became comprehensible when the secret information available to decision makers was taken into account. Thanks to the efforts of a number of scholars over the past two decades, there is now much greater appreciation of the often influential, sometimes dominant, role played by intelligence in foreign policy and military decision making.[2]

Intelligence, though intangible, is a component of national power, like an army or natural resources. Defined very generally as organized information required by an institution for the accomplishment of its goals, it is as necessary for the state in the international arena as reliable perception is to the brain. Intelligence is thought of as being produced from raw data that are deliberately collected by an assortment of means, secret and overt, active and passive.

To correct a possible misapprehension: intelligence is not synonymous with espionage. It may draw on intercepted or clandestinely acquired material, and without spies, it may be impossible to gain access to the target's innermost deliberations. Nevertheless, much of it has always been derived from open sources, whether travelers, diplomats, or plain observers. Today, special intelligence agencies are responsible for producing intelligence. In the past, intelligence was usually the responsibility of government officials in the course of their other duties.

Egypt and the Great Powers

Most of the intelligence material in the Amarna Letters is sent from Canaan to Egypt and reflects the administration's need for intelligence to maintain control of its Asian empire. It also reflects the arbitrary composition of the archive and not Egypt's overall intelligence priorities. However, the major importance of intelligence within the context of Egypt's international relations is suggested by the fact that two out of the three letters from Pharaoh to another Great King refer to intelligence matters.

In EA 1:77–88, Amenhotep III responds angrily to the Babylonian king's letter in which he is quoted as saying, "You said to my messengers, 'Has your master no troops?'" Taking this as an imputation on the quality of the information available to him, Pharaoh imperiously hints at his extensive intelligence capabilities: "Whether soldiers are on hand or not can be found out for me. What reason is there for asking about whether there are troops on hand belonging to you, whether there are horses on hand also belonging to you?" In other words, he had his own sources on Babylonian military movements and did not need to deign to question lowly Babylonian messengers on the subject.

A second explicit reference to intelligence material appears in EA 31:22–38, a letter sent by Amenhotep III to Tarhundaradu, the king of Arzawa, the Hittites' neighbor in southern Anatolia. In the context of negotiations for the hand of an Arzawan princess, conducted on the Egyptian side with uncharacteristic urgency, Pharaoh suddenly turns to the Hittite question: Together with the returning envoys, Tarhundaradu was to send him "people of the country Kaška," a region north of Hatti along the Black Sea. He continues, "I have heard that everything is finished, and that the country Hattuša [Hatti] is shattered."

The phrase "I have/the king has heard" is used as a marker for the quotation of intelligence material by Pharaoh. It appears in three out of the only ten messages emanating from the Egyptian court.[3] The request for Kaskeans is presumably in order to make contact and to question them about events in Hatti. Also suggestive is the offhand comment that Hatti had been "shattered," information that could hardly be news to the nearby Arzawan king. If Pharaoh were very eager indeed to acquire intelligence on the Hittites, whether from Arzawa or Kaska, he might well choose to parade his supposed knowledge of the subject. This is analogous to the practice, identified by Liverani, of sending luxury goods to their main supplier.[4] Certainly, in the intelligence field, it has always been easier to extract information if the potential supplier assumes one to be more knowledgeable on the point at issue than is really the case.

Moran interprets the Egyptian overture of a dynastic marriage to Arzawa as having the strategic purpose of impeding "the resurgence of the [shattered] Hittites."[5] Whether one adopts that view or not—and coalitions are usually formed when an enemy power is strong, not when it is weak—Pharaoh's request for Kaskeans and the reference to Hattusha certainly implies Egyptian interest in an ongoing exchange of intelligence between the partners.[6]

Beyond these two references, various items in the Canaanite correspondence suggest that northern Canaan was a natural and vital observation post on the surrounding Great Powers. It is to the role of Canaan that we now turn.

Egypt's Interests in Canaan

A glance at the map of the region covered by the Amarna system indicates why Canaan was so important from an intelligence perspective: It was the land bridge between Egypt and its brother Great Kingdoms of the ancient Near East. Through Canaanite territory or its harbors, troops, traders, and messengers, Egyptians and others, friend and foe alike, would have to pass. Egypt's Canaanite vassals would be well placed to gather information both on the local and wider international scene. Ports along the Levant coast and caravanserai along the main routes must have provided excellent tidbits of news about events in far-flung parts of the Mediterranean world and Fertile Crescent.

Egypt must also have had direct sources of information on the surrounding Great Powers, north and east. In a cosmopolitan center of commerce like Ugarit, where ships and caravans came and went, commercial and political information would have been readily available, a commodity like any other. In the same spirit, information has always been exchanged by states in a kind of intelligence marketplace. There is a hint of this in EA 31. We also know that envoys, like Keliya and Mane, old colleagues, often traveled together. Diplomats have always shared some news. Whether Pharaoh ran spies against his brother kings—and vice versa—is not known.[7]

Before considering the role of Canaan as an intelligence center, it is necessary to consider Egyptian interests in the region that intelligence would be intended to advance. Politically useful information is not gathered in a vacuum, for academic interest, but is produced to serve, in a timely manner, the ends of policy. Egyptian interests as reflected in the Amarna archive fall into four (albeit overlapping) categories: geopolitical, imperial, mercantile, and governmental-judicial.

First and foremost came the geopolitical significance of Canaan for Egypt. In the aftermath of Hyksos invasion and rule, it must have been, among other things, the wish to exercise direct control over the territory and resources of the area, while denying them to a potential enemy, that drew Thutmose III and his armies there in the first place. In the Amarna Letters, we pick up strong hints of a kind of "great game" being played in southern Syria by the Egyptians, Hittites, and Hurrians, uncannily like that played by the British Raj and Czarist Russia in the nineteenth century for control of Persia and Afghanistan. We read of troop movements, royal arrivals and departures, and a supple policy conducted by pivotal Amurru playing Egypt off against Hatti. "Do not you yourself know that the land of Amurru follows the stronger party?" Rib-Hadda asks Amanappa, the Egyptian commissioner, in a description of the buffer state shrewdly calculating its best interests (EA 73:11–16).

The Canaanite vassals well understand their geostrategic importance to Egypt. When Rib-Hadda writes (EA 109), "Whenever the king of Mittana was at war with your ancestors, your ancestors did not desert my ancestors," he is arguing to shared interest and his utility in the struggle with another Great King. Aziru, king of Amurru, also appeals to common geostrategic interest when he puts forward (EA 165:18–27) his fear of the presence of the king of Hatti in Nuhašše as a justifiable reason for not leaving home to appear before Pharaoh.

Egypt's interest in Canaan as a vital source of goods and services for the imperial army and navy derived, too, from Canaan's geostrategic role. Aitukama of Qadesh (EA 189:1–8) nicely defines the core obligation of a vassal towards the suzerain: "Thus do I serve you along with all my brothers, and wherever there is war against the king, I go, together with my troops, together with my chariots, and together with all my brothers." Elsewhere in the archive we read of the provision of supplies to Egyptian forces (EA 55, 226, 324, 325, 337), the preparation of "horses and chariots" (EA 141, 142), and the supply of ships (EA 153, 155).

Canaan was, in addition, an important economic resource and trading partner, and a vital traffic artery for Egypt. Thus, it was a source of materials and food (copper, timber, grain, oil, domestic animals, glass) as well as labor. Items were supplied both as tribute and on a commercial basis.

Canaan straddled the shipping and caravan routes up to Anatolia, Syria, and other parts of the Fertile Crescent. Maintaining these routes, and ensuring the safe and unimpeded passage of traders and messengers, were clearly vital Egyptian interests. Open communications are a condition of international life, then as now. Inland, vassals were responsible for the safe passage of the king's caravans through their lands. A breakdown of law and order immediately threatened the life and limb of Egyptian and other international travelers (cf. EA 8).

At sea, disturbances of various kinds—piracy, political turmoil—to the ports and sea lanes along the eastern Mediterranean coast would have disrupted shipping, as we see from EA 98 and 114, following the fall of Ṣumur. This would have serious mercantile and security implications. Finally, Egypt, like all Great Powers since ancient times, would be concerned for the welfare of its citizens living abroad. Egyptian residents of Levantine ports, doubtless including merchants, shipping and commercial agents, and officials, seem to have enjoyed some claim to protection, and Canaanite vassal rulers report giving them shelter in their hour of need (EA 62, 67, 105).

As suzerain, Egypt was responsible for order in Canaan. Without order, citizens are at risk, free passage in jeopardy, the payment of tribute and performance of other vassal duties in question. Imperial powers throughout the ages have always abhorred loss of control.

The Egyptian Intelligence Operation in Canaan

We have no means of knowing how intelligence was organized within Egypt, but if premodern structures of government were followed, it is likely that there was no separation of intelligence and administrative functions. Ibalpi-El, Zimri-Lim's ambassador to Hammurabi, personally supervises his embassy's espionage operation at court. In the *Arthashastra*, written in northern India in the fourth century B.C.E., Kautilya, a former chief minister, writes a treatise on the art of good government. His advice, presumably reflecting first-hand experience, is for direct royal supervision of the spies and agents believed essential for thwarting plots against the throne, maintaining domestic tranquillity, and defending the realm against its enemies. In the Amarna Letters, intelligence is made use of both by the authorities in Egypt proper and their commissioners in Canaan.

Evidence of this use is found in two places. In EA 162:22–29, in which Aziru, ruler of Amurru, is threatened with death by the axe, Pharaoh quotes evidence of Aziru's treacherous intercourse with an enemy of Egypt: "Now the king has heard as follows, 'You are at peace with the ruler of Qidša. The two of you take food and strong drink together.' And it is true. Why do you act so? Why are you at peace with a ruler with whom the king is fighting?" The source of this report, an account of the men meeting and eating together, must have been an observer at the court of one of the rulers—whether a guest at the ceremony or a spy is unclear—since Qadesh, an enemy of Egypt, would hardly betray a real or potential ally. In the circumstances, it seems unlikely that an Egyptian official or diplomat would be invited to or attend such an occasion.

In EA 333:4–18, Paapu, an Egyptian official, reports to one of the Egyptian magnates or commissioners in Canaan that two vassal kings were plotting against Pharaoh: "May you know that Šipti-Baʿlu and Zimredda are acting disloyally together, and Šipti-Baʿlu said to Zimredda, 'The forces of the town of Yaramu have written to me. Give me 11 bows, 3 daggers, and 3 swords. Look, I am about to sally forth against the land of the king, and you are in league with me.'"

Whatever the sources of information in EA 162 and 333, the letters graphically illustrate the use to which intelligence was put—in both cases, just as in the Kautilya *Arthashastra,* protection of the empire against external enemies and internal traitors. Note the orderly chain of transmission in EA 333: source (agent) → handler (official) → commissioner. Intelligence might be acted on locally and stop with the commissioner, or be passed on to Egypt, completing the string, → Egyptian administration.

The main conduit for intelligence in the Amarna Letters is the local "mayors" (vassal kings) writing directly to the Egyptian court. In thirty-eight documents that I consider to contain intelligence material from Canaan, twenty-eight are addressed by vassals to Pharaoh, six are addressed by vassals to Egyptian officials, one is addressed to Aziru in Amarna/Akhetaten, probably from his brothers, one is from Pharaoh to Aziru, one is from one Egyptian official to another, and in a final letter, the name of the addressee is lost. It should be noted that eighteen of the twenty-eight letters sent directly to the palace came from Rib-Hadda.

A sentence of Rib-Hadda in EA 116:6–16 suggests that passing on intelligence was one of the understood duties of the vassal: "But give thought to the fact that I am your loyal servant, and whatever I hear I write to my lord." Specific instructions to the vassal kings to gather information on particular topics are found in two places. In EA 145:22–29, Zimreddi, ruler of Sidon, cites the instruction to collect intelligence on Amurru: "The word you hear from there you must report to me." Again, in EA 151:49–58, Abi-Milku, ruler of Tyre, in a dispatch to Pharaoh, cites the instruction: "Write to me what you have heard in Canaan."[8]

Fortunately, we have the entire text of the message (embedded in a complaint about the actions of Abi-Milku's neighbor Zimredda of Sidon): "The king of Danuna died; his brother became king after his death, and his land is at peace. Fire destroyed the palace at Ugarit; rather, it destroyed half of it and so half of it has disappeared. There are no Hittite troops about. Etakkama, the prince of Qidšu, and Aziru are at war; the war is with Biryawaza." EA 151 is a classic intelligence report, concise and devoid of extraneous commentary, dealing with (1) the political situation in Danuna, a kingdom in eastern Cilicia within the Hittite sphere of influence; (2) a conflagration in Ugarit, the important trading entrepôt on the northern Levant coast; (3) the state of the forces of Hatti, Egypt's Great Power rival; and (4) a northern Canaanite conflict between Aziru, the ambitious ruler of Amurru (the key buffer state between the Hittite and Egyptian spheres of influence), his ally Aitukama, ruler of the important city-state of Qadesh on the Orontes, and Biryawaza, ruler of Damascus.

Intelligence reports are often prefaced by "may the king, my lord, be informed that," "may the king know that," "may the king, my lord, take cognizance," or some variation on the same. These tell-tale formulas are found in sixteen Amarna letters (EA 58, 68, 74, 75, 83, 86, 90, 114, 170, 174, 175, 176, 287, 335, 363, 366). A good example is EA 335:6–21, a dispatch from ʿAbdi-Ashirta to Pharaoh: "May the king, my lord, be informed that Turbazu and Yaptih-Hadda have been slain . . . and . . . Lakišu. May the king, my lord, be informed. And the rebel has taken all my . . . May the king, my lord, be informed that Lakišu is hostile, Muhraštu seized, Jerusalem hostile. And so may the king, my lord, send archers." Here we have intelligence exclusively about internal Canaanite affairs.

A dispatch from Tehu-Tessup to either Pharaoh or an official (EA 58:4–10) bears a similar hallmark, this time dealing with a military excursion by the Hurrian king: "Moreover, be informed that the king of Mittani came forth together with chariots and together with an expeditionary force, and we heard, 'At the waters . . .'."

Yet another example is EA 75:25–50, from Rib-Hadda to the king:

> The ʿApiru killed Aduna, the king of Irqata, but there was no one who said anything to ʿAbdi-Aširta, and so they go on taking territory for themselves. Miya, the ruler of Arašni, seized Ardata, and just now the men of Ammiya have killed their lord. I am afraid. May the king be informed that the king of Hatti has seized all the countries that were vassals of the king of Mittani. Behold, he is king of Nahrima and the land of the Great Kings, and ʿAbdi-Aširta, the servant and dog, is taking the land of the king. Send archers.

As in EA 335, there is no strict demarcation between intelligence and policy recommendation. (However, this principle of good government is even today seen more in the breach than in the observance.) This immediately raises the problem of tendentious reporting (see below).

The main topics of attention in the files are local affairs and Great Power activities. Many of the dispatches report on the situation in Canaan, local rivalries, internecine war, and mutual denunciations. Most of the letters coming from Rib-Hadda report on the turmoil in and around Amurru, ʿAbdi-Ashirta and later Aziru's machinations, the success of the latter pair in mobilizing local rulers and populaces, the plight of Gubla (Byblos), the siege and the suffering of the population, the fall of Ṣumur, and the death of the Egyptian commissioner. These events are presented as threats to Egypt's geostrategic position in the north, to loyal vassal cities, and, indeed, to Egypt's entire hold over the region. There is interesting news of the neighboring Great Powers of Hatti and Mittani: At one period, with the rise of ʿAbdi-Ashirta, we see the extension of Mittanian influence, signaled by visits by the Hurrian king to Amurru and Ṣumur, the important Levantine port and Egyptian administrative center, and a trip by ʿAbdi-Ashirta to Mittani. At a later period, when ʿAbdi-Ashirta's son Aziru ruled Amurru, it is Hittite expansion that is reported on. In EA 126, Hittite troops and allies are pictured as threatening Byblos.

Hittite military operations in the Bekaa Valley are reported on from two separate sources. In EA 174, 175, 176, and 363, allied rulers jointly report on the loss of cities to a Hatti-Qadesh coalition. A more conventional intelligence report is contained in EA 170:14–35, which Moran believes was sent to Aziru in Egypt by his brothers back home in Amurru. Note the intelligence markers "may our lord know this," and "we have heard the following":

> Moreover, troops of Hatti under Lupakku have captured cities of Amqu, and with the cities they captured Aaddumi. May our lord know this. Moreover, we have heard the following: "Zitana has come and there are 90,000 infantrymen that have come with him." We have, however, not confirmed the report, whether they are really there and have arrived in Nuhašše, and so I am sending Bet-ili to him. As soon as we meet with them, I will immediately send my messenger so he can report to you whether or not it is so.

Because this report was deposited in the Amarna archives, it clearly ended up in Egyptian hands. It may have been intercepted by the Egyptian authorities, but it most likely was passed on to them by Aziru, of his own free will. To do so would serve Aziru's purpose in two ways. First, news that one Hittite army had captured cities in the strategic Bekaa Valley and that another had arrived made up of ninety thousand foot soldiers, strikingly underlined Amurru's pivotal role as a buffer between Hittite and Egyptian spheres of influence. Had Amurru not existed, Egyptian forces or their proxies would be directly facing the troops of Hatti — an incendiary situation.

Second, it equally graphically demonstrated Amurru's key importance as a source of intelligence, an observation post on the Hittites. Not only does the dispatch contain vital military intelligence, it also depicts Amurru's indispensability as a source of information. Who was in a better position than the independent-minded Aziru and his brothers, possessing access to both sides, Egyptians and Hittites, to check up from the mouth of the Hittite general himself on the size of his forces? If EA 162, in which Pharaoh threatens Aziru with the axe because of his contacts with a Hittite ally, was the indictment, EA 170 was the effective case for the defense. And, indeed, Aziru returned home from Akhetaten a free man. Since it is farfetched to suppose that Aziru deceived the Egyptians about his activities (EA 170 does not conceal continuing Amurru-Hatti contacts), Pharaoh must have been convinced that Amurru was more useful to Egypt on good terms with Hatti than it could ever have been as an out-and-out Egyptian vassal, prohibited from remaining in touch with the Hittites.

Conundrums of Egyptian Intelligence

Just as Egypt sought intelligence on its neighbors and rivals, they, too, collected information on Egypt and its vassals. It would have been difficult for Egypt to maintain complete "field security," that is, to protect its secrets and those of its vassals from the prying eyes of potential enemies. The very geostrategic and demographic conditions that made Canaan so important a listening post for collecting information on others left Egyptian interests vulnerable to rival intelligence services. One local Canaanite ruler would find it difficult to conceal his plans and activities from his neighbors. The motive for espionage would be material gain or the concern of local Canaanite rulers to ensure their own survival in an uncertain environment.

In the Amarna Letters, there is no direct evidence of Great Power penetration of Egypt but a number of references to Amurru's intelligence-gathering activities in northern Canaan. EA 170, a report from Amurru on Hittite troop movements, has already been referred to. The picture conjured in EA 170, of an Amurru skillfully maneuvering between the Great Powers on the basis of sound intelligence, is confirmed by at least five other Amarna documents. In EA 87 and 92, Rib-Hadda complains that ʿAbdi-Ashirta had learned of his failure to coax military assistance out of Pharaoh, and that the ruler of Amurru had used the knowledge in two ways: to bring Batruna over to his side, and to take appropriate military steps to exploit Byblos' vulnerability: "I sent my messenger to the king, my lord, in regard to my cities that ʿAbdi-Ašrati had taken. ʿAbdi-Ašrati heard that my man had arrived from the king, my lord, and he heard that there was nothing with him. Since there was no auxiliary force that came out to me, he has now moved up against me" (EA 92:16–25). And again: "Then he heard that there were no troops with [the messenger] and as a result Batruna was joined to him. He has stationed the ʿApiru and chariots there, and they have not moved from the entrance to the gate of Gubla" (EA 87:15–24).

But the major intelligence coup reported in the Amarna archive is ʿAbdi-Ashirta's son Aziru's success in "turning" Zimreddi, ruler of Sidon. In EA 144, Zimreddi presents himself as an exemplary vassal of Pharaoh, preparing everything for the arrival of Egyptian archers. In other letters sent to the Egyptian king by Abi-Milku, ruler of Tyre, Zimreddi is depicted as an agent of Aziru passing on confidential information: "Zimredda, the king of Sidon, writes daily to the rebel Aziru, the son of ʿAbdi-Ašratu, about every word he has heard from Egypt. I herewith write to my lord, and it is good that he knows" (EA 147:61–71). In EA 149:54–73, Zimreddi is accused of having been instrumental in the fall of Ṣumur:

> The king, my lord, wrote me on a tablet, "Write whatever you hear to the king." Zimredda of Sidon, the rebel against the king, and the men of Arwada have exchanged oaths among themselves, and they have assembled their ships, chariots, and infantry, to capture Tyre. They captured Ṣumur through the instructions of Zimredda, who brings the word of the king to Aziru.

Finally, in EA 151:12–24, it is hinted that Zimreddi possesses intelligence sources within Tyre itself: "He heard that I was going to Egypt, and so he has waged war against me." If this is true, it points to a failure of counterintelligence and a leaking of vital information to Egypt's opponents.

The questions of veracity that a historian looking back on the Amarna period must consider when reading the reports of Egypt's vassals, particularly those where they denounce one another or implore Egypt for assistance in local quarrels, equally concerned the Egyptian authorities. Then, as now, a report possessing serious implications for Egyptian interests would only be acted upon (if at all) if found to be accurate. The principle is made clear in EA 170:19–35, where Aziru's brothers pass on information about Hittite troop movements with the proviso that "we have, however, not confirmed the report" and note that they would be checking it with the Hittite general.

Problems of falsehood and inaccuracy are referred to in several places in the archive. In EA 89:7–14 and 108:46–58, Rib-Hadda accuses other informants of Egypt of lying: "May the king heed my words. Their words are not true." And again: "Why do you listen to other men?" Rib-Hadda refutes an inaccurate report about the fate of Byblos in EA 84:11–31: "Moreover, as to men's saying in the presence of my lord, 'Gubla has been seized; its ruler is distraught,' my lord should know that they have not taken Gubla." Similarly, he corrects a misapprehension about Ṣumur in EA 116:6–16: "May the king, my lord, know that the war against us is very severe. As to its being told to you, 'Ṣumur belongs to the king,' may the king know that there was an attack on our garrison, and the sons of 'Abdi-Aširta seized it. And so there has been no one to carry word to the king. But give thought to the fact that I am your loyal servant, and whatever I hear, I write to my lord." Rib-Hadda again corrects an inaccurate report of the local situation in EA 362:40–59: "As to his having said before the king 'There is a pestilence in the lands,' the king my lord, should not listen to the words of other men. There is no pestilence in the lands. It has been over for a long time. My lord knows that I do not write lies to my lord."

Faced by a doubtful intelligence report, any consumer will consider two questions: the credibility of the source and the possibility of verification. When Rib-Hadda (as he does on a number of occasions) protests about his truthfulness, he is preempting or answering imputations on his credibility. In a number of other dispatches (e.g., EA 68, 69, 89, 90, 94, 102, 107), he proposes a sensible method for verifying the accuracy of his reports. His plea is for Pharaoh to corroborate the information he supplies on 'Abdi-Ashirta's activities and the threat to Egyptian interests by sending a commissioner or a messenger to investigate the situation on the spot. In EA 74:57–62, he proposes coming to Egypt in person, and in EA 108, he calls on Pharaoh to summon the Egyptian commissioner Haip home for cross-examination following the fall of Ṣumur.

Whatever Egyptian reasons for inaction against Aziru, and whatever the reliability of Abi-Milku and Rib-Hadda's reports, the correspondence presents a picture of a troubled intelligence operation at the period in question. Zimreddi's defection in the intelligence struggle against Aziru would have been a serious loss. That Egypt did not know that the important port of Byblos had not fallen, or that Ṣumur, the center of Egyptian operations in the north, had fallen, and that a plague had "been over for a long time" suggests that the collection and transmission of intelligence had been disrupted. It is surprising that Rib-Hadda had to continually suggest ways for the Egyptians to cross-check his reports, as though a Great Power had to be taught the elementary rules of intelligence appraisal. Another unusual aspect of the file is the lack of Egyptian interest in Rib-Hadda's news. This culminated in the reprimands: "Why do you keep writing to me?" (EA 117:1–9), and "You are the one that writes to me more than all the other mayors" (EA 124:32–40), expressions of irritation that hardly fit in with the evidence already cited of a pressing need for more — not less — information on events in northern Canaan.

It is possible that Rib-Hadda's offense was as much procedural as substantive — persistently bypassing normal Egyptian channels for the communication of intelligence (and policy making in general). Clearly, Pharaoh objected to Rib-Hadda writing directly to him with excessive frequency. Direct vassal communication with the Egyptian court would only make sense *if vital Egyptian geostrategic interests were at stake,* in the event, say, of Hittite or Hurrian troop movements, when urgency was of the essence. In other circumstances, direct communication would be unsound administrative procedure (and incongruous in a hierarchical system). Sound procedure would be, in the usual run of things, for officials on the ground in Canaan to collate information, comparing it with other sources, filling in blanks and following up leads as required. On local matters especially, they alone would be responsible for actually putting together a final intelligence product and making policy recommendations.

If this reconstruction is correct, it would explain the Egyptian complaint: "Why does Rib-Hadda keep sending a tablet this way to the palace" (EA 106: 13–22). According to this theory, the right way was for intelligence reports, of local rather than strategic interest, to be channeled through the local Egyptian commissioner. We see in EA 133 that the standard chain of transmission within the Egyptian administration was agent/source → handler/official → commissioner (→ court). Routine procedure for a vassal wishing to pass on information to the king would be vassal → commissioner → palace, exemplified by EA 98:1–26:

> Say to Yanhamu: Message of Yapah-Haddu. Why have you been neglectful of Ṣumur so that all lands from Gubla to Ugarit have become enemies in the service of Aziru? Šigata and Ampi are enemies. He has now stationed ships of Arwada in Ampi and Šigata so grain cannot be brought into Ṣumur. Nor are we able to enter Ṣumur, and so what can

we ourselves do? Write to the palace about this matter. It is good that you are informed.

Conclusions

There are various reasons for concluding that Egypt conducted organized intelligence activities in the Amarna period:

1. Several of the Amarna Letters are in whole or in part intelligence reports, pure and simple, having as their main purpose the transmission of information for the use of government. Intelligence reports do not occur in a vacuum.
2. At least 38 out of 329 documents in the vassal corpus, and two items in the Great King file, contain intelligence references.
3. Three out of only ten letters sent from Pharaoh refer to intelligence.
4. Egyptian instructions and vassal responses indicate that the collection of information was an explicit obligation of vassal rulers.
5. Rib-Hadda corrects others' inaccurate reports.
6. It is possible to detect standard operating procedures for the presentation of intelligence, including a certain form of words and a chain of orderly transmission.

Intelligence in the Amarna Letters mostly consists of odd snippets, brief, individual reports. But taken together, the various items accumulate into a set of materials of a recognizably intelligence character. Within the overall corpus of the vassal correspondence, this component is far from negligible, entitling us to conclude that Egypt invested a significant effort in the collection of intelligence at this period. We can imagine how the various items of information reaching the court from Canaanite rulers, commissioners, traders, diplomats, and returning messengers would be pieced together to form a larger intelligence tapestry.

In part, Egypt needed intelligence to run its Canaanite empire. Yet the deliberate collection of information on the Great Powers was surely of at least equivalent importance. It is significant that Pharaoh refers to intelligence matters in rare letters to the Babylonian and Arzawan kings. Rib-Hadda, Abi-Milku, and other vassals supply strategic information on the Hittites and Hurrians. Aziru is allowed home to Amurru, despite contacts with Hatti, after the arrival of the intelligence report from Amurru on Hittite troop strength.

Despite Egypt's wish to establish familial and fraternal relations with other Great Kings, it is clear that it needed to keep a close eye on brothers who, in the Near Eastern tradition of Cain and Abel, were also potential enemies. Some of the Great Power intelligence mentioned is of military movements and troop strengths; the rest concerns political matters. Adding one and one together: Estimates of military capability and political intention are the two classic components of threat assessment.[9]

An Egyptian sensitivity to potential threats to security along the northern periphery of its empire points to an acute awareness of the risk of war. It need not be taken to imply the precariousness of the Amarna system, however. On the contrary, vigilance and a reputation among the Great Powers for being well informed would be good ways to avoid surprise and deter aggression. Egyptian intelligence mastery, like that of the United States today, would be positively conducive to equilibrium. This is why, in two dispatches, Pharaoh does not bother to conceal his intelligence capabilities.

Egypt could not have conducted a far-flung network of international relationships, protected its trade and security, and maintained its sphere of influence had it not been knowledgeable about what was going on. Foreign-policy decisions cannot be made without organized information on the state of the world. Intelligence is needed to define the situation, identify constraints and possibilities, and delineate alternative courses of action. The Amarna Letters, then, not only demonstrate Late Bronze Age Egypt's diplomatic skill. They also hint at the orderly processes of information collection and, by extrapolation, of strategic and foreign policy making, that underlay Egypt's dominant Great Power role.

PART III

Imperial Policy

CHAPTER EIGHT

Imperial Egypt and the Limits of Power

WILLIAM J. MURNANE

The period between the fifteenth and eleventh centuries B.C.E. marks a sea change in Egypt's relations with western Asia—indeed, with the entire world beyond its borders. Up to that time, its foreign policy had rarely had aims any more ambitious than securing its frontiers and facilitating the acquisition of desirable products from abroad. Border fortifications had allowed Egyptian forces to monitor the local traffic and, when necessary, chastise troublemakers "who knew not Egypt." Never during the first fifteen hundred years of its history, though, had Egypt sought to control such turbulence beyond its borders with the mechanisms of imperial rule: until the fifteenth century B.C.E., in other words, Egypt seems to have asserted itself in the world abroad only so that it could enjoy the luxury of holding the world at arm's length.[1]

This pattern had already begun to change in the mid-sixteenth century, when Egypt emerged from its Second Intermediate Period. Having reclaimed the northern Nile Valley from the Asiatic Hyksos regime, which had dominated Egypt for more than a century, the new Eighteenth Dynasty showed a more daringly expansionist vision than ever before. This spirit first manifested itself in the south, where Egypt felt itself menaced not only by the kingdom of Kush (the Hyksos' former ally) but by other Nubian entities as well: by the early fifteenth century, Egypt would engulf all but the remotest of these potential enemies and had roughly tripled the greatest extent of its previous holdings in Nubia. Governing this conquered territory would be Egypt's first experiment in managing problems abroad by simply absorbing them.[2] Imperialism made slower progress in the Near East, where early Eighteenth-Dynasty Pharaohs, perhaps put off by the difficulty of controlling an area more alien and highly civilized than Nubia,[3] limited themselves to traditionally sporadic methods of intimidation and punishment. Starting with Thutmose III, however, Egypt began to define in western Asia a permanent sphere of influence where native rulers were forced to recognize Pharaoh's suzerainty, to the exclusion of all competitors. Over the next three generations this orbit would be consolidated and then regularized by agreement with the other Great Powers of the Near East, so that by the earlier fourteenth century, Egypt ruled over an Asiatic empire that stretched from the Sinai all the way up the Syro-Palestinian coast to Ugarit.[4]

That empire has left many traces in ancient records. In Egypt, it is reflected not only in official war monuments and campaign narratives but also in memorials left by private individuals, whose service in this "government of conquests" is attested by their titles and tomb autobiographies. Its presence is also manifest in the fragmentary archive that is the focus of this volume—these Amarna Letters, exchanged by Pharaoh with his vassals and the other Great Kings of the Near East, along with other cuneiform archives (mainly from the Hittite capital at Boghazköi and the port city of Ugarit in northern Syria), provide welcome insight into diplomacy and imperial government as they were actually practiced. Even so, what we learn from this combination of sources is still far short of the full picture we would like to have; and interpreting the remains is further complicated by the peculiarities of the period from which they come.

The Amarna Age takes its name from a site associated with one of the oddest experiments in all of ancient history.[5] There, on an obscure tract in Middle Egypt, Pharaoh Akhenaten founded the headquarters of a new cult; repudiating his earlier name, Amenhotep (IV), he declared his allegiance to a sole god, manifest as the solar orb *(Aten),* whom he put in place of Egypt's traditional gods until his successors restored the orthodox religion. Much about this period (including the precise drift of Akhenaten's creed) remains controversial, as does the assumed impact of the "revolution" on contemporary affairs.[6] The alleged beneficence of Akhenaten's regime, once believed to have dictated a pacifist approach to foreign policy, has been discounted, and in its place stand more "realistic" interpretations of his initiatives.[7] Unfortunately, there is not enough evidence to sustain any but the broadest outlines of what "happened" in the Amarna period, and attempts to "read" the heretic's personality or to forge connections between his foreign policy and his beliefs are unconvincing.[8] Still, with all these reservations in mind, an overall shape for Egyptian foreign policy can at least be inferred from Egyptian and cuneiform sources, if only to provide a setting (or, in some cases, another perspective) against which to project the more specialized discussions of ancient diplomacy in the rest of this volume.

The Egyptian Empire and Its Subjects

Early in Akhenaten's twelfth year on the throne, the king made a public appearance at Amarna, in order to "receive the deliveries (*inw*) of Kharu (Asia) and Kush (Nubia), west and east," while "the chieftains of every foreign territory were presenting [deliveries to the king and] begging peace from him, that [they might be] allowed to breathe the breath [of] life." This pronouncement, far from being the rhetorical boilerplate so common in Egyptian monuments, marks a genuine, dated event (one of the few we know from Akhenaten's reign) documented by two individuals who recorded different episodes of the ceremony in their tombs.[9] It seems logical that a public demonstration of this magnitude would mark an equally significant occasion, but our continuing inability to determine its precise significance (even with Egyptian and cuneiform sources combined at our disposal) only drives home how slender and anecdotal our information really is.[10] Even as a reflection of imperial might, moreover, this announcement significantly falsifies Pharaoh's relations with his vassals; although their chief function, from Egypt's perspective, might well be to approach submissively, "their products laden on their backs," not all tributaries were on the same level.[11] The "west" (implicitly Libya) seems to have been rather loosely bound to Egypt during the Amarna period. Nubia, however, was ruled by a military government headed by a viceroy. Egyptian ownership of landed property (by the crown or the main temples supported by the state) was widespread. Native princes, in the few places they had been allowed to survive, played only a limited role as intermediaries between their people and the ruling power. Nubia, therefore, was in effect a colony of Egypt, and the arrangement by which it presented its "deliveries" would have been quite different from that in the "west."[12]

Almost the complete opposite of the Nubian system held sway, moreover, in western Asia.[13] Direct government by Egypt was the exception there, with only a few areas being owned by Pharaoh or temples in the Nile Valley.[14] Local government elsewhere in Egypt's sphere of influence lay in the hands of native rulers, whose relations with Pharaoh might best be described as those of vassals toward an overlord. Making "deliveries," whether as the regularly expected tribute or the more irregular supplying of trade goods and emergency requisitions of matériel to Egyptian authorities, bulked large among their duties.[15] These obligations, though, operated in the wider context of the empire's role as a buffer zone between Egypt and the other Great Powers of the Near East. Vassals were expected to uphold their overlord's interests by reporting on their neighbors' activities, treating Pharaoh's enemies as their own,[16] and participating in military operations against such foes whenever required.[17] As pledges of their loyalty, they sent their sons to Egypt for "training" (though actually as hostages) and, on demand, their daughters as minor trophy wives for Pharaoh.[18] How well vassals fulfilled their obligations was a constant point at issue (as the Amarna Letters show) between them and their Egyptian overseers and, ultimately, the king—for Pharaoh was at perfect liberty to depose a ruler perceived as delinquent and to subject him, along with his family, to deportation or worse.[19] Moreover, although the commitment a local ruler made to his overlord was personal, his city's vassal status did not lapse with his death or at any other time; his successor, whoever he might be, received his office from Pharaoh and was expected to show the same loyalty in return.[20]

How relations between overlord and vassal were defined in Egypt's Asiatic empire is a complicated question. To be sure, the one-sidedness in Egyptian records (where foreigners show an unlimited subservience toward Pharaoh) is belied by the high incidence of complaints, evasiveness, and tacit negotiation emanating from vassals in the Amarna Letters,[21] as well as by references to what are clearly prices paid for trade goods sent to Egypt.[22] What remains elusive, however, is the mechanism that defined each side's relations with the other. One instrument that lay readily at hand was the treaty, widely used elsewhere in the Near East to establish mutual commitments, either in a hierarchic (overlord and vassal) or a parity relationship (among Great Kings and between vassals). No examples of such documents survive in the Egyptian sphere of influence, however, and even though we may assume that treaties were made between Egyptian vassals, these plainly were not used as a mechanism for enforcing a general peace among them; indeed, if the Amarna Letters show anything, it is that the Egyptians tolerated a good deal of independent action (including warfare and subversion) among their vassals in Asia, always providing that the overlord's interests suffered no damage in consequence.[23] Since the implication of this laissez-faire attitude is that Pharaoh (far from committing to protect all the vassals) intervened only at his convenience, Egyptian policy in practice also seems to contradict the assumption that Egypt regulated its relations with the princes of western Asia by formal treaty, with obligations mutually binding on both sides.[24] In fact, the existence of such obligations is never implied in the Amarna Letters. Not even Rib-Hadda of Byblos, the persistence of whose complaints so annoyed Pharaoh,[25] ventures to claim that the king's unresponsiveness amounts to a breach of promise: the case for Egyptian cooperation rests, rather, on the appellant's faithfulness (e.g., EA 108:18-25; 116:44-46), his need for help (e.g., EA 112:9-15; 118:34-44), and how it would profit the king to send it (e.g., EA 117:84-94; 126:43-60; 129:13-21; 131:57-62; 132:29-59). The prevalence of this strategy among princes anxious to enlist Pharaoh's aid suggests that whatever the instrument was that bound vassals to their overlord in the Egyptian empire, strict reciprocity played no part in the arrangement.

In the absence of treaties, it has been suggested that the binding instrument was a special fealty oath administered to princes who submitted to Egypt. In Egyptian records, this has been identified as an oath, called *sdf3-tryt*,[26] of which an example is presumed to survive in the promise sworn by the princes who surrendered to Thutmose III at Megiddo:

> We shall not repeat (doing) evil towards (King) Menkheperre — may he live forever and ever — our lord, in our lifetime, since we have seen his power and he has given us breath (i.e., life) at his pleasure. It is his father [Amun-Re, Lord of the Thrones of the Two Lands] who did it; it is surely no human action.[27]

It appears, though, that this may not be the all-encompassing fealty oath it was assumed to be, for the *sdf(3)-tr(yt)* is revealed as a more limited instrument by which actual or accused criminals normalized their relations with legitimate authority by "purging guilt," and it could thus have been confined to reconciling actual rebels rather than making peace with princes who surrendered on their own initiative.[28] That distinction might be illusory, however, because foreigners in the path of the Egyptian army would be tacitly "rebellious" before they submitted gracefully and might require the same absolving mechanism used later in more obdurate cases.[29] Besides, since vassals in the Amarna Letters do not assert rights consistent with those they could claim under the oath of formal treaty, it would seem to follow that they were bound by a mechanism less specific and conceptually more one-sided — that is, by an oath formulated on very similar lines to the promise made by the defeated rebels at Megiddo. If this is so, one can understand the strategy by which princes in the Amarna Letters invoked Pharaoh's aid, for their oath would be a unilateral promise made by each subject prince, formally committing the overlord to nothing except "his pleasure" and placing the onus of persuasion on the vassal. One might even sense here why princes might feel entitled to their overlord's care; in the Egyptian worldview the reward of submission was "breath/life," and it could surely be expected that Pharaoh would sustain what he had given so long as the vassal remained true to his oath.[30] Just such an understanding on a vassal's part seems to be implied by the only political guarantee one of them receives from his overlord in the Amarna Letters, when Addu-nirari of Nuhašše reminds Pharaoh (EA 51 obverse) of the historic bond between their ancestors and how Thutmose III swore to support the king he had enthroned in Nuhašše.[31] Expectations may also have been influenced by the mutual commitments vassals would normally have looked for in treaties; indeed, Addu-Nirari might well be hinting at this when he informs Pharaoh (EA 51 reverse:1–6) that he has just rebuffed the Hittites' offer of a treaty, although he, too, like other vassals, tries to influence Egypt's behavior by persuasion rather than a claim of right. This strategy, and the consistency of its application in the Amarna Letters, suggests that the vassals were well aware of their limited bargaining position. Since Egypt had ruled most communities in its Asiatic empire for at least four generations before the start of the Amarna archive, each side should have had enough time to develop a reliable notion of what it could expect from the other.

The novelty of the vassals' close ties with Egypt during the Eighteenth Dynasty is reflected by their anomalous situation in the empire. Though their obligations were indistinguishable from those of any other subjects of Pharaoh, particularly in the official Egyptian perspective, they still remained in a different category from the Egyptians who alone were truly "people."[32] Occupying an area at some distance from the Nile Valley, Asiatics were also not subjected to the type of overbearing foreign presence that virtually submerged native culture in Nubia while it was occupied during the New Kingdom. No significant Egyptian effort to implant its culture in western Asia is apparent: although a number of "Egyptian" temples have been identified in Egypt's sphere of influence, we have no clear idea of how they were used.[33] Neither on the ground nor in the Amarna Letters, moreover, is there any significant evidence that foreigners were encouraged to participate in Egyptian religion. The distinctively Egyptian notion of divine kingship, continuously present on earth to mediate between human society and the gods, seems to have made little impact on vassal princes.[34] Pharaoh, conventionally described as the "Good God" in Egypt, is generally called only the vassal's "lord" in the Amarna Letters, which also refer to the god Amun, not as Pharaoh's divine alter ego (as he was in the Nile Valley) but merely as his "lord."[35] This usage is too widespread in the Amarna archive to be confined to the relatively short period, late in Akhenaten's reign, when the heretic king also eschewed any explicit reference to himself as a "god" and called himself "Good Ruler" instead. Even then, moreover, the difference between the king and the supreme being continued to lie not in what each of them was but in what they did; whereas the Aten was the ultimate source of life for everybody, the king was the indispensable figure through whom that life was made effective in society. From the Egyptian subject's perspective, then, both Akhenaten and his divine father were gods, sharing in the same nature and performing the same life-giving functions, although in separate spheres and in different ways.[36] Foreigners, however, are almost totally excluded from these benefits; the god, in his infinite variety, has made special arrangements to accommodate their special needs, but foreigners remain distinct from real "people" (Egyptians) by language and nature,[37] and they are thus excluded from the social building by which Akhenaten advances the careers of his native subjects. These anomalies, which underscore foreigners' unequal participation in Egypt's world and their position as outsiders, may even have affected the treatment vassals received in practice from Egyptian authorities, in particular, the pattern of peremptory command and unresponsiveness to vassals' complaints, which may reflect (even if unintentionally) the style of the royal myth of Egypt, with its divine king "of whom there is no equal" among other human rulers.[38] Such dismissiveness toward foreigners dominates official rhetoric in Egyptian texts,[39] and on occasion we find it in colloquial utterances as well.[40] That such attitudes would have colored Egyptian thinking and behavior is credible enough, but to assume that both sides were held captive by their cultural predispositions, to the extent that (in the teeth of their long acquaintance by the Amarna period) they expected incompatible things of one another, seems hard to believe.[41] Egyptian rhetoric, as noted above, can falsify as well as illuminate, though it remains a useful background against which to project the Amarna archive's case studies of relations between Pharaoh and his vassals.

The Government of the Egyptian Empire

Once again, different aspects of reality are sometimes reflected in Egyptian and cuneiform sources. For instance, vassals in the Amarna Letters are given a title, *ḫazannu* (mayor), which corresponds to that held by a class of official (*ḥ3ty-ʿ*) who presided over local administration in Egypt, but this figurative description reflects only a partial truth, namely, the vassals' subordinate position under Egyptian control and not, as noted above, their independence in most areas of community government (unlike their Egyptian counterparts, whose roles were more fully integrated into the pharaonic system).[42] Still more discordant is the image of Pharaoh's government of conquests, as conveyed by Egyptian compared with cuneiform records. Vassals in the Amarna Letters take their orders from a class of officials with the generic title *rābiṣu* or "commissioner," but some of these men outranked the others (as internal evidence in the Letters can show),[43] and the style that obscures these distinctions in cuneiform records is, again, at odds with Egyptian sources that reveal a more rank-conscious hierarchy. It is now generally agreed that high commissioners (like Pawer, Maya, and Yanhamu in the Letters) would have held the title "king's envoy upon every foreign territory," an ancient rating adapted to the comparable rank borne by senior diplomats elsewhere in the Near East.[44] Symptomatic of the spotty preservation of records from this period is that only one of the high commissioners named in the Amarna Letters, Maya, is certainly known from Egyptian sources.[45] Junior commissioners, though similarly hard to identify in records from the Nile Valley, are nonetheless assigned titles in the Letters that identify them as military officers of middling though responsible rank;[46] they probably also shared the semi-honorific title "overseer of northern foreign territories," analogous to a similar title granted to important military officers in Egypt's Nubian empire.[47]

Plain as these broad lines are, much about the way Egypt's foreign service in western Asia actually operated continues to elude us. It is unclear, for example, whether the Asiatic empire was subdivided into provinces and, if so, how many.[48] The chain of command, moreover, remains incomplete in that we know little about how the Asiatic bureau was run. While we can be certain that command was divided, for example, we do not know how (or whether) the whole system was coordinated, either laterally or from the top down.[49] That Yanhamu, whose normal bailiwick was Canaan, was involved on occasion in affairs farther north might suggest that he outranked the other commissioners who were posted there;[50] but whether this was formally built into the empire's command structure for a significant length of time, or as a special and temporary commission, is all unknown. Indeed, it is frustrating not only that so commanding a figure remains unidentifiable outside of the Amarna Letters but also that his status in Pharaoh's administration is so unclear: the only title Yanhamu is ever given, "parasol-bearer of the king," is an honorific indicator of courtly rank that leaves open the official basis of his power, and thus also his historic role in Egyptian service.[51] Similar uncertainties becloud what happened at the highest level of government, where policy was set. Though decisions rested officially with Pharaoh himself, there must have been advisers able to ballast his judgment with expertise in foreign affairs. Indirect evidence for the operations of such a "foreign office" can even be inferred from parts of the Amarna archive itself, to the extent that the form and content of letters addressed to Pharaoh's diplomatic equals were designed to convey precise nuances of tone and meaning. The execution of well-honed diplomatic correspondence by a highly accomplished secretariat, however, tells nothing about how its work was directed or by whom.[52] Most probably, the composition of the council changed with each king, as advisers from the previous generation were replaced by current favorites; Akhenaten's chamberlain Tutu, who was importuned (as a sympathetic listener with access to the king?) by the wily Aziru, may have been a member.[53] The likeliest overall director of Egypt's foreign policy in Asia, however, would be the senior of Egypt's two prime ministers (customarily dubbed "viziers" in modern studies), who is designated "governor of Egypt" and "(*the?*) commissioner" in the Amarna correspondence.[54]

Eighteenth-Dynasty Egypt's greater involvement with Asia was marked by a growing cosmopolitanism. From this time on, we find Egyptians borrowing plentifully in the areas of religion and language, while influences from the Nile Valley spread widely through the Near East.[55] Regular contact with Asiatics — as captives and vassals, diplomats and merchants — bred not only familiarity but also more opportunities for "naturalized" foreigners to live in Egypt and work for Pharaoh's government; by the mid-Eighteenth Dynasty, such men are already found holding responsible positions in the administration,[56] and in the period of the Amarna Letters we not only find Yanhamu, an apparent Asiatic,[57] near the top of the Egyptian foreign service but perhaps others in comparably high office — Tutu, Akhenaten's chamberlain, might be one such favored Asiatic,[58] and it is even possible that one of Egypt's viziers on the eve of the Amarna period was of Asiatic stock. In 1979 a family tomb was discovered in the Memphite cemetery at Saqqara, belonging to a hitherto unknown vizier who seems to have served, in sequence, Amenhotep III and Amenhotep IV (apparently before the latter became Akhenaten). His name, spelled ʿprj3(r) in Egyptian, may be interpreted as West Semitic *Aper-El,* or "Servant of El";[59] as with Yanhamu, his retention of that foreign name is the sole basis on which his roots might be identified as Asiatic. In Aper-El's case, however, our dossier includes the burials of his wife and son (both of whom had Egyptian names) and the family's physical remains, none of which have traits that can be identified positively as foreign.[60] If Aper-El was an Egyptian with a foreign name,[61] the same might also be true of Yanhamu; the naming of both men, hitherto regarded as prima facie evidence of their foreign origins, might only reflect a fashionable taste for the exotic, which continued into the later New Kingdom.[62] The evidence for either case is fragile, and conclusions are subject to change. Nonetheless, despite clear indications of the growing acceptance of foreigners in Pharaoh's government, we cannot yet be sure that such cosmopolitan attitudes during the later Eighteenth Dynasty extended to entrusting "wretched Asiatics" with the highest and most sensitive offices in Egypt's imperial system.

Outlines of Egyptian Foreign Policy in Western Asia

Any comparison of Egyptian and cuneiform sources mentioning Egypt illustrates the gulf between pharaonic policy in practice and the monotonous triumphalism laid on, for home consumption, in the monuments. Pharaoh, though he occasionally found ways to impress his innate superiority upon other Great Kings of the Near East, was nonetheless forced to deal with them from a position of mutual respect and reciprocity quite alien to Egypt's traditional approach to lesser humans outside its borders.[63] To follow Egyptian policy closely is impossible, given the huge gaps in the record: how, for example, is one to decide whether Egypt's relations with Mittani took a decisive turn for the worse under Amenhotep III and his son, as opposed to undergoing merely some rough patches in what was otherwise a stable alliance? The evidence in this case seems compatible with either scenario,[64] underscoring the fragility of our efforts to reconstruct the period's history.

Still, several broad trends suggest themselves, the first being the caution Egypt displayed in charting its course in western Asia. Even after Mittani's collapse, and once the Hittites had withdrawn from Syria, Akhenaten disregarded the urging of local princes who wanted the vacuum filled by Egypt. Even when the Hittites took over two of Egypt's most important affiliates, Ugarit and Qadesh, Pharaoh failed to react until Qadesh was revealed as a Hittite catspaw, seeking to detach other Egyptian vassals — and even then, both Egypt and Hatti pursued limited war aims and remained formally at peace while actually engaged in cold war. What this pattern reveals is not the indecision of a pacifist Akhenaten but entirely reasonable caution on both sides. Neither would have wanted to repeat the half century of all-out war that had preceded the peace between Egypt and Mittani; if one could be pressured by the other, short of total alienation, an accommodation might be reached at a price each side was willing to pay. Closure, nearly achieved when the Egyptian queen offered to marry Suppiluliuma's son, was upset by the latter's sudden death (perhaps of plague, though the Hittites continued to suspect foul play), precipitating the open war neither party had wanted. This grudge match would be prolonged over the next sixty years, until domestic and foreign policy factors on each side allowed both to reach an acceptably face-saving accord and resume the entente cordiale that had existed formerly between Egypt and the previous superpower to her north.[65]

Hatti's drive to replace Mittani, moreover, put a fatal strain on Egypt's ability to keep its sphere of influence intact. Once the Hittites had seized Qadesh, the activities of their proxy, King Aitakama, challenged Pharaoh's control at the northeast corner of his empire, a situation hardly improved when two Egyptian efforts to recover Qadesh brought not only failure but also a carefully measured retaliation. Hittite activities in the north also imperiled Pharaoh's hold over Amurru, whose territory directly to the west of Qadesh was now on the front line of Egypt's crumbling position in Syria. Unable or unwilling to make an open-ended commitment of Egyptian military might, Pharaoh chose instead to rely on his own local proxies, men like Biryawaza in Upe (inland southern Syria, just south of Qadesh) and Aziru in Amurru. Allowing the latter to consolidate his power, even at the expense of vassals like Rib-Hadda, was a price the Egyptians, clearly, were willing to pay. As Aziru grew stronger, however, and the overall situation in the north failed to turn in Egypt's favor, the option of defecting became increasingly safe and profitable; eventually, Aziru did join Mittani's former vassals in north Syria as a client of the Hittite empire. Egypt, though it tried to recover its northern border provinces for another half century, would ultimately swallow the permanent loss of Qadesh and Amurru when Ramesses II made peace with Hatti.[66] The lessons Egypt learned from its bitter experience at the end of the Amarna Age are reflected, perhaps, in the tighter controls it would exercise over its vassals in the later New Kingdom. Imperialism in Asia, however, seems to have remained mostly a defensive expedient for Pharaohs: once the Late Bronze Age international system had collapsed in the twelfth century B.C.E., the empire was given up rather quickly.[67] This retreat, which must have seemed prudent at the time, ultimately cost Egypt dearly. One cannot help wondering if Egypt's long demise, under the shadow of the great empires later in the first millennium, was a price paid for being fundamentally uncomfortable with the give and take of interregional politics in the Near East and for acting, at crucial points in its history, as if the outside world could indeed be held at arm's length.

CHAPTER NINE

Egypt and Her Vassals: The Geopolitical Dimension

ALAN JAMES

Scene

The onset of the Amarna period found Egypt relatively well protected by its land frontiers against the advance of a hostile power. However, the deserts to Egypt's immediate northeast, the Sinai and the Negev, had been shown to be penetrable. Beyond that, along the eastern Mediterranean coast and its hinterland, lay a populous and prosperous area from which an ill-disposed power might launch an attack. This area was loosely called Canaan. Clearly, it was most important for Egypt that Canaan neither unite against it nor come under the domination of a great rival.

In this respect, geography worked both for and against Egypt.[1] In Egypt's favor was the fact that conditions in Canaan were not conducive to political unity. The coastal plain is discontinuous and often narrow; mountain ranges run parallel with the coast, making lateral communications difficult; and especially in the north, the wooded valleys—more appropriately, gorges— are often steep. Thus, there was little chance that a significant power, either indigenous or external, would emerge at Egypt's very gate. Authority was likely to be dispersed, and the resultant rulers would be much weaker than Egypt. By the same geographical token, the efforts of a large externally based power such as Egypt to exert authority would encounter logistical and tactical complications. Because the terrain was ideal for those who would later be called guerrillas, the checking of their activities would be a formidable task. Furthermore, other external powers might try to win the loyalty of some of the several hundred local principalities and their rulers who exercised authority in Canaan.

This was possible because of the area's geographical continuity with the northern part of the Fertile Crescent. Whoever dominated the great plain of Jazirah, and particularly the Syrian lowland to Jazira's west, was faced with several points of entry into Canaan, notably along or across the valley of the Orontes. A more difficult southward route could also be taken, heading for the coast along the lower Litani Valley or across the Plain of Esdraelon. Although Egypt could, therefore, entertain a measure of confidence about the security of her northeastern border, she could not, in a competitive international environment, take it for granted.

Indeed, the environment *was* competitive. Babylonia, at the eastern extremity of the Fertile Crescent, was a status quo power. But its northern neighbor, Assyria, was growing in strength. And to the west, the Hittites were emerging ominously out of Asia Minor. Between Assyria and Hatti lay Mittani, which had once dominated Canaan but had latterly been expelled by Egypt. A rapprochement was then established between these two powers, legitimizing Egypt's control of Canaan. Then, early in the second quarter of the fourteenth century, Hatti expelled Mittani from northern Syria and firmly entrenched itself in the Mittanians' former domain. Clearly, this might have an adverse impact on Egypt's position in Canaan or even directly threaten Egypt.

Whether and to what extent Egyptian hegemony over Canaan had been formally established through treaties is unclear. But Egypt's dominance had been displayed to devastating effect within living memory. The territorial entities of the region were Egypt's vassals and had to bear in mind the possibility of the dispatch of expeditionary forces with disciplinary intent. Logistically speaking, this would not be easy, especially to the north, but it could be done. During the period covered by the Amarna Letters, however, despite the emerging international threat to the north, Egypt's touch in Canaan was light. Egypt relied on the officials and garrisons that had been established in the more appropriate locations and sometimes dispatched other officials on special missions. Egypt also would have received regular reports from these sources. In additional, there was direct correspondence with vassals, to which the Amarna Letters provide bulky testimony. Though well aware that certain developments in Canaan did not speak encouragingly for its continued overall control, Egypt seemed to display little concern. Why was this?

The Vassals

Given the sparsity of the evidence, answers can only be adumbrated. By way of approaching them, I identify five disparate vassal elements.

The Vassals of the Nearby Coastal Plain

Patently, Egypt could most effectively exercise its strength over those who could be visited with comparative ease. Conceivably, armed men could have been moved eastward by sea from the Nile Delta, although the absence of natural harbors on Canaan's southernmost shore may well have discouraged this possibility. The large-scale overland crossing of Sinai was not the most straightforward of tasks, but it could certainly be done. It follows that the cities on the lush coastal plain to the immediate north of present-day Rafah must have been very mindful of their obligations toward Pharaoh. Concomitantly, they were far from alternative centers of significant power and therefore had virtually no political options. Furthermore, the nearness of these cities to Egypt must have discouraged any power-hungry cities or groups to their north and east from contemplating expansion in their direction.

One would therefore expect to find that this area was a belt of untroubled loyalty. Nothing in the Amarna Letters controverts this assumption. The relevant (albeit scanty) correspondence completely consists of protestations of fealty to Pharaoh of the day. One vassal king speaks of his guardianship of the gates of Gaza ([H]azzatu) and Yafo (EA 296). The ruler of Ashkelon sends assurances that that part of Pharaoh's domain is safe in his hands and that he is listening very carefully and obediently to what Pharaoh's commissioners have to say (EA 320–26). It would have been strange were it otherwise.

Inland Vassals in the Southern Region

As the distance from Egypt increases or the local topography becomes more difficult, it could be expected that a greater degree of independence on the part of the vassals might be found. Their day-to-day consciousness of the Egyptian yoke was presumably less keen than those who were more easily brought under its whip. There was fuller scope for local ambitions, of which there was unlikely to be a shortage. The hilly country, too, would not have obstructed and may even have facilitated low-intensity raids. Moreover, this area, roughly that lying to the south of the Galilee, would at this time surely have been effectively beyond the range of Hittite subversion. And while this meant the unavailability of external support, it also, more importantly, meant the absence of an alternative focus of authority.

Thus, it would not be surprising if this area was the scene of local turbulence. With it, there might well have been signs of tension between the indigenous rulers and the resident representatives of Pharaoh. So it proves.

Complaints come in about Egypt's commissioners from Gezer (EA 270, 292), Jerusalem (EA 285, 289), and Akko (EA 234). Shechem is at odds with Megiddo (EA 244) and Qiltu (EA 280). Jerusalem makes accusations against Gezer (EA 276, 289, 290), Shechem (EA 289), Gath (Gimtu), and Qiltu (EA 290). The latter asserts that it is isolated (EA 335), citing Jerusalem and Lachish as among its enemies (EA 335). And Lachish attracts the critical attention of Pharaoh's representative (EA 333). The Letters also contain numerous references to hostile action in an undefined area.

The charges of aggression contained in these reports are presented in the context of the territorial integrity of the pharaonic empire being undermined—with the clear suggestion that the innocent party is deserving of immediate imperial assistance. Routinely, all allegations are accompanied by flamboyant declarations of undying loyalty to the Egyptian throne. Such declarations should not necessarily be seen as meaningless. Most of these vassals, it is ventured, were fully cognizant and acceptant of the underlying reality of their vassalage (several of them paid, by way of tribute, "quite remarkable" sums to Egypt)[2] and of the benefits that, from time to time, such obeisance would bring. What they were bent upon, within that wider framework, was a local political and military game. Indeed, from one angle, the keenness with which it was pursued could be seen as a tribute to the protection against external threat afforded by the nearby hegemon.

Possibly, there is one exception to these remarks. Lab'ayu of Shechem and his sons (often allegedly in league with the 'Apiru; see below), seem to give their neighbors a disproportionate amount of trouble for a run-of-the-mill vassal (EA 244–46, 287, 289) and to be notably urgent in their protestations of innocence (EA 252–54; see further below).

The 'Apiru

This is a collective term referring to the warlords and brigands operating in and from the difficult and often mountainous terrain common to northern Canaan. These malefactors often trouble Egypt's vassals, and the Letters depict the 'Apiru as almost ubiquitous, archetypal outlaws. As such, they could not formally enjoy the status of vassalhood. But they operated in the area of vassalage and, with one exception (when, in EA 195, the ruler of Damascus claims to have lined them up against Pharaoh's enemies), are invariably presented as hostile to Egypt's interests.

The said ruler of Damascus may have been making the best of a bad job, for he is charged with having sided with the rebellious ʿApiru (EA 189), as are the rulers of Sidon (EA 148) and Gezer (EA 287). Other cities frequently claim to be endangered by them, such as Qiltu in the south (EA 271) and Hasi toward the north (EA 185). Many unspecified cities are said to have been lost to the ʿApiru, or to be on the point of that fate, and the rebels seem to have been particularly active and potent in and around the Bekaa Valley (EA 179, 185–86, 189). It is the constant complaint of Rib-Hadda of Byblos that the mini-state of Amurru, which lay in the northern Bekaa region, is in league with them.

This sounds like a familiar political ploy. "ʿApiru" seems to have become a general term of threat and abuse, a kind of political bogeyman employed in the hope of securing sympathy or support. Lacking, not surprisingly, is any hard evidence about the strength of the ʿApiru and the impact of their depredations. That Canaan may at this time have played host to roving bands of freebooters is entirely credible; so is the likelihood of such groups finding the fertile Bekaa especially rich in resources that, given the havens afforded by the high mountain ranges to both east and west, could conveniently be plundered. Whether the ʿApiru were, in their own right, a significant force seems much more open to question.

That by no means excludes the possibility of their having been drawn into the rebellious activity of more clearly identifiable actors, to the profit of both sides. One favorable locale for such interweaving was the north.

Damascus, Amurru, and the Adjacent Vassals

During the Amarna period, Egypt's vassals included two powerful mini-states in northern Canaan. One (which makes only a shadowy appearance in the Letters) was Damascus under Biryawaza. At the height of his power, he ruled a very large area "side by side with the Egyptian authorities."[3]

The other, to the northwest of Damascus, was Amurru. Based in the Orontes Valley in the northern Bekaa region, it extended toward the coast roughly between the latitudes of Arwad and Tripoli and was ruled by ʿAbdi-Ashirta, then by his son Aziru.

Amurru was in an expansionary mood, having designs on the coastal areas to the southwest of its inland core. Bases there would have given Amurru the opportunity to control traffic moving up and down what was here a very narrow coastal strip and to interfere with the parallel traffic at sea. It may also have wished to take over the sea-going trade of the generally prosperous Phoenician cities. From the Amarna accounts, the efforts of Amurru would appear to have been remarkably successful. Its influence extended as far south as the mouth of the Litani River, near Tyre. Thus, the ruler of that city reports that Sidon, a short distance to the north, is passing on intelligence to Aziru (EA 147), and then that the same city has marshalled Aziru's forces with a view to an attack on Tyre.

But it was from coastal Byblos, north of Beirut, that most accounts come of Amurru's expansion. Byblos's ruler was Rib-Hadda, who also claimed other cities. All of them, he complained in a long series of lamentations to the Egyptian court, were wrested from him by Amurru with the assistance of the 'Apiru. When Ṣumur, an Egyptian garrison city, falls (EA 76), 'Abdi-Ashirta explains that he in fact saved it (EA 62). 'Abdi-Ashirta also takes Ampi and Shigata (EA 76). He advances southward toward Baṭruna and eventually takes it, too (EA 88). Now all Rib-Hadda has left is Byblos. If Moran's order for the Letters is correct, Amurru then bypasses Byblos and becomes established in Beirut (EA 114, 116). In time, aided by the treachery of 'Abdi-Ashirta's brother (who may have been impressed by the likely threat of a pincer movement), Byblos goes over to Amurru's side (EA 136, 138). Evidently, it was not a happy decision, because Byblos's new ruler is soon complaining about the behavior of Aziru (EA 139–40). Meanwhile, Aziru also consolidates in the north, stationing ships at Arwad, beyond Ṣumur, so that (according to the ruler of Beirut, perhaps writing before his city came under Amurru's influence) the whole coast from Byblos to Ugarit (not far south of Antioch) is under Aziru's control (EA 98).

This account is substantiated by Singer, who writes that almost the whole coast "submitted to ['Abdi-Ashirta's] direct or indirect control." Later, under Aziru and his other sons, Amurru developed into "a (more-or-less) ordinary Syrian kingdom, with a centralized royal court and well-organized foreign relations."[4] In vain had Rib-Hadda repeatedly begged Pharaoh for help. What could the Egyptian court have been thinking? And how did the court feel about the power wielded by Biryawaza of Damascus? The answer to these questions may have partly depended on what was happening farther to the north.

The Northernmost Vassals

From Egypt's viewpoint, Canaan had all the advantage and disadvantage of a vertical (as distinct from a lateral) buffer zone. It was advantageous in that its front lines, being closest to or perhaps immediately facing one or more major rivals, were far from the domestic power base. Such distance spelled a comforting degree of safety. Its disadvantage lay in the possibility of vassals at the farther end of the zone displaying a disturbing measure of indiscipline, and if the opportunity was available, one or more of them might even transfer their allegiance to the other side. Given the technology of the time, which limited Egypt's immediate options on the ground, there was considerable scope for uncomfortable developments of this sort.

Supporting evidence for this idea is present in the Amarna Letters. Some vassals write to Pharaoh in insolent terms. Thus the ruler of Ugarit straightforwardly asks, among other things, for a physician (EA 49). A ruler in Nuhašše (inland from Ugarit) enjoins his lord not to be negligent in coming to his aid (EA 51). The ruler of Qatna, in the northeastern Bekaa, says baldly that he had heard that the king would not come forth (EA 53).

Such plain speaking very probably reflected Hatti's forward activity in the area, in the light of which some of the awe hitherto inspired by Pharaoh may well have evaporated. For the Hittites are said to have seized the vassals of Mittani (EA 75), to have moved into the inland region of Nuhašše (EA 165–67), and from there into parts that were indubitably within the Egyptian sphere of influence. Thus, out on the Syrian plain, the Damascene ruler calls for help against Hatti and charges that his enemies openly proclaimed their servility to Hatti's king (EA 196–97). From the coast, Rib-Hadda asserts that the Hittites had set fire to the country (EA 126). In between, Hatti's forces are said to have made headway in the Bekaa: Qatna has been successfully attacked (EA 55), and with the assistance of the ruler of Qadesh, an early recruit to the Hittite cause, other local cities have fallen (EA 170, 174–76, 363). The local Hittite general is reported to have been at the head of an infantry force of no less than ninety thousand men.

Most dramatically of all, some vassals — albeit alongside assurances of their continuing attachment to Egypt — openly refer to their diplomatic contacts with Hatti. These must have been very bold moves, which could easily have been taken amiss in Amarna. They suggest the impressive might of Hatti. Thus the ruler of Qatna says he has been invited (by a traitorous intermediary) to visit the Hittite king (EA 53). Ugarit's ruler is thought to have reported the receipt of a letter from him (EA 45). A king in Nuhašše unequivocally mentions such a letter, on no less explosive a topic (according to the restored text) than the making of an alliance (EA 51). It is said in almost as many words that Aziru of Amurru is in league with Hatti (EA 55). And Aziru himself does not deny that he has entertained a Hittite envoy (EA 161), suggesting that there was something, such as a treaty, to celebrate.

Manifestly, Egypt had a problem.

Egypt's Response

How Egypt reacted to events in Canaan would have depended on a variety of factors: its conception of its position and role, its knowledge and interpretation of what was happening to its northern region (both within and beyond Egypt's area of suzerainty), its assessment of its strength, and its other preoccupations. As a guide to these matters, the Amarna Letters are remarkably flimsy. What follows is therefore largely deduced from first principles.

Lesser Elements

Insofar as the cities of the coastal plain immediately to Egypt's northeast are concerned, it may be hazarded with some confidence that Egypt had little cause for concern. Necessarily, these vassals knew their place.

To the north and northeast, a good deal of political turbulence was apparent. But for a reason already mentioned — the presumed ready acceptance of vassalhood and its implications — Egypt probably was not too dismayed by what it heard. Provided that the cities in the area continued to facilitate the work of Egyptian administrators and the passage of Egyptian troops, their local rivalries and armed encounters were fully compatible with an assured Egyptian hegemony. Indeed, they may have strengthened it. For to the extent that the rulers were urgently focusing on their own parochial affairs — operating a local balance of power — they were that much less likely even to think about banding together against Pharaoh. *Divide et impera.*

However, the success of this policy depended on none of the immediate players coming to dominate all the others. The balance had to be maintained. If it swung too heavily in one direction, there would probably be trouble for Egypt. The ambitious ruler could well become resentful of aspects of Egyptian hegemony and make awkward demands. That would be a threat to Egypt's position and would create entirely the wrong impression, both in the region and among the neighboring Great Powers. Better to head off such an awkward development at an early stage.

It may well be that Lab'ayu's Shechem presented just such a disturbing case. There is very little evidence in the Letters of the extent of the problem or of Egypt's response to it. According to Albright, however, Lab'ayu secured control of much of central Canaan, from the trans-Jordanian Gilead Hills to the coast and southward from the Plain of Esdraelon to the frontiers of Jerusalem.[5] Power building of this order could not be ignored. Thus, a "counter-coalition, headed by the kings of Megiddo and Akko and supported by the Egyptian authorities, was formed in reaction and succeeded in bringing the [Shechem] offensive to an end."[6] Essential discipline was, it seems, restored.

The 'Apiru were a different type of case. They were disruptive locally, and their piecemeal distribution, their mobility, and the hit-and-run nature of many of their raids would have made them hard to pin down. They enjoyed the classic elusiveness of the guerrilla. But there must usually have been a question mark over whether Egypt needed to attempt a disciplinary exercise. Because the 'Apiru operated in small groups, the significance of their individual incursions would have been small. The lack of established governmental structures, both within each group and overall, meant that they were unlikely to be brought into any of Canaan's political equations. Moreover, their activity and the threat of it would have kept the vassals on their military toes (which would be helpful in the eventuality of Egypt having need of them) and may have discouraged political preoccupations of a perhaps disturbing character. On the whole, it may be supposed that the 'Apiru could, from Egypt's perspective, be fairly easily lived with.

One important qualification has to be made to this assessment. If, under the patronage of an established power, some of the 'Apiru underwent a measure of consolidation and control so as to add weight to their patron's cause, that could create a greater disturbance to the political balance than Egypt would find tolerable. Allegedly, some such process took place in the north, to the benefit of Amurru.

Amurru

In time, Amurru[7] emerged as a force in northern Canaan (possibly with the help of the 'Apiru). It might be thought that this would cause Egypt sharp concern. The charismatic 'Abdi-Ashirta had advanced from mere chieftainship toward the establishment of a substantial territorial domain, a process that involved the incorporation of nearby vassals. This suggests a certain deficiency in Egypt's ability to project its strength. Perhaps more telling from the Egyptian point of view was an associated consideration: that Amurru's aggrandizement might dilute its loyalty. Egypt's suzerainty, apparently, was under quite serious threat.

But on the face of it, the Amarna Letters show that Pharaoh does not seem to have been unduly disturbed. Rib-Hadda pours out a stream of warnings and supplications toward the Egyptian court, but the only answer was a complaint that Rib-Hadda was writing too much, presumably another way of telling him to shut up (EA 124). It has been suggested that Pharaoh was not in the habit of replying to vassals, so that no great significance should be attached to the absence of a response: it did not mean that the problem was not receiving due attention.[8] As against that, it is very clear from the correspondence that Rib-Hadda, who was presumably aware of the usual procedures, *was* expecting a reply. He may have had a reputation as a tiresome fellow who was best ignored. But the development that he repeatedly outlined was no figment of his imagination. So even if he, personally, was snubbed, surely some attention would be given to the events he was reporting. But there is no unambiguous evidence from the Letters of a campaign being mounted against Amurru. Could it be that the Egyptian court was really little concerned at Amurru's rise?

'Abdi-Ashirta, however, was himself brought to heel. He was taken to Egypt (EA 108, 117), and put to death (EA 101). Because this act was not followed by a direct attempt to undermine his state, it may be wondered whether Egypt's action was simply *pour encourager les autres*. An example had to be made of someone who had been notably unruly. The question posed above thus remains.

Possibly, Amurru's rise was not seen, at least for a while, as a significant threat and there may have been other, overriding considerations that led Egypt to accept the emergence of an entity that, in other circumstances, would have been seen as dangerously over-mighty. Such considerations are not hard to discern.

The Hittite Threat

At any time, a suzerain might not be too unhappy if one of its vassals at the far end of a sphere of influence was reasonably powerful. A frontier zone tends to fray at the edges, where it merges into adjacent territory. A strong vassal should help to stabilize the sphere of influence by discouraging raids into the area. Furthermore, such an area would normally be subject to an undesirable degree of skirmishing and indiscipline among the local vassals, who would know that it was inconveniently far for the suzerain to exercise the smack of firm government. The presence of a more powerful vassal might discourage this, for it would have its own interest in the maintenance of order and might even be encouraged by the suzerain to exert some authority. Of course, there could be danger here, in case the vassal in question began to take an inflated view of its position. But on balance, the emergence of such a power toward the extremity of a hegemon's reach might be reassuring. Moreover, it would be the least dangerous place, in a suzerain's eyes, for such an otherwise worrisome development to occur.

These general considerations are reinforced as a rival Great Power approaches the suzerain's sphere of influence. Such was Egypt's predicament as the Amarna period progresses. Hatti is on the march across and into the most northerly part of the area of Egyptian suzerainty. Naturally, Egypt looks for help from its Great Power ally, Mittani, which has an equal interest in repelling the Hittites. Reports speak of the cooperation and activity of Mittani, presumably in this cause (EA 56, 58; EA 100, n. 5). But Mittani is in decline and at about this time lapses into civil war. It cannot, therefore, be looked to for effective long-term assistance against the vibrant Hittites. In this perspective, the emergence of a relatively powerful domain in northern Canaan may have had positive attractions for Egypt and have helped to shore up the northern frontier. And if such forces as Mittani can deploy work in conjunction with Amurru, which is said to have received a visit from the Mittanian king (EA 95), so much the better.

Egypt's calculations may have run along some such lines. Crucial to the scenario is the continued allegiance of Amurru to the Egyptian throne. The danger is that Amurru might be tempted by the offer of an association with Hatti, which would certainly welcome Amurru's aid as a means of easing entry into northern Canaan. From Amurru's viewpoint, the likelihood of immediate gain might outweigh the hazard that in the longer term, it might be swallowed up by a suzerain close at hand.

In the event, Egypt's gamble, if that it was, went badly wrong. Egypt became uneasy about Aziru ('Abdi-Ashirta's son). He regularly declares his unswerving fealty (apparently in the light of suggestions to the contrary); offers help, if necessary, against Hatti (EA 157); and promises to rebuild Ṣumur (which had probably been destroyed in the course of Amurru's advance) (EA 159–61). But he shows a marked reluctance to accept what must have been pressing invitations to visit Egypt (EA 156, 162, 164, 166–67). He calls for the protection of an oath from the Egyptians (EA 164) and, succeeding where his father had failed, comes back from the subsequent visit alive (EA 169–70).

But all of this is of no avail to Egypt. Aziru's contacts with Hatti only deepen. Pharaoh rails against him, wanting to know why he communes with the ruler of Qadesh, who has already gone over to the other side (EA 162), and Aziru follows. There may have been an element of the short term about this decision, or Hatti may have made him an offer he could not refuse.

The Letters frequently speak of the vassals' readiness for the arrival of Pharaoh and his men. Such remarks could be no more than routine assurances of the vassals' cooperation and concern; they could refer to Egypt's annual tribute-gathering exercise; or they could indeed herald a campaign against the Hittites and those of Egypt's vassals who had joined them.[9] Aldred suggests that although a campaign was in fact mounted, it failed to change the situation in the north.[10] The balance of power was in flux.

Reflections

Once one achieves a modest familiarity with the principal characters and places in the Amarna Letters and imposes one's own order on the material, things fall very smoothly into place. Here were Great Powers behaving toward each other like Great Powers often do, aligning themselves in a multiple balance that represented such common maxims as "my enemy's enemy is my friend" and L. B. Namier's rule of "odds and evens" (that is, if powers are numbered in geographical sequence, the odd-numbered ones will tend to pair up against the evens). Here, too, were vassals, or clients, behaving as one would expect in the geographical and political context in which they found themselves. Here was a suzerain, a state with a well-defined sphere of influence, perhaps getting a little soft in its favorable geographical position and with a fading remembrance of an earlier lapse. And here was a Pharaoh, a powerful ruler, who was possibly getting carried away by a system of ideas. Plus ça change, plus c'est la même chose.

But two changes are evident. The first and obvious one is that formal suzerainty has gone out of fashion. Treaties of protection have been almost impossible to find for some decades. The second and associated development has to do with the use of force. It is part of the received wisdom in the study of international relations that since time immemorial, interrelating territorial units have used armed force to exert their will and expand their boundaries. In the second half of the twentieth century, however, this instrument (other than for self-defense) has become legally improper and politically unorthodox—which is not to say that it does not occur. But states now feel obliged to offer jesuitical justifications and to seek international legitimation for any such activity. And there is a marked reluctance to draw and redraw boundaries on the basis of influence.

However, it is arguable that these developments have only served thinly to obscure the scene, rather than alter its fundamentals. The essence of interstate relations remains the same and does not appear to have changed much since the Amarna period. A few centuries after the Letters were written, it was said that "there is no new thing under the sun" (Eccles. 1.9). So far as politics is concerned, the validity of the observation would not seem to have been eroded over the ensuing three thousand years.

CHAPTER TEN

The Egyptian-Canaanite Correspondence

NADAV NA'AMAN

Although the two sides to the correspondence are symmetrically presented in the title of this chapter, there is a marked difference in the number of their respective letters. Only six or seven Pharaonic letters sent to his vassals are known from the archive (EA 99, 162–63, 190[?], 367, 369–70) as against hundreds of letters sent by the vassals to Pharaoh and his officials. Moreover, there is a unified form to most of the Pharaonic letters (save for EA 162), as against a great variety among the vassal letters. Most of our information on Egyptian diplomacy in negotiating with its Asiatic province is gained from the vassal letters.

Details of the Egyptian messages are known from direct and indirect references in these letters. The many citations of written and verbal orders are due to the scribal practice of citing them briefly and then referring to them in detail. These references match the extant royal letters in word and content, indicating that they accurately reflect the nature of the Egyptian correspondence with its vassals.

When reading the Letters, it becomes clear that a considerable part of the relations between Egypt and Canaan was conducted by verbal orders and verbal negotiation. We may ask, when did the Egyptian court find it necessary to send written messages rather than verbal orders? Did the king send letters routinely, with no particular message, or did he send them only for a purpose, each letter carrying a specific message to the addressee? Also, how many letters did each vassal receive during a reign? Was the reception of a royal letter a frequent occurrence, or was it quite infrequent and an "event" for the recipient?

A new line of investigation into the vassal letters was outlined recently by Liverani.[1] He suggested what he calls a "procedure paradigm" in the historical interpretation of the Letters. Rather than written occasionally, whenever the situation demanded such action, there was a seasonal pattern for the correspondence: "The seasonal (or modular) patterning is based on the assumption that the administrative procedure into which the letters are set was basically a yearly procedure."[2] The key to the procedure was the preparation of goods in Canaan and their transfer to Egypt. The preparation of the tribute and specifically requested items would have taken place in the spring and their transfer in the late summer. Liverani calls letters preparing the collection tour "spring letters," and those closing the procedure "late-summer letters." He recognized that there existed other occasions for epistolary contacts than the standard collection tour, but in his opinion these were less frequent, and they, too, were assimilated to the standard tour in their epistolary language and procedure.

In the same volume in which Liverani published his thesis, I suggested an entirely different interpretation for a certain part of the assumed group of spring letters.[3] My analysis was based on chronological considerations and on the contents and literary expressions common to this group of letters. In my opinion, these letters refer to a specific event, the preparation of an Egyptian campaign to Asia in the late years of Akhenaten. It remains to be seen whether most of the Amarna Letters were written on a routine seasonal basis or whether they were drafted occasionally, whenever the rulers found it necessary to send a message to their lord.

The letters of Byblos pose a special problem. Their number far exceeds that of other cities, and most of them are long and detailed. We may ask, could the corpus of Byblian letters serve as a model for other Canaanite centers? Or does this corpus, with its narrative patterns and personal tone, reflect mainly the exceptional historical relations of Byblos with Egypt and the personality of its author, Rib-Hadda?

Another problem is the enormous difference in language, cultural background, and ideology between Egypt and Canaan. The divergence of the two sides of the correspondence raises the problem of communication. Did the Canaanite rulers fail to understand the intention of the Pharaonic letters and interpret them in a way that was markedly different from that of their author? Are there clear examples of misunderstanding of messages? Or did they understand the Egyptian messages quite well, and what looks like a misunderstanding is a deliberate representation of the situation? Also, how did the differences in ideology and perspective between Pharaoh and his vassals influence their perception of their mutual obligations? Were there considerable gaps in the interpretation of the obligations, and if there were, in which specific areas can they be located?

These problems, which are crucial for the interpretation of the vassal correspondence and the diplomatic measures taken by both sides, are systematically analyzed below.

Frequency of Royal Letters

Of the six or seven letters sent to vassals by Pharaoh, two order the preparation of supplies or troops before the arrival of Egyptian army (EA 367, 370); one orders the dispatch of a bride with her dowry (EA 99); and one deals with the acquisition of female cupbearers (EA 369). Two letters were written to Aziru, reflecting the Egyptian diplomatic pressure on the king of Amurru (EA 162–63). The seventh letter, sent either to Damascus or Qadesh (EA 190), is fragmentary but possibly deals with the preparations for a military campaign. Two royal letters sent to the rulers of Damascus and Shazaena and dated to the post–Amarna Age were discovered at the Egyptian center of Kumidi (Kamid el-Loz). They order the deportation of groups of ʿApiru from Canaan to Nubia.[4] Evidently, all royal letters carried a specific message to the addressee.

Pharaonic letters are often cited or alluded to by the vassals. The best known are the commands to be on guard or to guard oneself, to guard the place where the vassal is, and to obey the Egyptian commissioner.[5] Similar commands appear in all the pharaonic letters. But in addition to these elements, all the extant royal letters have a distinct message. We may ask, did the Egyptian court also send nonspecific letters that included nothing more than stereotyped phrases? The answer to this question is linked to another: on what occasions were royal letters sent to the vassals?

Since the Egyptian court expected answers to its letters, there is a good chance that we will be able to identify clear references to lost royal letters. It goes without saying that the investigation is marked by uncertainty, since it is founded mainly on inferences from something that is lost. But I believe that even though some of the inferences may be disputed, the overall picture that emerges is sufficiently unified to justify clear answers to the above questions.

Before starting the analysis, something must be said about the use of the verb *šapāru* in the Amarna Letters. The verb has two basic meanings: "to write" and "to send" (CAD Š/1 430–48). In the current translations of the Letters, the verb is usually rendered in the sense of "to write," except in passages where this interpretation is excluded by the context. This rendering gives the impression that the Egyptian court sent a large number of letters to its vassals. However, in many references in which the object of the verb is missing, the translation "to send (a message)" suits the context better than the common translation "to write (a letter)."[6]

We may further note that on many occasions, vassals sent several letters in response to a single royal letter. This is typical of the correspondence of Rib-Hadda but may easily be demonstrated in the dossiers of other Canaanite rulers (e.g., Abi-Milku, Ammunira, Aziru, Yidya, Milkilu, Shuwardata, Shubandu).

An analysis of the letters of Rib-Hadda indicates that no Pharaonic letter is alluded to in his correspondence with Amenhotep III. Evidently, Pharaoh did not reply to the stream of Byblian letters. But unlike his heir, Akhenaten, he showed no annoyance at the flood of letters. During Akhenaten's reign, Rib-Hadda received a few royal letters, each sent for a purpose. Many orders and instructions were received verbally through messengers.

The examination of many other letters from the coast of Lebanon and Palestine supports this conclusion. Royal letters arrived infrequently and, when dispatched, were always designed for a specific purpose. They were apparently sent only when the Egyptian court sought to emphasize the importance of a particular command. Routine messages were delivered verbally by Egyptian officials. Remarkably, the news of Amenhotep III's death and Akhenaten's accession were not delivered in writing. The main group of royal letters concerns the preparation for the arrival of the Egyptian archers. Only on that occasion were letters sent to all quarters of the Egyptian province in Asia, and direct answers arrived from southern Canaan (EA 65, 292, 324–25, 337), from northern Canaan (EA 55, 191, 193, 195, 201–6, 216–18, 227, and possibly 213), and from the coast of Lebanon (EA 141–42, 144, 147, 153, 362, and possibly 223 and 233). Other royal letters instructed the execution of certain military missions, the transfer of information, or the dispatch of special commodities to Egypt. Letters of admonition were addressed to rulers whose deeds endangered the stability of the Egyptian province in Asia (e.g., Lab'ayu and Aziru).

It is clear that most of the letters were written on the vassals' initiative. This conclusion may help explain the difference in the number of letters sent by individual vassals. No vassal received more than a few letters throughout his reign. Some rulers preferred to send only what was necessary, that is, responses to royal letters and sometimes also a reference to the visit of (important?) Egyptian officials. As a result, the number of their letters is minimal. Others took the opposite course and, for their own reasons, sent many letters to Pharaoh. Most remarkable is Rib-Hadda of Byblos. Other examples are the letters sent by Abi-Milku of Tyre and 'Abdi-Heba of Jerusalem, both educated in Egypt and enthroned by Pharaoh, thus having connections in the court and trying to make the most of them. It goes without saying that the number of letters does not necessarily reflect the political importance of Canaanite rulers. Some strong and influential rulers (i.e., those of Shechem, Hazor, and Damascus) sent only a few letters, whereas others, less important, sent quite a number of letters to Pharaoh.

Seasonal Procedure and the Vassal Correspondence

Are the payments of tribute and gifts to Egypt the key to the distribution of the vassal letters? To answer this question, I will first analyze the data concerning tribute and gifts in the vassal letters.

A remarkable feature in the correspondence of Rib-Hadda is the almost total absence of references to tribute and gifts. A payment of copper is probably mentioned in EA 69:25–30 and a request for copper and ingots(?) (*sinnu*) is discussed in EA 77:615.[7] It is rather Rib-Hadda who, again and again, asks for silver and provisions for subsistence, and for troops and horses to guard his city. It is hardly conceivable that he expected Egypt to send him all these for nothing. His words should be interpreted as a request for provisions in return for payment.

Ammunira of Beirut and Zimredda of Sidon do not mention either tribute or gift. At the request of Pharaoh, Abi-Milku of Tyre sent one hundred shekels of glass to Egypt. In another letter he reports sending tribute (five talents of copper and mallets) and a gift (a whip) (EA 151). The elders of Arwad, in contrast, ask the king to send them a gift as a sign of favor (EA 100). Somewhat exceptional is Aziru of Amurru. He undertakes to send everything requested by Pharaoh and his officials (EA 157:25–27; 158:17–19), and he prepares rich tribute to be sent to Egypt (EA 160:14–19, 41–44; 161:55–56). On his visit to Egypt, he brought a special gift to Pharaoh (EA 168:9–10) and received in exchange a royal gift, about which he complains that half of it was unlawfully taken by an Egyptian official (EA 161:41–46).

The place of tribute and gifts in Aziru's correspondence is easily explained. He started from a low position and sought Pharaoh's recognition. Later on he expanded, gained political and military strength, and occasionally operated against Egyptian interests. He tried to appease Pharaoh by sending him rich gifts, thereby emphasizing his loyalty. The same policy was followed by his father, 'Abdi-Ashirta (EA 60), and by Lab'ayu of Shechem (EA 253–54), both of whom expanded their territory and tried to appease Pharaoh by emphasizing that they were fulfilling all their obligations to Egypt. Aziru's policy of sending contributions did not go unnoticed by other rulers. Thus, Ili-rapih of Byblos wrote to Pharaoh as follows: "The king is to take no account of whatever Aziru sends him. The property that he sends are things that he coveted. It is property belonging to royal mayor(s) whom he has killed that he sends you" (EA 139:33–39).

Tribute and gifts are rarely mentioned in the letters of north Canaanite rulers. Ten prisoners of war were sent by an unknown ruler (EA 173). The ruler of Enishazi sent his daughter to the Pharaoh (EA 187), probably after receiving a letter similar to EA 99. Almost all the reports to prepare for the arrival of the archers refer to the planned Egyptian campaign to Canaan.

Finally, in a letter sent from Shamhuna, its ruler protests the imposition of a grain tax, claiming that it had not been imposed on his city since olden times (EA 224).

Tribute and gifts are more frequently mentioned in letters from southern Canaan. A series of letters report the preparation of unspecified commodities at the request of Pharaoh (EA 247, 267, 275–78). Four letters report the preparation of glass at the request of Pharaoh (EA 314, 323, 327, 331). The internal textual identity in each group is remarkable, and it seems that either a single scribe wrote them or that the Egyptian messenger dictated all these reports. Many other letters report the arrival of an Egyptian official, but preparations at his command are only sporadically mentioned (EA 302, 329).

Biridiya of Megiddo sent cattle and sheep, "what the king, my lord, requested" (EA 242). Tagi of Ginti-kirmil prepared a caravan (EA 264) and sent a gift (equipment for a chariot; EA 266) to Pharaoh. Milkilu sent various kinds of servants (EA 268) and complained about the extortion of the Egyptian commissioner, who had requested two thousand shekels of silver (EA 270). 'Abdi-Ashtarti sent women (EA 64). 'Abdi-Heba sent a caravan that was robbed (EA 287) and also gave the commissioner(s) various kinds of servants (EA 288). Shubandu sent girls and cattle (EA 301). Another ruler sent silver and servants (EA 309). And a southern ruler (possibly Shubandu) paid fourteen hundred shekels of silver as compensation for murdered Egyptian merchants (EA 313).

Summing up the discussion, it is clear that the payment of tribute does not play a major role in the Letters. It appears sporadically throughout the correspondence and is more frequent in the south Canaanite letters than from other parts of the Egyptian province. There are not enough data in the Amarna archive to build a picture of the contributions imposed by the Egyptians on their vassals.[8] Moreover, it seems that the routine payments of tribute were left out of the correspondence. What we have are reports of irregular payments, sent either after a special request from Pharaoh, after a certain delay in the delivery of the tribute, or in an effort to gain the favor of Pharaoh and his officials.

Redford suggested that the tax system imposed on the Canaanites was that of Egypt transported abroad.[9] Egyptian procedures were extended to Asia, and the Canaanite "mayors," like their Egyptian counterparts, were obliged to hand over their personal gifts (*inw*) every New Year's day, as well as to give a portion of the product of their labor. However, there is no evidence for this assumption in the Amarna Letters. The Canaanite rulers were neither part of the regular Egyptian system of tax collection, nor were they part of the Egyptian redistributive organization. Liverani is certainly correct when he suggests that there seems to be "an opposition between directly administered areas, whose revenues are regular in amount and time; and an external area with its own political authorities, from which goods come to Egypt more or less frequently . . . but cannot be planned ahead of time in amount, in time, or in their substance."[10] Indeed, the expression "year by year" does not appear in the Egyptian-Canaanite correspondence. I would question the assumption that the contributions to Egypt were paid on a yearly basis. True, the *inw*-contributions of Asia were presented in the parade of tribute offered by foreign emissaries on New Year's day, but the yearly display does not indicate the regularity of the payment of contributions. The criteria according to which the Egyptians imposed tribute in the different areas of Canaan remain unknown.

These conclusions contradict the assumption that the correspondence reflects a seasonal procedure of any kind. There is no evidence that the Letters refer to a yearly preparation of the tribute nor to any other periodical procedure. On the contrary, the correspondence is mainly concerned with the irregular and reflects the reaction of the vassals to either unexpected events in their immediate neighborhood or to verbal and written instructions from Pharaoh and his officials.

The Vassal Correspondence as "Business" Letters

The Akkadian title used to describe the local rulers of Canaan is *ḫazannu*, "mayor," which is the equivalent of Egyptian *ḥȝty-ʿ*, a mayor of an Egyptian town. It goes without saying that Egypt and Canaan were separate entities, and that the vassals were never regarded as Egyptian mayors in the full meaning of the term. The court administration treated them as Egyptian mayors in one important aspect: they held full responsibility for everything that happened in the town (or rather city-state) in their charge.

The self-image of the Canaanite rulers was quite different. They considered themselves to be kings (*šarru*) in their relations with their subjects and with their neighbors, and they sometimes applied the title unintentionally either to other city-state rulers or for themselves.[11] Even the kings of Babylonia (EA 8:25) and Mittani (EA 30:1) called them kings. However, the Egyptian conception of the Canaanite rulers was strictly maintained in all the formal contacts with Egypt and is reflected in the official aspects of the correspondence.

The most prominent obligation of the mayors was the defense of the city put in their charge by Pharaoh. There are innumerable variants of the reports of guarding the city and its territory. But the statements of guarding are only one aspect of the theme of defense. All the complaints of vassals about encroachments on their territories and their neighbors' expansion; about attacks by the 'Apiru and Sutu, and the general insecurity in the land; and statements about the expected arrival of Egyptian archers and garrisons — all these are aspects of the major theme of guarding. The vassals interpreted the obligation to defend their towns and territories in a very broad sense and developed it as a central theme around which they directed all their complaints concerning the state of insecurity in their territory and in neighboring areas.

Closely related to the theme of defense is another: the mayor as a loyal servant (*arad kitti*) of Pharaoh. Moran has convincingly demonstrated that the ideal of loyalty unifies the entire correspondence of Rib-Hadda.[12] Such self-presentation appears in many other letters, though not expressed in so many words and details, or in such dramatic tone, as in Rib-Hadda's letters. Even rulers who operated against the Egyptian interests in Canaan praised their own loyalty and condemned the treachery and faithlessness of their enemies. No ruler ever admits his disloyalty, no matter what he has actually done. To judge from their letters, all the rulers were loyal servants, devoted to their posts in their towns, whereas it was their enemies who conspired against Egypt and broke their oath to Pharaoh.

If guarding the city and territory was the major theme in the vassal letters, some other obligations, all derived from their status as mayors, are sporadically mentioned. These include the payment of contributions, the housing and feeding of Egyptian troops and officials, the dispatch of military units and ships to help the Egyptians in their campaigns northward, the safe passage of foreign caravans, the cultivation of the lands of the Egyptian garrison cities, and the guarding of certain installations therein. Most (if not all) of these obligations were performed on an irregular basis, and their execution is mentioned in the letters.

With this background in mind, it is possible to define the circumstances in which vassals may have written to Pharaoh. A letter from Pharaoh was answered immediately, and we may assume that the messenger who brought it carried back the reply. The execution of verbal orders may have also been reported. But unexpected events in their neighborhood were the most important motive for writing. The vassals believed that the theme of guarding was reciprocal and all inclusive, comprising all aspects of security and territorial integrity. They also knew that their rivals might send a contradictory account of the new event. They therefore dispatched their own version of the episode in an effort to justify themselves, to emphasize that they were the victims of aggression, and, if possible, to persuade Pharaoh to intervene in their favor (or at least to gain his neutrality). They learned from experience that attracting the attention of Pharaoh was not an easy task. They therefore aggrandized the episode and emphasized that what looked like a local event was a threat to the Egyptian control of the land. Some vassals repeated the same message in several consecutive letters, much like the repetition of a single message in the modern mass media.

We may conclude that local events were the main impetus for dispatching letters to Egypt. The vassal letters are mainly genuine "business" dispatches, written in an effort to deliver certain messages and, if possible, to gain the support (or, in other instances, the neutrality) of Pharaoh and his officials. This would explain why, unlike the international correspondence, they refer so often to political and military events.

Egyptian Obligations: Two Conflicting Viewpoints

As is well known, Egypt adhered to a monocentric ideology in which Pharaoh occupied the central position. Liverani has demonstrated that in accordance with its ideology, Egypt conceived its relations with its vassals to be one-sided, the latter being regarded as outsiders to the Egyptian system. The supply of nourishment was confined only to the Egyptian redistributive organization.[13] Indeed, all vassals acknowledged their status as outsiders; the only requests for provisions from Egypt appear in the letters of Rib-Hadda of Byblos. It is possible, of course, that in situations of severe famine and shortage of grain, some vassals would also appeal to Pharaoh for help. After all, at a later date, even the king of Hatti, by then an ally of Egypt, appealed to Pharaoh in such a situation. But these would have been ad hoc requests and did not reflect an effort to be integrated into the Egyptian distributive system. Egypt and Canaan were separate economic entities, and the vassals were never regarded as Egyptian mayors in the full meaning of the term.

Of the many differences in ideological and political outlook between Pharaoh and his vassals, the one that had the most important consequences for their relations was the disagreement on the guarding issue. As Liverani has shown, there was a large gap between the Egyptians' and the vassals' perception of the relationship.[14] The latter's interpretation of the theme of guarding as reciprocal and all inclusive was not agreeable to Pharaoh. This is clear from the correspondence of Rib-Hadda, in which the impatience of Akhenaten with the former's requests is vividly expressed.

Liverani suggested that the vassals misunderstood the Egyptian viewpoint due to linguistic differences: the divergent connotations of the Akkadian verb *naṣāru* ("to guard," "protect") and its equivalent in Egyptian (*sȝw*). "The bureaucratic pressure of Egyptian origin was completely misunderstood as we can see in the answers."[15]

The evidence presented in support of this argument is taken entirely from the correspondence of Rib-Hadda. But Rib-Hadda's rhetoric is exceptional and does not properly represent the corpus of vassal letters. The letters of other mayors answer the command to guard in clear terms and occasionally elaborate on it, for the reasons explained above. As far as I can see, there is no evidence to support the assumption that by the verb *naṣāru*, the Egyptian bureaucracy meant anything other than "to guard." Moreover, the order to guard was part of a formula that appears again and again in pharaonic letters and in official verbal instructions. It is inconceivable that this formal request, which carried no operative command, remained unclear to any vassal in Canaan.

The administrative measures taken by Egypt to rule Canaan were already about a century old in the Amarna period. After such long experience, the Canaanites must have become well acquainted with the Egyptian system of government and its requests. Egyptian orders were delivered mainly verbally, by officials, and even royal letters were brought by experienced messengers, who were able to elaborate on obscure points. Given this situation, I very much doubt the assumption that due to cultural and ideological gaps, the vassals frequently misunderstood the Egyptian orders. (But occasional slips are self-evident.) What looks like a misunderstanding is no more than deliberate manipulation by the vassals, who tried to get the maximum results from their correspondence with Egypt while refusing to adopt the Egyptian monocentric view of the relationship.

Finally, it is evident that Pharaoh's silence about local matters does not always means "no." There is evidence for Egyptian intervention in local affairs (e.g., EA 92:30–37; 126:4–6; 155:35–45; 245; 280:36–40), and this may be the result of either verbal instructions of the royal court in Egypt (messages exchanged between the royal court and the Egyptian commissioners in

Canaan did not come down to us), or of the initiative of local commissioners in Canaan. How indifferent was the Egyptian court to vassals' complaints cannot accurately be established.

Egyptian Officials as Translators of the Royal Commands

The Egyptian commissioners (*rābiṣu*) played a central role in the negotiations with the local rulers. Royal letters being infrequent, they were responsible for the transmission of orders and their implementation. To carry out their mission, they traveled from the Egyptian garrison cities to the seats of the vassals, conveying messages or collecting contributions. Other messengers arrived from Egypt and, after transmitting their messages, returned home. These agents translated the pharaonic policy and commands into action, and their role as intermediaries gave them much power and influence.

This is not the place to discuss the role of the commissioners in the chain of events, nor to analyze the opposing stands which they adopted in local conflicts. What matters are the reports of the vassals on the functioning of those agents and how the vassals reacted to situations in which they did not see eye to eye with the Egyptian authorities.

On many occasions, vassals reported to Pharaoh about particular instructions they had received from officials. Such reports must have had a double message: on the one hand, to confirm that they obeyed the transmitted orders and thereby manifested their loyalty and, on the other hand, to check on the commissioner. Accusations against certain officials, or efforts to persuade Pharaoh to reverse their decisions, appear quite frequently in the correspondence. The best-known examples are the many accusations raised by Rib-Hadda against Egyptian officials who operated in his area. Since Rib-Hadda's letters are exceptional and have been extensively discussed, I will restrict my analysis to letters sent by other mayors.

'Abdi-Heba of Jerusalem was in conflict with the Egyptian authorities in southern Canaan (Addaya, Puwuru, Yanhamu), and his whole correspondence is overshadowed by these muddy relations. The bone of contention was the Egyptian garrison stationed in his town. Following the conflict, the garrison was transferred to Gaza and later sent back to Egypt (EA 285; 286: 25–33; 287:32–52, 71–75; 289:30–36), and 'Abdi-Heba was denounced before Pharaoh (286:16–21). He fought back by denouncing the Egyptian commissioners (notably in the words in EA 286:17–19, "I say to the commissioner of the king, my lord: 'Why do you love the 'Apiru but hate the mayors?' ") and recounted in detail his version of the garrison episode. He further emphasized that he had been elevated to the throne of Jerusalem by the intervention of Pharaoh, that he bore Egyptian titles, and that he was a loyal servant of Pharaoh.[16] Thanks to his background, he had former connections in the Egyptian court. Four of his letters have postscripts addressed to the royal scribe, asking him to support his case before Pharaoh. Finally, he strove to appear before his lord in order to bypass the barrier of the Egyptian authorities in Canaan (EA 286:39–47; 288:30–32).

The complaints of Abi-Milku of Tyre are associated with the coastal town of Usu, once in the possession of Tyre and later captured by Zimredda of Sidon (EA 149:47–53). The conquest severed the island of Tyre from the continent, depriving it of its sources of water, grain, and wood. Abi-Milku wrote again and again to Pharaoh, asking him to restore his captured town. He emphasized the severe situation of his city, deliberately using words and images derived from the Egyptian vocabulary (EA 147:65–66; 148:11–13; 150:14–21; 151:37–40; 155). He further tried to denounce his enemy, Zimredda, accusing him of conspiring against the king's land and against the city of Tyre (EA 147:66–69; 148:38–45; 149:57–70; 151:64–67; 152:7–8; 154:11–23). When at last Abi-Milku appeared before Pharaoh, the latter ordered the restoration of the town to Tyre. However, his order was not carried out by the commissioner, and Abi-Milku reported the nonperformance of the command to his lord (EA 155:7–13, 31–46).

Another set of complaints came from vassals who operated against Egyptian interests in Canaan. In an effort to vindicate themselves, they blamed certain commissioners of slandering them before Pharaoh. The accused rulers are 'Abdi-Ashirta (EA 62:42–49), Aziru (EA 158:20–31; 161:4–10, 35–46; 171), and Lab'ayu (EA 252:13–16; 254:10–19). Each of the three had a commissioner who supported him and who was cited as a witness to his innocence. Thus, 'Abdi-Ashirta was supported by Pahamnata (EA 60; 135:34–36; 132:41), and Lab'ayu by an unnamed $r\bar{a}bisu$ (EA 253:32–35; 254:10–15). Aziru was supported by Haip, who was accused of treacherous deeds by the mayors of Byblos and Tyre (EA 131:47–48; 132:42–43; 149:37–40).

Several letters reflect disputes between vassals and commissioners and the efforts of the former to persuade Pharaoh that they were justified. The points of disagreement vary: a failure to execute a commissioner's order (EA 207) or the arbitrary decisions or unlawful deeds of particular commissioners (EA 234, 239, 270, 292, 294). Some of these accusations suggest corruption on the part of Egyptian officials (EA 161:41–46; 270; 292:41–52; 294:16–26). But it is difficult to verify accusations, and in some situations we can do no more than present the conflicting claims of the two rivals.

The many charges directed against the Egyptian officials reflect above all the complexity of the situation in Canaan, where so many elements were involved in the chain of events. The commissioners were caught in the middle of many local and external powers, and there was no likelihood that their decisions would be accepted by all parties to the conflicts. The contradictory positions of officials on various issues, and the denunciations or approval of their decisions voiced by rival vassals, were the direct result of this situation. Corruption and incompetence, which are inseparable from any bureaucracy, were secondary to the basic problems that emanated from the structure and political culture of Canaan at the time.

Conclusions

The complex nature of the Egypto-Canaanite relations sometimes worked in favor of those who were able to manipulate it and make the most of their remoteness from the center of government. It enabled some vassals to expand their territories and strengthen their power. Pharaoh was slow to react, but once he made up his mind and decided to operate, he was able to carry out his decision with no real opposition. Following such a decision, ʿAbdi-Ashirta was caught and killed, and Ṣumur restored to Egyptian hands. At roughly the same time, Labʾayu was caught and killed on his way to Egypt. When Egypt was less determined, however, as in the early years of Akhenaten, some rulers were able to gain power and even dared to contact a rival empire (i.e., Hatti). The number of internal conflicts increased at that time, in particular in southern Canaan. Again, once Pharaoh decided to operate and start organizing a campaign to Asia, internal conflicts abruptly ended. Only the northernmost vassals were then able to carry out their former plans, though not openly, since they could rely on the power of another empire (Hatti). Real power was in the hands of Egypt, and its policy decided the internal affairs in Canaan.

Egypt concentrated on major issues and the exploitation of its province, ignoring minor episodes that occurred in many parts of Canaan. The lack of response to so many vassal letters exactly reflect the order of priorities at the Egyptian court. The perspectives of the ruler of the empire were entirely different from those of his vassals, and differences of political perspective, combined with a unique ideology and distinctive cultural tradition, produced conceptual gaps between the two sides of the correspondence.

Royal letters played a secondary role in the current administration of Canaan. They were sent infrequently, when it was deemed necessary to emphasize the importance of a message. Verbal orders by officials played a central role in the administration of the province, but the majority of these remain unknown, other than orders to which vassals referred in their letters.

The Egyptian officials operated at the juncture of two different cultural and administrative systems. The center of government was in Egypt, and they functioned as its ears and eyes and carried out its orders. The province of Canaan was divided among many entities, each with its own interests and policy. Each city-state had its social structure, economic resources, and cultural background. The set of prohibitions incumbent upon the vassals was oral and was subject to different interpretations and political manipulations. The vassals were able to bypass certain officials, either by direct communication with Pharaoh or through the support of other officials. In such a multicentered system, with so many players and no strict rules of the game, it is no wonder that conflicting voices were always heard and that there was no consensus about the officials and their functioning.

Different officials sometimes carried out their missions in opposite directions. The job of these officials must have been quite difficult, and the Letters clearly illustrate the many problems that confronted the Egyptian authorities in Canaan.

Vassals had a direct line of communication to Pharaoh, but this line was quite ineffective in view of Pharaoh's silence. Ostensibly, they could appear before him and submit their claims in person. However, there are no indications that the direct approach was effective. Also, a long absence from home might have been dangerous, as is evident from EA 263, in which a vassal complains that he was robbed of everything when he appeared before Pharaoh. The complaints of many rulers that they were unable to leave their towns to appear before Pharaoh, on account of external or internal threats, are quite understandable. Appearance before Pharaoh and the reception of gifts might bring prestige in external and internal relations, but diplomatically, it was quite ineffective.

What effective channels were open to the vassals? No single channel could guarantee success, and vassals operated by combining all channels but probably with little illusion. The dispatch of tributes and gifts to Pharaoh and his officials might occasionally have been effective, but there are no concrete data to evaluate the effect on decisions. Moreover, this channel was open to every ruler, and the gift of one could be neutralized by that of his adversary. The situation invited all kinds of manipulation. Reading the Letters makes it clear that some rulers found their way despite the many obstacles, whereas others lost their way and paid the full price for their failure.

PART IV

International Transactions

CHAPTER ELEVEN

The Interdependence of the Great Powers

CARLO ZACCAGNINI

The intense network of interactions between great Near Eastern powers during the Late Bronze Age is attested by the Amarna and Boghazköi epistolary
archives, the latter covering the entire thirteenth century.[1] In both cases, the
overall scenarios are closely similar regarding geopolitical horizons, insti-
tutionalized procedures of interstate relationships, and standardized instruments of formal interaction and communication. The core of the interrelated
and often conflicting contacts concerns the so-called Great Powers' Club,
that is, Egypt, Mittani, Assyria, Babylonia, Hatti, and Alashiya (= Cyprus).
In what follows, I will concentrate on the Amarna documents and make use
of the pertinent or related Boghazköi material only as comparative or related
evidence.

It has long been noted that a basic feature of the Near Eastern scenery
ca. 1600–1200 B.C.E. is a wide-ranging web of political, cultural, commercial and military interactions, encompassing the entire Fertile Crescent but
also involving peripheral areas such as central and western Anatolia and the
Levant. These interactions are attested, in different and at times contrasting ways, both by archaeological findings and written sources. In contrast to
earlier periods, in which different and separate areas of interactions are attested, or to later periods that are marked by the presence of all-embracing
state formations (see, e.g., the Neo-Assyrian or Achaemenid empires), the
Late Bronze Age is characterized by the presence of many "actors," all of
whom know almost everything about each other and, to a great extent, are
fully engaged in a complex and intricate political game. To judge in a somewhat telescoped historical perspective, one gets the clear impression that
there are no hegemonic powers acting on the Near Eastern stage (Egypt's
role is briefly discussed below); rather, the fluctuating fortunes of the various

state formations were always part of a wider and internally changeable set of international dynamics. Thus, the concept of interdependence seems most appropriate for a general understanding of the international relations of this period and for a detailed analysis of the behavioral patterns and ideological implications that gave shape to the structure and dynamics of those relations.

Independence and Interdependence

The statement of Burnaburiash II, king of Babylonia, is lapidary: "And, as I am told, in my brother's country everything is available and my brother needs absolutely nothing: also in my country everything is available and I myself need absolutely nothing" (EA 7:33–36).[2] "(However) [the Babylonian king continues] we have received good relations of long standing from (earlier) kings: to send 'greetings' (*šulmu*) to each other. These same relations should be lasting between us" (EA 7:37–39).[3]

For an adequate understanding of Amarna international relationships, emphasis must be laid on the relevance and implications of this short passage. The basic principles and the rhetorical elaboration of the arguments presented by Burnaburiash are paradigmatic. In the first section of the letter, the king of Babylonia complains that Pharaoh did not show immediate concern for him: he failed to send a messenger to inquire about his health and forward his "greetings" (*šulmu*) (cf. lines 21, 23, 30). Having accepted the Egyptian explanation that the only reason for such a delay was the great distance between the two countries—a distance that Burnaburiash claimed not to know[4]—the bitter protests at the lack of timely "greetings" are withdrawn (lines 8–32). Here follows, somewhat abruptly, the statement concerning Egyptian and Babylonian self-sufficiency in subsistence and luxury goods; however, this peremptory statement is joined to the reminder of inherited good relations and the habit of exchanging "greetings" (again, *šulmu*). The semantic range and ambiguity of the term *šulmu*, which is obvious in this passage but can also be observed in other Amarna letters, allows us to follow the rhetorical development of Burnaburiash's message.

The *šulmu*s that are mentioned or evoked in lines 33–48 (but lines 42–48 are badly broken) certainly denote or allude to material tokens of "greetings," that is, "(greeting-)gifts."[5] My proposal finds convincing support in the following two sections of the letter. In the former (lines 53–62), the king of Babylonia responds to Pharaoh's arguments for not having sent his "greetings" (namely, the long distance between Egypt and Babylonia) and announces a small shipment of "(greeting-)gifts" (*šulmānu*), "since I have been told that the journey is difficult, water cut off and the weather hot." He then adds that as soon as the weather improves, he will send many beautiful (greeting-)gifts to Egypt, whatever Pharaoh may request. In the following section (lines 63–72) Burnaburiash asks for "much fine gold" and complains about an earlier shipment of the precious metal, the quality of which turned out to be totally unsatisfactory.[6]

I have dwelt at some length on the structural organization, rhetorical devices, and last but not least, linguistic subtleties of EA 7 because this letter represents a paramount example of the multinuanced and far-reaching concept of interdependence within the Amarna setting. The starting point is a proud statement of principle ("you need nothing and I need nothing"), but the conclusions are quite concrete ("send me much fine gold" ["and do not try to cheat me as you did the time before"]).

Interaction

Between these two extremes, there is ample space for developing an intense network of interactions: one of its most distinctive structural features is that all members of the so-called Great Powers' Club are more or less distant partners of the king of Egypt, in a strictly geographical sense. More precisely, there is no direct contact (i.e., a border) between any of the Asiatic countries and the land of Egypt: the Syro-Palestinian buffer states separate and affect the nature of relations between the (Syro)Anatolian state formations (of Mittani and, later, Hatti) and Egypt. In brief, Babylonia and Mittani (also Assyria) often experience problems with acts of hostility, robberies, and blockades perpetrated by Egyptian vassal states but never have to face a direct military challenge from Egypt.[7]

An entirely different pattern is displayed in inter-Asiatic relations, as far as we can judge from the very few illuminating bits of information recorded in the Amarna correspondence. Conflicts between bordering countries, such as Mittani and Hatti (EA 17) or Assyria and Babylonia (EA 9:31–35) directly concern the parties involved but hardly affect their respective relations with faraway Egypt. Rather, they are instrumental in the effort to promote privileged partnerships at the expense of other competitive relationships.

In this connection, the post-Amarna pattern, especially as concerns Egyptian-Hittite relations, entirely confirms the pattern of Near Eastern interactions outlined above. When the two countries came face to face on Syrian territory, eventually to fight at Qadesh, the only way to restore friendly relations was to draft a treaty of peace—the only one ever signed by Egypt (in spite of some unclear and doubtful allusions to previous formal agreements between Egypt and Hatti).[8] Only after this could an entente cordiale be resumed, with exchanges of greetings and gifts, marriage(s), etc., in accordance with the well-established diplomatic practices of the Amarna Age.

The Boghazköi archives, which are our main documentary source for international relations during the Ramesside period, also attest to Hittite-Assyrian and Hittite-Babylonian interactions. It is certainly no surprise that the progressive growth of Assyria was perceived as an ongoing serious menace to Hatti: the exchange of letters between the two courts bears unquestionable witness to this state of affairs.[9] Relations with more distant Babylonia are a matter of lesser concern and conform to the repertoire of contemporary diplomatic correspondence.[10] Interestingly enough, in the letter KBo I 10 + KUB III 72, sent from Hattusili III to Kadashman-Enlil II, one explicit reference and one allusion to Assyria are made, and in both cases, strong anti-Assyrian feelings come to the fore.[11] Hattusili urges the king of Babylonia to react against an alleged Assyrian blockade that would prevent Babylonian envoys from reaching Hittite land. He further suggests making a *razzia* into enemy territory — most probably, even if not explicitly mentioned, Assyria — slaying as many people as he could, then reporting back the good news to the Hittite sovereign.

Love and Gifts among Brothers

Let me enlarge upon the evidence of EA 7. In the international relations of the Amarna period and, more generally, of the Late Bronze Age, positive interactions among foreign partners are best expressed through the metaphor of the family group, whose members are reciprocally bound by blood, moral, social, and economic ties.[12] Of course, some adaptation is called for: in the absence of a paterfamilias, interactions between kings of equal rank are patterned according to brother-to-brother relationships, whereas interactions between subjects of different rank (e.g., a Great King vs. a small king) follow a lord-to-servant schema, at both the formulary and procedural levels. Father-to-son relationships are reserved for less politically defined interactions, in which official position, prestige, authority, and age combine to create an objective disparity between partners.[13]

According to the logic of a closed family group, correct and functional interactions among brothers (that is, the Great Kings) should express "friendship" (*atterūtu, râmuttu* [lit.: love]), "(good) friendship" (*ṭābūtu*), "good relationships" (*amātu banītu*), "concord" (*salīmu*), etc.[14] On a practical level, brotherhood, friendship, love, and so on, become evident only if supported by a constant and adequate flow of material exchanges, that is, "(greeting-)gifts" (*šulmānu*, less frequently *qīštu*), at times labeled or hinted at as "greetings" (*šulmu*).

One of the most explicit formulations of this vital connection between good diplomatic entente and the dispatch of luxury goods can be found in another letter of Burnaburiash: the king of Babylonia wishes to receive much gold from Egypt and adds, "May the neighboring kings hear the following statements: 'There is [much] gold. [Among] kings there are brotherhood, friendship, peace and [good] relations [if/since he (i.e. the king of Babylonia)] is well provided (lit.: heavy) with (precious) stones, well provided with silver, well provided with [gold]" (EA 11: Rev. 21–23).[15] Similarly, Tushratta, king of Mittani: "May my brother send me much gold that has not been worked. . . . May Teshup and Amon grant that my brother show his love for me, that my brother greatly glorify me before my country and before my foreign guests" (EA 20:71–74). In general, the functional link between friendship, love, etc., and dispatches of gifts is a true leitmotif of the Amarna correspondence; see, for example, "From the time my ancestors and your ancestors declared a mutual friendship, they sent beautiful gifts to each other and did not refuse each other any request for beautiful things" (EA 9:7–10 [letter of Burnaburiash]). For a different formulation, albeit expressing the very same concept, see this passage of a letter from Tushratta: "Mane, my brother's messenger, [came and] I heard the greeting (or well-being?) (*šulmānu*) of [my brother] and I rejoiced greatly. I saw the goods (*unūtu*) that my brother sent and I rejoiced greatly" (EA 27:7–8).[16] It is unnecessary to quote in extenso the many other variations on this theme.

Commercial Interests and Interconnections

Having ascertained that economic exchanges were almost entirely embedded in an overall standardized pattern of high-level diplomatic interactions, whose customary metaphor was that of brotherhood, love, and friendship, we can further inquire about the material assumptions, dynamics, and consequences of these exchanges. Regardless of Burnaburiash's statement that both Egypt and Babylonia were totally self-sufficient (EA 7:33–36; cf. above), it is well known that throughout the Late Bronze Age, Egypt was the exclusive source of gold for the entire Near East.[17] Thus it is no surprise that the most recurrent topic dealt with in the Amarna international correspondence is the shipment of Egyptian gold abroad. Among other merchandise, Egypt was also the exclusive or main supplier of ivory, ebony, and alabaster. But it depended entirely on foreign countries for its supplies of silver, lapis lazuli, other semi-precious stones, and copper. Thoroughbred horses were mainly sought in Babylonia, as the later Boghazköi correspondence shows. Already in the Amarna period and even more in the course of the thirteenth century, iron (and possibly steel) artifacts were exclusively produced in the south-western Anatolian region, under Mittanian and, later on, Hittite suzerainty.

Thus, simply from the viewpoint of the procurement of the most prized luxury items of trade (while the role of Cyprus as copper supplier should not be overlooked), a dense network of reciprocal ties was firmly established. However, this synthetic picture runs the risk of oversimplifying and requires qualification.

1. In the Alashiya correspondence, the insistent requests for silver forwarded to Pharaoh do not contradict the well-known fact that Egypt was totally lacking in sources of this metal: these requests should be judged in the light of the overall mercantile tone of the letters.[18] "Silver" simply means "price" or "(equivalent) value" of any item traded, and this affects the ceremonial level of the exchanges and thus the long- or short-term balance of trade rather than its economic content.[19]

2. Within the category of luxury goods that were transferred from one court to another, special mention should be made of expert personnel, first of all physicians (asû) and specialists in diagnosis and exorcism (ašipu). The Amarna correspondence attests only to a request for a physician from the king of Ugarit (EA 49: 22–25) and for an expert in vulture augury from the king of Cyprus (EA 35: 26).

More compelling is the evidence of the Boghazköi Letters, which fully confirm the renowned prestige of Egyptian physicians, followed by Babylonian physicians and exorcists.[20] However, I call attention to Tushratta's letter EA 23, in which he announces the dispatch of a statue of Shaushka (= the Hurrian equivalent of the Akkadian Ishtar) of Nineveh, probably to heal the old and suffering Amenhotep III.[21] Elsewhere, I have pointed out that one of the premises behind allowing qualified experts to travel to foreign courts was that they would be sent home as soon as their professional tasks were completed.[22] In fact, this prerequisite was very seldom satisfied.

3. Another paramount category of luxury goods—indeed, the most prestigious of all—was foreign princesses (daughters or sisters of Great Kings) for whom international marriages were concluded. Although I do not address the subject in this chapter, it does represent a true cornerstone of Amarna (and post-Amarna) international relationships.

Dynamics of Ceremonial Bargaining

The diplomatic formalities that governed the exchange of goods among the Great Powers of the Amarna Age show distinctive peculiarities that have been dealt with elsewhere.[23] Therefore, I will limit myself to pinpointing some of the most evident features that characterize the dynamics of Amarna gift-giving, most of which find parallels in the Old Babylonian evidence pertaining to international and domestic exchanges.[24]

1. There is the well-attested practice of sending (modest quantities of) luxury goods from countries that notoriously had no direct supply of the commodity to countries that were themselves current exporters thereof. Elephant tusks sent from Cyprus (imported from Syria?), gold and ebony sent from Babylonia and Mittani to Egypt, and silver and even lapis lazuli sent from Egypt to Babylonia, should not be judged as "irrational" aspects of Amarna commerce.[25] Rather, they were a means to demonstrate that some of the most prized items of foreign import were already available at home and could even be sent as provocative gifts to a primary exporting country.[26]

2. A recurrent technique used to overcome or minimize the embarrassment of making or repeating requests is to allege specific circumstances that required the goods in question to be available at short notice and for a limited time only: this technique is a stylized formula in almost every Asiatic request for Egyptian gold. In a one-to-one relationship and in the wider international setting, where everyone knows everything about everyone else, it would have been morally inappropriate and demeaning to give the impression of mere acquisitiveness.[27]

3. Complementary to this is the recurrent statement that what was requested from the other party should be of little concern to him, since the desired goods were abundant in his country. In this case, too, Egyptian gold is the most recurrent trade item that is referred to in the letters sent from Asia: the standard metaphor is that in Egypt "gold is as plentiful as dirt," further enlarged in EA 16:15–16: "One simply gathers it up. Why does it stick to your eyes?"[28]

4. In counterpoint to these motives, we have many instances of temporary refusal or delay in satisfying the partner's requests. Due to the high level of these international exchanges, the protocol of which diverges from that of bare commercial interactions, recurrent discontent at the unsatisfactory proceedings and (outcome of) transactions is expressed in terms of astonishment, sorrow, moral reproach, and the like.

In this context, I call attention to two well attested techniques used as means of pressure: the detention of foreign messengers, awaiting favorable moves from one's counterpart; and the declaration of a temporary inability to fulfil the other's requests. In either case, more or less plausible explanations are proffered in order to reaffirm a noncommercial, nonutilitarian gloss on the overall relationship.[29]

5. "Never look a gift horse in the mouth." But horses and all other gift items were always meticulously inspected and evaluated, by both the sender and the recipient. I have investigated elsewhere the various techniques used for describing the goods that were dispatched and the reactions — in most cases negative — of the recipients.[30] Suffice it to say that the general attitude of the donors is to emphasize the quality and quantity of the gift items that were dispatched abroad. Recipients frequently disagree.

Considering the Egyptocentric nature of the Amarna archives, and given that gold was the main item of export, it is no surprise that it is an almost compulsive subject of requests, protests, and quarrels.[31]

6. As I have mentioned before, a regular chain of exchanges provided the basis for and reflected positive international relationships. A constant rhythm of comings and goings of messengers and their caravans not only reassured the parties about their friendship but also implied the dispatch and arrival of material goods. Despite the various distances between Amarna and the other Near Eastern capital cities, it seems reasonable to infer that a one-year turnaround was considered, in principle, appropriate for regular contacts. In this regard, see a passage in a letter from Alashia: "And year by year let my messenger go [into your presence] and, on your part, year by year let your messenger come from [your country ?] into my presence" (EA 33:27–32).[32]

Differences apart, it is tempting to compare an ideal yearly rhythm of interaction between the Great Powers of the Amarna Age with the contemporary (and later) yearly rhythm of compulsory material services, primarily the delivery of goods, imposed on the Syro-Palestinian princelings both by the king of Hatti and Pharaoh, in their respective spheres of Asiatic suzerainty.[33] Nevertheless, the Amarna Letters furnish consistent evidence of frequent deviation from the convention of maintaining regular and possibly yearly contacts. Kadashman-Enlil I, Burnaburiash's predecessor, strongly censures Pharaoh's behavior:

> Previously, my father would send a messenger to you and you would not detain him for long: you would immediately send him off and you would also send here to my father a beautiful gift. But now when I sent a messenger to you, you have detained him for six years and for (these) six years you have sent as my gift (only) 30 minas of gold that was worked with silver (?). (EA 3:9–15)[34]

Leaving aside some dramatic requests for immediate shipments of gold, the regular exchange of caravans transporting consistent amounts of precious items was a fundamental requirement for positive, profitable interaction.[35] A bitter remark of Burnaburiash closely resembles that of his father, Kadashman-Enlil (EA 3:9–15):

> From the time of Karaindash, since the messengers of your ancestors came regularly to my ancestors, up to the present, they [i.e., the ancestors] have been friends. Now, although both you and I are friends, three times have your messengers come here but you did not send me one single beautiful gift and therefore I did not send you one single beautiful gift. (EA 10:8–15)

Many other examples could be adduced to show the Great Kings' pervasive concern for keeping in close touch and, what is more, for being reassured about constant and generous supplies of valuable staples. I will simply recall the brief and pointed message sent by Assur-uballit, king of Assyria, on the occasion of his bold entry into the Great Powers' Club:

> I send my messenger to you to visit you and to visit your country. Up to now, my predecessors have not written: today I write to you. I send you a beautiful chariot, two horses and one date-stone of genuine lapis lazuli as your gift. Do not delay the messenger whom I sent to you for a visit. He should see what is your mood and what is the mood of your country and then leave for here. (EA 15:7–22)

Dynastic Rank and International Prestige: Pride and Prejudice

The existence of an exclusive circle of Late Bronze Age monarchs is clearly attested by the Amarna (and Boghazköi) epistolary evidence. The ideal, if somewhat utopian, model of interstate relations foresees exclusive, or at least privileged, bilateral relationships being maintained without interference from third parties. Such a rigid scheme, which is best formulated in many Late Bronze Age Syro-Anatolian vassal treaties, by no means fits the complex and varied Amarna network of Egypto-Asiatic diplomatic relations. Of course, Pharaoh's foreign partners are well aware of and have to face this state of affairs; however, at times they react in protest. Interestingly enough, the arguments that support these complaints always concern business and profit. The most explicit statement is that of the king of Alashiya: "You [i.e., Pharaoh] have not been put (by me) on the same level with the king of Hatti or the King of Babylonia: as for me, whatever gift he [i.e., Pharaoh] sent me, I have returned back to you double" (EA 35:49–53).[36]

Comparing past and present transactions between Egypt and other foreign partners prompts Assur-uballit's drastic statement about the present unsatisfactory balance of Assyrian-Egyptian exchanges:

> When Ashur-nadin-ahhe, my ancestor [lit.: father], wrote to Egypt, they sent him 20 talents of gold. When the king of Hanigalbat wrote to your father in Egypt, he sent 20 talents of gold to him. [Now] I am [the equal] of the king of Hanigalbat, but you have sent me [(only) x talents/minas (?) of] gold, and it is not enough for the pay of my messengers on the journey to and back. (EA 16:19–31)

This very interesting passage deserves some comment. The assertion of earlier contacts between Assyria and Egypt at the time of Ashur-nadin-ahhe[37] is not supported by any other textual evidence and, in addition, is patently contradicted by Assur-uballit's earlier letter to Pharaoh quoted above (EA 15:9–11).[38]

Concerning the mention of the two extraordinary deliveries of twenty talents of gold, it is worth pointing out the cleverly nuanced difference between the two statements, a difference that possibly is not at all fortuitous. In the former case (lines 19–21), Ashur-nadin-ahhe "wrote to Egypt" and "they sent" twenty talents of gold; in the latter case (lines 22–25), the king of Hanigalbat "wrote to your father [i.e., Amenhotep III] in Egypt" and "he sent" twenty talents of gold. All in all, one gets the strong impression that the allusion to an enormous shipment of Egyptian gold to Assyria during the reign of one of Assur-uballit's predecessors is nothing but a self-serving fairy tale. The latter reference to twenty talents of gold allegedly sent to the king of Hanigalbat requires a different explanation. As correctly pointed out by Moran, EA 16, which is somewhat later than EA 15, refers to an advanced stage of Assyrian-Egyptian relationships, as is plainly reflected by the Babylonian reaction in EA 9:31–35.[39] The twenty talents sent to Mittani could well be an echo of the twenty talents (= 1,200 minas) of gold objects sent by Akhenaten to Burnaburiash as bridal gifts for his marriage with a Babylonian princess (see the inventory EA 14:II 34).[40] No corresponding inventories related to Egyptian marriages with Mittanian princesses are preserved. Therefore, one can only hypothesize that twenty talents was the standard amount of gold delivered by Pharaoh on the occasion of his marriages with foreign princesses.[41]

Assyria's appearance on the scene did not go unobserved; Babylonia strongly reacts to Pharaoh: "Now, it was not I who sent the Assyrians, my own subjects, to you. Why have they come on their own authority to your country? If you love me, they should not make any business whatsoever. Drive them away (to me) empty handed!" (EA 9:31–35).[42]

Jealousies and rivalries among foreign Great Kings characterize the complex and evolving network of Asiatic relationships with Egypt. To a certain extent, this state of affairs parallels inner conflicts that so often mark the Amarna correspondence of the Syro-Palestinian princelings subject to Egyptian suzerainty. In both cases, there is no trace of Pharaoh's reaction to denunciations and pleas of rival kings, be they great or small. However, there is one instance of Egypt taking a stand in a manner that is fully in line with comparable reactions of the Asiatic kings. Commenting on the unfair behavior of the Babylonian messengers, Amenhotep III states: "I have quarreled because of your messengers since they report to you saying: 'Nothing is given to us who go to Egypt'. Those who come to me: does one of the two (messengers) go (away) [without] taking silver, gold, oil, cloaks, every sort of finery, [more than i]n any other country?" (EA 1:66–71).[43]

Satisfactory treatment of foreign messengers on their missions abroad is a prime ingredient of the Amarna—and also earlier and later—diplomatic code. Frequent allusions to high-quality hospitality and offers of gifts and, at the same time, protests or coy explanations for the detainment of foreign envoys are common themes of Late Bronze Age court-to-court interactions.[44]

It is significant that the presence of foreign guests, together with high-ranking dignitaries and other domestic personnel, is sometimes mentioned in connection with the actual or anticipated arrival of caravans bringing gifts from abroad. The king's personal enthusiasm or disenchantment was amplified by the very fact that these public scenes were witnessed by a number of selected individuals who would report their impressions to their respective audiences at home and abroad. First of all, there is the passage in EA 11:Rev. 21–23, already commented on, concerning foreign kings' learning of the great quantity of gold sent from Egypt to Babylonia. However, the most significant statements about the political implications of the satisfactory (or unsatisfactory) exchanges of gifts are found in some of Tushratta's letters; see, for example, EA 29:80–90, where the king of Mittani describes the great celebration that he had staged for the arrival of an Egyptian caravan carrying gifts. Court magnates, foreign guests (*ubāru*), and the Egyptian ambassador were all assembled amid great rejoicing. Later in the same letter, Tushratta sketches his ideal model of Egyptian-Mittanian relations. Despite the poorly preserved text, the contents of Tushratta's wishes are clear: mutual, uninterrupted "love" and "joy" will make both countries "happier [than all other countries]"; every foreign land will see this mutual happiness and will acknowledge that such a state of affairs had no equal in any other international relationship.[45]

Similar effusions can be found in other letters of Tushratta; see, for example, EA 20:71-79, in particular lines 73-74: "May my brother let me be greatly resplendent before my court and before my foreign guests"; EA 24:II 15-18: "When earlier Mane [= the Egyptian ambassador] brought what my brother had dispatched [as] my gift, I assembled my entire land and my nobles, as many as there are"; and ibid., III 71-73: "May my brother make me rich in respect to the kings, my vassals (?) (and) the other lands."[46]

At the same time, the reciprocal fame and prestige that redound to donors for sending presents to foreign courts are magnified in the eyes of international audiences if the receiver celebrates the arrival of gift-bearing messengers; see again a passage in the Hurrian letter of Tushratta, in which the king of Mittani announces the arrival of his daughter Tadu-Hepa together with her lavish dowry. Pharaoh should

> assemble the entire land, and may all other lands and the nobles (and) all (foreign) envoys be present. And they may show the dowry to my brother, and they may spread out everything in the view of my brother. ... And may my brother take all the nobles and all the (foreign) envoys and all other lands and the war charioteers whom my brother desires, and may my brother go. And may he spread out the dowry and may it be pleasing. (EA 24:III 21-34)

Personal joy, national pride, and international prestige are transformed into distress, shame, and disrepute if foreign gifts do not conform with the partner's expectations. Personal disillusion and dismay are worse if witnessed by a wider foreign audience; see again a passage in a letter from Mittani in which Tushratta depicts the scene upon the arrival of an Egyptian embassy and the opening of the sealed parcels containing gold. The event took place in the presence of all the foreign guests, who had been assembled by the king for this express purpose. In a general state of consternation, everyone burst out crying, saying: "All this is not at all made of gold!" They added: "In Egypt gold is more abundant than dirt. Moreover, 'my brother' loves you very much. (But if) he is a man who loves he would not give him [= Tushratta?] such things" (EA 20:51-54).[47]

Rivalries and jealousies among Great Kings over their standing in Pharaoh's eyes are a striking facet of the Amarna correspondence and provide insight into the nature of interdependence in the Amarna system. The complaint of Rib-Hadda of Byblos, who protests to his overlord because the messenger of the king of Akko was honored in Egypt more than his messenger (EA 88:46–48), shows that even among vassals, an overall competitive climate was fully operative. More serious would have been the case of Great Kings put on the same level as vassal kings. An isolated yet paradigmatic episode of this kind is recorded in a reply sent by Amenhotep III to Kadashman-Enlil: the king of Babylonia had protested because "he [i.e., Pharaoh, his brother] put my chariots amid the chariots of the *ḫazannu* [= the Asiatic kinglets subject to Egyptian rule]: you did not review (lit.: see) them separately. You insulted (?) them before the country where you are (?): you did not rev⟨iew⟩ them separately" (EA 1: 89–92).[48]

Conclusion

The selected items of textual documentation commented on highlight some pertinent features of diplomatic relations between the Great Powers during the Amarna (and post-Amarna) period. The interactive scene displayed by the Amarna (and Boghazköi) Letters testifies to a wide-ranging diplomatic network whose dynamics and formalities attain an almost unique level of sophistication and routine. Thus, it can safely be maintained that the Amarna and Ramesside Ages represent a true peak in the long history of Near Eastern diplomacy and diplomatic practice. It is certainly no accident that this very same period is marked by a true blossoming of international treaties issuing from the Hittite chancery. In a way, they represent the practical implementation of the stream of ad hoc messages that mark relations between the Great Kings themselves, and between the Great Kings and their vassals.

CHAPTER TWELVE

Reciprocity, Equality, and Status-Anxiety in the Amarna Letters

KEVIN AVRUCH

An anthropologist asked to contribute to the elucidation of the corpus of fourteenth-century B.C.E. texts called the Amarna Letters—and who is not a specialist in the history or languages of the ancient Near East—faces a dilemma. Used to the authority that ethnographic fieldwork confers, the anthropologist can hardly function in the present endeavor as specialist in the ethnographic sense; one is not especially privileged by "inside" knowledge of the Amarna cultures. The insiders in this volume are those specialists in ancient Near Eastern history and languages who have metaphorically resided in these and similar texts from other recovered archives (or triumphal stelae or war reliefs), almost in the way that an ethnographer resides in village or ward.

I am certainly not a resident in these texts, perhaps at best a tourist. When I began to think about metaphor and symbol in the Amarna Letters, and when I first opened Moran's translation of them—immediately lost in a blooming and buzzing world of unfamiliar names and locutions and ellipses, just like a tourist—I felt my limitations keenly. For the contemporary cultural anthropologist takes symbolism and metaphor very seriously as part of a discourse *constitutive* of culture and not simply accidental, reflective, or epiphenomenal to it. From my perspective, the nuanced, close, or fine-grained interpretation of a culture's symbolism or metaphor demands precisely that sort of linguistic and contextual knowledge—*cultural* knowledge—that I lack. If the goal of contemporary ethnography is to produce "thick description," then I am here starting from a very thin base.[1]

Some Uses of Naïveté

My reading of the Amarna Letters is culturally naïve[2] and, thus, essentially defective. But the defects need not be lethal, and perhaps there may even be some virtue in them. First, a naïve observer, unable to see nuance, is struck by the most obvious and robust of forms—those that can come through the blooming and buzzing. These forms may be obvious and robust for a reason—their centrality to the system, perhaps. I shall return to this notion of robustness and of symbols and metaphors.

Second, tourists can pose questions about matters unseen by long-term residents. One question appeals especially to the anthropologist: it is clear that the societies of the Amarna Letters are culturally quite distinct.[3] In a multicultural setting, problems in intercultural communication—misunderstandings and misapprehensions—are to be expected. In fact, an Amarna specialist has written brilliantly on this matter.[4] Yet it is also clear that despite cultural differences, the Amarna Letters do depict a larger sociopolitical system. By acknowledging it to be a *system,* one can also ask about what holds the parts together.

To begin with, it is clear that the Great Kings are engaged in fairly large-scale trade among themselves (for example, gold from Egypt, copper from Alashia, lapis lazuli from Babylonia and Mittani) and that raw materials flow from the vassals to the center (timber from Byblos, glass from Tyre, for example). In the Letters, this trade is conflated with more archaic-looking gift exchange, so that commerce appears in the guise of reciprocity.[5] But sometimes straightforward payment for goods in silver is demanded outright, in the same tablet filled with fraternal/familial symbolism (e.g., EA 35 and 37, from Alashia). And some of the Letters refer specifically to safe- or duty-free passages for merchants, their ships, and cargoes (EA 8, 39, 40).

Gift exchange, the language of family and kinship, and reciprocity are related to the meaning of symbol and metaphor. I turn to this topic below, focusing particularly on the Mittanian correspondence.

Two Views of Metaphor

The importance of symbols in understanding culture has long been accepted by anthropologists, and from very different theoretical camps—from neo-evolutionist and social anthropological to psychoanalytical approaches.[6] But a truly symbolic anthropology emerged as part of the poststructural movement of the 1970s, when many (though of course not all) anthropologists turned from one form or another of causal or functional explanation toward

interpretation and a Weberian-inflected emphasis on meaning and understanding.[7] An interest in metaphor, per se, followed and was part of this larger
movement toward symbolic analysis.[8] The main thrust here consisted of re-
vising the traditional, Aristotelian view of metaphor as something limited to
poetics or rhetoric, something peripheral to the main tasks of language and
communication, merely "figures of speech" that embellish or prettify. Now,
metaphor is seen as something central to communicational performance. It
is constitutive of discourse (hence, culture), and ultimately of human cogni-
tion and reasoning.[9]

Which view of metaphor we take will affect how we see it in the Amarna
Letters. By the lights of the first view, the Letters are remarkably poor in
metaphor. After all, they are not, on the face of it, the sort of texts in which
one expects to find rich symbolic or metaphorical veins to mine: they are not
mythic, ritual, religious, panegyric, or "literary" texts. They are records of
diplomatic exchanges, proposals of treaty or marriage, requests for military
assistance, inventories of gifts or trade goods. In this view, they are utilitarian and, on the whole, rather sparse or terse. The only sustained exception to
this (in my reading) is EA 147, a letter from Abi-Milku of Tyre to Pharaoh;
I note that editor Moran must also have felt the exceptional sense of poetry
about this letter, because he titled it "A Hymn to Pharaoh." Otherwise, the
"classical" metaphors are scattered and banal.

For example, how many times does Tushratta, importuning Pharaoh for
yet greater quantities of gold, remind him that it is well known that in Egypt
"gold is as plentiful as dirt?" (e.g., EA 19:ff.; EA 20:46–59; EA 27:45–51, 104–
9; EA 29: 143–47). Could this figure of speech have sounded as hackneyed to
fourteenth century B.C.E. ears as it does today? Was it young and vigorous
then, or already, in the *ancient* world, a dead or dying metaphor?[10] It brings to
mind how the richness of America was characterized for potential East European immigrants to it earlier in this century as a country whose "streets were
paved in gold." Other than three millennia, is this what separates Amarna
Egypt from the Lower East Side—the paving of their respective streets?

Tushratta provides the most consistent metaphor (in the traditional sense)
in the Letters, but certainly others are scattered about. Second to Tushratta
is the unfortunate Rib-Hadda. Indeed, I suspect it is their different (but ultimately convergent) insecurities that drives them to metaphor. As his situation worsens, Rib-Hadda several times quotes the proverb, "For lack of a
cultivator, my field is like a woman without a husband" (EA 74:13–19; EA 75:
15–17; EA 81:37ff.; EA 90:42ff.). Several times, as his enemies close in, he also
refers to himself (and the people of Byblos) "like a bird in a trap" (e.g., EA 74:
45–50; EA 81:34–36). Finally, defeated and close to his end, "an old man in

exile," as editor Moran puts it, he characterizes his abandonment to his enemies by his lord, Pharaoh, in these terms: "and there was no breath from the
mouth of the king for me" (EA 137:65–77).

No doubt there are other such "classical" figure-of-speech metaphors in
the Letters, and for the ancient Near East specialist, it is worthwhile to find,
and compare them philologically to similar metaphors in other texts. But as
I have indicated above, the traditional view of metaphor, which peripheral-
izes it, has been supplanted for most contemporary anthropologists by a view
that centralizes it as a core constituent of discourse. If the Letters seem rather
poor in the first sort of metaphor, they are relatively rich in the second. However, my limitations as a nonspecialist tourist in these texts (a reader of the
texts in English translation) are especially apparent in elucidating this other
sense of metaphor. I am limited, in fact, to those symbols that are particularly robust. They come through time and culture and translation because of
their repetitive occurrence in the Letters, their possible similarity to my own
cultural understanding of the world, or most profoundly, their ontological
and existential basis in and signification of transcendently *human* experience. These, then, are the key or dominant symbols, the root metaphors, to
be found in the Letters. They have to do with status, prestige, equality (or the
lack of it), and authority. Within the Great Kings' correspondence, at least,
these timeless qualities are metaphorized through the symbols of blood, kinship, marriage, and the family. Before turning to this, however, I discuss
briefly the Letters in general, highlighting their political context.

The Amarna Letters in Context

The Amarna corpus as a whole divides unevenly into two segments, the
Great Powers and the vassals; each letter is also separable into two unequal
segments. The first part of each letter is a heading, an address: salutations
among the Great Powers, "prostration formulae" for the vassals.[11] The headings are like ritual: formalistic, relatively unvarying, and predictable. The
main body of the Letters are less formal (though, as we noted above, metaphors and other tropes can be sprinkled within it) and less predictable. In
the body of the letter lies the utilitarian "point" of the message: the specific
request, proposal, démarche, complaint, inventory, arrangement for commercial transaction, or laissez-passer—the very stuff of diplomacy that led
Cohen to see in the Amarna archive "irrefutable evidence of a fully-fledged
diplomatic system," that "remarkably . . . reflects many features present in
the classic European diplomacy of three millennia later."[12]

I concentrate first on the ritualistic heading, or address, of the Letters. One can go hunting here for robust symbols and root metaphors. I start with the observation noted above — that within the Great Powers' club, salutations are exchanged, whereas vassals symbolically throw themselves at Pharaoh's feet.

Robust Symbols and Root Metaphors

"Say to Namhurya [Pharaoh], the son of the Sun, my Lord: Message of Akizzi, your servant. I fall at the feet of my lord 7 times" (EA 55:1–3).

"Say to the king, my lord: message of ʿAbdi-ashtarti, servant of the king. I fall at the feet of my king, my lord, 7 times . . . and 7 times, here and now, both on the stomach and on the back" (EA 64:1–7; also EA 65).

"Say to the king, my lord, Sun of all countries: Message of Rib-Hadda, your servant, footstool for your feet. I fall at the feet of the Sun, my lord, 7 times and 7 times" (EA 84:1–7).

"Say to the king. . . . Message of Abi-Milku. . . . I fall at the feet of the king, my lord, 7 times and 7 times. I am dirt under the sandals of the king, my lord" (EA 151:1–5).

These four examples of headings from letters written to Pharaoh by vassals vividly illustrate just what scholars of the ancient Near East call "prostration formulae." In their discussion of some fundamental metaphors found cross-culturally, Lakoff and Johnson recognize a class they call "orientational metaphors," having to do with spatial orientation (up-down, in-out, front-back, etc.). They note that *having control or force is up; being subject to control is down,* and also that *high status is up; low status is down.*[13] The prostration formulae derive their meaning from this basic up-down metaphor. Note that secondary metaphorical elaborations, building off of up-down, also occur: Rib-Hadda is a "footstool" for his lord's feet, while Abi-Milku further debases himself as "dirt under the sandals" of his king. And the self-debasement can take on other metaphorical forms: in addition to being "mud under your feet," for example, ʿAbdi-Ashirta also calls himself "a dog of the house of the king, my lord" (EA 61:1ff.). Of course, this metaphor is not simply *animal is low status; human is high status,* since (say) to be a *lion* is in many cultures a good thing. The negative valorization has to do with the qualities of *dog* in this context.

It is important to recall that these headings are ritualistic. The self-debasement that formally occurs within them might well be compromised or even subverted by the tropic qualities of the message itself, which might show exasperation,[14] irony,[15] sarcasm,[16] or even outright insolence.[17] To borrow a terminology introduced into the study of the Amarna Letters by Cohen, itself taken from negotiation and game theory, I am not so much interested in the "minor issue subgames" of the messages, which have to do with the actual issues under negotiation, as I am in the "major relationship metagames," in which the parties negotiate their relative status and standing vis-à-vis one another.[18]

In the vassal correspondence, the nature of the relationship between the center and periphery is presumed to be that of superior to inferior, of dominance to submission. The metaphors used in the headings — up-down, footstools and dirt, dogs in the household, and so on — both reflect *and* constitute this essential asymmetry. The heading in the Great Kings' correspondence, by contrast, consists of a salutation that refers to the addressee explicitly as "my brother," then reports on one's own well-being ("For me all goes well"), and then expresses good wishes for the addressee ("May all go well with you"), his extended household, army, property, etc.[19] The notion of brotherhood and fellow-caring is supposed to connote a relationship very different from superior-inferior and dominance-submission. In the correspondence between the Great Kings, the nature of the relationship is presumed to be one of equality or parity.[20] And the root metaphor here is *family,* symbolized by a constellation of kinship relationships, especially fraternity through blood and marriage, that is held together (in the ideal) by such ties of moral community as blood and love, and maintained through repetitive cycles of reciprocal gift-giving.

Although all the Great Kings share the familial (particularly fraternal) metaphor, they do not seem equally committed to (or apprehensive about — see below) it.[21] In the two letters of the Assyrian correspondence, for example (EA 15–16), the term "brother" does not appear in the first letter, when Assuruballit is tentatively proposing the establishment of relations with Egypt. He does, of course, send a greeting-gift (*šulmānu*) with this letter, so the first move in an exchange system has been made.[22] In the second letter, in which Pharaoh has agreed to Assyria's entry into the club, the Assyrian does call the Egyptian "my brother" but is also already complaining about the quantity of reciprocated gifts (compared to past Egyptian-Mittani exchanges), as well as the mistreatment of his messengers in the sun.[23]

In the Alashiyan correspondence (EA 33–40), fraternal concern and fellow-feeling seem entirely subordinated to the reciprocal gift-giving, which itself seems subordinate to demands surrounding the commercial trade. "Let me inquire about my brother's health" is followed one line later with, "Send me pure silver." Elsewhere, the Alashiyan king combines both levels of exchange in the same sentence: "My brother, the payment is due" (EA 37:17–19; EA 35:29). The Arzawa correspondence (in Hittite) concerns the negotiation of a marriage, proposed (in EA 31) by Amenhotep III to a daughter of the Arzawan king, who seems (in EA 32) a little mistrustful about the whole thing.[24] The Hittite letters (EA 41–44) include at least one from Suppiluliuma to Akhenaten or Tutankhamun offering greeting-gifts and recalling the good relations previously enjoyed between the two countries. This was, clearly, a communication seeking to maintain or re-establish stable relations after a change of regime in Egypt.

To a greater (Hatti) or lesser (Alashiya) extent, then, the familial metaphor and the use of reciprocal gifting can be found in the above Great Kings' letters. But in my reading, at least, the two sets of Great Kings' correspondence where the principles of reciprocity and family/marriage/kinship come together most interestingly, even (in Tushratta's case) poignantly, is in the Babylonian and Mittani correspondence. Here, the problematical nature of the claims to equality and parity, supposedly inherent to reciprocity and kinship, is most evident. In the Mittani correspondence, the nature of the "major relationship metagame" in these letters, to use Cohen's phrase, is most starkly exposed. The Great Kings' letters are also — whatever the putative or manifest topic of any given message — *negotiations* about the nature of their relationship. They are all about claims, sometimes anxious, to validate status, prestige, and authority vis-à-vis the Egyptians. And none is so anxious as Tushratta's.

Hierarchy, Anxiety, and the Limits of Reciprocity

Ever since Malinowski traced the clockwise and counterclockwise movements of necklaces and armbands, called the *kula,* in Melanesia, and Mauss drew together comparative data from a variety of "archaic" societies, anthropologists have been interested in linking forms of exchange with kinds of social structures and with genres of morality as well. The insight of the economic historian Polanyi, that exchange systems took on three main forms — reciprocity, redistribution, and market — was extended by anthropologists like Sahlins, who refined the notion of reciprocity on a continuum of three subforms (generalized, balanced, and negative), based on the expectation of return and the closeness of the tie linking the parties to the exchange.[25] The model for generalized reciprocity (where no immediate return is expected) is the family, characterized by close ties of a moral, not transactional, type. The three major forms of exchange were also correlated to the sociopolitical variables of equality, hierarchy, and stratification. In general, reciprocity implies egalitarian social relations.[26]

Scholars of the Amarna Letters have hardly ignored the findings of the anthropologists I have mentioned in approaching the problem of trade and politics. They have been especially concerned with disentangling (as

Liverani put it) the "rational" (commercial, transactional, commodified, profit-seeking) elements of the trade from its "irrational" ones (reciprocative, moral, "pure gift," prestation).[27] In this they are continuing, in the Amarna material, a long argument in the scholarship of exchange, between the utilitarian views of Adam Smith or Hobbes—that exchange, including reciprocity, is a means to self-interested ends—and the Maussian view that exchange not reducible to self-interest is a social-moral end in itself.

Not surprisingly, this tension is strongly present in the Letters themselves. First, one can broadly distinguish the redistributive from the reciprocal forms by comparing the Great Kings' letters to the vassals'. The vassals are responding to Egyptian requests for *tribute*—timber, glass, slaves, or women.[28] (The vassals are also requesting stuff from the Egyptians—military aid and supplies, mostly—which is not, on the whole, forthcoming.) By contrast, the Great Kings seek to engage one another in cycles of reciprocal exchanges of (as Mauss would put it) "pure gifts," total prestations, for example, the "greeting-gift" (*šulmānu*). No strings are attached to pure gifts; they are truly ends in themselves. In the ideal, the reciprocity displayed by the Great Kings would be, *as in a family*, generalized reciprocity, free of the anxieties of immediate (*balanced*) return. If the system were harmonic, then the familial metaphor of the Letters' address, the repeated idiom of "my brother," would be reinforced by the generalized reciprocity of their gifting.[29] And if the exchanges were purely reciprocal, both the exchange and the familial metaphor of fraternity would work together to express an essentially egalitarian—*symmetrical*—construction of their relationship. But the system is far from harmonic, and the relations between the other Great Kings and Pharaoh are (in this period) not really symmetrical. Instead, the letters of the Great Kings (especially the Babylonian and Mittani) express anxieties about relative status and hierarchy, and seek—in Tushratta's case, almost obsessively—to negotiate them.

How can we discern the disharmony of the prestation system? First, by noting that the reciprocity never achieves generalized form. At best, it is balanced (a return of about equal value is expected immediately), and worse, the letters are filled with the complaints of the Great Kings to Egypt that it is in fact *negative*—that the "generosity" of the kings has been taken advantage of. Expected solid gold statues are in fact only coated wooden ones (EA 26–27); gold claimed to weigh forty minas, when melted down weighs barely ten (EA 7:63–72); gold arrives that looks suspiciously like silver (EA 3:13–22; EA 20: 46–59 [?]); gold arrives too late (EA 4:36–50; EA 41:14–15); and gold comes in quantities (given that it is "as plentiful as dirt" in Egypt) that are, finally, much too small (EA 9:6–18; EA 16:22–34; EA 19; EA 27:45–51, 104–9; EA 29.

Thus, the Letters are filled with complaints about the asymmetry of the relationship. There are two sorts of complaints. First, there are complaints about one's absolute status vis-à-vis the Egyptians. Second, there are complaints about one's relative status vis-à-vis the other Great Kings. For the latter, consider the following: the Babylonian king complains that their dominance of the Assyrians is not being respected by the Egyptians (EA 9); that the Egyptian escort accorded his daughter is insufficient and insulting; that his "neighboring kings" would hear of it and he would lose prestige (EA 11: 16–22, also 19–23); and that his gifts and chariots were humiliatingly placed for Pharaoh's review among those of the vassal mayors rather than the Great Kings (EA 1:88–98). The Assyrian king compares his greeting-gift from Egypt to that received by Mittani and finds it wanting.[30] And Tushratta of Mittani, who speaks compulsively of love throughout his letters, complains that Akhenaten is not according him the same respect and affection as did his father, Amenhotep III (or, for that matter, as Tushratta's father, Shuttarna, received from Egypt!).[31]

What is interesting about all the above complaints is that they concern, as I noted, jockeying for status vis-à-vis the Egyptians *relative* to the other Great Kings. Jockeying for status vis-à-vis Pharaoh himself is rarer. It is as if the ultimate superiority of Pharaoh among the Great Kings is accepted. So all "brothers" are not equal. Tushratta tries perhaps to temper the asymmetry by reminding Pharaoh that the latter is not just his "brother" but also his son-law and, thus, Tushratta is his father-in-law. However, it does not appear that this appeal to alternative kinship terms mitigates in any way the asymmetry. It is vital to understand that when Tushratta calls himself Pharaoh's father-in-law, he is not so much stating a kinship fact as making a claim; it is a bargaining stance, a proposal. *Only if* Pharaoh acknowledges this claim (acting toward Tushratta as a son-in-law should) does then the claim become a (social) fact. In all the Letters, in fact, I find only the vigorous Suppiluliuma, Great King of Hatti, who questions this basic asymmetry. He complains testily about the placement of his name below Pharaoh's on a tablet and asks him bluntly, "Is this the accepted practice? My brother, did you write me with peace in mind? . . . Why have you exalted your name, while I, for my part, am thought of as a corpse."[32]

The second way in which what I have called the "disharmony" of the system, its claims to familial equality in face of asymmetry, is expressed is in the way marriages are formed by the correspondents. Indeed, the marriage system is the key to reading the status negotiations in the Letters. Zaccagnini has remarked that "gold (immediately after women) was the most appreciated item in non-commercial transactions."[33] I think he has the order just right. Clearly, in the vassal correspondence, Pharaoh asks for women as part of tribute, along with timber, glass, and so on. In the Great Kings' correspondence, women are used through marriage to Pharaoh explicitly to forge "blood-relationships" (as in EA 31). Tushratta never tires of reminding Amenhotep III, Akhenaten, and the Queen Mother Tiye of the history of marriage ties that bound Mittani peaceably to Egypt. He always adds "son-in-law" and "father-in-law" to the epithet "brother" in the headings of his letters. He constantly offers (and claims) the prerogatives that "love" brings forth, as it would in a family. However, while marriage ties do create political alliances, serve as opportunities for large-scale commercial trade, and in general "grease the wheels" of exchange, they ultimately fail to achieve symmetry among the Great Kings for the elementary reason that Egypt has structured the exchange of women such that they will take women from others, vassals and Great Kings alike, but give no sisters or daughters of the Nile in return.

It was Claude Lévi-Strauss, following Mauss's powerful insights about gift exchange, who argued that the fundamental, indeed primordial, social exchange was that of women between social groups.[34] Lévi-Strauss also understood that the purported egalitarianism at the heart of reciprocity could only exist in situations of what he called "restricted exchange," where women are exchanged directly between two groups, resulting in isogamy. In "generalized exchange" (not to be confused with generalized reciprocity), each group does not symmetrically receive women from the others; some groups "give" their daughter and sisters, and other groups "take" them. Now, any rule of generalized exchange results in asymmetry between those groups that receive and those that provide sisters and daughters as wives. Cross-culturally speaking, in fact, wife-givers are usually superior to wife-takers; women in effect "marry down" (hypogamy). The exception is where women are regarded as tribute.[35] There, one group refuses to gives its daughters in marriage, while taking the women of other groups, who, from this perspective, are "marrying up" (hypergamy). And this describes precisely, of course, the position of Pharaohs vis-à-vis the other Great Kings.[36]

What do the other Great Kings think of this?

The Babylonian king, Kadashman-Enlil, when asked for his daughter by Amenhotep III, tries to establish isogamy — equality — by asking for an Egyptian princess in return (EA 2). Pharaoh responds: "From time immemorial no daughter of the king of Egypt is given to anyone."

Rebuffed, Kadashman-Enlil then makes an astonishing counter-proposal: "Someone's grown daughters, beautiful women, must be available. Send me a beautiful woman as if she were your daughter. Who is going to say, 'She is no daughter of the king!'?" But the Babylonian monarch does not even wait for a reply to this remarkable proposal. Later in the same letter, he is resigned to the hypergamous way things are: "If, during this summer . . . you send the gold I wrote you about, I will give you my daughter" (EA 4:4–22, 36–50).

Tushratta never even attempts to question the asymmetry. He tries repeatedly to invoke love as a basis for symmetrical equality, apparently in vain. He tries to invoke his other familial claim, as a father-in-law, to obtain some leverage vis-à-vis Amenhotep III; but alas, for fathers of the bride, this works best in hypogamous exchange systems, not hypergamous ones. In the end, he is reduced to writing to Akhenaten's mother to try to get him only to connect—it appears, in vain.

Conclusions

Later in history, when the position of Egypt deteriorated, a daughter of the king of Egypt did marry out, to Solomon. But that is beyond the purview of the Amarna Letters proper. In the correspondence of the Great Kings, there is a treasurehouse of diplomatic history and process. But whatever else these kings are negotiating over, they are carrying on metanegotiations over relationships—over status, ranking, and prestige, both in absolute terms, vis-à-vis Egypt, and in relative terms, vis-à-vis each other *relative* to Egypt. The root metaphors involve gift-exchange and family/blood/kinship ties, reciprocities that ideally symbolize equality but in reality do not. First, because the fundamental marriage tie is, in this period, asymmetrical, hypergamous in Egypt's prestige-favor. And second, because the reciprocal gifting never quite achieves and, certainly, never sustains the purity of Mauss's ideal *don,* an end in itself.

CHAPTER THIRTEEN

Diplomacy and International Marriages

SAMUEL A. MEIER

Any discussion of marriage in the Amarna Letters must be seen in the context of the entire Late Bronze Age and, to some extent, of the ancient Near East as a whole. Nevertheless, very few reliable generalizations are possible for all periods and all locales. If one focuses only on the cultures that spoke Semitic languages, the diversity in marriage laws and customs—not to speak of the position of women, laws of inheritance, determination of royal succession, roles of women in the palace—in even one place is hardly surprising, given a two-millennia span of history characterized by frequent political and cultural upheavals.[1] Marriage in Assyria had different features from those attested in Babylonia.[2] These East Semitic marriages in turn presupposed different expectations from those attested in the West Semitic world.[3] When one expands the horizons of the Near East to include the cultures of ancient Egyptians,[4] Hittites,[5] and Hurrians,[6] one cannot simply extrapolate features of marriage from a particular place or time and expect them to reappear elsewhere.

In this light, it comes as a surprise to find that it is marriage between royal houses that is a clearly defined activity uniting, not dividing, these diverse cultures at the end of the Late Bronze Age. As Pintore demonstrated, the rules of the international marriage game are already in place, and the players usually know their moves. But it is only a recently formulated game.[7] It is true that marriage between royalty is not an innovation of this period, for Old Babylonian interdynastic marriages in the Upper Tigris and Euphrates area, amply illumined by the Mari texts, take place for the most part between royalty in a cultural continuum (Qatna, Aleppo, Mari, and their smaller neighbors).[8] But political marriages on such a grand scale as in the

Late Bronze Age, persistently crossing cultural and linguistic lines, have no comparable attestation in the ancient Near East.[9] In light of the variability of marriage customs, the ease of interdynastic marriage in the Late Bronze Age should give us pause. It may be that ease of communication and ideals of tolerance in our cosmopolitan world have blinded us to the impressive difficulties working against the ease of Late Bronze interdynastic marriages, difficulties that may be superficially masked in the ancient sources.[10]

In order to begin to uncover factors working against Late Bronze international marriages among royalty, it is appropriate to begin with the notion of royalty, which is itself problematic. An international ritual and vocabulary associated with royalty (couched in Akkadian, the lingua franca) is already fully developed and in use in the Amarna texts. But it is an artificial vocabulary. "Artificial" does not mean that the words and concepts are a de novo creation, for they have a respectable history in Mesopotamia. What is meant, rather, is that these words and rituals associated with royalty are being used in a cosmopolitan environment that strips the words of their cultural moorings in order to attain a more generic utility, transcending specific cultures and inevitably weakening the semantic content.[11]

A case in point is the application of the language of family relationships to the frankly mercenary and self-seeking political machinations of the Great Powers at this time.[12] Kinship structures and obligations of brothers to brothers to fathers to sisters to sons to daughters are not identical in Egypt, Hatti, Mittani, Babylonia, and Assyria. Brothers who constantly must be reminded that they are brothers are not good brothers; the persistent reminders in international relations underscore that this family life is a fiction. "Love" and "brotherhood" among kings at a thousand miles removed mean less than love and brotherhood among close kin, but the ideological bonuses that such words bring are considerable. What is not sufficiently appreciated is the ideological sacrifice that was also required in adopting the rules of the game and its accompanying vocabulary.

The very notion of kingship is a paramount example. Kingship in second-millennium Egypt was a far different phenomenon than kingship in Hatti, which differed in turn from kingship in Mesopotamia. In the latter, the king was selected from among humans by the gods,[13] whereas the king of Egypt himself was a god, "an epiphany,"[14] in contrast to the Hittite king, who became a god when he died. It is thus remarkable that Pharaoh allows himself to be described in the lingua franca as a šarru, "king," the same term that is used to describe the kings of Hatti, Babylonia, Assyria, and Mittani. When Pharaoh's letters refer to Pharaoh with this term, he means something much different than what his correspondents in Hattusha or Babylon mean. But the semantic playing field has been impoverished by applying a single word to a variety of phenomena;[15] the very real cultural differences have been erased, and Pharaoh gives up his distinctiveness to join the international game. When a non-Egyptian Great King sensed a supercilious Pharaoh, it is stunning to find Pharaoh himself protesting equality, as in Ramesses II's reply to Hattusili III:

> Now [I have heard] these [words] that are not good which you have written [to me]: "Why do you write these many words to [me like a slave]?" That I [had written to you like] a slave among [my] slaves [is not the case]. Have you not received kingship (*šarrūta*), and do I [not know it?][16]

Pharaoh's surrender of uniqueness is even more surprising when it is recalled that Pharaoh accepted a designation (*šarru*) that was in common currency among petty kings to describe themselves.[17] It is crucial to observe how Pharaoh's vassals usually avoid applying the term *šarru* to themselves when writing to Pharaoh, for they know their status.[18] But inevitably, they leveled everyone in rulership positions, vassals and sovereign, with the term *šarru:*

> My lord, just as I love the king (*šarri*), my lord, so too the king (*šar*) of Nuhašše, the king (*šar*) of Nii, the king (*šar*) of Zinzar, and the king (*šar*) of Tananab; all of these kings (*šarrānī*) are my lord's servants. (EA 53:40–44)

Such inadvertent humiliation, suggesting that Pharaoh's position was in some way commensurate with insignificant vassals, was ameliorated by the adjective "great" to distinguish that elite class of kings who moved in a more rarified atmosphere. But even among the elite, the terminology underscored that each of these kings had peers, that there was a brotherhood of equals. Despite this democratizing, the terminology was willingly adopted, and each king condescended to acknowledge regularly with his "brother" king the social equality that they share. Such verbiage marked a compromise for a king such as Pharaoh for whom, in Egyptian ideology, there was no peer; indeed, no other country had a Pharaoh.[19] It is telling that the international verbiage was not reproduced in Egyptian inscriptions: "The best that a foreign king could be expected to be designated was *wr* 'prince,' 'chief.'"[20]

In the context of marriage, this compromising of royal ideology in order to communicate on an international level was exacerbated when the daughter of a foreign Great King married another Great King. The king who gave his daughter might waste no time in exploiting the psychological leverage that accompanied the now very real family ties, stressing repeatedly that he is "father-in-law" (*ēmu*) to the married king, now his "son-in-law" (*ḫatānu*). Among the correspondence of the Great Kings, this is a peculiar feature of the Mittani letters of Tushratta to Pharaoh.[21] For Pharaoh to treat with foreigners in such a fashion is a remarkable compromise of centuries of intolerance of foreigners. Egypt was a culture where "Egyptians were people; foreigners were not."[22]

Real kinship resulted from such marriages between Great Kings. Once again, however, as with kingship, the terminology of kinship was too impoverished and debased to convey adequately the meaning brought by each participant to the international dialogue. The kinship verbiage was sufficiently vague as to invoke notions of extended family relationships without necessarily corresponding precisely to kinship patterns that actually were found in each of the participating cultures. Consequently, as with the verbiage of kingship, a Great King could use the terminology and mean one thing that could be understood in quite a different sense by another Great King.

This reality is evident in international marriages. Whether Pharaoh married the daughter of a petty king of Canaan in the fifteenth century B.C.E.,[23] or the daughter of a Great King in the thirteenth century B.C.E.,[24] the official Egyptian presentation of the event for internal consumption depicted the transaction as tribute of inferiors to Pharaoh. But when corresponding with the same thirteenth-century B.C.E. Great King, the language of vassalage is nowhere to be found, replaced instead with the international verbiage of equality and kinship. Pharaoh and his chancery had surrendered on the international level their self-image in order to communicate with second-class humans. What Egypt gained was coexistence with powerful neighbors on the northern fringes of their empire. The public compromise of Egypt's image — demotion from uniqueness to membership in an elite club — suggests that Egypt was not dealing from a position of strength.

This posture of compromise marks a real surrender on Egypt's part that is confirmed on other levels. Not only in the areas of kingship and kinship is Egypt publicly (i.e., internationally) compromising its image. One must also not overlook the fact that Egyptians are corresponding in a non-Egyptian language. Instead of foreigners learning Egyptian standards, it is Egypt who learns the mechanics of international communication from others. It is not suggested that there was any competition in this regard. It is simply that when Egypt began to join in the dialogue, the tools for diplomacy had already been forged, and Egypt had to learn the rules set up by others.[25]

With respect to marriage in particular, the same compromise by Egypt can be discerned. Egyptian envoys are sent to pour oil upon the head of the princesses destined to become Pharaoh's wife in the courts of Babylonia

(EA 11:16–18, Rev. 15), Arzawa (EA 31:11–14), and Hatti (Edel, *Korrespondenz*, 51.14–16; 53.5–8; 107.4′–7′). In the past, such texts had been used to suggest the Egyptian antecedents of anointing ceremonies in the Semitic world. But it is essential to observe that these Egyptian anointings occur on foreign soil, as a recent reevaluation of anointing with oil in Egypt affirms:

> An indication that the Egyptian kings often followed native customs when dealing with the Hittites and the rulers of the Syro-Palestinian states is found in the practice of anointing a woman prior to marriage. There are several references in cuneiform documents which mention that a representative of Pharaoh poured oil on the head of a future Asiatic bride of the king, possibly to indicate her betrothal to the Egyptian monarch. There is no evidence of this being an Egyptian custom; but there are references to such a practice attested in Asia in cuneiform documents. It is likely that in these instances the representatives of Pharaoh were engaging in a ceremony common among Asiatics.[26]

As with kingship and kinship, so Egypt is once again submitting to foreign ways in order to participate in the international arena. If this submission is voluntary, it represents a remarkable reversal of centuries of momentum in aversion to all things foreign. More likely, this and other compromises represent a necessity if Egypt is to participate on the international scene.

Finally, we come to the problem of the direction in which princesses moved in forming interdynastic marriages among the Late Bronze Age palaces. More specifically, how was it possible for Egypt to be a magnet for foreign princesses, while at the same time Egypt resisted sending its princesses to foreign courts in marriage?[27] No other Great King is as reticent as Pharaoh to see Egyptian princesses in foreign courts: "From time immemorial no daughter of the king of Egypt is given to anyone" (EA 4:6–7).[28]

Schulman summarized one solution succinctly in noting that Egyptian marriages

> represented . . . its claim to be the leading "great power" . . . and . . . a tacit recognition of the power, if not the claim, by the weaker but still important other "great powers." . . . If the daughter of an Egyptian king were to be given in marriage to a foreign ruler, this would not only imply a loss of face and prestige for Egypt, but it would also, though intangibly, elevate such a foreign ruler to the level of Pharaoh.[29]

Schulman has here overlooked the fact that the international language of brotherhood and kingship among the Great Kings has already placed Pharaoh on the same level as these other monarchs. Pharaoh has already accom-

modated himself to the marriage rites of non-Egyptians. We have not even
discussed here the parity treaty (a non-Egyptian genre that clarifies a relationship of mutual expectations of respect and defense) that is accepted by
Ramesses II as a legitimate expression of his international status: even though
"an agreement with Pharaoh-god is excluded a-priori . . . , Pharaoh comes to
a formal agreement with another party."[30] The reasons for Schulman's perspective have already been compromised, for Pharaoh has been shown to be
a functional equal with the other Great Kings, and the other Great Kings harbor no suspicions that Pharaoh is actually a primus inter pares.

It is not difficult to discern when Pharaoh or any Great King is dealing
with inferiors, as the abundant vassal correspondence from Amarna testifies.
If a vassal has peculiar marriage customs at dissonance with the sovereign, it
is the vassal who must bend:

> (King of Hatti:) This sister whom I, My Majesty, have given to you as
> your wife has many sisters. . . . For Hatti it is an important custom
> that a brother does not take his sister or female cousin (sexually). It is
> not permitted. In Hatti, whoever commits such an act does not remain
> alive but is put to death here. Because your land is barbaric, it is in con-
> flict(?). (There) one quite regularly takes his sister or female cousin. . . .
> You shall no longer take (sexually) the wives of your brother. . . . You
> shall not take a woman from the land of Azzi as (an additional) wife.
> Divorce the one whom you have already taken. (Beckman, *Hittite
> Diplomatic Texts*, 3.25, 29)

Pharaoh does not so treat the other Great Kings in this supercilious manner characteristic of a superior. It is true that the Great Kings make demands
of one another, but as has been established by Pintore with respect to marriage and Zaccagnini with respect to gift exchange, any resistance and demands are all a part of the game of diplomacy between functional equals.[31]
Those Great Kings who corresponded with Egypt saw little of Egyptian royal
ideology distinct from their own international blend. Which brings us back
to this singular deviation: What are the implications of the Egyptian refusal
to send princesses abroad in marriage?

In the same way that the term "king," *šarru*, in the international milieu
meant something different to the various kings who used it, so the exchange
of princesses did not necessarily mean the same thing to all the international
players. The most commonly attested bestowal of princesses outside of Egypt
takes place where a lord gives his daughter in marriage to a vassal. Indeed,
some of these marriages are arranged with impoverished, landless, and fugi-

tive figures.[32] This is not an aberration of the Late Bronze age or the accident of discovery, for the same pattern applies to the earlier interdynastic marriages of the Old Babylonian period.[33] It is quite appropriate to perceive such marriages as a manifestation of vassal status, for King Zimri-Lim is advised to "send his daughter so that he might exercise kingship in Karanâ."[34]

Into this environment walks Egypt as a latecomer to the international game of diplomacy. From Egypt's perspective, giving royal offspring to non-Egyptians is demeaning (EA 4). At the same time, incorporating foreign princesses into Pharaoh's harem is quite acceptable, something Pharaoh does regularly as a sign of sovereignty over his vassals.[35] This Egyptian peculiarity can be integrated into the diplomatic game with little fuss. Where Egypt regularly receives princesses in marriage as a sign of sovereignty, the other players regularly give princesses in marriage as an expression of sovereignty. Marriage of princesses carries quite distinct implications for the parties involved. As with the international compromise on (and even weakening of) the term *šarru*, so the activity of marriage is successful in cementing kinship ties, but each culture may bring to the event nuances not shared by all.

What results is the climax to any successful bargain: the buyer and the seller walk away with good feelings about the transaction, both thinking that they have the better part of the bargain. On the one hand, the non-Egyptian kings are pleased and perhaps enjoying the status that comes from having once more given a daughter, as they do so often to vassals, to a new member of the extended family. From this non-Egyptian perspective, it is Pharaoh's loss if he does not wish to take advantage of his status as a Great King and give his daughters in marriage to others. Pharaoh, on the other hand, is also satisfied with the successful, extended family bonding that takes place when he marries a foreign princess. But from his perspective, he sees it as the non-Egyptian's loss that they do not gain an Egyptian princess. Both sides walk away claiming (under their breath) that they had a better deal: Ramesses II's Marriage Stela is explicit from the Egyptian side, for this text depicts the marriage as incorporating tribute from Hatti. Is the non-Egyptian perspective on marriage with Egypt available?

By inspecting the correspondence prior to the marriage itself, one can discern that foreigners are not treating with Pharaoh as inferiors. When Ramesses II corresponds with Hittite royalty, the future status of the Hittite princess is agreed to be that of "mistress (*bēltu*) of Egypt" (Edel, *Korrespondenz*, 62.5), and the Hittite queen insists:

As for the daughter that [I will giv]e to my brother . . . , [I want] to make her superior [to all the other daughters of Great Kings]; no [one should be able] to find (another) beside her. Should I compare [the daughter that] I will someday give to my brother to the [daughter of the king of Assyria or t]he d[aught]er of the king of Zulabi? (Edel, *Korrespondenz*, 106.5′–9′)

Great Kings negotiate to have their daughters become queens in Egypt, not simply a part of the harem. This is reminiscent of the vassal treaties in which the Hittite kings insist on a privileged status for their daughters in their new home. Ramesses II writes reassuringly to the Hittite king, Hattusili III:

The king of Babylonia and the king of Hanigalbat [wrote to me]: "They are sending [the daughter of the king of Hatti] to the king of Egypt and [the king of Egypt will make her queen of Egypt]. Put my daughter in her place!" [So those kings wrote to me. I will not consent to giv]e the queenship, which the king of Ba[bylon desires, to his daughter].[36]

Great Kings are aggressively competing in the thirteenth century to give their daughters to Pharaoh so that they may rule as queens.

There is no opprobrium or sense of a lower status when a Great King's daughter becomes a queen in Egypt. Indeed, the fact that Pharaoh elevates the daughter of a foreign king to the status of queen confirms that from his perspective also, she is a very valuable individual. Ramesses II's Hittite queen, under her new name, Maat-Hor-Neferure, "was given a full share in the honors of the palace with her Egyptian compeers . . . [appearing] on the monuments of Pi-Ramesse, as a full queen on royal statuary."[37]

One finds the non-Egyptian Great Kings bargaining with Pharaoh until an equitable marriage arrangement is agreed upon. Threats to delay (EA 11: 13–18) or withhold the daughter from Egypt, and advice to Pharaoh on how to treat the princess as befits her royalty, are not comfortable on the lips of individuals who sense their inferiority.

(King of Babylonia to Pharaoh:) You could send me 3,000 talents of gold, and I would not accept it. I would send it back to you, and I would not give my daughter in marriage. (EA 4:49–50)

(King of Mittani to Pharaoh:) And now when the wife of my brother comes . . . the entire land may my brother assemble, and may all the other lands and the nobles and all envoys be present. (EA 24:21–26)

It is no inferior who refuses multiple requests to marry his daughter:

He asked for the daughter of [my grandfather, the sister] of my father. He wrote 5, 6 times, but he did not give her. When he wrote my grandfather 7 times, then only under such pressure did he give her. (EA 29:16–18)

This "antagonismo ceremoniale," so lucidly analyzed by Pintore,[38] is probably something Pharaoh had to learn and to which he had to adapt (similar to the anointing of brides), for a Pharaoh who bargains with non-Egyptians is at dissonance with the profile of Egyptian royalty. Indeed, the preceding text may even provide the learning curve documenting Pharaoh's adaptation to the international scene, as it continues:

When Nimmureya, your father, [wro]te to Šutt[arna], m[y] father, and asked for my father's daughter, my own sister, he wr[ote] 3, 4 times, but [he did not giv]e her. When he wrote 5, 6 times, only under such pressure did he g[iv]e [her]. W[hen Nimmureya, [yo]ur [fa]ther, wrote to me and asked for my daughter, I did [not] say n[o]. The [very] first ti[me] I said [to] his messenger, "Of course I will give her." (EA 29:18–22)

In sum, this discussion has focused on the deceptive aspects of the international language of diplomacy and marriage in the Late Bronze Age. The various ethnic and linguistic entities knew that their neighbors had different customs and saw the world from a different (inferior!) point of view. The lingua franca and international marriages allowed sufficient ambiguity and imprecision so that those who participated as equals could actually appear so on the international stage. But the ambiguity and cultural games allowed each of the Great Kings to rest satisfied that the others did not really measure up to the stature that each envisioned for himself.

CHAPTER FOURTEEN

A Social-Psychological Analysis of Amarna Diplomacy

DANIEL DRUCKMAN AND SERDAR GÜNER

The Amarna Letters provide rare insight into the diplomatic relations among the Near East kingdoms of the fourteenth century B.C.E.. Given the large amount of scholarly work already completed, Mario Liverani asks whether there is anything more to be studied. He answers his own question by remarking that there is always room for more studies "because the methods of analysis have been improved, the frontiers of historical interest have widened, our cultural trends are changing, and every document can always be studied again and again."[1] It is in this spirit that we offer another, perhaps new but tentative, approach to the analysis of the Letters. This chapter adopts a social-psychological perspective on international relations (IR), drawing on structural and processual concepts and the connections between them. Although each concept stands on its own, taken together, they illuminate the Amarna period.[2] Following a brief discussion of research methodology, the key features of the context and interactions of Amarna diplomacy are described. This description is then used to highlight certain themes, including the role played by values and interests, the emphasis placed on reciprocal exchanges, the consequences of strategic choices, and the way that the players attempted to manage the impressions that they conveyed through their messages. The chapter concludes by considering the implications of the analysis for the development of cooperative regional institutions.

On Research Methodology

Content analysis is the method preferred by analysts of international negotiation. To a large extent, our knowledge about negotiation processes is based
on the results of studies using this methodology.[3] Its use, however, is limited
to negotiations in which complete transcripts are available or the material
consists of a sample taken from a known "population" of negotiating interactions. Neither of these conditions exists with regard to the Letters. Severe
sampling problems limit the kinds of inferences that can be drawn from the
available material.[4] We simply have no way of knowing the extent to which
the surviving correspondence is representative of the sum total of letters or
events. This leads to the question of whether the missing (or "uncoded")
data differ qualitatively from the data that are available (or "coded"). Any
inferences made from this limited and possibly unrepresentative material are
suspect and, at the very least, subject to systematic biases that are difficult to
estimate and, thus, take into account or correct.

Although some of the more interesting uses of content analysis deal with
the inferential questions "Why?" "How?" and "With What Effect?," the technique has also been used to address such descriptive questions as "What?"
"Who?" and "To Whom?" The latter questions are less sensitive to sampling
problems, and their answers can provide a running commentary on the body
of available Letters. For example, it would be possible to document the key
types of arguments or tactics used by each of the kings. But even here, there
are some limitations. One concerns the repetitiveness of the kings' requests
and arguments. Another is the one-sided communications, usually from the
kings to Pharaohs, that characterize the material. Both these features limit
the range of distinctions that can be made among coding categories; only a
few categories are likely to be used frequently.

Further, even if the data requirements were satisfied, content analysis
would only illuminate processes reflected in the words of the kings. Aspects
of diplomatic interaction not captured by these rhetorical exchanges would
be hidden from view. Also missing are the exchanges among messengers and
kings that may have provided insights into the manner in which intermediaries exerted influence on the court.[5] More generally, by focusing attention
on the messages per se, we may miss the way that the international context
shapes those communications as well as the larger meanings, referred to as
the "meta-game," implied by the texts.[6]

Another issue concerns the relevance of social-psychological approaches
to and negotiation analyses of the Letters. For social psychologists, the most
interesting questions concern the factors that influence attitudes and behav-

ior in face-to-face interactions among individuals or small groups over time. Factors include structural aspects of groups, elements in the immediate situation, and demographic variables, such as gender. For negotiation analysts, the most interesting questions are those asked about factors that influence a process in which two or more negotiators, usually accountable to agencies or constituencies, exchange offers and make concessions or work together to find solutions to joint problems. Many of these questions are difficult to answer with the information provided by the Letters, reducing the relevance of many of the findings in these fields. However, some research is pertinent, and these topics are identified following a description of the situation that existed. The description makes it possible to set bounds on the analysis by bringing proper analytical perspectives to bear on the diplomatic exchanges.

The Situation

Based on a selective reading of the Letters and some interpretive articles, we conclude that these kingdoms played a competitive game for status conferred by the kinds of exchanges made and the wealth accumulated and displayed. It seems clear that the kingdoms were not a "brotherhood" in the sense of a communal system in which each king acted to secure the welfare and security of the other kingdoms.[7] Rather, they operated as if they held views on IR consonant with a Realpolitik framework. This conclusion derives from the following observations.

First, the kings functioned largely as unitary actors. They were not elected from below but selected from above, by the gods. Although they depended in part on the support of certain elites in their countries, they appeared to have considerable latitude in negotiations with other kings. Second, the international negotiations consisted of exchanges of material items (gold, horses, brides) in which attempts were made to enhance one's own benefits *relative* to gains made by the other parties. Such relative-gain motivation is emphasized by Realist perspectives on IR.[8] Third, as negotiators, the kings frequently insisted on *reciprocal* exchanges but seemed mostly concerned with the symbolic implications of these exchanges for their status or prestige. The instrumental value of the exchanges was evident even in the occasional use of such ingratiating communications as the repetitious salutations that appear at the beginning of letters. We note, especially in the Babylonian correspondence, a softening of positions and even unilateral concessions (see, for example, EA 3, 4, 7, 9). These moves, we would contend, were not demonstrations of concern for Pharaoh's welfare but were tactics employed to encourage reciprocation of the favor in order not to jeopardize the (Babylonian) king's regional status. And, fourth, there appears to be a status differentiation be-tween Egypt and the other kingdoms.

These features served to perpetuate or reinforce conflictual relations among the kingdoms, making it difficult, if not impossible, for them to de-velop norms, regimes, and institutions that would ensure long-term coopera-tion. By constantly jockeying for advantage, the kings avoided confronting the larger issues (values, relationships) that could have altered the norma-tive climate in the direction of cooperation and community. By insisting on a rather strict reciprocity, they were subject to partisan biases that would, more often than not, lead to exchanges judged to be unfair. By being overly strategic, resolving conflicts of interest in favor of the more powerful party, they precluded the possibility of integrative or optimal solutions to their problems. And by managing the impressions they projected, the kings risked being viewed, at best, as appropriately tactical or, at worst, as manipulative or devious. Each of these points is elaborated further below.

Interests and Values

Maneuvering for competitive advantage, the kings focused on trading items that had "market value." Acting strategically, they were aware of the con-nection between a shifting balance of power and the relative value of the exchanges arranged through negotiations. A similar process is observed in modern arms-control negotiations, where an urge for symmetry makes "states hypersensitive to newly perceived inadequacies (which they) tend to correct by leveling up to parity in a variety of force categories."[9] Like arms-control negotiators concerned about the size of their arsenals, they bargained over such narrowly defined interests as their stocks of gold, horses, and other material objects.

Trading relationships such as these typically focus on objects that have a known trade or monetary value, over which a bargain can be readily struck. Indeed, the notion of "fractionating" issues by reducing their size or their nonmeasurable properties has been proposed as a tactic for getting agree-ments; the evidence suggests that agreements do occur on "smaller" points.[10] The agreements are, however, limited and are usually achieved at the cost of ignoring larger value-laden issues that may also divide the parties.

The only apparent reference to common values in the Letters is made when the kings acknowledge their ancestral ties and shared aims. The issues over-whelmingly concern distributive matters.[11] There is virtually no discussion of preferred political or economic systems, nor did the kings address issues con-cerning the design of international institutions or regimes. By ignoring these issues, the kings avoided confronting organizational matters other than security alliances. One consequence of this emphasis was to preserve the existing competitive system, ruling out the benefits of cooperation that occur in communal systems.[12]

Reciprocity and Equivalence

In trading relationships, the parties must gauge the equivalent values of commodities. Some sense of the difficulties involved in assessing equivalence is evident in the Letters, where few deals are closed. (Exceptions are EA 19 and 32.) The problem evident in most of the messages was agreeing on a fair exchange: The players regularly insisted on reciprocal deals, frequently made conditional offers, and often complained about unfair proposals. The absence of Pharaohs' replies complicates the analysis. We can only surmise that had they reached agreement on equivalence, a deal would have followed. Why, then, was it so difficult for these kings to agree on the terms of trade?

Several reasons may be suggested. First, since perceived status was always at issue, the kings were highly sensitive to any deal that might have reduced their status. Second, the kings were subject to the well-known tendency to judge their own offers as being more valuable than the counteroffers made by others; such partisan biases have been found to be very prevalent in bargaining relationships.[13] And, third, it was unclear which of the many forms of reciprocity was to serve as a trading standard — whether strict equality, equity, compensation, or compound justice. Although these distinctions refer to final outcomes, the question of fairness arises also with regard to the negotiation process or its procedures. Yet this was largely ignored in the Letters.[14] The kings' insistence on the need for reciprocal trades has implications for the "relationship meta-game,"[15] for example, when Kadashman-Enlil offered his daughter on condition that Pharaoh send gifts and not detain the Babylonian delegation (EA 3). These kinds of contingent offers have been shown to contribute to a deterioration rather than an improvement in relationships. They do so by raising questions of equivalence: Is the other's response to my offer an equivalent concession? What is an equivalent response to the other's initiative? When, however, Kadashman-Enlil also invited Pharaoh to a festival, despite having been snubbed by him earlier, he made an unconditional offer that, if not viewed as being tactical — as an attempt to "sweeten the pie" — avoided the issue of equivalence, thereby contributing to an improved relationship.

There may have been other problems as well. The protracted delays in responding through messengers (note here the two-year detention of messengers in EA 7) complicate the task of gauging the appropriate response to the original initiative. Negotiators have been shown to monitor the recent moves of contestants, paying much less attention to moves taken over longer periods: Their own concessions are responses to the relative size of the concessions made in the previous round.[16] Furthermore, the climate of mistrust, made evident by the large number of threats and accusations, makes it likely that any attempt to reciprocate will be misinterpreted. Suspicions about Pharaoh's motives may have led to a denial that they constituted a fair counteroffer to the other king's proposal.

Interpretations of reciprocity are complicated further by the competitive game being played. The players could be construed as tacticians who calculate the consequences of their moves or choices. These consequences are the result of the combined choices of the players, where the best outcome for one may be the worst for the other. In this game, each player searches for his best outcome, which may be neither mutually beneficial nor optimal. Such a dilemma is illuminated in the next section.

In the analysis to follow, we reason backward from known outcomes described in the Letters to the processes leading to those outcomes. The analysis is construed as a thought experiment in the form of an "if-then" simulation of a possible path that would have led to the decisions that were made. *If* we assume that the kings — referred to here as players — were acting strategically, *then* this is a plausible depiction of the processes; however, it may not have been the actual process, about which the Letters provide little information.

Four kinds of information would provide evidence for the postulated strategic calculations. First, it should be shown that the kings thought about these issues in dichotomous terms, as "either-or." Second, it should be clear from their statements that they ranked possible outcomes in the postulated order. Third, there should be indications that they were attentive to one another's preferences and choices. And fourth, it should be evident that the options exhaust the possible outcomes without recourse to side payments or deals made with other kings. Since the Letters are not clear on these points, we offer the game as a model of the processes leading to the outcome.

Strategic Choices

At stake in most of the transactions was relative status. This was a competitive game in which one player's status was gained at the expense of the other player(s). Thus, the players had conflicting interests, defined as different preferences for the distribution of status, a scarce resource. The conflict of interests could be resolved through a compromise whereby each player

Figure 14.1

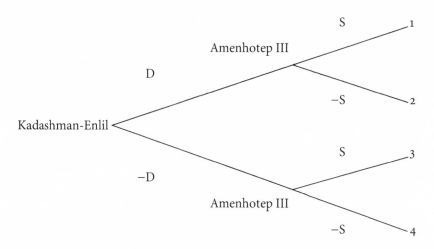

settled for less but neither settled for his worst outcome, in other words, a non-zero-sum game. When power is asymmetrical, however, it is likely that the less powerful player will settle for less than his more powerful opponent. This situation is illustrated by an analysis of the exchange described in EA 1. This is one of the few cases in which an actual interaction occurs between Pharaoh and another king.

The players in this game are Amenhotep III (called "Nibmuarea" in this letter) and Kadashman-Enlil. Both have two courses of action: Amenhotep III chooses between showing the Babylonian Princess (S) or an impostor (-S), and Kadashman-Enlil chooses between sending dignitaries (D) or not sending dignitaries (-D). Kadashman-Enlil chooses first. Observing his choice, namely, whether Babylonian dignitaries were sent to Pharaoh's court, Amenhotep III chooses between showing or not showing the Princess.

The four possible outcomes of this interaction are shown in Figure 14.1. The Princess is identified by the dignitaries in outcome 1. In outcome 2, Amenhotep III is caught in a lie; while knowing that the dignitaries can identify the Princess, Pharaoh presents someone else to them. (Given this outcome, the game could take another twist were Kadashman-Enlil to respond to the detection by breaking off relations with Egypt.) Amenhotep III claimed the third outcome, namely, that he had no incentive to present someone other than the Princess: "But if your sister were dead, what reason would there be for one's concealing her death and presenting someone else?" (EA 1). He further says, "Did you, however, ever send here a dignitary of Yours truly, who knows your sister, who could speak with her and identify her? Suppose he spoke with her. The men whom you sent here are nobodies. . . . There has been no one among them who knows her, who was an intimate of your father, and who could identify her" (EA 1). Kadashman-Enlil claimed the fourth outcome by accusing Pharaoh of not showing his sister to his low-ranking messengers.

Amenhotep III's insistence that he "has no reason whatsoever to show someone else" suggests that he had a dominant choice—to show the Princess to any messengers sent by Kadashman-Enlil. If we take him at his word, we can assume that he valued outcomes 1 and 3 more than 2 and 4. Knowing this, Kadashman-Enlil could "prune the branches," leading to outcomes 2 and 4. Outcomes 1 and 3 in Figure 13.1 then become the possibilities. Choosing between these outcomes, we have reason to believe that Kadashman-Enlil preferred outcome 3.

The first outcome does not serve Kadashman-Enlil's objective of denying Pharaoh his daughter. He complains in EA 2 that Pharaoh would not send him an Egyptian princess. By using his sister's "disappearance" as a pretext, he refuses to send his own daughter to Pharaoh. Here he conditions his response on Pharaoh's willingness to send him a daughter. In this game, with complete information, Pharaoh knew Kadashman-Enlil's objectives. Realizing that Pharaoh knows that he—Kadashman-Enlil—knows his preferences, he should have understood that his insistence on outcome 4 (the Princess is not shown and dignitaries are not sent) would not have helped him to deny a daughter to Pharaoh. Thus, by reasoning back in this way, we can understand why outcome 3 was inevitable.

This was an easy solution to discover. One player had dominant choices (outcomes 1 or 3) and the other, moving first, had to decide on his best reply in the light of those choices. We assumed that Amenhotep III was informed of the messengers' rank prior to making his choice of showing or not showing the Princess. Now, let us relax that assumption. Suppose that Pharaoh decided to reveal the Princess without knowing which messengers were sent by the Babylonian king. Here each player moves without knowing each other's prior choices. Such interactions involving imperfect information are analyzed by games in "strategic form": each player devises his strategy before knowing what the other will do.

Analysis in Strategic Form

The players, their alternative choices, and the possible outcomes can be depicted as shown in Figure 14.2.

Figure 14.2

		Kadashman-Enlil	
		Send Dignitaries	*Not Send Dignitaries*
Amenhotep III	*Show Princess*	Outcome 1	Outcome 3
	Not Show Princess	Outcome 2	Outcome 4

Preferring outcome 1, Amenhotep III realizes that when the Princess is correctly identified, Kadashman-Enlil can no longer deny him a daughter. Although the Princess cannot be accurately identified by the messengers in outcome 3, they can report to Kadashman-Enlil that Pharaoh attempted to show someone. There is, then, a probability that the one presented is indeed the Princess. Kadashman-Enlil takes advantage of this situation by insisting that the one presented is, in fact, not the Princess. Outcomes 2 and 4 are of lesser value for Amenhotep III. Since no one is presented to the Babylonian messengers in outcome 4, this gives Kadashman-Enlil a stronger hand (than in outcome 3). Outcome 2 is particularly undesirable since Pharaoh is caught cheating. Thus, Amenhotep III's preference ordering is $1 > 3 > 4 > 2$.

Preferring outcome 2, Kadashman-Enlil realizes that he would gain bargaining power if Pharaoh is caught in a lie. Although Pharaoh's cheating cannot be detected in outcome 4, the fact that the Princess (or a surrogate) was not shown also serves the Babylonian king's interests. Still less preferred is outcome 3, whereby Pharaoh shows the Princess whose identity cannot be verified. Least preferred is outcome 1: The Princess is identified, and the Babylonian king loses leverage in the bargaining for his daughter's hand. Thus, Kadashman-Enlil's preference ordering is $2 > 4 > 3 > 1$. This is a reversal of Amenhotep III's preferences, resulting in a pure conflict of interest between the players.

We can now construct a game matrix (see Fig. 14.3). The first and second entries are Amenhotep III's and Kadashman-Enlil's ranking of the outcome, respectively. For example, by showing the Princess, Pharaoh obtains either his best outcome (4), if Kadashman-Enlil sends dignitaries, or his second-best outcome (3), if the Babylonian king sends low-ranking envoys. By not sending dignitaries, Kadashman-Enlil obtains either his second-best outcome (3),

Figure 14.3

	Kadashman-Enlil	
	Send Dignitaries	*Not Send Dignitaries*
Show Princess	$(4, 1)^*$	$(3, 2)$
Not Show Princess	$(1, 4)$	$(2, 3)$

Amenhotep III

*The higher the ranking, the more favorable the outcome.

if Pharaoh does not show the Princess, or his third-best outcome (2), if Pharaoh shows the Princess.

Amenhotep III's strategy of showing the Princess is dominant: he obtains either his best or second-best outcome. Had he decided to choose the dominated (inferior) strategy of not showing the Princess, he would have obtained either his worst or second-worst outcomes. Whether Kadashman-Enlil decides to send dignitaries or not, Amenhotep III comes out better by showing the Princess. Thus, Kadashman-Enlil must choose his best reply to Pharaoh's dominant strategy: since he can only obtain either his worst or next-to-worst outcomes, he chooses the latter, that is, not to send dignitaries.

The third outcome is thus the equilibrium solution to this game. By equilibrium solution, we mean the outcome that neither party expects to improve on, given what each knows about the likely choices of the other player. When interests conflict, as they do in this case, the equilibrium outcomes are not the same as the parties' optimal outcomes (outcome 1 for Amenhotep III, and 2 for Kadashman-Enlil). Knowing that the second row of the game matrix is eliminated, Kadashman-Enlil chooses his preferred strategy of not sending dignitaries. By so doing, he forces Amenhotep III to settle for his second-best outcome (3). In a sense, Kadashman-Enlil's choice becomes obvious once it is realized that Pharaoh has no incentive to present anyone other than the Princess. Then, knowing that Kadashman-Enlil was going to send low-ranking messengers, Amenhotep III was not surprised to see them at his court. He was entertained by declaring in EA 1, "Here is your mistress who stands before you."

The game analysis illuminates a relationship between the structure of an interactive situation and the choices made by the contestants.[17] In the situation described in EA 1, players of unequal power had conflicting interests indicated by their different preferred outcomes. The choices made in this situation produced a nonoptimal compromise that favored the more powerful player (Pharaoh).

Managing Impressions

An analysis of options does not include the attempts made by players to influence one another's choices or to persuade the others to make advantageous decisions. By focusing only on strategy, an analyst ignores the way players communicate their intentions and the impact of those communications on the others' choices. Influence tactics used by the kings are revealed, at least to some extent, by the Letters. It would, therefore, be useful to examine them for insights into the way that impressions were managed.

By impression management, we refer to communications intended to influence another's perceptions, evaluations, or decisions.[18] Although a wide variety of tactics have been discussed in the literature, we can divide them into those that reward others for behaving in desired ways and those that punish them for behaving in undesired ways. Reward tactics include such attraction-seeking communications as ingratiation (compliments, flattery, esteem-enhancement) and agreeing with the other's opinions, as well as making promises about positive consequences for taking desired actions and reciprocating or making unilateral concessions. Coercive tactics include issuing threats or warnings, making commitments that prevent the other from achieving his or her goals, and depriving the other from receiving benefits, as when requests are ignored or concessions are not reciprocated. Many of these tactics are used in exchange transactions, referred to in this context as the "issue subgames," as well as in the psychological status/recognition games referred to as the "meta-game."[19] We use these terms as interpretive concepts in examining the Letters, focusing especially on EA 1–41.

Whether one kind of influence tactic is more or less effective than another depends on the structure of the situation in which they are used. The dependency context in which the kings interacted—each depended on Pharaoh (and each other) for recognition—may have led them to employ certain approaches. When one party is dependent on the other, *and both know it*, an effective strategy is to mix agreements with disagreements (rather than to agree consistently) in order to avoid appearing manipulative.[20] This seems to have been the approach used by many of the kings. They were cautious to convey the impression that nonreciprocated exchanges would be unac-

ceptable, nor were they eager to convey the impression of being overly ingratiating or obedient. (These types of communications were rare.) However,
there were also differences among the kings in their emphasis on rewards or
punishments.

Despite his frequent complaints and occasional threats (e.g., EA 8), the
Babylonian king conceded often (EA 3, 4, 7) and offered compliments that
can be interpreted as ingratiation (EA 9, 11). In EA 16, the Assyrian king asserted demands for equal or better treatment to that given to the Mittanians.
The Mittanian king used various tactics. In an act of apparent desperation,
he settled for less (EA 19) but then expressed dissatisfaction with the deal
(EA 20). Of particular interest was his attempt to use a "go-between" (the
Egyptian Queen Mother) to influence Pharaoh (EA 26), while conveying a
compellent threat in EA 27 (urging Pharaoh to act). He also resorted to
shaming by unfavorably comparing recent Egyptian actions to those taken
by Pharaoh's ancestors (EA 28). He then softened his approach by issuing
promises. When this did not work, he saved face by blaming Pharaoh for his
troubles (EA 29).

Reacting to a common enemy, Hatti, Pharaoh struck a rare deal with the
king of Arzawa (EA 31, 32). A very different approach was used by the king of
Alashiya. His nonthreatening appeals for equal exchanges (EA 33), unilateral
concessions (EA 34, 35, 37), and compliance with Egyptian views (EA 38)
left him open to being exploited. This king presented himself as a dependent
player who hoped that his cooperation would be rewarded by Pharaoh.[21] In
contrast, Suppiluliuma, the Hittite king, conjures up images of sibling rivalry
in EA 41 when he asserted his claim that he was in a stronger bargaining position than Tushratta, the Mittanian king. These tactics are similar to
those used in modern international negotiation, especially during the Cold
War. Various studies have documented the frequent use of coercive strategies and tough rhetoric by negotiators in both inter- and intrabloc talks.[22]
Like these modern negotiators, the kings alternated between hard and soft
communications, occasionally even ratcheting up the level of demands and
threats when earlier attempts at being cooperative "fell on deaf ears." (Note,
in this regard, the Babylonian king's escalating sequence, going from rewards
to issuing warnings about an Egyptian loss of reputation, appealing to guilt,
then threatening to call off giving his daughter in marriage as well as with-
holding his own gifts if none were received from Pharaoh [EA 1–11].)

Although distributive issues remain on the contemporary international
agenda, a good deal of activity has shifted toward shared goals, problem
solving, and cooperative relationships. This theme has gained momentum
in post–Cold War theorizing, largely as a reaction to Realist approaches.[23]

It emphasizes attitudes toward conflict that were absent during the Amarna period: namely, that many disputes are based on misperceptions and misunderstandings rather than conflicting interests, that quick fixes are less important than enduring resolutions, and that integrative solutions—outcomes that are best for all parties—can be found. The conditions for effective problem-solving include showing a concern for the other's payoffs as well as one's own, exchanging information about real priorities and needs, and being willing to put in some hard thinking in order to identify integrative outcomes.[24] Despite the frequent references to brotherhood and family, the kings showed no inclination toward this kind of problem-solving. Nor did they seem eager to consider issues with broad (regionwide) substantive implications. Indeed, it has been argued that international negotiators have only began to consider the cognitive sources of conflict—as opposed to interests—over the past thirty years.[25]

Effective problem solving depends also on the way negotiators view one another. Modern conflict theorists emphasize the importance of images in negotiation and strategic thinking. Complex images of other nations facilitate the search for integrative solutions; relatively simplistic images accompany the sorts of competitive tactics used by the kings. However, we can only speculate about what the kings thought about Pharaohs and how the Egyptian kings viewed the others. Could a "superior" Egypt have viewed the other kingdoms as being comparable to them in strength yet culturally inferior, leading Pharaohs to consider those kingdoms fair prey? This attitude enables a nation to rationalize aggressive postures or to take aggressive actions against the "inferior outgroups."[26] The Letters suggest that Egypt had a sense of superiority to the surrounding peoples and was mostly indifferent to communications from them but not aggressively imperialistic. Could the "inferior" kingdoms have viewed the Egyptians as being superior in military and economic capabilities but not superior in culture? This view leads a nation to view the hegemon as being dangerous, serving to temper hasty aggressive actions.[27] The Letters suggest that most kings were cautious in dealing with Pharaohs, preferring the softer reward tactics over the harder coercive approaches. (The strong postures taken by the Assyrians were an exception.) However, as discussed above, these tactics were instrumental, serving to further selfish or national interests. This posture is consistent with the Realpolitik orientation that guided the kings' behavior.[28]

Conclusions

The perspective taken in this paper suggests that the kings were engaged in a competitive game for status. By jockeying for competitive advantage, they avoided confronting the larger substantive issues that had ramifications for the broader regional system. By insisting on reciprocity, they were often unable to agree on a formula for exchange on which agreements could have been based. Although their tactical communications were intended to persuade Pharaohs to compromise or concede, their disadvantaged power position would lead (at best) to nonoptimal equilibrium solutions that favored Pharaoh. But few deals were made, and those that did occur resulted from concessions made by the kings in desperation or to preserve an alliance that bolstered security in the face of a common enemy.

These interpretations are based solely on available communications. They are not the result of applying systematic methodologies such as content analysis. Unavoidably, it is difficult to decide whether they reflect our own bias rather than the views of the kings themselves.[29] This discussion does, however, have the advantage of stimulating a debate among scholars from different disciplinary backgrounds. Although the varied interpretations are unlikely to converge on "the truth," they can be regarded as equally plausible ways of conceiving of relations during the Amarna period.

With regard to our own interpretation, we welcome challenges to the Realpolitik framework from which we believe the kings were operating. In particular, other analyses and other information may reveal more about the perceptions that are hidden from our view. They may provide "missing" information that would, for example, suggest a willingness by the kings to engage in the sort of problem-solving processes that would enable them to make the transition from an exchange to a communal regional system.

In an effort to broaden our analysis, it would be advantageous to learn more about several aspects of the communications and about other interactions that probably took place. First, it would be useful to have more information about the Pharaohs' initiatives and responses to offers made by the kings. Second, a better rendering of the chronological flow of the communications would clarify the response-counterresponse sequence. Third, ruminations by the kings in the form of thinking out loud would have provided a window on their images of the other nations. Fourth, messages among other kings would have illuminated further their relationships in the context of a dominant power. Fifth, missing are the internal communications that took place between the kings and their advisers or constituents; these could have provided insights into the way strategies were developed and images formed. And, sixth, we would have benefited from more information about the messengers' interactions with their kings as well as with the targets of their messages; some evidence suggests that they performed numerous critical functions in their boundary roles, including acting as interpreters.[30] These "data" would broaden the framework that guides a social-psychological analysis of the diplomatic interactions.

PART V

Diplomacy

CHAPTER FIFTEEN

Diplomatic Signaling in the Amarna Letters

CHRISTER JÖNSSON

Communication is the essence of diplomacy. The contemporary diplomatic system may be described as a universal communications network in which the exchange of signals is a professional preoccupation.

All acts, verbal or nonverbal, intentional or unintentional, are potential signals that feed into the network and are liable to reach all listeners and be read by them for the messages that they convey. Moreover, any message may be read together with and understood in the light of the collective body of evidence already communicated or later to be communicated.[1]

Diplomatic signaling typically aims at persuasion; that is, communication is designed to influence others by modifying their behavior or beliefs and attitudes.[2] Attempts at mutual persuasion are of the essence. In other words, bargaining and negotiation processes are at the heart of diplomacy.[3] In effect, diplomacy can be defined as "the conduct of international relations by negotiation rather than by force, propaganda, or recourse to law, and by other peaceful means (such as gathering information or engendering goodwill) which are either directly or indirectly designed to promote negotiation."[4]

Diplomatic negotiations are generally seen as the only alternative to warfare in resolving conflicts among autonomous states.[5] Other forms of collective decision making, such as voting or adjudication, violate the principle of sovereignty. Only through bargaining processes, whereby sovereign states are left to themselves to sort out their differences, can the states come to a common decision.

In these bargaining processes, signaling may be either verbal or nonverbal. For states, as well as individuals, "body language" complements and adds to verbal communication. In fact, both behavior and nonbehavior may constitute messages. "Activity or inactivity, words or silence, all have message value: they influence others and these others, in turn, cannot *not* respond to these communications and are thus themselves communicating."[6] This, in a nutshell, is a common way of looking at signaling and bargaining in contemporary diplomacy.

To what extent is the contemporary perspective on diplomatic communication applicable to the Amarna Letters? In other words, what are the timeless, and what are the transient aspects of diplomatic signaling? In addressing these questions, I first consider the diplomatic codes and conventions that render meaning to the exchange of signals and then identify similarities and differences in communication techniques.

Diplomatic Codes and Conventions

The very word "communication" stems from the Latin verb *communicare,* "to make common or shared." It reminds us that what is made known in any social communication is contingent on some kind of "architecture of intersubjectivity."[7] The meaning of a signal, in short, is not fixed and objectively given but rests on social convention. Semioticians argue that successful communication presupposes a common *code,* which is part of the (often unconscious) preknowledge necessary for understanding a message. A common code establishes what German hermeneutic philosophers call *Interpretationsgemeinschaft,* or initial commonality with respect to interpretation.[8]

Modern diplomacy rests on a code and conventions shared by members of the profession. Diplomacy can thus be seen as "the construction of an intersubjective reality."[9] While facilitating communication across cultures, diplomatic codes and conventions render communication between professionals and nonprofessionals more difficult. In addition, codes and conventions differ over time. All this calls for humility in any effort at uncovering the codes and conventions of Amarna diplomacy. Yet some elements of the intersubjective architecture of the Amarna Letters seem fairly obvious even to modern-day readers. As in today's diplomatic world, the Amarna exchanges appear to have been governed by protocol and diplomatic etiquette. I shall limit myself to a discussion of three components of the underlying code—the use of ritualized language and symbols, the quest for recognition, and concern with reciprocity—and how these could be used to convey signals that are not immediately and superficially evident.

Ritualized Language and Symbols

The backbone of modern diplomacy is a carefully deliberated diplomatic language with courteous, nondramatic, and sometimes ritualistic phrases. The American writer Caskie Stinnett has characterized a diplomat as "a person who can tell you to go to hell in such a way that you actually look forward to the trip." And when a diplomatic communiqué speaks of "frank" exchanges, we know that a row has taken place. Circumlocution, such as understatements and code phrases, permits controversial things to be said in a way understood in the diplomatic community but without needless provocation.[10]

Similarly, the language of the Amarna Letters is ritualized, replete with courtesies and other set phrases, suggesting a honed and well-established diplomatic code. The greeting phrases are highly standardized, and deviations from the established practice are noted. When a new monarch succeeds to the throne there are pledges of, or demands for, "ten times more love" than for the predecessor (e.g., EA 19, 26, 27, 29). For a *demandeur*, who wants to deflate the size of requested concessions from the more powerful Egypt, it is commonplace to use the phrase "gold is as plentiful as dirt" in Egypt (e.g., EA 20, 26, 29).

In the same vein, one might infer that the recurrent references to brotherhood and family are part of a ritualized diplomatic language rather than a constitutive paradigm, in the same way as today's diplomats may allude to "the family of nations" on ceremonial occasions.[11] As is argued by Avruch in this volume, the family metaphor derives its strength from its ontological and existential basis in human experience. And as is pointed out by students of contemporary Arab culture, references to brotherhood remain common in modern political language.

However refined, verbal language cannot convey all the nuances of diplomatic signaling. There are several aspects of international relations that require symbolic representation. Therefore, symbols have always played a prominent role in diplomatic exchanges. Expressions of *status* and *power* have traditionally been symbolic. Thus, the Peace of Westphalia of 1648 was delayed for half a year because of a dispute concerning the order in which delegates were to enter and be seated at the table; similar problems of relative status at the Potsdam meeting in 1945 were solved by having Churchill, Stalin, and Truman enter the signing ceremony simultaneously through three different doors; and the Paris talks seeking an end to the Vietnam War in 1968 were long stalled because of an argument about the shape of the negotiating table that revolved around the status of the South Vietnamese Liberation Front (Vietcong).

In this respect, little has changed since the days of the Amarna Letters. As discussed above, greeting phrases and gifts are generally understood as symbols of status and power. To be addressed as "brother" is a symbol of being accepted into the club of Great Powers.

Expressions of friendly or hostile *relations* between states are equally symbolic. In the current diplomatic system, for example, a handshake is an accepted visual sign of friendly relations. The Rabin-Arafat handshake is but one of the latest in a long history of graphic conciliatory symbols. The exchange of gifts appears to have been the Amarna counterpart of today's handshake as a symbol of good relations. And in the same way as a refusal to shake hands is today taken as an indication of hostility, the absence of gifts or the delivery of inferior gifts were seen as signs of deteriorating relations in the ancient Near East. Amenhotep III's dispatch of gold (objects) that turned out not to be of the expected quality was seen by Tushratta to signify souring relations; no longer was he able to tell others that "my brother, the king of Egypt, loves me very, very much" (EA 20:46–59). And Akhenaten's refusal to honor his father's promise to deliver statues of solid gold symbolized a further deterioration: "Is this love? I had said, 'Naphurreya, my brother, is going to treat me 10 times better than his father did.' But now he has not given me even what his father was accustomed to give" (EA 26:30–48).

In sum, the diplomatic dialogues described in the Amarna Letters obviously rested on ritualized language and symbolic expressions that were well understood by all the participants and thus formed part of a shared diplomatic code.

Recognition and Status

The desire for recognition by others is a basic human need, central to our sense of who and what we are. Social and organizational selection occurs largely by mutual empowerment. Actors create their own environment by preferring and tolerating only certain types of actors and organizations. Today, recognition is an essential aspect of sovereign statehood. The state needs external authorization to be the ultimate claimant within its territory; this is not an attribute of the state but is attributed to the state by other state rulers. To be granted or denied statehood is central to participation in contemporary international relations.

Beyond acknowledged statehood, international recognition concerns status. The conception a state has of its own role in the world accounts for little, unless it is matched by similar role expectations by other states. For instance, a central theme in Soviet foreign policy from the late 1950s was the quest for recognition of Soviet superpower status, especially by the rival superpower, the United States.[12] In the same vein, Russia today covets a seat on the G-7 as a recognition of its continuing Great Power status. In neither case are the desires for recognition necessarily granted by the relevant others.

Similarly, the diplomatic correspondence in the Amarna Letters reflects a keen and jealous preoccupation with recognition and status. In Cohen's words, "The most crucial game of all concerned acceptance and recognition as a Great King, as this was the condition of diplomatic and strategic activity."[13] As already alluded to, recognition and nonrecognition usually found symbolic expression.

Thus, the king of Assyria, reminding the king of Egypt how much gold his predecessor had sent to the Egyptian king's father, points out that "now I am the equal of the king of Hanigalbat." By linking this with a complaint about the amount of gold the king of Egypt has sent him — "not enough for the pay of my messengers on the journey to and back" — he implies that his proper status has not been recognized (EA 16). Similarly, when Amenhotep III's gifts to Tushratta proved not to be solid gold, this was a blow to the latter's status and prestige, aggravated by the fact that the gifts were delivered in the presence of foreign guests who realized that no one would give such humiliating gifts to someone he "loves," that is, recognizes as equal (EA 20:46–59).

The address of the Amarna letters constituted another symbolic expression of status: only if the sender was superior or the equal of the addressee did he name himself first.[14] Deviations were noted and given sinister interpretations:

> And now, as to the tablet that you sent me, why did you put your name over my name? And who now is the one who upsets the good relations between us, and is such conduct the accepted practice? My brother, did you write to me with peace in mind? And if you are my brother, why have you exalted your name. . . ? (EA 42:15–26)

The language and symbols of the Amarna Letters may seem alien, but the diplomatic quest for recognition and status appears to be strikingly familiar. Decisive influence rests with a "club" of Great Powers with certain values in common but also mutual conflicts (a bargaining relationship, in short). The Great Powers guard against usurpers of power and are wary of admitting new members into the inner circle. Perhaps the nineteenth-century Concert of Europe or today's G-7 can be seen as distant parallels.

Reciprocity

Norms of reciprocity are today codified in current international law and are often invoked in international negotiations. Concessions are to be returned, and retractions to be retaliated. The distinction between *specific* and *diffuse* reciprocity is pertinent in this connection.[15] Specific reciprocity refers to "situations in which specified partners exchange items of equivalent value in a strictly delimited sequence," whereas in situations of diffuse reciprocity, "the definition of equivalence is less precise, one's partner may be viewed as a group rather than as particular actors, and the sequence of events is less narrowly bounded."[16]

Buyers and sellers of houses or cars practice specific reciprocity; families or groups of close friends rely on diffuse reciprocity.[17] The ideal of international cooperation ought to be diffuse reciprocity, where the participants do not insist on immediate and exactly equivalent reciprocation of each and every concession, on an appropriate "quid" for every "quo." However, in contemporary international relations "stable patterns of specific reciprocity are often the most one can expect," whereas "genuinely diffuse reciprocity is rare."[18] The kind of trust that binds families together is simply lacking in the relations between sovereign, egoistical states. What about diplomatic relations in the Amarna period? Does the frequent use of the family metaphor imply greater reliance on diffuse reciprocity and more widespread expressions of trust than is the case today?

The first observation one can make is that reciprocity definitely appears to have been a prominent norm in the Amarna diplomatic exchanges. There are many expressions of expected equivalence of behavior in bilateral relations, variations on the theme "do to me what I have done to you." For the most part, however, these expressions seem to reflect expectations of specific rather than diffuse reciprocity. This applies across a whole spectrum of issues, ranging from security matters to the exchange of gifts and other symbolic measures.

Thus, the mutual defense pact, referred to by the Mittanian king Tushratta in his letter to the Egyptian pharaoh Nimmureya, was obviously based on specific reciprocity:

> If only an enemy of my brother did not exist! But should in the future an enemy invade my brother's land, then my brother writes to me, and the Hurrian land, armor, arms, . . . and everything concerning the enemy of my brother will be at his disposition. But should, on the other hand, there be for me an enemy—if only he did not exist!—I will

write to my brother, and my brother will dispatch to the land of Egypt, armor, arms, . . . and everything concerning my enemy. (EA 24:III 110–18 = sec. 26)

Specific reciprocity also seems to have governed the exchanges of gifts. "My gift does not amount to what I have given you every year," complains the Babylonian king to the Egyptian Pharaoh (EA 3:13–22). Tushratta voices similar complaints about his gifts: "In comparison with mine they are not equivalent"; moreover, "my brother has not given to me the equivalent of what he dispatched to my father" (EA 24:III 68–70 = sec. 25). The treatment of messengers is another aspect of relations in which specific reciprocity was expected. Tushratta repeatedly tells the Egyptian Pharaoh that he will detain Pharaoh's messenger, "until my brother lets my messengers go and they come to me" (EA 28). "As soon as he lets my messengers go, . . . and present their report to me, I will let Mane go and I will send Keliya back to my brother as before" (EA 29:148–54). In short, behind the professed brotherly love, one can discern a preference for hard-nosed tit-for-tat strategies.

Only when one party makes a bid for friendly relations do vague offers of diffuse reciprocity appear: "Write me for what you want from my country so that it may be taken to you, and I will write you for what I want from your country so that it may be taken to me," the king of Babylonia proposes to Pharaoh (EA 6:13–17). And when Tushratta wants to forge friendly relations with Akhenaten, the son and successor of the recently deceased Amenhotep III, he points out that his relations with Akhenaten's father had rested on diffuse reciprocity. Whereas in earlier generations, daughters had not been given in marriage until after prolonged haggling, Tushratta had given his daughter to Amenhotep III immediately without asking anything in return, and the bride price paid by Amenhotep III had been "beyond measure" (EA 29:16–27). Once friendly relations were established, however, specific reciprocity seems to have reigned. Thus, contrary to the idealized picture given to Akhenaten, Tushratta in his correspondence with Amenhotep III had in fact complained about the lack of specific reciprocity (EA 24).

Conventions and Signaling

Only if the underlying conventions of recognition and reciprocity are taken into account can otherwise puzzling dispatches be understood.[19] For instance, in EA 4, the Babylonian king recounts an incident that would seem to put him in an unfavorable light. His initial bid for Pharaoh's daughter had been refused with reference to a marriage taboo—"From time immemorial no daughter of the king of Egypt is given to anyone." The Babylonian king had then requested the daughter of a commoner instead: "Someone's grown daughters, beautiful women, must be available. Send me a beautiful woman as if she were your daughter." Pharaoh again refused. Why should the Babylonian king recall a seemingly humiliating episode like this in his dispatch?

The key to a possible answer can be found in the latter part of the letter, where the Babylonian king offers his daughter to Pharaoh in marriage: "Should I, perhaps, since you did not send me a woman, refuse you a woman, just as you did to me, and not send her? But my daughters being available, I will not refuse one to you." He goes on to demand a heavy bride price in gold and set a deadline for payment. If the main purpose of the Babylonian king's letter was to bargain for the highest possible bride price in return for his daughter, the references to Pharaoh's dual snubs make sense. The king probably knew that his request for Pharaoh's daughter would be refused. And the following offer of a ruse might have been a tactic to expose Pharaoh's hypocrisy — the second refusal to provide a bride could not be accounted for by religious or traditional taboos — and gain the moral upper hand. The Babylonian king, in short, made cunning use of the convention of strict reciprocity between Great Kings. By reminding Pharaoh of his failure to maintain the customary reciprocity, he hoped to increase the compensation for offering his daughter in marriage.

In EA 7, the Babylonian king also makes tactical use of prevailing conventions. He starts by recording his anger at receiving no "get well" message from Pharaoh when he was ill, as the convention of recognition required. An Egyptian messenger ostensibly managed to appease him by referring to the great distance between the countries. Why did the king bother to relate this non-incident to Pharaoh in terms that made the king look foolish and ignorant? The king was hardly unaware of the distance between Egypt and Babylonia, for envoys had been exchanged between the two courts for many years.

If the king's proclaimed ignorance is merely a sham, and he knows that Pharaoh knows it is a sham, the account has a tactical purpose that becomes clear in the latter part of the letter. The king takes the distance and the difficulty of the journey as a pretext for sending smaller gifts: "Furthermore, as I am also told, the journey is difficult, water cut off, and the weather hot. I am not sending many beautiful greeting-gifts." The excuse is again a sham that ought to be obvious to Pharaoh. The hidden message seems to be that the Babylonian king was discontented with the Egyptian Pharaoh and wished to express this symbolically by sending a smaller gift than usual. At the same time, he wished to avoid impressions of stinginess or poverty. The fiction of difficult conditions then came in handy. The Great King, however, wanted to avoid loss of face from showing weakness in the face of natural difficulties. The phrase "as I am also told" then becomes of key importance. The informant must be the Egyptian messenger, which means that the Egyptian side had already admitted to such weakness. The Babylonian king, in sum, made good use of the earlier incident in building up an argument in his own favor. By alluding to the conventions of symbolic expressions, recognition and reciprocity, he turned his seeming foibles into sources of strength, in a veritable diplomatic jujitsu.

Communication Techniques Then and Now: Similarities

As we have seen, there are parallels between ancient Near Eastern and modern diplomatic signaling in terms of its foundation in shared codes and conventions that lend nonobvious meanings to messages. In addition, several features of the Amarna Letters are reminiscent of modern diplomatic communication techniques. I dwell on four of these: the practice of incurring commitments, the use of precedents, the concern with credibility, and the role of messengers/diplomats.

Commitments

To persuade an opponent, spoken or written proposals and arguments may not be sufficient; accompanying measures that demonstrate seriousness and resolve may be needed. This is what Thomas Schelling, in his seminal analysis, calls "the art of commitment."[20] By means of commitments, actors underscore their current position by making it more difficult for them to yield. Thus, the art of commitment rests on "the power to bind oneself."[21]

Commitments may be either unconditional or conditional. Troops who "burn their bridges" behind them as they advance, display their determination to fight by physically excluding a retreat. Negotiators frequently try to convince their opponent that a binding public opinion at home renders a change in position impossible. In both instances, unconditional commitments are incurred. Conditional commitments, on the other hand, make one's course of action contingent on what the opponent does. Threats and promises are examples of such conditional commitment techniques that are considered useful in bargaining situations. Threats are dissuasion attempts, promises persuasion attempts. Whenever the alternatives are more than two, threats and promises are often used in combination.

The Amarna Letters indicate that the art of commitment is a timeless feature of international bargaining. The statesmen of the ancient Near East knew well that the spoken word had to be backed up by other gestures that made their bargaining position credible to the other side. The quality of gifts and the selection and treatment of messengers were used as commitment instruments. Also, the usefulness of combining threats and promises was well understood. In a difficult marriage negotiation, the Babylonian king used this technique in an exemplary way:

> If during this summer, in the months of Tammuz or Ab, you send the gold I wrote you about, I will give you my daughter. . . . But if in the months of Tammuz or Ab you do not send me the gold and with it I do not finish the work I am engaged on, what would be the point of your being pleased to send me gold? Once I have finished the work I am engaged on, what need will I have of gold? Then you could send me 3,000 talents of gold, and I would not accept it. I would send it back to you, and I would not give my daughter in marriage. (EA 4:49–50)

Tushratta employed a similar tactic when he tried to persuade Akhenaten to release detained messengers. Threatening to keep the Egyptian messengers as long as Akhenaten detained the Mittanian messengers, Tushratta added the promise that if Akhenaten released the messengers, he would not only reciprocate but also send a large mission to Egypt (EA 29:166–72).

Precedents

Related to the art of commitment is the practice of referring to precedents in diplomatic communication. "Precedent seems to exercise an influence that greatly exceeds its logical importance or legal force," Schelling notes.[22] Earlier behavior and relations are considered to commit the actors to similar behavior and relations in the future. There are two sides to this in international relations. On the one hand, states have to assess what kind of precedent a certain course of action may create. Thus, the domino theory, which guided U.S. foreign policy during the Cold War, precluded the abandonment or loss of any of its allies or clients for fear of the precedent and chain reaction it might create. On the other hand, states frequently try to convince their opponents in negotiations that they are bound by previous behavior, that they have committed themselves to a certain course of action.

There are several manifestations of the latter technique in the Amarna Letters, especially in connection with regime changes, when there is a felt need to remind the new king of the commitments his predecessor has ostensibly made. Thus, Tushratta, as we have seen, tried hard to convince Akhenaten that his father had made a commitment to deliver golden statues and that he was bound by the precedent of good Mittanian-Egyptian relations (esp. EA 29:50–54, 61–64). Similarly, the king of Hatti reproached the new Pharaoh: "Why, my brother, have you held back the presents that your father made to me when he was alive?" (EA 41:14–15). These and other statements invoke a tacit norm that commitments should be honored, *pacta sunt servanda,* which remains one of the foundations of modern diplomacy.

Credibility

To be persuasive, diplomatic signals need to be not only communicated but also deemed credible. The problem of credibility has received considerable attention in the bargaining literature. The manifest possibility of deception creates an intrinsically insoluble credibility dilemma.

Because signals derive their meanings from tacit or explicit agreements among the actors, an actor can lie as easily as he can tell the truth. A signal used to convey an accurate message can also convey a misleading one. It is logically impossible to design a signaling system that does not have this attribute.[23]

There are several indications that credibility was indeed a concern for ancient Near Eastern statesmen as well. In response to actual or imagined doubts about the credibility of his messages, Tushratta implores Amenhotep III not to trust other sources than the tablets and the messengers: "And an evil word that anyone may say about me or about my land, may my brother not hear those words if Mane and Keliya do not say them. But the words that Mane and Keliya say about me and my land, they are true and right, and may my brother hear them" (EA 24:IV 16–23). However, the word of a messenger might not always be enough; it had to be backed up by some sort of commitment:

> Behold, concerning the fact that Kalbaya has spoken this word to me, "Let us establish a blood-relationship," in this matter I do not trust Kalbaya. He has indeed spoken it as a word, but it was not confirmed on the tablet. (EA 32:4–6)

Credibility problems became acute for Tushratta, when Amenhotep III died before having delivered on his promise to send gold statues. He wrote to Tiye, Amenhotep III's widow, who was "the one . . . who knows much better than all others the things that we said to one another," and asked her to remind the new king Akhenaten of the commitment (EA 26). In addition,

Tushratta wrote to Akhenaten himself on several occasions and pleaded with him to listen to Tiye, his own mother (EA 27, 28, 29). At the same time, he referred to his own messengers as witnesses; they "saw with their own eyes" how "your father himself recast the statues in the presence of my messengers, and he made them entirely of pure gold" (EA 27:19-27). Yet, in the end, Tushratta's efforts to boost the credibility of his demand for the golden statues seem to have been in vain. At any rate, credibility appears to have been as much of a problem in the diplomatic signaling of the ancient Near East as it is today.

Messengers/Diplomats

Most international negotiations take place through representatives, agents who are authorized to represent their principals. As noted above, these agents — messengers in the ancient Near East, diplomats in the modern world — assume symbolic significance. The way the agents are treated reflects state relations. In his eagerness to forge friendly relations with Egypt, Tushratta points out that he has treated the Egyptian messengers "with great distinction," showing them "very great honors" and exalting them "like gods" (EA 20, 21). He also goes out of his way to praise the Egyptian messengers — "I have never seen men with such an appearance" (EA 21:24-32). He especially praises Mane: "There does not exist a man like him in all the world" (EA 24:II 95-96 = sec. 17).

In addition, principals can use agents either to facilitate or interrupt communication. The Amarna Letters repeatedly refer to the detainment of messengers for long periods. Today, ambassadors are called home for consultations. Both practices indicate an unwillingness to communicate with the other party.

The selection of messenger/diplomat can also have symbolic significance. For example, the selection of Averell Harriman to lead the U.S. negotiating team in the test-ban talks in Moscow in the summer of 1963 was one in a series of conciliatory signals on both sides. Harriman was well known to the Soviets and had become well acquainted with Khrushchev during the Soviet leader's visit to the United States in 1959. In the words of an official from the Soviet embassy in Washington, "As soon as I heard that Harriman was going, I knew that you were serious."[24] Similarly, Tushratta made it abundantly clear in his correspondence with Amenhotep III that the selection of messenger was of importance. In his opening bid for a renewed alliance, he sent no less a person than his chief minister, Keliya, as messenger (EA 17). Later, he made it clear that the Egyptian selection of messenger mattered to him as well:

And may my brother send Mane along, so he can leave together with my envoy! Any other envoy may my brother not send. May he send only Mane. If my brother does not send Mane and sends someone else, I do not want him, and my brother should know it. No! May my brother send Mane! (EA 24:IV 52–57 = sec. 31)

In another letter, the Egyptian Pharaoh complains to the Babylonian king who, instead of sending "dignitaries," had dispatched a delegation of "nobodies," one of whom was an "assherder" (EA 1). Again, it is obvious that the selection of envoys was a serious matter, as it remains today.

Negotiation Techniques Now and Then: Differences

It is not difficult for students of modern diplomatic signaling to identify "surprisingly familiar stuff" in the Amarna Letters.[25] But one should not underestimate the dissimilarities. Changes in communication technology have brought about significant changes in diplomatic signaling and negotiation. I will point to just two aspects of these changes.[26]

First, the speed of diplomatic communication has increased dramatically. In our century, first nuclear weapons and then the advent of electronic media have contributed to the accelerating speed of communication. Nuclear weapons added urgency to crisis management efforts; television introduced "real-time" coverage and a demand for immediate diplomatic reactions to unfolding events.

In the Amarna Letters, there is reference to a messenger being detained, and thus communication being interrupted, for six years (EA 3). Before the advent of telecommunications, the exchange of diplomatic messages could take weeks or months. Still, in 1962, during the Cuban missile crisis, it took four hours, with luck, for a formal message to pass between Washington and Moscow.[27] And whereas in 1961, President Kennedy could wait eight days before making a public policy statement on the erection of the Berlin Wall, President Bush was compelled to make a statement within hours of the dismantling of the wall in October 1989.[28]

The accelerating speed is not necessarily beneficial from the viewpoint of diplomatic signaling. As Hans Morgenthau noted before the communication revolution, "Diplomacy owes its rise in part to the absence of speedy communications in a period when the governments of the new territorial states maintained continuous political relations with each other. Diplomacy owes its decline in part to the development of speedy and regular communications."[29] Another student of the evolution of diplomacy argues that "as time replaces space as the significant mediation of diplomacy, crisis-management takes the place of reflective decision-making." [30]

Another important dimension of change in diplomatic communication concerns the ever-widening audience. The diplomatic tablets contained in the Amarna Letters were read by no one other than the intended addressees. In the seventeenth and eighteenth centuries, diplomats were still, by and large, members of an "aristocratic international" with a sophisticated communication system between themselves but little contact with other sections of society. The advent of electronic media in combination with the elevation of public opinion as a significant factor in foreign policy have made the differentiation among audiences more difficult. Diplomatic signals are intercepted and interpreted by a variety of audiences across and within states. The expansion of multilateral at the expense of bilateral diplomacy adds to this tendency.

This represents a problem for the finely calibrated signaling of classic diplomacy, which was characterized by constructive ambiguity to allow varying interpretations among strictly delimited audiences. There were obvious drawbacks to the exclusively bilateral communication system of the Amarna Letters, however. For one thing, the lack of a wider audience made it more difficult to incur commitments. For instance, Tushratta's problems in convincing Akhenaten that his father had indeed made a vow to send gold and establish good relations stemmed in part from the fact that "no one else" beside the Queen Mother, Tiye, knew about the commitment (EA 26, 27, 28). While making communication simpler in many respects, a strictly delimited audience at the same time narrows the register one can play upon in employing various commitment tactics.

In summary, modern-day diplomats would have recognized many of the basic communication and negotiation techniques had they been transferred in time to the era of the Amarna Letters. No doubt they would have missed many of the things that they have become used to in the wake of technological changes, such as speedy and reliable communication links, diplomatic immunity, and permanent embassies. But they would certainly find things to envy their ancient counterparts, such as the absence of obtrusive TV cameras and constant time pressures.

CHAPTER SIXTEEN

The Diplomatic Service in Action: The Mittani File

PINHAS ARTZI

Around 1415 B.C.E., Egypt and Mittani reached an understanding that divided the northwestern region of the Near East into spheres of influence. The principal reason for the understanding was a common aim — to repel Hittite expansion into Syria. This relationship, perhaps never enshrined in a formal treaty, led to the most intensive dynastic and state relations of the Amarna Age.

This intensity finds a supremely fitting expression in the style of the Mittani correspondence (EA 17–30). The aim of the style was to create the basis for indissoluble relations with Egypt, so as to ensure the survival of King Tushratta and of the state of Mittani itself.

The stylistic matrix of the Mittani correspondence is a richly elaborated variant of the international diplomatic "family language" used in the great majority of the Amarna Letters and concentrated in the opening address of the Letters: an exchange of greetings between brother kings and their families. The Mittanian version always adds greetings based on real family relations: to his daughter, the wife of the king of Egypt, "my son-in-law." But Tushratta actually goes far beyond that by introducing into his letters the all-pervasive elements of love and religion, as well as the concepts of union and mixing of the peoples of Egypt and Mittani. The considerable material expression of this envisaged unity — the course of negotiations over gifts and dowry — is so clear and well organized that even after the penetrating study of Kühne, the order of the Letters, EA 17–30, remains virtually unchanged from that of their first scientific edition.[1] We should not, however, be deceived by appearances; apart from the marriages themselves, the letters reveal a number of acute problems, in particular:

1. Tushratta's relentless efforts to ensure the stability of his shaky throne by a constant flow of gifts of gold extorted from Pharaoh, because it is vital to him to display to international and internal public opinion Pharaoh's personal esteem.[2]
2. Hidden efforts, formulated only in EA 24 (see below), to reach a mutual defense treaty against the Hittites.

All this intensive, sometimes highly emotional, and near-panicky activity is conducted through the excellent joint channel of the combined Egyptian-Mittanian diplomatic services, unparalleled in their efficiency. The Mittani correspondence represents a hard-pressed ruler of strong but at the same time emotional character, whose foreign policy is nonetheless coherent and always primed to provide the appropriate response. In this, he is ably assisted by the contemporary diplomats — of both sides, it must be emphasized. I propose to follow analytically the development of relations between Mittani and Egypt, with special attention to the diplomatic service.

Improving Relations

1. Mittani's diplomatic relations with Egypt had begun with Tushratta's grandfather, Artatama I (mentioned in EA 24: III 52 and EA 29:19). Relations were excellent under the latter's son, Shuttarna II, who gave his daughter Kelu-Hepa to Pharaoh in marriage. What happened after Shuttarna's reign is described in EA 17, in which Tushratta, in a personal-historical account, introduces himself and gives his credentials. Tushratta's older brother, King Artashumara, was murdered by a certain Uthi, who then ruled — illegally — as regent. (It is important to note that although Egypt did not intervene, it evidently suspended relations at this point.)[3] Tushratta now assures Amenhotep III that he has succeeded in freeing himself from Uthi, who did not allow Tushratta, a minor, to remain in contact with anyone who loved him. (This is the first appearance of the central motif of "love.") As proof of his awareness of Egypt's needs, he reports on a successful skirmish with the Hittites and sends samples of the booty.[4]

The letter concludes with an all-important entry — the revival of the diplomatic mission to Egypt, in a "credentials section" marked by the term "herewith" (in the phrase "I herewith send Keliya . . ."). Keliya will become a central figure, forming, with his Egyptian counterpart Mane, a diplomatic team. He is elevated to the rank of *sukkallu*, "minister" (= ambassador), while

Tunip-ibri, perhaps an interpreter, serves with him; this is the nucleus of the reestablished mission.

2. Evidence of the regularity of diplomatic relations between the two countries at this time is provided by EA 30, a diplomatic laissez-passer that served as a standard document of the Egyptian and Mittanian diplomatic services.[5] This small tablet is written according to an agreed procedure. The addressees, the "kings of Canaan," were, in their capacity as officials of the Egyptian administration, responsible for the safe transfer of the (on this particular occasion) "super-express" messenger. The messenger evidently carried several such documents with him, according to the zones or staging posts through which he passed on his way to Egypt. The "herewith" section of this tablet, in which his credentials are given, matches the "herewith" section of the letter that he is delivering, thus proving his identity and assuring his safe transfer into the hands of the Egyptian officials.

3. With EA 19 there begins a diplomatic waltz that continues down to EA 24. On the basis of long-standing mutual "love" (quoting from Pharaoh's letter), blessed by the gods Amun of Egypt and Teshup of Mittani, a request arrives from Egypt for a (further) marriage. Tushratta stresses his immediate consent (a standard motif of the letters) because he does not wish to cause distress (a further standard motif). He requests, however, much "raw" gold (which is "as plentiful as dirt" in Egypt)[6] for the promotion of his own dynastic status—the erection of a dynastic mausoleum—and for the most impressive bride price, vital for his personal standing.

EA 19 also marks the debut of the famous team Mane (Egypt) and Keliya (Mittani). Mane presents *orally* the marriage request of Pharaoh. Keliya *reads* (translates?) it to Tushratta and Tushratta, *hearing* it, is happy. Mane has already "viewed" the daughter and praised her profusely. The Akkadian verb for "praise" in this instance is that used of gods and goddesses.

In the "credentials" section, Tushratta sends back Keliya, characterizing his mission in a richly rhetorical sentence and returning again to the plea for the blessings of the highest national gods. The next stage would, of course, be to receive Pharaoh's answer to Tushratta's consent and requests.

4. The agenda for the agreed marriage is pursued in EA 20, which includes a dramatic interlude: an aptitude test of the Egyptian diplomatic service. Tushratta confirms the return of Mane, who has come to take the new bride back with him. Tushratta expects that his daughter will be the "Mistress of Egypt," an obviously exaggerated expectation or misformulation; Queen Tiye is the only "Mistress of Egypt" (cf. EA 26). Nonetheless, it fits the style, because, the union motif, another exaggerated declaration, follows: "On that day (i.e., of the wedding) shall Hanigalbat and Egypt be one."[7]

Evidently, Mane had brought with him the bride-price, or at least a part of it, but Tushratta argues that he is still not ready with the dowry and detains *both* ambassadors for six months (EA 20:18–22). At the same time, it is decided that both ambassadors will bring the new bride to Pharaoh.

The credentials section is important, because it shows the complete integration of the Egyptian and Mittanian diplomatic services (EA 20:33–38). Tushratta sends back Haaramashi, an Egyptian (express) messenger, with a letter—with the obvious aim of continuing the gift negotiations over the six-month interim period.

Once he has disposed of the current agenda, Tushratta returns to the subject of the gifts that have already arrived. Here a dramatically colored scene is staged, with the ultimate aim of showing Tushratta's brotherly understanding and restraint. Tushratta had convened all his foreign guests (ambassadors, according to Na'aman), together with the leadership of his state (i.e., public opinion) to observe the important occasion of unsealing a consignment of Egyptian gold. To his dismay, the gold turned out to be debased. However, the Egyptian delegation (Mane and his party) reacted correctly: they were also dismayed and wept; moreover, with eloquent rhetoric, they defended the good intentions of their Lord. Tushratta now expresses his complete satisfaction with Mane, honoring him and his "troops." The diplomatic test of the Egyptian envoy had been resolved to the Mittanian king's satisfaction.

5. The conclusion of the extremely complicated marriage/gift negotiations is recorded in EA 21, with the blessing of the (Hurrian) gods Shimige and Shaushka. The tangible results of those negotiations are presented in EA 22 and EA 25, which list not only the dowry sent by Tushratta on the occasion of giving his daughter in marriage to Amenhotep III but also personal gifts to Pharaoh, whom Tushratta refers to both as his brother and son-in-law. The Egyptian delegation of Mane and Hane, his interpreter, emerges from its mission (according to EA 21:24–31) covered in praise. Tushratta declares that he never saw men of such stature, blessing them by the gods of both sides. The diplomatic service—on both sides, in my view—excelled in the art of conciliation.

6. The marriage festivities were accompanied by many events, but perhaps the most important of them was the visit of the goddess Shaushka who, according to EA 23, expressed (mantically) her wish to visit her beloved Egypt and then return. With Moran, I consider that the purpose of the visit was not to heal the sick Egyptian king but to bless the marriage, as had been done earlier in the time of Shuttarna II (see EA 23:18–25). Moreover, there is a parallel gesture of piety by Pharaoh himself: in EA 24:I 83–108 (= sec. 9), Keliya reports that Amenhotep III sent a gift to Shimige, the Hurrian sun goddess.

The gift was sent from Ihibe, "the city of Shimige," but Ihibe is none other than Heliopolis (= biblical On, cf. Gen. 41:45), center of the cult of the *Egyptian* sun god. The letter ends with the invocation of a common prayer by the two kings to the goddess. Thus, we have here evidence of integration of national religions and a further step toward union.

7. The peak of Tushratta's efforts to seal an (indissoluble) union with the Egyptian dynasty and especially with Amenhotep III (and his queen, Tiye: see EA 26) is reached in EA 24, the "Mittani/Hurrian Letter." A diplomatic démarche was to be launched on the occasion of the wedding festivities. The purpose of the letter was, in my understanding, to instruct Keliya and the Mittanian delegation on the course to be adopted in their discussions with the Egyptian court. This letter is the best example of the coherent policy of dynastic and political union mentioned above. Initially, the letter surveys in detail the historical background to the new marriage (and its precedents), which Tushratta values as the prelude to fulfillment of his goal of political integration.

The following are the key political and diplomatic proposals in the letter that are expected to result from this warm, loving, family relationship:

1. Hittite Enemy. According to a new reading of Wilhelm,[8] the Hittites are mentioned twice at the beginning of Tushratta's letter. There then follows their definition as "his enemy." In other words, the Hittites are to be regarded as the mutual enemy.
2. Interchange of Rulers. In sec. 15 (II 71ff.), there is "an astonishing statement of Tushratta,"[9] namely: "I (= Tushratta) am the lord (not "king") of the land of Egypt and my brother (= Amenhotep) is the lord of the Hurrian land." This interchange, symbolizing the unity of the two dynasties, is reminiscent of a famous pre–World War I photograph showing the emperors of Germany and Russia exchanging uniforms.[10]
3. Mutual Defense Treaty. Sec. 26 (III 108–18) continues in the same vein of solidarity: "If the enemy invades my brother's land, my brother writes to me and the Hurrian land, armor, arms . . . will be at his disposal" (and vice versa). Note that the enemy is unnamed, but his identity should be obvious from the beginning of the letter. For the reasons given above, I consider this to be a *proposal* for a defense treaty, not a reference to an existing treaty.
4. Diplomatic Service. As a defense against "evil words," Tushratta proposes an agreement that only the words of Keliya and Mane, the diplomatic team, will be accepted as reliable by both kings (sec. 27, IV 1–29; cf. EA 26). Tushratta favors only Mane and will refuse to receive any other

envoy (sec. 31, IV 52–57). By this means, Tushratta wishes to establish a secure line of communication, the two diplomats being the very foundation of mutual trust between the states. Furthermore, the movement of the envoys must be unhindered and swift (sec. 29, cf. EA 28; EA 30).

Deteriorating Relations (EA 26–29)

Political Situation

At the death of Amenhotep III, Akhenaten ascended the throne. Almost immediately, the change reverberated throughout the whole area: there was a sharp decline in gift (gold) transfers.[11] For Mittani, it marked the end of the diplomatic waltz.

Tushratta, in despair, felt himself cheated and endangered.[12] In EA 26, 27, 28 he tries to approach Akhenaten through his mother, Tiye, who was privy (with the knowledge of Keliya and Mane) to all the secret talks between Tushratta and Amenhotep III. In EA 26, he implores her directly to influence Akhenaten to keep his father's obligations. Although in EA 27 there is some improvement, in that a seemingly positive message arrived from Akhenaten, practically nothing changed. The promises of Amenhotep III were cast aside.

In EA 27:32–36, Tushratta exclaims despairingly:

> But my brother has not sent the solid (gold) statues that your father was going to send. You have sent plated ones of wood. Nor have you sent me the goods that your father was going to send me, but you have reduced (them) greatly. *Yet there is nothing I know of in which I have failed my brother.* Any day that I hear the greetings of my brother, that day I make a festive occasion.

The frantic movement of express messengers was also interrupted. Akhenaten refused to let them return; consequently, Tushratta, despite his desire to keep communications open, could not let Mane return (EA 28:12–41).

Finally, in a lengthy telescopic review, Tushratta appeals to the paternal connection (EA 29). He wishes to influence Akhenaten through a highly emotional recapitulation of the entire relationship of the two dynasties, interwoven with a recital of current problems such as the free movement of envoys and the delivery of promised gifts. Especially impressive, beautifully formulated subsections are the descriptions of Amenhotep III's joy on the eve of his marriage with Tadu-Hepa, stressing the Egyptian king's excellent relations with the diplomatic service (EA 29:28–35), and of Tushratta mourning Amenhotep III's death (EA 29:55–60).[13]

Diplomatic Service

In EA 26, it is Keliya who throws a lifeline to Tushratta. Through him, a worried Queen Mother Tiye sends a message to Tushratta, imploring him to be a quasi-father to Akhenaten. This plea served as a heaven-sent opportunity to Tushratta, which he used both in this letter and in EA 27 and 28. It seems that the Egyptian ambassador Mane also made efforts to alleviate the anxieties of Tushratta: in EA 27:7–8, he brings greetings and goods from Akhenaten, and Tushratta rejoices greatly. Given the generally unfriendly attitude on the part of Egypt, I would surmise that this encouraging démarche was the personal initiative of Mane.

EA 28 deals almost exclusively with the scandal of the detainment of express messengers, accurately describing the predicament of the messengers and the damage caused by the disruption of ordinary, everyday communications (EA 28:20–28). The disruption, indeed, is of the whole system of diplomatic exchange exemplified by the laissez-passer of EA 30.

Almost symbolically, EA 29 ends with swift judicial action by Tushratta, accepting the complaint of Akhenaten against two members of the Mittanian diplomatic service who "broke the law" in Egypt; they were severely punished. The damage to the diplomatic service itself was equally severe.

Conclusions

Tushratta's "coherent policy" and the brilliant performance of the diplomatic services of both sides were of no avail. With Akhenaten and his ministers, there came a momentous turning-point in Egyptian foreign policy. By the reception of an Assyrian delegation — an act equivalent to the opening of diplomatic relations — Assyria, an active participant in the destruction of Mittani, its former overlord and the (quasi-)ally of Egypt, was now recognized as fully equal (EA 15, 16).[14]

Abandoning Mittani to its fate, Egypt and Hatti set out upon a long, tortuous path of alternating peace and war, to arrive finally at a form of coexistence never really reached by Egypt and Mittani — a binding mutual defense treaty.

CHAPTER SEVENTEEN

Amarna Diplomacy:
A Full-fledged Diplomatic System?

GEOFFREY BERRIDGE

It is clear that a diplomacy of sorts was a feature of the relations between the chief political entities of this period. Kings communicated with each other on a basis that was in some measure both regular and regulated, chiefly to promote commerce but occasionally to conclude alliances and sign peace treaties as well. It is, however, one thing to maintain, as Cohen does, that the Amarna archive permits us "to observe in detail a constitutive phase in the development of a central feature [diplomacy] of Western civilization"; it is quite another to claim, as he also does, that it "provides uncontestable evidence of the existence of a sophisticated and effective mechanism for the management of international relations."[1] That Cohen is convinced of the latter point is evident from his comment that Martin Wight's description of the Amarna diplomatic system as " 'rudimentary' " was a "noteworthy lapse."[2] At the end of the same piece, he concludes that "there is no doubt that the Amarna archive provides irrefutable evidence of a fully fledged diplomatic system."[3] In this chapter I argue that, on the available evidence, Wight's characterization is more accurate than Cohen's, substantially because the full conditions for a "sophisticated and effective" diplomacy were not adequately approached in the Amarna period.

How Sophisticated Was Amarna Diplomacy?

Diplomacy is essentially a means of communication designed to promote negotiations, gather information, and clarify intentions, in relation to enemies as well as friends. What features does a "sophisticated" diplomacy exhibit? I suggest that they include the following: immunity of the envoy, continuous contact, well-qualified if not necessarily professional personnel, bureaucratic direction, provision for mediation, a method for underpinning agreements, and flexibility of form and procedure. The most sophisticated systems of the modern period are probably to be found, first, in the essentially European system that followed introduction of the telegraph in the late nineteenth century and was celebrated, with reservations, by Harold Nicolson,[4] and second, in the world system operating since the middle of the 1980s.[5] To what extent did the features of sophisticated systems such as these exist in the Amarna period?

The Immunity of the Envoy

The immunity of the envoy from local jurisdiction (together with the duty of the receiving government to accord special protection to his dignity and security) constitutes the most fundamental feature of diplomacy. It must extend not only to the person but also to the entourage, private residence, papers, and means of communication and transport of the envoy. It must cover him in third countries as well. There are two main reasons for diplomatic immunity. First, an embassy of only modest efficiency, especially if from an unfriendly state, may, by virtue of its duty to gather information on local conditions and sometimes deliver unwelcome messages, excite the wrath of the government to which it is accredited as well as sections of its people. Second, without special guarantees that among other things, physical protection will be provided and that charges of law-breaking will not be manufactured against it, the embassy will be unable to do its various jobs properly. In short, the rule of diplomatic immunity is a response to functional necessity in circumstances that are, at worst, life-threatening.[6] A diplomatic system can survive occasional lapses from this norm, even when the culprits are not pursued with energy and even if they are states themselves. But these lapses must only be occasional, and there must be widespread acceptance that they are indeed the exception and not the rule. How did the Amarna system measure up on this fundamental point?

Cohen states baldly that in the Amarna period, "the person of the envoy was inviolate and he enjoyed diplomatic immunity."[7] Others come to the same conclusion,[8] and the most impressive explanation of such special protection for diplomats as existed at this time is that it was a function of the "laws of hospitality." However, a number of considerations make it difficult to conclude that these accounts provide evidence of the kind and extent of diplomatic immunity characteristic of a developed diplomatic system.

To begin with, envoys were temporary rather than resident (see further on this below). This had two important implications for the significance of diplomatic immunity in the Amarna period. First, messengers were sent in general only by friends or prospective friends, because receiving an enemy envoy, unless to engage in the ritual preliminaries to war, was certain to create dismay among the allies of all concerned.[9] Second, limited in scope by virtue of being limited in time, missions were also small and not well resourced. The significance of all this is evident: the Amarna envoy was intrinsically unthreatening. As a result, and notwithstanding the phenomenon of the detained messenger (see below), there was little incentive to subject the envoy to cruel treatment or take drastic measures in order to impair his functioning. And as a result of this, diplomatic immunity in the Amarna system, where international embassies were, by definition, "embassies of joy" (EA 1), was the largely exclusive privilege of those who did not need it. Amarna diplomacy, in other words, was rarely put to the real test of a developed diplomatic system: the granting of immunity to envoys—especially resident envoys—of hostile states. When it was tried on one occasion recorded in the Amarna Letters, it not surprisingly failed. Thus Rib-Hadda, the woeful ruler of Byblos, complained to Pharaoh that when he sent a messenger to Yapa-Hadda, the mayor of Beirut who had seized his property and thrown in his lot with Aziru, "he bound him" (EA 116).

Special protection for diplomats may have cost rulers little to grant in the Amarna period, but even so, the practice was affected by norms flagrantly inconsistent with the modern notion of immunity. First, as in the earlier Mari period, envoys were still not permitted to return home without the permission of their hosts (on whom they were dependent for supplies and a return escort), and permission was often refused.[10] (During the Amarna period, Egypt had a particularly bad reputation for this.)[11] Second, there appears to have been no rule—quite vital in a developed diplomatic system—that envoys were entitled to unhindered passage through third countries, despite some feeble attempts to encourage it.[12] In short, the principle of free communication enshrined in Article 27 of the Vienna Convention on Diplomatic Relations (1961) was not a prominent feature of the Amarna system.

Continuity of Contact: Permanent Embassies

A sophisticated diplomatic system must feature continuous rather than episodic or even regular contact between the parties, unless they are actually at war, and preferably even then. Among other things, this makes information gathering vastly more efficient, multiplies the opportunities for lobbying, and enables new initiatives to be taken without attracting attention.[13] In practice, this means permanent embassies and, in principle, either frequent rotation of personnel or efficient communications between foreign missions and home. Permanent embassies in the absence of efficient contact with home are at best of limited use and at worst counterproductive, not least because of the well-known tendency of diplomats long stationed abroad to "go native." What is the evidence on these points concerning the diplomacy of the Amarna system?

Cohen acknowledges that "most of the envoys mentioned in the Amarna Letters are visitors and not resident,"[14] but he is quick to emphasize that "there are hints of the existence of resident embassies, too."[15] We are told initially that "it is likely that this central feature of developed diplomacy . . . was first introduced by Shamshi-Adad of Mari circa 1800 B.C.E., so that by the time of Amarna the institution was long established."[16] This striking and unelaborated claim cannot, as it stands, be regarded as persuasive, not least because it contradicts the conclusion of the exhaustive work of Munn-Rankin on the diplomacy of the Mari period (see below).

Nor is the second piece of evidence more compelling: "Ambassadors of Egypt's vassal Tunip spent 20 years at court."[17] There are at least three problems with this. First, according to Moran, "The 20 years here and in line 44 are round numbers meaning nothing more than 'a long/considerable time,'" so for all we know, this figure could be a considerable exaggeration.[18] Second, the minor north Syrian kingdom of Tunip was a vassal state and not one of the other Great Powers, and it is at least plausible that its messengers would have been treated differently, as were its messages.[19] At best, the example would appear irrelevant. Third, and most important, there is no evidence in this letter of any expectation (certainly not on the part of Tunip) that its "messengers" would remain at Pharaoh's court for a long time. On the contrary, they appear to be complaining either that they had been detained or, more likely, that they remained so long simply because Pharaoh refused to give any reply! Institutions are nothing if not sets of expectations.

Cohen's third hint of the existence of resident embassies is the evidence from the letters that foreign messengers frequented the dwellings of princesses of their own courts married to Pharaoh;[20] that, in effect, the households of these princesses constituted a special kind of permanent embassy, with the princess herself playing a role crudely analogous to head of mission. The chief example cited by Cohen is the household of Tadu-Hepa, the Mittanian princess first married to Amenhotep III and subsequently transferred to the harem of Akhenaten.[21] He also mentions evidence of a similar kind concerning contacts between the messengers of the Babylonian king and those of his daughters married to neighboring potentates.[22] It seems clear, as Cohen suggests, that princesses may well have been instruments as well as objects of diplomacy, especially when backed by fathers able to make their weight felt in their daughters' adopted countries.[23] Nevertheless, there is no indication in EA 29 that the Mittanian messengers who were "in residence in (to?) the quarters that [were established] for Tadu-Hepa" were doing anything other than killing time while waiting for replies or gifts (though they would presumably have had diplomatic opportunities of other kinds). The evidence on Babylonian emissaries from EA 1 carries no suggestion of residence with their king's daughters installed in foreign harems but merely indicates that they made a habit of visiting them in order to check on their treatment and, more especially, to secure gifts from them for their master. In general, this point is interesting and possibly justifies more investigation, but unless either the princess was a harem favorite or unusually qualified and externally supported, it seems unlikely that she could have fostered an embassy in any true sense.

The fourth hint is said to suggest "the existence of a collective diplomatic corps" and consists in this: "King Tushratta of Mittani uses the significant expression 'nobles [and] all envoys' for an assembly at court."[24] Similar references have been found in the Mari archive, from which it is also clear that envoys of different kings at the same court exchanged information and even traveled together for extra safety.[25] This is even more striking evidence of the existence of a "diplomatic corps" in the narrow sense. However, a diplomatic corps can be constituted by temporary as well as resident envoys, so this point is not persuasive, either.

Of course, it is clear that envoys sometimes spent considerable periods at foreign courts.[26] This was sometimes because a special task could not be completed overnight;[27] because practical considerations—acquiring provisions and protection for the homeward journey, for example—could cause delay, as might inauspicious omens;[28] or, more usually, because the receiving king wished to exert pressure on the sending king.[29] But does a temporary envoy forced to linger make a resident ambassador? Manifestly not. Such an envoy will not have been charged with the general functions of a resident ambassador and is likely to be temperamentally as well as practically ill equipped to play this role. This is even more likely when it is considered that this envoy will be distracted by the priority of securing his own release, which in itself is likely to make him fawn even more on the local ruler.

Finally, it should be noted that even if genuine resident missions had been a feature of the Amarna system, it is unlikely that they would have been in efficient communication with home. It is true, as Munn-Rankin tells us, that in urgent circumstances, tablets and oral messages could be carried in the Mari period by relays of runners,[30] that boats could be used on the Tigris and the Euphrates in Mesopotamia,[31] and that the domestication of the horse by this time had quickened communications dramatically.[32] Moreover, it appears to have been customary for the receiving government to provide a military escort for returning messengers, provided they represented a friendly state that was not too distant.[33] However, speed of communication in these conditions was obviously a function of the roads and their security, which were both generally bad;[34] the weather, which was uncomfortably wet in winter and intensely hot in summer (EA 7); and geographical distance, by which some of the Great Powers in the Amarna period were widely separated. In addition, free communication was seriously impeded, as we have already seen, by the right of the local king to veto the envoy's return home and the absence of a norm of unhindered passage through third countries — vital in that period to communications between all except the littoral states of the eastern Mediterranean.[35] In any case, neither clay tablets nor memories could carry long, complicated, and nuanced messages.[36] And because the tablets were not encrypted, their authors would in any case have been naïve to confine truly sensitive information to them. Necessity may, of course, have left them no choice, for suspicion of the deliberate distortion of oral messages (in order to curry favor with the recipient) was widespread.[37]

The Qualifications of the Personnel

In order to work effectively, a diplomat must obviously be highly intelligent, well briefed, properly schooled in procedure, and persuasive in both the spoken and written word. He should be as honest as possible but not naïve, which is why Abraham de Wicquefort recommended Machiavelli as essential reading.[38] Because the core function of diplomacy is negotiation, which is a creative activity, such a person must also be capable of imaginative thinking and not be temperamentally hostile to the possibility of compromise. In order to speak for his sovereign, he must carry confirmation of his position, or "letters of credence." Finally, and though in significant degree this depends on the political temper of the age, it is, as Wicquefort says, "a great Ornament to the Embassador" if he is a member of "an illustrious House, or a noble Family."[39]

There is certainly evidence of well-qualified diplomats at work in the Amarna system.[40] A significant number are mentioned by name in the archive,[41] as they are in the earlier one found at Mari. It also seems possible that some, at any rate, were professionals in the loose sense that diplomacy was either their regular calling or a substantial part of it; there is also evidence of specialization on certain countries and cultures.[42] Individuals such as Mane and Keliya were important in their own right, skilled in pleading, trained as scribes and linguists,[43] and bearers of easily recognizable letters of credence. For diplomacy involving what in a later age was known as "high" politics, it seems that there was also a preference for envoys of "noble" position, including the sons of kings and even vassal kings themselves.[44] Nevertheless, it is also clear that in the Amarna system diplomacy was intimately linked with trade, and it seems that much, if not most, diplomatic work was carried out by people who were simultaneously merchants.[45] This is not least because trade, which was extensive, was an important subject of negotiations. Wise in the ways of foreign lands as a result of their regular journeys, dealing with matters close to the hearts of the kings, and direct servants of the latter to boot, merchants were the obvious choice to double as diplomats in the absence of a regular diplomatic service—as they were in lesser degree in much later periods, for example, in the service of the trading states of Venice and Britain.

If most Amarna diplomats were simultaneously merchants, does this disqualify them as the agents of a "full-fledged diplomacy"? Wicquefort was contemptuous of the use of merchants as ambassadors in seventeenth-century Europe, though principally because their employment was likely to be regarded as an insult by the prince to whom they were sent or because making money was likely to be too much of a distraction.[46] Nicolson echoes the second of these points in connection with the Byzantine envoys, who were expected to finance their missions from trade.[47] Merchants, who generally traveled in caravans, were also too slow for the transmission of urgent messages.[48] It might also be imagined that they would have been at a disadvantage if interrogated on the broader nuances of a tablet they had delivered or on some quite unrelated topic, and the limitations of tablet correspondence meant that interrogation of the envoy was an important element in diplomatic communication, as Meier has emphasized.[49]

But despite his reservations on this point about Byzantine diplomacy, Harold Nicolson is also well known for his insistence that diplomacy was fostered by the pragmatism of the trader and the centrality of bargaining in the trader's work.[50] Bearing in mind, too, the importance of commerce in Amarna diplomacy, as well as the possibility that for this reason, as well as because merchants were palace officials,[51] they had more social prestige than their European counterparts three millennia later, on balance it seems probable that the conduct of diplomacy by merchants in the Amarna period was no bad thing.

A final point here should be added about the honesty of the Amarna diplomat since, on the evidence quoted at the end of the last section, this was not pronounced. Furthermore, Sir Herbert Butterfield made the "moral code" of the professional diplomat the distinguishing feature of "true" diplomacy, and on this ground he flatly disqualified the activity conducted by Amarna envoys.[52] "The Tell el-Amarna letters," he wrote in 1970, ". . . have acquired great fame as early documents of foreign policy. They no doubt deserve their fame; but one can brood over them at dead of night without finding a trace of the diplomatic craft, though there were occasions when diplomacy was sorely needed."[53] Butterfield, however, admits in the same breath that the European diplomats of his ideal were themselves the most fervent supporters of this doctrine, and he adds that "they may have protested too much, for an ambassador does have to promote the interests and the ideals of his own country."[54] This seems, and I think rightly, to water down the significance of the moral criterion and weaken its ability to dismiss the Amarna envoy as a true diplomat. Having said this, it remains apparent that the messengers of the Amarna period, with certain notable exceptions, were routinely suspected of lying and that this impeded their work.

Bureaucratic Direction

Did the Great Kings have their own foreign ministries? In other words, was the formulation of foreign policy and the conduct of diplomacy in the Amarna period supported at least by archives of correspondence and treaties, together with a body of permanent officials charged with the assessment of intelligence and the provision of coordinated advice? The evidence is not clear, nor can a positive answer be deduced from the indisputable fact that the conduct of diplomacy was patterned and disciplined. Most Great Kings appear to have formulated their own foreign policies and issued personal instructions in order to give them effect.[55] Of course, they listened to opinion (some no doubt more than others) but their key advisers appear to have been senior envoys such as Mane and Keliya, who were constantly on the move and thus not always available.[56]

At the same time, the palaces of the Great Kings kept archives, which were presumably preserved by the small scribal caste. These included copies of outgoing tablets of importance as well as incoming ones, otherwise we should not have the raw material for this book. And archives containing correspondence and treaties are, as we know, the kernel of any foreign ministry. Meier has rightly noted their value to the diplomacy of the Amarna period.[57]

Provision for Mediation

Mediation, the intervention in a dispute of a third party motivated by a desire to promote a diplomatic settlement, is an essential and therefore prominent feature of a sophisticated diplomatic system, not least in our own day. It is therefore of great interest that there is evidence of its occurrence well before the Amarna period, though it is sometimes unclear as to whether the surviving tablets, as well as subsequent commentary on them, are referring to mediation or arbitration.[58] This distinction is, however, not lost on Munn-Rankin, who explicitly argues that a case of genuine mediation is revealed by the Mari archives.[59] Unfortunately, other than the unheeded pleas of vassals to Pharaoh for adjudication on disputes between them, there is no evidence of mediation in the Amarna Letters themselves. It seems, therefore, unlikely that the practice was extensive, certainly in relations between the Great Powers.

Methods for Underpinning Agreements

All diplomatic agreements are underpinned in greater or lesser degree, and either directly or indirectly, by reciprocity: enjoyment of the fruits of an agreement is more likely if they are shared, as promised, with the other side. However, for any number of reasons, one or more of the parties to an agreement may subsequently feel less pulled by this calculation. As a result, a sophisticated diplomatic system has well-understood methods for reinforcing agreements. One is to present them in especially impressive forms; a second is to provide for their formal ratification by sovereign bodies; a third is to seal the agreements at public ceremonies of high moral significance; a fourth is to agree that they create obligations that are enforceable, either by a court or a nominated arbitrator; and a fifth is to arrange for guarantees by third-party Great Powers, which may or may not be dressed up as some kind of "universal body" like the contemporary U.N. Security Council.

In this regard, it would seem that the Amarna system probably scores highest of all. Agreements were made impressive by embodiment in writing,[60] and a little later, in 1258 B.C.E., a treaty between Egypt and Hatti was inscribed on tablets made of silver.[61] Ceremonial rituals were also employed that symbolized the nature of the arrangement concluded.[62] In addition, a system of hostage-holding (not unknown in more recent times) was commonly used as well, not least in connection with messengers.[63] Most significantly, however, agreements were "sworn to by the parties concerned in the presence of divine witnesses,"[64] and this was repeated in a process of ratification by the king.[65] Sacrifices to the gods embellished these ceremonies, and ritual acts testified to the acceptance of a system of enforceability which turned upon the threat that divine retribution of an invariably fatal nature would be visited upon any oath-breaker. Of course, oaths were broken then, as they have been ever since, and the inconsistency of the gods in acting in the manner envisaged in these circumstances no doubt weakened the system. Nevertheless, in view of the significance of religious thought in that period and the ease with which otherwise inexplicable personal and natural disasters could be attributed to the wrath of the gods, it would seem obvious that this was at least as good a method for underpinning agreements as any later one. Agreements between minor states accepting the same Great Power as suzerain could also be enforced following arbitration by the latter.[66]

Flexibility

Finally, a sophisticated diplomacy is flexible, with forms and procedures sufficiently varied and malleable to cope with varying numbers and sorts of states in all circumstances, provided there is a will to communicate. Among other things, and although the mix will depend on the demands made on the system, there will be provision for unofficial as well as official communication, multilateral as well as bilateral encounters, summits in addition to meetings between officials, well-understood devices for preserving the momentum of a negotiation as well as for prevaricating, and a host of different ways of packaging agreements.

On this point, it would seem that the Amarna system does not score as badly as might at first be thought. Envoys of different sorts were available for missions of greater or lesser importance, and for the former, rulers themselves might be employed.[67] Messages could be committed to memory or inscribed on tablets. And some variation in the speed with which they were delivered was possible, depending on the urgency of the circumstances. All of these points have already been noted. Different codes had also evolved to cope with the different demands of diplomacy between Great Powers and between Great Powers and their vassal states, a feature already apparent during the Mari period.[68] Of multilateral diplomacy, however, except in the informal settings of caravans and places where temporary envoys sent to the same palace were gathered, there is no evidence. Nor is there any evidence in the Amarna years of that institution which, throughout the modern period, has been so expressive of the indispensability of diplomacy when, in theory, this has failed: the protecting power. Since, however, there were no resident embassies, this is hardly surprising.

To summarize so far, the evidence strongly suggests that it is misleading to describe Amarna diplomacy as a full-fledged diplomatic system. It is true that its personnel were in general adequate to their tasks, that its methods for underpinning agreements were impressive, and that a suitable degree of flexibility of form and procedure (associated in this case perhaps with its very underdevelopment) was apparent. Nonetheless, it was marred by an incomplete and weakly held norm of immunity, an absence of resident missions other than those — stunted and crippled — of special envoys temporarily detained, incomplete bureaucratic support, and little in the way of a reflex for mediation between the Great Powers. Most significantly, diplomatic communication between hostile states — the real test of a developed diplomatic system — appears to have been virtually nonexistent.

Weak or Nonexistent Conditions

The explanation of this state of affairs is straightforward: the full conditions for a full-fledged diplomatic system did not exist in the Amarna period. What are these conditions? First, there must be a plurality of states which are believed to be very roughly equal in power; second, mutually impinging interests of an urgent kind; third, a minimal toleration of cultural (including religious and ideological) difference; and fourth, technically efficient international communication. With regard to the first and the third conditions, the Amarna period was not wanting. However, in connection with the second, and despite the relative international turmoil of the later half of the second millenium, there is room for considerable doubt and, with reference to the fourth, room for none at all.

Diplomacy was important to the Great Powers of the Amarna system because they certainly had mutually impinging interests. These included control of trade routes and ports, commerce, security, and, as Cohen has emphasized, recognition.[69] It seems reasonable to suggest, however, that in contrast to the relationships that produced the febrile, paranoid climate of late fifteenth-century Italy and fostered the invention and spread of the resident embassy,[70] gratification of these interests was not permanently and transparently a matter of life and death. They were not, in other words, vital interests. One overriding reason for this suggests itself. International politics during the Amarna period was focused on the struggle for control of a large, complex buffer zone — Syria/Palestine — that not only absorbed the energies of most of the Great Powers but cushioned their relations with distance. The means of warfare were also primitive and long supply lines difficult to sustain. As a result, and while there were notable exceptions, the Great Powers did not generally present direct security threats to each other. Hence the incentive for that great hallmark of the developed diplomatic system, resident embassies, which would have represented permanent eyes and ears at each other's courts, was reduced.[71] Alliances and political intelligence were certainly on the Amarna international agenda, but secure for the most part in the knowledge that any fighting was a long way from home, most of the international diplomacy was concerned with commerce. As Moran points out, the international correspondence is almost devoid of political discussion.[72]

If diplomacy remained underdeveloped in the Amarna period because it was not permanently, as opposed to sporadically, urgent in relations between the Great Kings, the role of technological limitations seems quite beyond doubt. The technical obstacles to quick, secure, and secret communication were just too formidable to support any but the most rudimentary form of diplomacy. Most of these obstacles have already been discussed above. However, it is necessary to add something about language.

Diplomacy in the Amarna period was certainly made possible by the fact that rulers and diplomats speaking different mother tongues were able to communicate with the assistance of interpreters, whose importance was recognized.[73] Furthermore, they were also often able to communicate in Akkadian, and much is made by some scholars of the existence of this "diplomatic language." However, Liverani, who has studied this question closely, is obviously not convinced that Akkadian was well understood, even by the scribes of the Armana diplomatic system. "In the Amarna archive," says Liverani, "the forced or imperfect translations are so evident and so substantial that they cause a reaction on the part of the very people involved. The high percentage of perplexed answers," he continues, "the denunciations of an impossible obedience, or of the difference from the real situation to that imagined or prescribed by Pharaoh and, on the other hand, the high percentage of excessively acquiescent and resigned answers are, in my opinion, the obvious result of a substantial difficulty in communication between two different worlds."[74] Misunderstanding, it barely needs to be added, is invariably corrosive in its effect on diplomacy.

Effective Nevertheless?

Amarna diplomacy may not have been sophisticated, but it is important not to overlook the obvious fact, also stressed by Cohen, that it was still able to achieve results. Intentions were conveyed; information was gathered; and negotiations were successfully concluded. And there is a view that if the procedures involved were slow and simple, this was precisely because international relations at the level of the Great Kings were, on the whole, uncomplicated and rarely touched vital interests. Amarna diplomacy, on this argument, was adapted to its environment.

As far as it goes, none of this is exceptionable. The issue, however, is not whether Amarna diplomacy was effective but how effective it was, and in view of the limitations of the evidence, it is by no means an easy one with which to grapple. This is because a convincing answer would require firm pointers on the following questions. First, what were the aims of the foreign policies of the Great Powers of the Amarna period? Second, what was the contribution of diplomacy, as opposed to force, propaganda, and secret intelligence, to their achievement? Third, what effect did existing limitations of diplomatic machinery have on the formulation of Great Power aims in the first place? These questions are, in any case, the proper field of diplomatic historians of the period. The student of diplomacy can nevertheless offer at least one general observation.

There is a difference between adequacy (or adaptation to the environment) and "effectiveness." To argue for a moment by analogy, countries that rarely get severe winter weather have only rudimentary arrangements for clearing snow from the roads. These arrangements are nevertheless regarded as adequate because the costs of infrequent transport paralysis are judged to be less than those of investment in fleets of snow ploughs. However, no one would claim that the snow-clearing capacity of such countries is remotely effective when major blizzards actually shroud the land, or that short-lived and localized snowfalls could not be much better handled. And so with Amarna diplomacy: it may well have been adapted to its environment, but it does not follow that it was very effective. Clearly, a diplomacy honed by the perpetual negotiation of vital interests would have been more effective at coping with the sleet of commerce as well as with the rare blizzards of high politics.

Conclusions

Judged by modern standards, and even by the standards of ancient Greece, the diplomacy of the Amarna period was certainly not sophisticated. On the contrary, it was quite crude. It was in general slow, fitful, less than comprehensive in its coverage, and incapable of maintaining a high level of clear and nuanced communication even in those channels where it flowed most smoothly. In the circumstances of the time, this was hardly surprising. Nevertheless, that it existed at all demonstrates once more that however unpropitious technological conditions may be, a balance of power among minimally interdependent states, especially ones engaging in extensive commerce, will generate pressure for a modestly effective diplomacy of sorts.

CHAPTER EIGHTEEN

Conclusion: The Beginnings of International Relations

RAYMOND COHEN AND RAYMOND WESTBROOK

Originating in a friendly talk between a political scientist and an Assyriologist, the project from which this book derives consisted of an encounter between students of the social sciences, particularly international relations, and students of the ancient Near East. Although we lacked a common research methodology or even an agenda, we possessed a shared interest in trying to make sense, from our different disciplinary perspectives, of a collection of enigmatic yet fascinating administrative and "diplomatic" records, the Amarna Letters. Random and incomplete, these texts seem to be the remnants of a set of working files from the Egyptian royal archives of the Eighteenth Dynasty loosely centered on the affairs of Egypt's West Asian empire. Unfortunately, their chronology cannot be conclusively determined, and it is unclear how representative a picture they present of ancient Egyptian governance and "foreign policy," or of the overall conduct of ancient Near Eastern diplomacy and foreign relations. They are tantalizingly silent or ambiguous on fundamental historical questions. They clearly tell us something important about Egyptian imperial policy and international relations at an embryonic stage of its development. Just what is open to debate.

In the spirit of scientific investigation described by Nobel physicist Werner Heisenberg (discoverer of the Uncertainty Principle), the participants in the Bellagio conference engaged in a series of discussions about their contending readings of the documents. We accepted as our point of departure that no one person (or specialization in this case) can have a monopoly of knowledge or understanding but that the results of science "are attained through talks among those who work in it and who consult one another about their interpretation[s]. . . . Science is rooted in conversations."[1] Thus our method of investigation was dialectical: a give-and-take of hypothesis and query, answer and counterexplanation. Unlike Heisenberg's community of scientists, who could ponder and debate the results of laboratory experiments performed under controlled conditions and subject to replication, aiming ideally to arrive at a generally accepted interpretation, our own discussions of texts could only hope to map out the range of alternative interpretations and explanations. Sometimes, but not always, we succeeded in narrowing the parameters of disagreement. What follows is therefore a summation rather than a definitive conclusion. We have attempted to collate the diverse contributions to this volume with the aid of their substrate text: the oral interactions that took place between the contributors at the Bellagio conference.

An Exchange System

One thing that all participants could agree on was that, as Kevin Avruch emphasizes, the glue holding the Amarna system together was exchange — commercial, dynastic, and cultural. The correspondents want things from each other and request, demand, haggle, offer, and beseech that they might get them. Carlo Zaccagnini demonstrates that while proclaiming their self-sufficiency, Great Kings in fact depended on each other for the supply of various key items, such as gold, iron, and horses. They also highly valued, without necessarily depending on, foreign princesses, experts (such as physicians and augurs), cultural items, and luxury artifacts. Thus, in Zaccagnini's words, "a dense network of reciprocal ties was established." *Diplomacy by means of the regular exchange of messengers was the essential mechanism for managing these ties and transactions.* Pinhas Artzi's detailed reconstruction of the Egyptian-Mittanian diplomatic channel shows just how diplomacy worked as the vehicle for negotiating exchange (in this case, of gold, gifts, and military aid). It is no coincidence that the rhythm of diplomacy and the exchange of commodities were intimately connected, with messengers and traders often accompanying each other in the caravans that traveled to and fro across the region.

The acute interest of Great Kings in exchange explains the centrality of gift-giving in the Amarna archive, which includes long lists of presents. Gifts, as Marcel Mauss showed in his pioneering study, "which are in theory voluntary, disinterested and spontaneous . . . are in fact obligatory and interested."[2] They are given in the expectation of reciprocation and on the basis of economic self-interest. Systems of *total prestation* (= benefit, service rendered), in which everything is exchanged, from women, via wealth, to military assistance, are characteristic of archaic cultures.³ Although the remote, tribal societies Mauss investigated were usually premonetary, he did not rule out the possible parallel existence of market mechanisms. Indeed, in the case of Amarna, we observe the Great Kings' aspiration to maintain an exchange system, untainted by commerce, between themselves, while at the same time considerable international trade was being conducted by merchants through the medium of silver.

In his chapter on dynastic marriage, Samuel Meier points to the incongruity at the heart of the Amarna world: the language of family relationships alongside "mercenary and self-seeking political machinations." Christer Jönsson, too, notes the contradiction involved in demanding specific reciprocity—quid pro quo—when between brothers the expectation should be of general reciprocity. In fact, exchanges are made in systems of total prestation with only the pretense of generosity. As Evans-Pritchard argues, however, this element of deception does not at all preclude exchange in archaic societies constituting "not a mechanical but a moral transaction, bringing about and maintaining human, personal, relationships between individuals and groups."⁴ Exchange relationships are interested, but they also entail moral obligations, mutual claims grounded in nonmaterial values. Only transactions freely contracted by individuals in an exclusively money economy are devoid of moral sentiment.

The moment the centrality of exchange is grasped, it immediately becomes clear why Great Kings are so preoccupied by reciprocity: Without it, the system fails. Reciprocity is the sacred ground rule of exchange systems. It is also, by the same token, as Mario Liverani notes, "the only possible starting point for the functioning of an international community."

"Primitivists" versus "Modernists"

A fundamental albeit implicit discussion in this volume is between "primitivists" and "modernists." At stake is the issue of whether we can view the remote past through present-day eyes, meaningfully comparing, among other things, ancient with modern diplomacy. The primitivist approach, advocated by Liverani, cautions against anachronism and argues that the Amarna Letters and the phenomena they describe can only be understood on their own terms within the context of the worldviews and cultures of the peoples of the ancient Near East. The reader is obliged to resist reading the logic of modern thought and preoccupations backward into remote periods. For Liverani and Zaccagnini, it is of the essence that "international relations" during the Amarna period were understood in terms of the small community, whether the family, the neighborhood, or the village. This model was constitutive and not simply expressive. As Liverani remarked at the conference, at some points in the correspondence it is as though the Great Kings think that they are leaning out of their upstairs windows talking to each other across the street. He wondered whether the ancient Near East was relevant to the study of modern international relations at all. For Zaccagnini, the leitmotif of the letters is therefore the theme of brotherhood, the insistence of Great Kings that they should express "friendship" or "love" to each other. This familial relationship was to be made manifest in a constant exchange of women and gifts.

Advocacy of a primitivist perspective was by no means the exclusive preserve of Assyriologists. Avruch noted the grave obstacles to substantive analysis inherent in the complete absence of observational data. There is a limit to what ethnographers can say on the basis of epigraphic or archaeological material about a culture that they can never actually visit and see with their own eyes. Goeffrey Berridge, as a diplomatic historian, was skeptical of the anachronistic claim that the Amarna correspondence provided evidence of a sophisticated or full-fledged diplomatic system. He was particularly critical of the supposed identification of such modern phenomena as diplomatic immunity, resident ambassadors, a foreign office, or a diplomatic corps. Berridge's advice is to avoid measuring Amarna diplomacy with the yardstick of modern diplomatic standards but to evaluate its effectiveness in terms of contemporary requirements. By that criterion, he concluded at Bellagio, Amarna diplomacy was indeed adequate to the needs of the times.

On the whole, though, political scientists tended to a modernist approach, recognizing modern international phenomena in ancient disguise. While accepting the prevalence of domestic, household metaphors, Rodolfo Ragionieri applied present-day concepts to find evidence for an international society in the making, underpinned by rules of the game and state interests. Jönsson recognized techniques of communication and negotiation, commitment and credibility that are familiar from relations between the superpowers. Steven David detected clear signs of the working, in effect if not intention, of an international system governed by Realpolitik and maintained in equilibrium by the balance of power. Alan James applied classic tools of geopolitical analysis to explain the varying degrees of control Egypt exercised over its Canaanite sphere of influence. Raymond Cohen argued that many of the documents contained intelligence material, purposefully collected on the military threat posed to Egypt by the other Great Kings. He inferred from this the existence of a security dilemma — the fear of war circularly provoked and then reinforced by each side's defensive measures — and a machinery for strategic decision making in such an environment of fear. Daniel Druckman, who was unconvinced that "brotherhood" was anything more than a rhetorical flourish, identified a Realist, anarchic system of unitary actors bargaining to achieve their best interests. Royal decisions, he demonstrated, could be elegantly and convincingly explained using methods of rational choice analysis developed during the Cold War.

The Ontology of the Ancient Near East

In any hermeneutic exercise comprising the attempt to interpret and understand a product of human culture, whether a text, an institution, or an activity, we are probably bound to use both primitivist and modernist tools. As William Murnane pointed out at the conference, interpretation poses a double challenge: to reconstruct the mind-set and ideology of a past civilization on its own terms, inevitably a primitivist exercise; then to uncover the practice or reality behind the words, by definition a modernist exercise, because it steps back from the texts. Imagine, Murnane remarked, researchers several thousand years from now trying to interpret four hundred recently discovered Soviet diplomatic texts of all kinds—propaganda and business, Great Power and vassal correspondence. As we know, in the USSR, pragmatic politics and the dictates of power did not necessarily coincide with marxist rhetoric, though they might be clothed in its guise. To make sense of these "Kremlin Letters," ideology would have to be reconstructed. But without also introducing modernist concepts—critical, comparative criteria—it would be difficult to make sense of the material and reveal the gap between rhetoric and action.

Before revealing contradictions there must be understanding of what was believed at the time to constitute reality. The first step in interpreting Amarna has to be a reconstruction of the ontology of the ancient Near East, that is, recovery of the categories, ideas, and things to which the Amarna correspondents attributed objective existence. Mythological characters, magic forces, and an entire pantheon of gods and goddesses were as real for the ancients as tables and chairs.[5] Seemingly familiar ideas, too, had unusual semantic fields that have to be mapped out. Take the concept of "peace," since ancient times a condition and aspiration central to international relations. To what precisely does the term refer? By piecing together fragmentary and elliptical artifacts and writings, Betsy Bryan is able to reconstruct the semantic field of the Egyptian hieroglyphic for peace, *ḥtp.* Found in inscriptions describing Egyptian-Mittanian relations, the hieroglyphic had, as we would expect, diplomatic and commercial connotations. Zaccagnini, indeed, points out that peace, *salīmu,* was synonymous with the exchange of the peace offerings, *šulmānu,* that were part of every diplomatic mission. Bryan suggests why this should be so, demonstrating that *ḥtp* also possessed the important religious/ ideological meaning of propitiation of the gods. In both political and sacred contexts, appeasement-propitiation required the giving of gifts, in one case to Pharaoh, the god-king, and in the other, to the gods themselves.[6] Peace to the ancient Egyptian mind, achieved by mutual propitiation through gift giving, was a harmonious, metaphysical balance on earth and in the heavens.

What of other diplomatic and legal concepts, central to international relations at least since the time of Cardinal Richelieu, such as "state," "border," "territory," and "sovereignty"? Did these ideas "exist" in the minds of the Amarna Great Kings? Raymond Westbrook, from the perspective of a jurist and Assyriologist, shows that such modern categories of thought did not exist as such in the ancient Near East but were substituted for by metaphors of household ties—Liverani's small community. Although the modern abstract concept of the state was unknown, even without it the household metaphor was sufficient to permit the emergence of an early form of international law. International law was the system of rules regulating relations between kingly households. It was possible, in other words, to establish an effective legal apparatus on different but functionally equivalent ontological foundations. Westbrook adds that it is impossible to understand the Amarna world without emphasizing the very real presence of the gods. Moreover, since divine sanction rather than national consent gave ancient international law its obligatory quality, it was in some respects more feared and binding than modern international law. In disputes between kings, divine tribunals were courts of first instance. Equally, sovereignty, or exclusive legal jurisdiction over a defined territory, was not curtailed by international treaty, because rulers by their sacred oaths were submitting to the gods and not other kings.

A Balance of Power?

Many of our contributors were exercised by the puzzle of whether the Egyptian kings conducted foreign policy on balance of power principles, in other words, whether they sought to negotiate coalitions, particularly by means of dynastic marriages, as a strategic counterpoise against a potential opponent. If Egypt did so, this would be a remarkable confirmation of the timeless validity of the theory of Realism in international relations: the view that states act on the basis of fear, the pursuit of power, and calculated self-interest, and that only opposing power can restrain aggression.

The most explicit case for the Realist thesis and its balance of power corollary is made by David. In his view the Amarna system, like the modern international system, lacked any central authority. In an anarchic world, each Great King had to fend for himself. Notwithstanding the belief in divine retribution and the rhetoric of family, treaties were broken and war licit. Power realities rather than normative restraints determined behavior. In these circumstances, he argues, Great Kings may not have known the term "balance of power" but acted as if they did. Thus "balances of power regularly formed, dissipated, and reformed during the Amarna era." Druckman, too, argues that Great Kings might speak of brotherhood but "operated as if they held views of international relations consonant with a realpolitik framework." A similar perspective is adopted by James, who sees the Great Powers of the time "aligning themselves in a multiple balance." The whole logic of his geopolitical analysis rests on the Realist assumption that the ability to project power is in inverse proportion to distance.

In opposition to these views, Ragionieri denies that there is any hard evidence for the actual working of the balance of power. He points out that if Egypt viewed Mittani as a strategic asset in a balance of power game against such rising empires as Hatti and Assyria, it is hard to understand why it abandoned Tushratta to his fate in the end. As for the proposed dynastic marriage between Egypt and Arzawa, Ragionieri argues that there is no particular reason to assume that it was directed against Arzawa's Hittite neighbors. At Bellagio, he added that in his view, a balance of power alliance was beyond the Great Kings' "intellectual powers." More convincing, he believes, is the hypothesis that Egypt's dynastic policy was intended to engage other Great Kings in an inclusive brotherhood rather than construct exclusive, opposing alliances.

Other contributors took views somewhere between the opposing positions. Artzi portrays a situation in which the Mittanian king, Tushratta, conducted a calculated diplomacy, couched in the idiom of love, to ensure his survival against internal and external enemies. Negotiations with Egypt were aimed, among other things, at establishing an alliance against Hittite expansion. An unexplained change in Egyptian but not Mittanian policy occurred following Akhenaten's accession to the Egyptian throne. Bryan explains Akhenaten's coldness toward Tushratta as "contempt for a weakened foe." At Bellagio, Artzi was inclined to explain the Egyptian-Arzawan negotiations as aimed at an anti-Hittite alliance. Both Artzi and Bryan accept that Great Kings were certainly no strangers to power calculations.

Murnane and Cohen do not accept that the Egyptian kings thought in balance of power terms because they believe that such a concept was outside the conceptual universe of the latter, not part of their ontology. Egypt did anticipate and prepare for the eventuality of an Asian war. Its foreign policy, however, was based on archaic tactical thinking and not considerations of political-strategic equilibrium. Murnane sees Egypt's West Asian empire as serving as a listening post and, in effect, a defensive glacis protecting Egypt proper from incursions by the other Great Powers. He doubts whether the Great Kings possessed a cartographic, horizontal sense of space. Distance, we may add, was intelligible in terms of traveling time, not spatial extension. (At the conference, Meier reflected that the Great Kings seemed to have no idea of how large the world was.) In the absence of a sense of space, it is hard to imagine the Great Kings acting in conformity with balance of power logic. They thought in hierarchical rather than geographical terms of the vertical control of vassals.

Cohen finds that Egyptian preoccupation with military and political intelligence provides convincing evidence of a concern with potential security threats. He argues that the Arzawa connection was meant to provide Egypt with much-needed information on the Hittites without the intention of establishing a full-blown anti-Hittite alliance. Besides which, Egypt probably did not have the means to project military force in support of an ally in Asia Minor. Pharaoh was thinking tactics, not grand strategy. Cohen agrees with Murnane that Egypt's Canaanite vassals were great assets in the intelligence war. Nadav Na'aman, for his part, strongly emphasizes the broad range of logistical services provided by the vassals. Refuting Liverani's argument that Egyptian missions to West Asia were regular and seasonal, he reconstructs preparations for a major military campaign toward the end of Akhenaten's reign. (These measures do not appear to have had a diplomatic dimension.)

The Amarna Brotherhood

It is reasonably clear that Great Kings were members of some kind of social collectivity linked together by shared norms and not simply a set of entities involved in mechanical, albeit regular contact. Liverani is in no doubt that "the Amarna letters are the product of an international community of mutually independent polities, whose long lasting and rather intensive contacts generated precise norms regulating their interactions." Westbrook goes on to describe the ontological basis, nature, and working of the rules governing relations between kingly households. The question that arises is how best to characterize the Amarna collectivity. Liverani uses the term "community" and Ragionieri talks of a "society." But Avruch objects that the sparseness of metaphor in the letters and a certain poverty of expression or cultural "thinness" suggest that Amarna was at best an embryonic society. Meier is also unhappy with the concept of community and argues that the use of Akkadian whitewashed cultural differences rather than established a transcendent common culture. Rejecting Ragionieri's Constructivist thesis, he maintains that the most one can conclude is that the system of dynastic marriages indicates that Great Kings adopted certain external forms and practices. There is no proof that they internalized shared norms and values, let alone constructed an intersubjective reality.

Another term that has acquired common currency is that of a "Great Powers' club." The objections to this concept, put by Artzi at the conference, are that it misleadingly suggests that Great Kings were a closed group of royal cronies passively sitting around with no particular purpose in mind except aimless socializing. In fact, Artzi insists, the opposite was the case. This was, historically, a new kind of collectivity that bound its members in active, ongoing relationships based on equality and reciprocity. Most important, it was a framework for peaceful relations between peoples, the expression of a common conception of humanity.

In the circumstances, the best term for the Amarna collectivity is surely the one suggested by the letters themselves: *aḫḫūtu,* that is, brotherhood or "collective of brothers," in the figurative sense of friendly society. A lively discussion of the term at the conference, stimulated by Liverani, established that *aḫḫūtu* had a rich semantic field going beyond the sense of children of the same parents.[7] Brothers, Liverani reminded the conference, might certainly quarrel. The term caught the ambiguous interplay of power and sentiment. James agreed that brotherhood referred to formal equality of status, not power. It also implied that Great Kings could make claims against each other as equals, not that they necessarily lived together in harmony and tranquillity. The resemblance between the Amarna brotherhood and the relations between members of the present-day Arab League, which also call themselves brothers but are sometimes riven by tension and hostility, was not lost on us.

The conditions for the existence of the Amarna collective of brothers were both structural and normative. On the one hand, we learn from Zaccagnini, no single state possessed a monopoly of either military power or the luxury goods that constituted the basis of international trade. So no Great King could impose his will on the others. On the other hand, there was an exclusive sense of being civilized, for example, in having the arts of writing, in enjoying a taste for luxury goods, in conducting relations in conformity with certain conventions. Outside the brotherhood were uncivilized barbarians. Membership, with its entrée into the exchange system of total prestation, was therefore highly prized. To qualify, monarchs had to possess military strength and rule over vassals, and their equal status had to be acknowledged by other Great Kings.

The Longevity of the System

The most remarkable feature of the Amarna system of international relations was its survival for more than two hundred years. Despite competition for power and prestige, vigilance to potential threats, and the domestic glorification of prowess in battle, the Great Powers mostly succeeded in avoiding war. They negotiated rather than fought, with rare exceptions, and succeeded in accommodating each other's needs and ambitions while facilitating trade and cultural contact. How did they do it?

One factor was the absence of a dominant actor, as noted: No single state acquired a decisive advantage in military terms or cornered the market on the commodities that were the basis of international trade. The system was multipolar and, to some extent, interdependent. The brotherhood also contributed to the sense of solidarity. Once a ruler was recognized as a Great King and brother, he became subject to constraints and obligations. Though a Great King could well be the enemy of another Great King, he could not be the enemy of all, or even most of his brothers, and stay in the collective.

Brotherhood, however, posed a serious dilemma because it contradicted the myth of the warrior-king. Domestically, regimes depended for their survival, or at least their stability, on legitimacy. Legitimacy derived from various sources, including divine grace and success in combat. War was presented in a positive light, as a manly activity that demonstrated the vigor of the ruler and pushed away the forces of chaos, the barbarians beyond the pale of civilization. In their inscriptions, rulers constantly laud their victories in war, but none ever seeks praise for his skills at compromise and peace-making.

How are the contradictory ethics of belligerence and brotherhood to be reconciled? In the final analysis, the Amarna states avoided war out of necessity and force of circumstance. Pharaoh entered into diplomatic relations with other Great Kings, notwithstanding the ideology of Egyptian supremacy and pharaonic omnipotence, because he was left with no choice. By abandoning isolationism and acquiring a Canaanite empire abutting on other great empires that he could neither ignore nor subjugate, he had to find a way to accommodate to reality. Not all foreigners could be subjected to his all-powerful will in the real world as they were in the wall paintings.

The prohibitive price of war and a strong stake in the exchange system provided Great Kings with an incentive to settle their differences peacefully. Motives for conflict might always arise, including disputes over territory, resources, ports, and trade routes. There were also dynastic ambitions, jealousies, and rivalries. Brotherhood certainly did not preclude enmity, as we learn from the stories of Cain and Abel, and Jacob and Esau. In the Amarna Letters, competition for status and prestige is marked; domestic disarray risked external intervention; loss of control over vassals might drag Great Kings into unintended confrontation.

Thus while the game of "happy families" is being played in the Great Power correspondence, with its rhetoric of brotherhood, there is another "great game" for high stakes in southern Syria involving Hittites, Egyptians, and Mittanians, mirrored in the clash at the local level of buffer states and vassals struggling to survive and even expand at each other's expense. Egypt's intelligence interest in the area leaves no doubt that it fully grasped the potential dangers inherent in the grinding contact between the tectonic plates of the great empires and their proxies.

Among the Amarna Great Powers, the prevention of conflict was preferred to its resolution. Spheres of influence and buffer states worked to reduce friction; intelligence and diplomacy could reduce the possibility of surprise attack and reinforce deterrence, through knowledge of the consequences of aggression. Proxy wars might act as a substitute and a warning. Arguably, a "royal peace" played the role of the "democratic peace" in our own time. That the Great Kings were all despotic monarchs and possessed a strong personal interest in trade and family ties was an antidote to unrestrained competition. Should differences arise, they were dealt with by resort to diplomatic negotiation and conciliation, appeal to international law, and judicial inquiry. Grievances resulting from acts of illegality or violence could be settled by legal remedies, such as payment of financial compensation.

Religion may be another reason why this uniquely polycultural system remained intact for so long. In the modern era, monotheistic religion has often been a source of dissonance, even between sects of the same faith. In contrast, polytheism, by definition, accepts the existence of many gods and has no reason to proselytize or persecute. Gods were recognized to be worshiped under different names in different places. Idols, believed to possess therapeutic power, were exchanged. Great Kings therefore honored each other's deities and acknowledged their potency.

The existence of a neutral interlanguage, Akkadian—like English today—helped to integrate the system. As an international means of communication, an interlanguage is useful precisely because most correspondents are non-native speakers. For them, the interlanguage is an instrument for conducting business, a precise tool for technical purposes, and lacks the resonance of their first language. It therefore allows them to manage their affairs in a reasonably objective way. In the ancient Near Eastern case, it also helped the Great Kings to insulate chauvinist domestic ideology, expressed in the vernacular, from the embarrassing necessity of external commitments and constraints, expressed in Akkadian.

Expertise in the interlanguage helped to promote another cohesive factor: Akkadian demanded years of training in professional scribal academies, producing a cosmopolitan elite conversant with the same classical canon (the classics of Mesopotamian literature). When this elite is also responsible, as a professional component of the diplomatic corps, for managing relations and resolving conflicts between members of the system, its integrative function will be readily appreciated.

Ultimately, diplomacy played a crucial role in managing international relations in the Amarna period. Without it, there could have been no brotherhood of Great Kings. Despite its shortcomings, exchanges were conducted, disputes contained, dynastic ties promoted, and on the whole, peace preserved. Diplomacy created the conditions for international relations to flourish.

Notes

Chapter 1. Introduction: The Amarna System

1. See Gianto, *Word Order Variation,* 10–11.

2. We are grateful to Dr. Avi Segal of the Department of International Relations, Hebrew University of Jerusalem, for this distinction.

Chapter 2. The Great Powers' Club

1. Bezold, *Oriental Diplomacy.*

2. The relevance of the new documents for reconstructing the international relations of the "Tell-Amarna-Zeit" or "Tell-Amarna-Periode" was already emphasized in the first report: Winckler, *Ausgrabungen,* 1–59.

3. See especially Nougayrol, *Palais Royal d'Ugarit.*

4. Wiseman, *The Alalakh Tablets.*

5. On the international relations of that period, cf. Munn-Rankin, "Diplomacy," 68–110; Zaccagnini, "Gift-Exchange," 189–253.

6. The famous treaty between Ebla and Abarsal has been published by Sollberger, "Treaty," 129–55, with fig. 28a–g; cf. Edzard, "Vertrag," 187–217.

7. On the early stages of the debate, see Finley, *The Bücher-Meyer Controversy;* on further developments, see Lepore, "Economia antica," 3–33. For recent evaluations in the context of Near Eastern studies, see Renger, "Probleme," 166–78; Zaccagnini, "Les échanges," 213–25.

8. See, e.g., Korošec, *International Relations;* and, more recently, Kestemont, *Diplomatique.*

9. This holds especially true for Zaccagnini, *Lo scambio,* and Pintore, *Il matrimonio.*

10. This was my position in *Three Amarna Essays,* 21–33.

11. This is the basic thesis of my *Prestige and Interest.*

12. On the main features of the persuasive message, see Perelman and Olbrechts-Tyteca, *Traité de l'argumentation.* One of the most influential studies on political language is Lasswell and Leites, *Language of Politics.*

13. On the technical meaning of this title, see Artzi and Malamat, "The Great King."

14. Liverani, *Prestige and Interest*, 21, 197–202, 211–17. Accepted also by Cohen, "All in the Family," 11–28.

15. Wiseman, "Is it Peace?" 317–22.

16. Cf. in particular Tushratta's use of the terms "father-in-law"/"son-in-law" in the opening address (EA 19–21, 23–24, 27–29), and his mention of Gilu-Hepa (EA 17) and Tadu-Hepa (EA 23, 26–29).

17. In fact, it was used to say that one is perfectly well, even when later on in the same letter, it will emerge that the sender had a lot of problems.

18. A similar (Egyptian) protest is hinted at in EA 34 (from Alashiya).

19. The Babylonian scribes in particular seem to have considered it a rule to start their letters (immediately after the opening address and greetings) with a reference to past behavior as a model for solving present problems: EA 6:8–12; EA 8:8–12; EA 9: 6–10; EA 10:8–10.

20. See the emblematic statements in EA 19:9–14 (tenfold love), 68–69 (tenfold return); and cf. the analysis by Zaccagnini, *Lo scambio*, 139–47.

21. Cf. EA 8:11–12 (quoting the agreement between Burna-Buriash and the newly enthroned Akhenaten); EA 26 (Tushratta to Tiye, on the same occasion); EA 33 (the king of Alashiya to a new Pharaoh, probably Akhenaten); EA 41 (Suppiluliuma to the newly enthroned "Huriya," probably to be identified with Akhenaten: Meyer, "Hurija und Piphururija," 87–92). Cf. also EA 6 (newly enthroned Burna-Buriash to Amenhotep III).

22. Cf. Liverani, *Prestige and Interest*, 44–65, 79–86; on Egyptian royal inscriptions, see now Galán, *Victory and Border*.

23. Liverani, *Prestige and Interest*, 87–105.

24. Cf. ibid., 95.

25. This expression was introduced into Amarna studies by Tadmor, "Decline of Empires," 3.

26. For a detailed treatment of this principle, see Liverani, "Storiografia," 267–97; cf. Zaccagnini, *Lo scambio*, 100–108.

27. Cf. EA 11:Rs 22–23 for a paradigmatic statement: "Among kings there is brotherhood, amity, peace and good relations [if] there is abundance in precious stones, abundance in silver, abundance in [gold]." (Moran's translation differs in part.)

28. Cf. Liverani, *Prestige and Interest*, 218–29.

29. Ibid., 150–59.

30. Liverani, "Seasonal Pattern," 337–48.

31. Cf. the evidence and somewhat optimistic calculations in Kühne, *Chronologie*, 105–24.

32. See Meier, *Messenger*; Holmes, "Messengers," 376–81.

33. EA 16:29–31. For the king of Alashiya suggesting a regular annual pace, see EA 33:27–32.

34. Note that EA 39 contains no "message" at all and was probably intended to accredit a merchant as if he were a royal messenger (in order to avoid customs problems); the same is true of EA 40, whose message is purely commercial.

35. Cf. the discussion between Kadashman-Enlil and Amenhotep III in EA 1: the two Babylonian "messengers" mentioned in lines 18–19 were probably a trading agent and a caravan leader (dismissed as an "assherder").

36. Cf. Liverani, *Prestige and Interest,* 95–105, with further bibliography.

37. The concept of "ceremonial contention" has been used by Pintore in particular: *Il matrimonio.*

38. On the norms of gift exchange, see Mauss, "Essai sur le don," 30–186; on hospitality, see Pitt-Rivers, *Fate of Shechem,* chap. 5.

39. Cf. the "new palace" of Assur-uballit (EA 16:6); the "work in the temple" of Burna-Buriash (EA 9:15; cf. 4:40–47; EA 7:63–65; EA 11:Rs. 30); and the mausoleum of Tushratta (EA 19:44–58; EA 29:146–63).

40. For this procedure, see Liverani, *Prestige and Interest,* 250–51.

41. Cf. especially the plague in EA 35:10–15. Note that Egypt follows a different line, in that it cites ideological reasons (EA 4:6–7; EA 7:33–39) and not diplomatic excuses.

42. Zaccagnini, *Lo scambio,* 83–85.

43. Sahlins, "Exchange-Value," 112, 118.

44. Liverani, *Prestige and Interest,* 224–25.

45. Beckman, *Hittite Diplomatic Texts,* 128 (KUB XXI 38: 47–56).

46. On both problems (disappearing princesses and "mixed" gifts), see most recently Liverani, "Hattushili," 209–10.

Chapter 3. International Law in the Amarna Age

1. The earliest account of a border dispute, between the Sumerian states of Lagash and Umma in the twenty-fifth century B.C.E., is a dramatic tale of treaties, breach, and consequences: Cooper, *Reconstructing History.* Although individual legal systems varied greatly, there was a common legal tradition throughout the ancient Near East that continued into the first millennium B.C.E. As a result, it is possible to draw examples of a legal principle from different periods and countries.

2. Kelsen, *General Theory,* 181–82, 191–93, 197–99.

3. Legal historians have, it is true, suggested that their role was no different from that of a modern ruler. Korošec called the Hittite emperor "der oberste Funktionär des Staates" (*Staatsverträge,* 46). Similarly, Kestemont states that "en matière juridique publique, le chef d'État et la communauté nationale constituent deux pôles d'une seule et même personnalité morale: la communauté nationale est le siège réel des droits et obligations et le chef d'État en est le répresentant" (*Diplomatique,* 48). All that these authors are doing, however, is unconsciously imposing the corporate model upon ancient polities, the result being jarring anachronism.

4. For the lay reader, it should be emphasized that the term "domestic" in this

article has nothing to do with family or family law; it is simply used as defined above, in opposition to international law.

5. E.g., Cohen, "All in the Family," 11–26; Artzi, "Mourning," 167.

6. See Stager, "Archaeology of the Family."

7. EA 162:1, rightly translated "ruler" by Moran. This was not an innovation of the Amarna Age; in the Old Babylonian period we find references such as "Hammurabi, the man of Babylon."

8. The theoretical picture is complicated somewhat by the existence of vassal kings—see below.

9. EA 162, 367, 369, 370. See Moran, xxvii, nn. 73, 74. The term "mayor" (*ḫazannu*), not used in the formal address, refers to their function in the Egyptian administration.

10. Kestemont, *Diplomatique*, 201–4.

11. Translated by A. Goetze, in ANET, 394–96; cf. Houwink ten Cate, "Hittite Royal Prayers," 97–98.

12. There was no such thing as a spiritual sphere into which human courts would not enter: they saw it as within their jurisdiction to punish even "victimless" crimes against the gods, such as incest.

13. E.g., an Old Babylonian diplomatic dispatch reports that King Atamrum of Andarig, a vassal of King Zimri-Lim of Mari, has seven vassal kings of his own! (Joannès, "Atamrum," 172).

14. Laws of Hammurabi 229–30: "If a builder builds a house for a man and does not make his work strong, and the house that he built collapses and causes the death of . . . the houseowner's son, the son of that builder shall be killed."

15. For the crime of treason and blasphemy, Naboth was executed along with his sons: 1 Kings 21; 2 Kings 9:26.

16. The Amarna letters reveal a series of obligations that were taken very seriously but that were clearly no more than etiquette: e.g., inquiring after the health of a brother monarch, inviting a brother monarch to a special festival, sending greetings on accession to the throne, and declaring official mourning on the death of a brother monarch. See Korošec, *Staatsverträge*, 47–48; Artzi, "Mourning," 167.

17. On passports for envoys, see Meier, *Messenger*, 89–93.

18. Ibid., 229–45.

19. As illustrated in the biblical account of the shameful treatment of King David's envoys. Half their beards were shaved off and their clothes cut off at the middle. David responded with an armed expedition: 2 Sam. 10:1–14.

20. Following the interpretation of Redford, cited by Moran, 41, n. 16.

21. Green, "Wenamun's Demand," 116–17.

22. PRU IV 17.146: 154–57.

23. See Westbrook, *Studies,* 39–83.

24. See, e.g., the detailed provisions of the Egypt-Hatti peace treaty: Beckman, *Hittite Diplomatic Texts,* No. 15, paras. 12–19, pp. 93–94.

25. The Hittites sometimes conceded limited extradition rights to their vassals in

the vassal treaty. See, e.g., Treaty between Mursili II of Hatti and Kupanta-Kurunta of Mira: Beckman, *Hittite Diplomatic Texts*, No. 11, para. 22, p. 75.

26. E.g., Westbrook, *Marriage Law*, 137 (YOS 8 51), and Falkenstein, *Gerichtsurkunden* II, No. 17, pp. 27–28.

27. E.g., Falkenstein, *Gerichtsurkunden* II, No. 17, pp. 27–28.

28. Beckman, *Hittite Diplomatic Texts*, No. 8, para. 22, p. 59.

29. Two agreements that were identical in substance could be domestic or international, according to the status of the parties. The Assyrian emperor Esarhaddon designated as his successor a younger son and feared that disparate elements in the empire would revolt against the son after his death. He therefore concluded a series of treaties taking an oath of loyalty to his successor from members of the royal family, high officials, and vassal kings. The treaties are all identical in form, whether with internal subjects or with vassal kings (Parpola, *Neo-Assyrian Treaties*, No. 6, pp. xxviii–xxxi, 28–58). But where the Hittite kings dealt with primitive countries that had no monarchy, they contracted with the leading householders as representatives of their community, who were thus elevated to international status (Beckman, *Hittite Diplomatic Texts*, No. 3, pp. 22–30).

30. Art. 2(1)(a) of the Vienna Convention on the Law of Treaties (1969, am. 1980) defines a treaty as "an international agreement between states in written form and governed by international law." Korošec considered the ancient treaty document dispositive (*Staatsverträge*, 15–16), but so much evidence has since accrued of purely oral treaties that writing cannot have been a condition of legal validity. See, e.g., Charpin, "Alliance," 109–16. The law was the same for domestic contracts: Renger, "Sealing," 75–76.

31. ARM 26/2 404:60–63: Joannès, "Atamrum," 175.

32. See, e.g., Charpin, *Archives*, 144–45, 179–82; Charpin, "Zimri-lim," 144–45; Eidem, "Old Assyrian Treaty," 185–207. Thus, in a reciprocal treaty, there could initially be two tablets, each containing unilateral obligations. The practice of interleaving the mutual obligations on a single tablet also existed, however, as can be seen already in the Ebla treaty from the twenty-fifth century: Edzard, "Vertrag."

33. The two extant versions of the treaty reflect the procedure, although the tablets already contained the obligations of both parties. The version from the Hittite archives is an Akkadian original drafted by the Egyptian chancery, whereas the version on the temple at Karnak is an Egyptian translation of the Akkadian original drafted by the Hittite chancery (Spallinger, "Treaty," 299). Although almost identical in substance, their difference in format reflects the insistence of each side on drafting the text to which the opposing monarch had to swear.

34. Moran's objections (122, n. 2) to Altman's surmise ("Justification Motif," 30) are therefore unfounded, although there might have been a further tablet drafted as a record of the treaty, had it come to fruition.

35. E.g., Korošec, *Staatsverträge*, 12–15.

36. Ibid., 24–25.

37. See Altman, "Historical Prologue," 180–82, 203–5.

38. Liverani, "Storiografia."

39. E.g., Schachermeyr, "Wertung," 182.

40. Lorton, *Juridical Terminology,* 138, Nos. 2 and 3, cf. 111, No. 4 (Tutankhamun). Cf. the ruse of the Gibeonites in Jos. 9:3–27.

41. Cf. the letter of the Hittite king Suppiluliuma to the king of Ugarit, offering him a treaty of vassalage as one of the rewards for giving military support: Beckman, *Hittite Diplomatic Texts,* No. 19, pp. 119–20.

42. See the Hittite Instructions to Temple Officials, Sturtevant, *Chrestomathy,* 2.28–33, pp. 148–49.

43. Edgerton, "Strikes," 141.

44. Cf. Parpola's remarks on Assyrian vassal treaties (XV–XVI).

45. Zaccagnini, "Forms of Alliance," 51–67; cf. Liverani, "Political Lexicon," 49–51.

46. Thutmose III from the Canaanite rulers at Megiddo (*Urk.* IV 1234:17–1236:1); Amenhotep II from the ruler of Qadesh (*Urk.* IV 1304:2).

47. Beckman, *Hittite Diplomatic Texts,* No. 22D, pp. 124–25.

48. Ibid., No. 15, paras. 7, 9, p. 93; cf. No. 11, para. 18, pp. 73–74. In this volume, Artzi argues that Egypt's failure to intervene when the Mittanian king was murdered by a usurper (EA 17) is evidence that it had no treaty relations, since protection of the partner's dynasty was a standard treaty obligation. But the usurper did not ascend the throne himself; instead, he ruled as regent for the murdered king's son. To me, this suggests a concern to avoid triggering the terms of a treaty, by conserving the outward form of dynastic succession.

Chapter 4. The Amarna Age: An International Society in the Making

1. The term *international society* reflects the use of state and nation as synonyms in English. *International society* is to be understood in its general sense, not as a society of nations per se.

2. Bull, *Anarchical Society,* 13.

3. Wight, *Systems of States,* 33. He tends to use the expression "international society," but in his *Systems of States* introduces the equivalent term "states-system."

4. Ibid., 25.

5. James, "System or Society," 275–78.

6. Keohane, *International Institutions.*

7. Neorealism and Neo-liberal Institutionalism differ in many respects, such as relative and absolute gains, the impact of time, and the possibility of learning, which deeply affect the possibility of effective and stable cooperation. Nevertheless, in this context we are interested in their common points rather than in their differences.

8. Buzan, "International System."

9. Wendt, "Anarchy."

10. Morgenthau, *Politics among Nations.* Another example of a great realist thinker

who can be interpreted from the point of view of constructivism is E. H. Carr: see Dunne, "Social Construction."

11. Quoted in Morgenthau, *Politics among Nations,* 237.

12. "Intersubjective" refers to a subjective, socially constructed reality shared by all concerned parties.

13. Buzan, "International System," 343–44.

14. Ibid., 344–45.

15. See Wendt, "Anarchy."

16. See, for example, Walker, *Inside/Outside.*

17. The Indus valley and the Aegean area could probably already be included in the system.

18. Liverani, *Antico Oriente,* 372–402; on interstate relations, see particularly 384–90.

19. This is evident in most of Rib-Hadda's messages (EA 73–96).

20. Cohen, *Rules of the Game,* 8; Luard, *International Society,* 201.

21. Kratochwil, *Rules, Norms and Decisions,* 69.

22. Liverani, "Political Lexicon."

23. There is some uncertainty in this respect. Artzi, "Middle-Assyrian Kingdom," maintains that the Egyptian king here is Tutankhamun.

24. Liverani, *Antico Oriente,* 604.

25. Keohane, *International Institutions,* 163.

26. Bull, *Anarchical Society,* 71.

27. See ibid., 97–121, 178–93.

28. No reference to past Egyptian hostility is mentioned in the historical introductions to the vassal treaties imposed on the component parts of Arzawa after its defeat and dismemberment by Mursili II. Nor is special mention made of Egypt as a potential enemy, as would surely be the case had the two powers clashed in the past (Beckman, *Hittite Diplomatic Texts,* 64–88).

29. Liverani, *Antico Oriente,* 461–67.

30. Wight, *Systems of States,* who had correctly identified the Amarna Age as a "secondary states-system," in my opinion missed the point when he wrote about a balance of power system with Babylonia, and Crete holding the balance.

31. Hellenistic kingdoms formed a subsystem because the interstate system stretched at the time from Rome and Carthage in the west to the Indian kingdoms in the east.

32. It would be interesting to see what kind of conditions (technological, geographical, ideological, etc.) made the construction of a balance of power possible in the subsystem of Greek city-states.

33. See Liverani, *Guerra e diplomazia,* 131–61.

34. Wight, *Power Politics.*

35. Cohen, *Rules of the Game,* 100.

36. See Liverani, *Guerra e diplomazia.*

37. Wendt, "Collective Identity," 385.

38. See Liverani, *Guerra e diplomazia.*

Chapter 5. Realism, Constructionism, and the Amarna Letters

1. The following description draws from the two standard works of realist thought, Morgenthau, *Politics among Nations,* and Waltz, *International Politics.* This section is also guided by an excellent discussion of realism and constructivism (as well as other challenges to realism) put forth by Mearsheimer, "False Promise." In general, Morgenthau pursues a more classical form of realism emphasizing flawed human nature, whereas Waltz and Mearsheimer are neorealists, that is, they focus on the impact of the distribution of state power in an environment of anarchy to explain behavior.

2. On the continuity of world politics in the realist vision, see Layne, "Kant or Cant," 10–12.

3. This list draws from Mearsheimer's description of realism in "False Promise."

4. A good, concise view of constructivism can be found in Wendt, "Constructing International Politics."

5. Wendt, "Anarchy."

6. Cohen, "All in the Family."

7. For a similar argument that asserts that feudal Europe also behaved consistently with realism, see Fischer, "Feudal Europe."

8. Schulman, "Diplomatic Marriages," and "Some Remarks"; Liverani, "Political Lexicon," and *Prestige and Interest;* Singer, "Concise History"; Artzi, "Middle-Assyrian Kingdom"; and Frandsen, "Egyptian Imperialism."

9. Kaplan, "Coming Anarchy."

10. For more on the desire of Assyria to understand Egyptian intentions, see Artzi, "Middle Assyrian Kingdom."

11. Liverani, "Political Lexicon," 49–50.

12. Ibid., 51. Although aligning with a patron to ensure your survival is consistent with realism, aligning with a patron (e.g., Pharaoh) to ensure your survival after death can be construed as being more in tune with constructivism. We have no way of knowing whether the attractiveness of an alliance with Egypt stemmed more from traditional realist motivations of surviving in this world or from the hope of everlasting life, which would be better explained by the constructivist approach.

13. Artzi, "Middle-Assyrian Kingdom," 32.

14. Schulman, "Some Observations," esp. 65.

15. See also Singer, "Concise History," for more on this point.

Chapter 6. The Egyptian Perspective on Mittani

1. This view discounts the claim for Amenhotep I made by Redford based on a Karnak temple inscription of an unnamed ruler. Tunip is mentioned on it, but the

text has variously been assigned to the early Eighteenth, the mid-Eighteenth, and the Twelfth Dynasties. Redford, "A Gate Inscription," 270–87.

2. Breasted (*Ancient Records* II, 31, sec. 73) translates *mw ḳd* as Euphrates and notates it as such. However, challenges to this view (Vandersleyen, *L'Egypte*, 257–59, with references) have emerged because the term *inverted water* appears in later New Kingdom references to Nubian toponyms and to the route to Punt: for example, one Ramesside letter mentions Shasu of *mw ḳd* attacking the gold mines in Nubia in the far eastern reaches of the Wadi Allaqi. In addition, *mw ḳd* appears as a toponym on an ostracon listing the Nubian localities of Kush, Miu, Ibhet, *Mw ḳd*. Vandersleyen, 258; Zibelius, *Orts- und Völkernamen,* 197; Posener, "Mwḳd-V," 39.

3. Bradbury, "Tombos Inscription," 6–9.

4. Vandersleyen, *L'Egypte,* 303–6, makes an elaborate argument for a different itinerary. Although he may or may not be entirely correct, his point that the Euphrates region cannot be definitely identified is a valid one.

5. Vandersleyen, *L'Egypte,* 300ff, argues that the river in question is the Litani, but he is unconvincing.

6. Simons, *Handbook,* passim.

7. See the useful discussion in Liverani, *Prestige and Interest,* 257–60, esp. 259–60.

8. "Accounting relating to the gold of honor: lion; *shebiu* (gold collar of rings): 2; flies: 2; rings: 4" (*Urk.* IV 892). "Accounting relating to the gold: *shebiu* collars: 2; rings: 4; flies: 2; lion: 1" (*Urk.* IV 893).

9. Tomb of Dedi, Number 200, PM I² 1, 303–304; tomb of Suemniwet, Number 92, PMI² 1, 187–89 (in process of publication by the author). Suemniwet wears the lion and fly pectoral twice in the tomb.

10. Schulman, "Hittites," 54, pl. 14.1. Kendall, "Helmets," 201–31, esp. 215–19, and 219–21 for the production of such helmets in Egypt. According to the studies cited, these helmets would have been Syrian in type.

11. TT 42, 74, 84, 85, 86, 88, 92, 100, 131, 155, 200. In 84, the chief of Naharin is included among Asiatics generally designated in text as "defeated Retenu," while in tomb 86 direct references to the defeat of Mittani (*Mtn*) and the Great Bend River (*Pḫr wr*) occur (*Urk.* IV 930–31). In 100, Rekhmire pictures the Syrian captives in several scenes as they were put to work back in Egypt.

12. Garis Davies, *Ken-Amūn,* 30–31, pl. XXII.

13. Ibid., 29–30, pls. XVIII, XX.

14. See the excellent study of Lilyquist and Brill, *Glass,* esp. 10–12, 25–27. Lilyquist mentions that the imitation of marble was a distinctively Near Eastern, not Egyptian, style and is found in Egypt only in early imported glass and imitations thereof.

15. For year 33, *Urk.* IV 699; for references to "flat bottomed dishes," Annals Years 23 (Megiddo and the Lebanon), Year 24 (Retenu), Year 38 (Syria, mentioned "flat dishes, and with heads of goats and heads of a lion, vessels of all the work of Djahy"), Year 39 (Syria, flat dishes of gold and silver, and one with the head of an ox), Year 42 (unknown Syrian toponyms, including both flat dishes and ones with heads of bulls), *Urk.* IV 665–732.

16. Simpson, "Reschef," 244–46; Leclant, "Astarte," 499–509.

17. See ibid.

18. Dr. C. Lilyquist is republishing the finds from the tomb of these three queens. Her work on glass and gold (see note 14 above) has been precipitated by this important effort. For earlier publication, see Winlock, *Princesses*. The women's names in Egyptian were Menwai (*Mnw3i*), Meleti (*Mlti*), and Menhet (*Mnḫt*).

19. Murnane, *Coregencies,* 44–48, *Urk.* IV 1287–1316.

20. A deben, as weighed with actual marked Egyptian weights, was approximately 91 grams, or 2.9 ounces troy, there being approximately 31.1 grams to the troy ounce and twelve ounces to the troy pound.

21. *Urk.* IV 1309 and also later, *iw n.f wrw Mtn inw.sn ḥr psdw.sn r dbḥ ḥtpw sb.tw t3w.f ndm n ꜥnḫ, Urk.* IV 1326. "The Chiefs of Mittani come to him, their deliveries upon their backs, to request offering gifts of his Majesty, and in quest of his sweet breath of life." The verb *iw* may be a Second Tense form, while *sb.tw* must be a circumstantial. The translations in Liverani, *Prestige and Interest,* 231–322, are slightly incorrect, in that there is *no* indication of "in return for" implied by *sb.tw* "in quest of," literally, "that one might send." Rather, it indicates the actual aim of the diplomatic mission bringing gifts, i.e., further and stable diplomatic relations. From his discussion of the ideology of life, Liverani would agree with such an assessment: see *Prestige and Interest,* 230–39.

22. Lorton, *Juridical Terminology;* Liverani, *Prestige and Interest,* 230–39.

23. "I found the ruler of Yam, he having gone himself (*šm r.f*), to the land of Tjemeh (Libya) in order to smite (*ḥḥw*) the Tjemeh people at the western corner of heaven. I went out after him to the land of Tjemeh, and I propitiated him in order that he might praise all the gods on behalf of the sovereign" (*Urk.* I 125–27).

24. For uncountable examples, see Baines, *Fecundity.*

25. Compare the text of Harkhuf acting on behalf of the king in an area where state hierarchies were unimportant.

26. For a discussion of Egyptian relations with Syria during this reign, see Bryan, *Thutmose IV,* 336–44.

27. PM I² 1, 187; 153–54; 185.

28. Unpublished as yet. See Letellier, "Thoutmosis IV," 36–52 for bibliography.

29. In my opinion, all the scarabs were manufactured much later for the first *sed* festival in Year 30. Their texts may have been disseminated in other forms much earlier, however. See, most recently, Berman, *Egypt's Dazzling Sun,* with full bibliography.

30. Pestman, *Marriage,* 65–71.

31. Ibid., 106–07; 143–46.

32. Ibid., 153–54; 162–64. Allam, "Ehe," 1162–81, esp. 1176.

33. A brief summary in Allam, "Women," 123–35.

34. Some of the following discussion is adapted from the author's essay "In Women," 25–46.

35. Schmitz, *Königssohn*, 33, 37, 117–33, for the Old Kingdom, and Spalinger, "Remarks," 103–15.

36. Spalinger, "Remarks," 114.

37. Robins, *Women*, 30–36, esp. 32.

38. In general, see Schulman, "Diplomatic Marriages," 177–93.

39. See the important insight of Liverani, *Prestige and Interest*, 279, with regard to Ankhesenamun or Meretaten.

40. Vandersleyen, *L'Egypte*, 376–776; Simons, *Handbook*, 132a5.

Chapter 7. Intelligence in the Amarna Letters

1. For a rare study of intelligence in the ancient Near East, see Follet, "Deuxième Bureau."

2. The best general introduction to intelligence is Herman, *Intelligence Power*.

3. See EA 5:13–33 and EA 162:22–29. In the latter, it precedes secret information about contacts between Amurru and Qadesh.

4. Liverani, "Amarna Trade."

5. Moran, 102, fn. 2.

6. There are examples in modern history of *intelligence alliances,* or partnerships for intelligence cooperation, including the exchange of information. Such agreements need not have a *military assistance* dimension.

7. However, it would be surprising if he had not. The Mari archives of four hundred years before give firsthand evidence of the extensive espionage activity of Ibalpi-El, the ambassador of Zimri-Lim, king of Mari, at the court of Hammurabi (ARM, 26/2, 159–86). There is also the suggestion of *Mittanian* espionage against Egypt in EA 29. Relations are at a low point between the countries. Two Mittanian diplomats (one an important scribe), having already been allowed to return home from a crucial mission to Egypt (EA 24), are charged by Pharaoh with committing a serious unspecified crime, by implication against the Egyptian state. Though refusing to divulge details of the charge, he asks for their execution. Tushratta sends them only into exile. I read the episode as a spy scandal. Pharaoh is coy because he cannot reveal counterintelligence information. As long as relations are good, great powers turn a blind eye to each others' intelligence activities.

8. Note, in these examples, the intelligence marker "hear."

9. Kent, *Strategic intelligence.*

Chapter 8. Imperial Egypt and the Limits of Power

1. For Egypt's relations with Asia during the Old and Middle Kingdoms see Helck, *Verwaltung*, 4–84; Redford, *Egypt, Canaan, and Israel*, 3–97. Nubia, where Egypt moved its border south to the Second Cataract during the Middle Kingdom, is still

covered most thoroughly in Säve-Söderbergh, *Ägypten und Nubien,* 5–116, though cf. Adams, *Nubia,* 163–92, and O'Connor, *Early States.*

2. The rise of Egypt's empire in Nubia is treated broadly by Adams, *Nubia,* 217–45, adding Bradbury, "The Tombos Inscription"; and cf. O'Connor, "The Land," for the elusive land of Irem, which lay beyond Egypt's zone of control.

3. Note the astute comments of Frandsen, *Egyptian Imperialism,* 177–79.

4. The broad lines of Egyptian policy in western Asia during the early Eighteenth Dynasty are well discussed by Redford, "A Gate Inscription," and Weinstein, "The Egyptian Empire," 1–12. On the formation of Egypt's empire in the Near East see, in general, Helck, *Beziehungen,* 107–67, and Redford, *Egypt, Canaan, and Israel,* 125–91.

5. Ancient "Akhet-Aten" or "Horizon of the Solar Orb"; in Arabic, "(Tell) el-Amarna."

6. See Kemp, *Ancient Egypt,* 216–317, for a recent and even-handed treatment of the period. Current controversies on Akhenaten's beliefs are discussed by Murnane, "Nature of the Aten."

7. Against the classic statements on the pacifist Akhenaten (Breasted, *History,* 379–95; Wilson, *Burden,* 207, 230–31), see Schulman, "Some Remarks," Several, "Reconsidering," and Murnane, *Road to Kadesh,* 2–21.

8. E.g., Redford, *Akhenaten,* 195–97, on Akhenaten's "vacillating" nature and its impact on foreign policy, for which cf. Murnane, *Road to Kadesh,* 7–8.

9. Murnane, *Texts,* 134–35 [sec. 66.6], 162–64 [sec. 71.1], with references.

10. E.g., Aldred, *Akhenaten,* 178–81, and (more circumspectly) Redford, *Akhenaten,* 186.

11. The rhetoric of imperialist nationalism in Egyptian records is covered by Lorton, *Juridical Terminology* and Grimal, *Termes;* cf. Liverani, *Prestige and Interest,* 51–58, 115–25, 144–49.

12. On imperial government in Nubia see, in general, Habachi, "Administration of Nubia." Nubian princes are discussed by Edel, "Zur Familie," Säve-Söderbergh, "Tomb of the Prince," and Simpson, *Heka-nefer,* esp. 26–27. For Libya, see Kitchen, "Arrival of the Libyans," 15–16; and cf. the observations of Liverani, *Prestige and Interest,* 240–46, on "deliveries" to Egypt from remote or unincorporated areas.

13. On the functioning of the Asiatic empire see, in general, Frandsen, "Egyptian Imperialism," 174–80; and Redford, *Egypt, Canaan, and Israel,* 192–213.

14. For these areas and their administration see, for convenience, Ahituv, "Economic Factors," and Na'aman, "Economic Aspects" and "Biryawaza of Damascus."

15. The literature on such interactions, and on the vexed term *inw* ("deliveries"), is large: see, most recently, Galán, "Heritage," and Bleiberg, "Official Gift," along with the illuminating comments of Liverani, *Prestige and Interest,* 240–46, 255–64.

16. Cf. EA 162:22–29 in which Pharaoh rounds on Aziru, king of Amurru, for consorting with his overlord's enemy, the king of Qadesh.

17. This obligation, implied in a number of letters specifying that the vassal is to stand ready with his warriors to join an oncoming Egyptian force, is discussed by

Naʿaman, "Praises" — although note the alternative (and, in this writer's opinion, less convincing) interpretation by Liverani, "Seasonal Pattern."

18. The taking of hostages, first established as a policy by Thutmose III (see *ANET*, 239), is occasionally reflected in the Amarna Letters (e.g., EA 162:42–54, 296:23–99); and the same is true for "diplomatic marriages" (EA 99, 187; cf. Schulman, "Diplomatic Marriages").

19. Deportation was practiced both by the Egyptians (e.g., *ANET*, 245–47; cf. Spallinger, "Historical Implications," and Janssen, "Beuteliste") and the Hittites (Beckman, *Hittite Diplomatic Texts*, 39 [sec. 4], 96 [sec. 4], cf. 99–100 [secs. 4–5]); and cf. EA 162:33–38, where Aziru is warned that noncompliance will mean that "you, along with your entire family, shall die by the axe of the king."

20. E.g., EA 51 obverse, 296:23–29. The assumptions underlying these relationships seem to be the same as those set out in treaties, where the contract made by two rulers results in peace between their lands (Théodoridès, "Les relations," 113, n. 100, and 117, n. 115). The assumption that vassals were legally free to change overlords at the end of a stated term (Helck, *Beziehungen*, 247; Frandsen, "Egyptian Imperialism," 175 and 187, n. 55) rests on a misinterpretation of clauses in a Hittite treaty (Beckman, *Hittite Diplomatic Texts*, 14–15 [secs. 2–8]) and is inconsistent with the relations otherwise observed between Great Powers and their subordinates.

21. See, in general, Liverani, "Contrasti"; and cf. EA 162:42–54.

22. See EA 369; and cf. the Egyptian "report" of Wenamun (translated by Wente in Simpson, *Literature*, 142–55 [where an emissary sent from Egypt to Byblos near the beginning of the eleventh century is reminded that earlier Pharaohs had paid for the wood they obtained from there]: cf. Liverani, *Prestige and Interest*, 247–54).

23. See Liverani, "Pharaoh's Letters."

24. References to "tablets" documenting past relations between Egypt and its vassals (EA 52:5–7, 74:10–12) could as easily refer to past correspondence as to treaties.

25. See Liverani, "Pharaoh's Letters," 10–11.

26. E.g., Abdul-Kader, "Administration," 134–35; Helck, *Beziehungen*, 256–57; Lorton, *Juridical Terminology*, 132; Redford, *Akhenaten*, 25; Liverani, *Prestige and Interest*, 144–49.

27. Gebel Barkal Stela of Thutmose III (*ANET*, 238). The god's name in brackets was erased during the Amarna period.

28. Morschauser, "End."

29. See Liverani, *Prestige and Interest*, 126–34.

30. See esp. ibid., 230–39, on the "ideology of life" in official rhetoric from Egypt.

31. This seems to be the sense (Moran, 122), although the end of the line is cut off.

32. See, in general, Yurco, "Painted Reliefs."

33. Wimmer, "Egyptian Temples."

34. See, most recently, the articles by Baines and Silverman in O'Connor and Silverman, *Ancient Egyptian Kingship*.

35. References to Pharaoh as a "god" occur exceptionally and only in greeting for-

mulas (e.g., EA 52–53, 144, 147–52, 168, 174–77, 179, 181–83, 185, 192). The more common address "my Sun" may reflect the influence of Egyptian solar epithets (Lorton, *Juridical Terminology*, 8–10, 21; Grimal, *Termes*, 359–75; and cf. its widespread use by Hittite kings in Beckman, *Hittite Diplomatic Texts*). Amun, wherever mentioned, is the king's "god" (EA 20:26, 71:4–6, 77:3–12, 86:3–11, 87:5–11, 95:3–6, 369:29–32); EA 24, iv:118, from Mittani, which speaks of "Teshup and Amanu, our lords, our fathers," is unusual and probably hyperbolic. Akhenaten's god, the Aten, occurs only in the name of Akhenaten's daughter Meritaten ("Mayati" in EA 155), though it may be implicit in Aziru's oath "to my gods and to (god)^{d}A" (EA 164:40; cf. Moran, 252, n. 3, and see Galán, "EA 164").

36. This is a point Akhenaten's servants repeatedly make in their tomb inscriptions—e.g., Panehsy (Murnane, *Texts*, 171 [sec. 77.1]) and Tutu (ibid., 197 middle [sec. 89.11]), both late: cf. Murnane, "Nature of the Aten," 36–40.

37. Thus explicitly in the Great Hymn to the Aten in the tomb of Ay (Murnane, *Texts*, 114–15 [sec. 58.B.4]).

38. Liverani, "Contrasti," 1983, and *Prestige and Interest*, 187–96.

39. See Lorton, *Juridical Terminology*, for Eighteenth Dynasty examples; comparanda for later periods are in Grimal, *Termes*, esp. pp. 50–60, 322–35.

40. For example, in the letter that a tipsy Amenhotep II (ca. 1426–1400 B.C.E.) sent to his viceroy of Nubia, with its expressions of open contempt for Asiatics and Nubians: see Manuelian, *Studies*, 155–58.

41. See Frandsen, "Egyptian Imperialism," 185–87, nn. 49–50, for a discussion of this case and objections to it.

42. See Moran, xxvii, n. 73; Gardiner, *Egyptian Grammar*, 1:31*–32*.

43. See, for example, EA 292:26–40; and cf. Zorn, "The Role."

44. See Helck, *Beziehungen*, 249–50, for the "high commissioners" known from Egyptian records. On royal messengers, see Vallogia, *Recherche*.

45. Kitchen, "Review"; Vallogia, *Recherche*, 105–7 (secs. 47, 49). Other proposed identifications (e.g., in Helck, *Beziehungen*, 251) are more tenuous.

46. E.g., transcriptions such as *ihri-pita* (Egyptian *ḥry pḏt*, "archer/troop commander": Moran, 181, n. 1); and Akkadian terms translatable as Egyptian *ỉmy-r ỉw'yt*, "garrison commander" (ibid., 338, n. 6) and *ḥry ỉḥw*, "stablemaster" (ibid., 365, n. 2).

47. Discussed at length in Murnane, "Overseer." Unfortunately, we know too little about individual careers and the principles underlying promotion in Egypt to be sure how regularly such indicators of status were awarded.

48. E.g., Hachmann, "Verwaltung" (four); Helck, *Beziehungen*, 248–50 (three); Na'aman, "Political Disposition," 166 ff. (two); and Marfoe, "Between Qadesh," 494–98 (none until after the Amarna period).

49. To the incidence of high "commissioners" outranking their juniors, add the isolated title of one Djehuty (under Thutmose III), who called himself "overseer of a part of the northern foreign territory" (*ỉmr-r'n ḫ3st mḥtt*: see Lilyquist, "Gold Bowl," 13).

50. See EA 83:38–42, EA 116:73–80, EA 117:60–64, EA 71; cf. Hachmann, "Verwaltung," 42–46.

51. For the equivalence of his Akkadian title (in EA 106:38 = Moran, 179–80 with n. 9) with Egyptian *ḥbsw-bht,* "fan-carrier," see Helck, *Verwaltung,* 281, n. 5.

52. For the "Bureau for the Correspondence of Pharaoh" at el-Amarna, see Campbell, *Chronology,* 32–36, with the references collected in Kemp and Garfi, *Survey,* 93 (Q42.21, the "records office" discovered by Petrie in 1894).

53. For Aziru's letters, see EA 158, 164, 167, 169. Tutu, although formally a court official, enjoyed an ambiguous preeminence over a wide range of clergymen, treasury bureaucrats, and army officers, "all officials and chief men of the entire land" who were commanded to contribute some of their own perquisites to fatten Tutu's reward from the king (see Murnane, *Texts,* 193–94 [sec. 89.9]).

54. Helck, *Beziehungen,* 248; cf. Moran, 113, with n. 1 (EA 40, written by the prime minister of Alashiya to his "brother" and opposite number in Egypt), and 140, with n. 1 (EA 71, sent to the senior vizier by Rib-Hadda). The double vizierate is discussed by Helck, *Verwaltung,* 1–24; Gardiner, *Egyptian Grammar,* 1:19* (A 73). For Rib-Hadda's correspondent, "Haya the vizier" (known in Egypt as Huy/Amenhotep), see Gordon, "Tomb," 1989.

55. See, in general, Helck, *Beziehungen,* 495–581; cf. Stadelmann, *Gottheiten,* for religious imports; and on borrowed vocabulary, see Hoch, *Semitic Words.*

56. E.g., major domos, fan- and sealbearers: see Helck, *Beziehungen,* 352–56.

57. Generally presumed to be an Asiatic on the basis of his West Semitic name: see ibid., 249; Moran, 385.

58. Moran, 353 (I.8), 355 (III.20), although his identification as an Asiatic is uncertain: see Albright, "Cuneiform Material," 22 (62).

59. Cf. in Egyptian sources the names Aper-Anat (Martin, *Egyptian Administrative Seals,* xxi [D.15.1]) and Aper-Ba'al (Caminos, *Miscellanies,* 26; Helck, *Beziehungen,* 355 [IV.3]).

60. For Aper-El and his tomb see Zivie, *Saqqarah,* with earlier bibliography. The physical remains are discussed by Strouhal, "L'Etude" (for which reference I thank Christine Lilyquist).

61. Cautiously suggested by Zivie, *Saqqarah,* 172–75.

62. Cf. the fairly common Egyptian names Pakharu, "The Syrian," and Panehsy, "The Nubian" (Helck, *Beziehungen,* 352–53); and the West Semitic name Bint-Anat, "Daughter of (goddess) Anath," which Ramesses II would later give to his eldest daughter (Kitchen, *Ramesside Inscriptions* I, 916 [sec. 381.1], 923–24 [secs. 389–90] and *Ramesside Inscriptions II,* 598, 603–4).

63. See, in general, Liverani, *Prestige and Interest,* 33–43; and for Pharaoh "pulling rank" on the king of Babylonia, see EA 4:4–23, with the comments of Schulman, "Diplomatic Marriages," 179–80.

64. Worsening relations between Mittani and Egypt are suggested by Redford, *Akhenaten,* 195–96; a troubled but essentially solid partnership is argued in Murnane, *Road to Kadesh,* 2–11.

65. For all this, see Murnane, *Road to Kadesh,* 11–38; Schulman, "Ramesside Diplomacy."

66. See Murnane, *Road to Kadesh,* 139–44.

67. Ibid., 67–71.

Chapter 9. Egypt and Her Vassals: The Geopolitical Dimension

1. For modern comment on the significance of geography for the relations of states, see, for example: Mackinder, *Democratic Ideals,* chaps. 3 and 4; and Sprout, *Foundations of National Power,* pt. 1.

2. Naʿaman, "Economic Aspects," 183.

3. Naʿaman, "Biryawaza of Damascus," 187.

4. Singer, "Concise History," 146, 158.

5. Albright, "Amarna Letters," 116.

6. *Anchor Bible Dictionary,* 176.

7. As Amurru figures so prominently in the Amarna Letters, the following discussion focuses on it. But it may be supposed that Egypt's response to Biryawaza's Damascus would have been much the same.

8. See Liverani, "Pharaoh's Letters," 3, 5. It may also be noted that in EA 59, the citizens of Tunip apparently complain of having waited twenty years for an answer to their letters. Moran notes that this is not meant to be an accurate statement of the time that had elapsed (131, n. 5). But it nonetheless underlines the point that Pharaoh could not be relied upon for an answer to a vassal's letter.

9. See Moran, xxxiii, n. 118.

10. See Aldred, "Egypt," 84.

Chapter 10. The Egyptian-Canaanite Correspondence

1. Liverani, "Seasonal Pattern," 337–48.

2. Ibid., 39.

3. Naʿaman, "Praises to Pharaoh," 397–405.

4. Edzard, "Kamid el-Loz," 55–60; Naʿaman, "Biryawaza," 179–93.

5. Moran, xxx–xxxi.

6. For example, among the Amarna references cited in *CAD* Š/1 444a, at least four (EA 280:7; 53:60; 234:23; 82:12) should be translated "to send (a message)" rather than "to write." Also, in Rib-Hadda's early letters, the verb *šapāru* sometimes refers to verbal messages rather than to writing (e.g., EA 73:26; 74:30; 92:35–40). When the verb *šapāru* appears with no object, context alone is our guide for deciding which translation should be preferred. My analysis is based on this contextual approach.

7. EA 126:4 should, in my opinion, be rendered SI.LA (for SI.IL.LA) = *piqittu,* "delivery (of goods)." The letter does not refer to an Egyptian request of *taskarinnu* wood, as scholars assumed on the basis of Knudtzon's decipherment (^{giš}K[U-m]a). See Moran, 206, n. 2.

8. Naʿaman, "Economic Aspects," 172–85.

9. Redford, *Egypt and Canaan,* 40–42, idem, *Egypt, Canaan and Israel,* 209.

10. Liverani, *Prestige and Interest,* 259.

11. Naʿaman, "Biryawaza," 182–83, n. 18. For the correspondence of Ugarit with the Phoenician coast, see Arnaud, "Les ports de la 'Phenicie,' " 179–94, with earlier literature.

12. Moran, "Job at Byblos?" 173–81.

13. Liverani, *Prestige and Interest,* 230–39.

14. Ibid., 205–66.

15. Liverani, "Political Lexicon," 49–51 (cited from p. 51). For a systematic discussion of Liverani's arguments and an entirely different interpretation of the evidence, see Moran, "Amarna Politics," 559–72. Unfortunately, Moran's article (whose conclusions on this point are identical to my own) was available to me only after my article was sent for publication.

16. Moran, "Syrian Scribe," 155–56.

Chapter 11. The Interdependence of the Great Powers

1. The study, as a whole, is a result of the joint research project "Gift and Trade in the Ancient World" that I direct at the Istituto Universitario Orientale of Naples with the financial support of the Italian Ministry of Universities.

2. Cf. possibly the unclear passage in the Mittani letter EA 24 III 5–7: "What the Hurrian land does not want at all, what the land of Egypt does not want at all." All quotations from EA 24 follow Wilhelm's translation in Moran, 63–71. See previously Bush, "Grammar," 123, 203–4, 249–50; for a different interpretation see, however, most recently Girbal, "Der hurritische Ausdruck." Cf. perhaps also another statement of the same Burnaburiash: "For me nothing is scarce ((w)aqru) and for you nothing is scarce" (EA 10:16–17), if Moran's interpretation (p. 19 with n. 3 and quote of AHw, p. 1460b) is accepted (but note that von Soden's understanding of the passage is very different from that of Moran). The current rendering of these lines is: "There was nothing precious for me and (so) there was nothing precious for you" (cf. *CAD* A II, p. 208a). Although Moran's rendering looks attractive, especially if related to EA 7: 33–36, I wonder whether the logical connection of lines 16–17 with the arguments dealt with in the preceding lines 8–15 rather favors the traditional interpretation. (In Moran's opinion, lines 16–17 represent a "parenthetical remark," and in his translation they are put in brackets.)

3. Differently Oppenheim, *Letters,* 114.

4. But cf. EA 16:35: "We are countries far apart": the king of Assyria to Pharaoh.

5. Cf. Zaccagnini, *Lo scambio,* 203, s.v. *šulmānu.*

6. For similar Babylonian complaints, see EA 3:13–17 and 10:18–22; cf. Zaccagnini, *Lo scambio,* 83–84.

7. See, e.g., EA 7:73–82; 8; 16:37–42; cf. EA 30. For the Mittani–Amurru re-

lationships see, most recently, Liverani, "Abdi-Ashirta," and previously Zaccagnini, "Tudhaliya IV," quoting earlier literature.

8. See, most recently, Zaccagnini, "Forms of Alliance," 46–50.

9. Cf. Hagenbuchner, *Korrespondenz*, 241–280, nos. 188–203.

10. See especially KBo I 10 + KUB III 72; cf. Hagenbuchner, *Korrespondenz*, 281–300, no. 204.

11. Obv. 43–54; Rev. 49–55: cf. Hagenbuchner, *Korrespondenz*, ibid.; Oppenheim, *Letters*, 146; Zaccagnini, "Forms of Alliance," 43–44, n. 18.

12. See, most recently, Cohen, "All in the Family."

13. Cf. Zaccagnini, *Lo scambio*, 149–60.

14. I have dealt with the metaphorical use of the concept of brotherhood in Zaccagnini, *Lo scambio*, 108–17. For an explicit refusal to accept a brotherly relationship between Hatti and Assyria, regardless of Hittite full acknowledgment of an equal rank with the Assyrian king, see the Boghazköi letter KUB XXIII 102: cf. Hagenbuchner, *Korrespondenz* 1989, 260–64, no. 192, and previously Zaccagnini, *Lo scambio*, 44–45 and nn. 110–11.

15. This passage has been differently restored and translated: in addition to Moran, 22, see, e.g., *CAD* K, p. 26a; A I, p. 57a; AHw, p. 418a; Pintore, *Il matrimonio*, 63. In any case, the concept expressed by Burnaburiash, who ingeniously resorts to quoting an anonymous utterance, seems perfectly clear.

16. Note the word pair *šulmānu-unūtu*, which corresponds to the word pair *šulmu-šulmānu* in EA 7, already commented on.

17. Cf. Edzard, "Beziehungen."

18. Cf. Zaccagnini, *Lo scambio*, 121–22.

19. Cf. Liverani, "Elementi 'irrazionali,'" 307–12 ("L'intervento dell'argento"). See, however, the requests for "refined silver" (EA 37:18) and "the very best (?) silver" (EA 35:20), which might specifically allude to actual shipments of this metal.

20. Cf. Edel, *Ägyptische Ärzte*; Zaccagnini, "Patterns of Mobility," esp. 250–56.

21. I do not share Moran's perplexities (62) about the widely accepted and most plausible explanation for this episode, especially in the light of a much later but cogent piece of parallel evidence (the Bentresh stela), commented on in the literature cited in the previous note.

22. Zaccagnini, "Patterns of Mobility," 253–56.

23. In addition to Zaccagnini, *Lo scambio*, I would refer to some of my other contributions: "Ceremonial Exchange"; "Dono e tributo"; "Lo scambio dei beni."

24. Cf. Zaccagnini, "Gift Exchange."

25. As ingeniously pointed out by Liverani, "Elementi 'irrazionali,'" esp. 299–304 ("Lo scambio di un prodotto contro sé stesso").

26. Consider again the statement of EA 7:33–36, concerning the respective total self-sufficiency of Babylonia and Egypt, and see the most illuminating passages of EA 27 and 29, in which Pharaoh perfidiously reproaches Tushratta for only (!) asking statues of gold and promises to send him also statues of genuine lapis lazuli: "Never mind giving them (i.e., Tushratta and Tadu-Hepa) statues just of solid cast gold! I will

give you ones made also of genuine lapis lazuli" and adds: "and in addition I will give you, along with the statues, much other gold and goods beyond measure" (EA 27:21–23); "What are statutes of just gold with nothing else that my brother has asked for? Come on! I will make ones of gold but also of genuine lapis lazuli and send them to you" (EA 29:51–52). My translation of these passages is slightly different from that of Moran, 87, 94, and Adler, *Das Akkadische*, 215, 237.

27. Cf. Zaccagnini, *Lo scambio*, 68–69; Liverani, *Prestige and Interest*, 218–23.

28. Cf. Zaccagnini, *Lo scambio*, 66–67. See also KBo I 10+ KUB III 72: Obv. 41: "In the country of my brother (= the king of Babylonia) horses are more plentiful than straw," to be related to a detailed request for tall fine horses in the final section of the letter (Rev. 62–65); cf. Hagenbuchner, *Korrespondenz*, 282, 289, no. 204.

29. Cf. Zaccagnini, *Lo scambio*, 70–78 ("Contrasti, rifiuti, dilazioni"), esp. 72–74, with previous literature; Liverani, "Elementi 'irrazionali,'" esp. 301, n. 12, for the well-known practice of sending "soliciting gifts," a practice that often characterizes the Amarna (and Boghazköi) dynamics of exchanges.

30. Zaccagnini, *Lo scambio*, 78–89; Zaccagnini, "Ceremonial Exchange," esp. 60–61.

31. Cf. Zaccagnini, *Lo scambio*, esp. 83–87. For complaints concerning the quality of horses and lapis lazuli sent from Babylonia to Hatti, see KBo I 10+ KUB III 72: Rev. 62–66, 67–72 (Hagenbuchner, *Korrespondenz*, 287, 294, no. 204).

32. Cf. Moran, 105, n. 10, and see also EA 4:37, commented on below.

33. Cf. the well-known clauses concerning the annual tribute that had to be personally delivered to the Hittite sovereign, and the most recent interpretation of the Amarna "tributary" rulership over Syria-Palestine, by Liverani, "Seasonal Pattern." In this latter case, a yearly rhythm has been convincingly proposed. Note that Liverani's view has been challenged (but not discussed) by Moran, xxxii–xxxiii, with nn. 111, 118.

34. For alternative translations of line 15, cf. Moran, 7, with n. 6.

35. See, e.g., EA 4:37–39: "before your messenger [comes] to me, right now, in all haste, this summer, either in the month of Tammuz or in the month of Ab (i.e., mid-June–mid-August)"; the same final deadline is emphatically repeated in the lines that follow. I wonder whether the specification in line 37 ("before your messenger [comes] to me") may hint at a regular (i.e., yearly) time schedule of messengers' journeys to and from Egypt. See further EA 11: Rev. 27–30.

36. See, most recently, Zaccagnini, "Lo scambio dei beni," 55, and previously Zaccagnini, "Forms of Alliance," 107 with n. 8, citing earlier literature.

37. It is not clear whether Ashur-nadin-ahhe I or II is meant; cf. Moran, 40, n. 9.

38. Irreconcilable contradictions about historical events and circumstances, as presented by Near Eastern sources, even stemming from one and the same archival milieu, should cause no surprise. This particular feature of Late Bronze Age sources is found most of all in the so-called historical preambles of the Hittite vassal treaties; for an illuminating example, cf. Zaccagnini, "Tudhaliya IV." See also Zaccagnini, "Forms of Alliance," 67–71. The deep intricacies and the politico-ideological implications of the common practice of cunningly manipulating "facts," in the absence or even in

the presence of documentary sources available to the players in the game, cannot be illustrated here.

39. Moran, xxxv, n. 123.

40. Note that the name of the addressee of EA 16 is broken (line 1): it could either be Akhenaten or, according to Moran (39, n. 1), Aya.

41. Moran, 40, nn. 9–10.

42. Note the derogatory qualification of the Assyrian-Egyptian interchange: *šimātu,* "business, purchase," instead of *šulmānu* "(greeting-)gift."

43. For the rendering of line 69, I follow Rainey, "Amarna Letters," 110.

44. On the quality of gifts and hospitality, see, e.g., EA 20:64–69; 21:24–32; 29: 32–37; cf. 27:99–103; etc. As regards messengers, there is sometimes concern for their very survival: see EA 20:69–70, interpreted differently by Moran, 48, and Adler, *Das Akkadische,* 141–43. See also the unique passage of EA 16:43–55, for which cf. Moran, 39, with nn. 16–18; Liverani, "Review," 169–70; Zaccagnini, "Lo scambio dei beni," 57 with n. 36.

45. EA 29:119–35, following the free but plausible restorations of Moran, 95.

46. CF. III 88: "May my brother make me rich in respect to my land."

47. The interpretation of lines 53–54 raises several problems: cf. Moran, 48, with nn. 11–12; Zaccagnini, *Lo scambio,* 132; Pintore, *Il matrimonio,* 110; Liverani, *Prestige and Interest,* 214; etc. I do not consider the expression "my brother" (line 53) as a scribal mistake for "your brother" (cf. Adler, *Das Akkadische,* 141; Moran, 48, with n. 10) but rather as an ironic and sarcastic quotation of Tushratta's speeches addressed to his people: cf. already Zaccagnini, *Lo scambio,* 132, n. 191.

48. Line 91 is difficult. For the various renderings of the passage see Moran, 2, and previously Pintore, *Il matrimonio,* 26; Liverani, "Dono," 15–16; Moran, "Amarna Lexicon," 302; Liverani, *Prestige and Interest,* 265–66.

Chapter 12. Reciprocity, Equality, and Status-Anxiety in the Amarna Letters

1. The *locus classicus* of "thick description" in interpretive anthropology is Geertz, "Thick Description: Toward an Interpretative Theory of Culture," in *Interpretation,* 3–30; see also "Deep Play: Notes on the Balinese Cockfight," ibid., 412–53.

2. My reference is to Gluckman and Devons, who warned about nonspecialists' extradisciplinary wanderings, in *Closed Systems and Open Minds.*

3. See Albright, "The Amarna Letters," 109.

4. Liverani, "Political Lexicon," 54–55.

5. The intertwining of these two "levels" is analyzed by Liverani in "'Irrational' Elements."

6. See, for example, White, *Science of Culture;* Turner, *Forest of Symbols;* Spiro, "Collective Representations," 45–72.

7. Once again, the exemplar here is Geertz; see fn. 1.

8. For example, Fernandez, ed., *Beyond Metaphor.* For an example of metaphor

analysis in contemporary international relations theory, see Chilton, *Security Metaphors.*

9. See Lakoff and Johnson, *Metaphors;* Lakoff, *Women, Fire.*

10. *Chicago Assyrian Dictionary,* under ḫurasu (gold), lists its figurative uses to include "wisdom" and "constancy," as well as value; and, in homeopathy, as a cure for "heartbreak"—something that Tushratta, at least, seemed at times to have suffered: Vol. H, 245–47.

11. See Moran, xxii–xxiii (great powers), and xxix–xxx (the vassal letters).

12. Cohen, "On Diplomacy," 266.

13. Lakoff and Johnson, *Metaphors,* 14–21.

14. E.g., EA 106 or EA 117. Rib-Hadda becomes a study in mounting and frantic exasperation.

15. EA 112, and see Moran's comment, 186–87.

16. EA 117, and see Moran's comment, 194.

17. "Look, as to the king, my lord's, having written, 'Troops have indeed come out,' you spoke lies." Thus Rib-Hadda, very near the end of his rope, caught between a rock and a hard place, to Pharaoh, EA 129:34ff.

18. Cohen, "All in the Family," 11–28.

19. See Moran, xxii–xxiii. Incidentally, the consistent linkage of the state of well-being of the country with the state of well-being of the king, a linkage assumed a priori in these letters, is a classic example of the trope metonymy—the *country/ nations/polity is the king*—and a good indication as to how the notion of sovereignty was understood in these cultures. Certainly, it was not understood in abstract, legalist, historicist, or—god knows—the liberal-consensual terms of modern states. The Great Kings owned their countries; in a sense they *were* their countries. Having said this, however, one must recall Liverani's arguments about the different parsing of sovereignty, and the responsibility of sovereigns to their subjects, as between Egyptian and Asiatic cultures; see Liverani on the notion of "protection" in "Political Lexicon," 337–48.

20. Under the entry for aḫu (brother), the *Chicago Assyrian Dictionary* (195) lists also composite forms of the kinship term that indicate relative rank within the kinship category: aḫu rabû (oldest brother) and aḫu ṣiḫru (younger brother). It is significant that these rank-marked terms are not used in the letters but simply "brother," thus emphasizing the egalitarian message of the term. Likewise, the more abstract notion of "brotherliness" (aḫḫūtu) itself connotes a group of people of equal status (186).

21. I should note that a kinship metaphor is used in the vassal correspondence—tellingly—by Rib-Hadda. In EA 73 and EA 82, he writes to Pharaoh as "your son. . . . I fall at the feet of my father." Rib-Hadda thus combines kinship with self-abasement. As Rib-Hadda's appeals for help continue to flow forth yet more desperately, it is clear that he is deeply hurt (and puzzled?) because he genuinely expects more paternal succor from the lord to whom he has given such filial fealty.

22. According to the *Chicago Assyrian Dictionary,* the šulmānu ("greeting-gift")

can connote either parity, as an exchange between kings of equal rank, or asymmetry, as a gift sent by vassals to their masters (245).

23. The Assyrian's comments about the size of Egyptian-Mittani exchanges points to the issue of intelligence gathering by the Amarna messengers and to the whole problem of the Amarna Letters and intelligence or, more narrowly, espionage. See, for example, EA 31:24–29.

24. Though here (EA 32:1–3) the point is made explicitly that the marriage would establish a "blood-relationship" between the two kings. The mistrust seems to have to do with the *verbal* nature of the proposal as rendered by one Kalbaya; the Arzawan king wanted it "confirmed on the tablet" (i.e., in writing).

25. Elsewhere in this volume Christer Jönsson makes a similar point, using "diffuse" for *generalized,* and "specific" for *balanced, reciprocity.*

26. Malinowski, *Argonauts;* and Mauss, "Essai sur le don." 'Polanyi, "Instituted Process," and Sahlins, *Stone Age Economics.*

27. See Liverani, " 'Irrational' Elements"; also Zaccagnini, "Ceremonial Exchange," 57–65.

28. E.g., EA 99, for the whole list in a single letter.

29. Recall that "brother," minus any indication of relative ranking (older or younger), is used in the letters.

30. EA 16:19–34. The Assyrian asserts: "I am the equal" of the Mittani monarch. And once again, the issue of intelligence is raised: Assur-uballit clearly knew exactly what the Mittani king had received.

31. E.g., EA 26–27, EA 29. Moran notes that in the Amarna period " 'love' unquestionably belongs to the terminology of international relations" ("Love of God," 77–87, 79), and that it "may be defined in terms of loyalty, service, and obedience" (82). He cites furthermore the Assyrian practice "of demanding an oath of allegiance from their vassals expressed in terms of love" (84).

32. EA 42:15ff. Moran aptly calls this letter "a question of honor," p. 115. It is also one of the more vigorous of traditional uses of metaphor in the letters.

33. Zaccagnini, "Ceremonial Exchange," 59. The key work on marriage in this period is Pintore, *Il Matrimonio.* See also Zaccagnini's critical review of the same ("Recensione").

34. Lévi-Strauss, *The Elementary Structures of Kinship.*

35. See Fox, *Kinship and Marriage.*

36. During the conference, Betsy Bryan objected to this passage. To her, it implied I was saying that Pharaoh never gave women in marriage because this would be interpreted in Egypt as giving tribute; she pointed out that women are known to have possessed independent means in ancient Egypt. I did not mean to imply that giving women would have been interpreted as giving tribute, but certainly that for "internal Egyptian consumption," royal marriages to the daughters of the other Great Kings— *taking* women—was in fact presented (as in stelae) as tribute directed to Pharaoh. I thank Professor Bryan for helping me to sharpen this distinction.

Chapter 13. Diplomacy and International Marriages

1. A helpful survey of the bibliography in this regard can be found in Zaccagnini, *Lo scambio,* 12–14.

2. Compared to nearby Babylonia, "il est évident que les gens d'Eshnunna avaient connaissance de beaucoup d'autres règles concernant le mariage" (Sauren, "Le mariage," 84). The Kassite domination of Babylonia intervenes between Old Babylonian and Middle Babylonian, the latter's sources on marriage representing "an entirely different tradition" (Westbrook, *Marriage Law,* 1) with further innovations traceable in Neo-Babylonian (Abraham, "Dowry Clause," 311–20). Even the sparse Neo-Assyrian evidence reveals new practices compared to the preceding Middle Assyrian period (Jakobson, "Neo-Assyrian Law," 118–19; Saporetti, *Status of Women,* 5–17).

3. The procedure of Ruth 4 compared to Deut. 25:5–10, for example, continues to bewilder biblical scholars.

4. Evidence for marriage in the New Kingdom depends heavily for reconstruction upon later Egyptian documents (Allam, "Stellung der Frau," 155; Goody, *Systems of Marriage,* 319–41). The problem of royal succession, often a significant element in treaties, is a complex issue in the New Kingdom (Robins, "Female Line," 67–77).

5. Lebrun, "Considérations," 109–25; Westbrook, "Mitgift," 283.

6. The rich and idiosyncratic material from Nuzi represents the mingling of Semitic and Hurrian cultures.

7. *Il Matrimonio.* Evidence points to the fifteenth century for the beginning of this international exchange (Drower, "Amarna Age," 486).

8. Durand, "Les dames," 385–435; Lafont, "Les filles," 113–23. "Il semble, cependant, que Zimri-Lim n'ait vu aucune de ses filles recherchée en mariage par les fils d'un des principaux monarques de l'époque" (Charpin and Durand, "Zimri-Lim," 335).

9. This is not an isolated fact but is accompanied by related international phenomena of unparalleled intensity: "Precisely in this period the practice of exchanging letters between monarchs (and officials), and that of stipulating international treaties, reach a true peak in the entire Near Eastern history" (Zaccagnini, "Forms of Alliance," 38).

10. The schema outlined succinctly by Artzi ("Political Marriages," 23–26) for marriage between Great Kings masks serious problems. Crucial issues requiring resolution before a marriage uniting Great Kings are typically not addressed in the documents presently in our possession, such as succession of offspring, status of the future wife in relation to other wives, consequences of childlessness, inheritance of the woman's property, or grounds for divorce, topics that were hot issues in various parts of the ancient Near East. We possess legal documents regarding royal divorce ex post facto in the Late Bronze; can we expect to find someday a royal marriage agreement, and if so, will it most resemble Old Babylonian models?

11. Liverani suggested linguistic misunderstandings between Egypt and Canaan in this period ("Political Lexicon," 41–56). For a different perspective, however, see Moran, "Amarna Politics," 550–72.

12. For the basic issues see Cohen, "All in the Family," 11–28, although he does not feel that this was simply a "pragmatic relationship of mutual benefit" (16).

13. Frankfort, *Kingship and the Gods,* 237–43.

14. Ibid., 5. For the specific context of the Eighteenth Dynasty, and in particular Amenhotep III and IV, see Redford's and Silverman's comments in O'Connor and Silverman, eds., *Ancient Egyptian Kingship,* 69–80, 85–86, 157–84.

15. For some kings, such as Pharaoh, the self-designation *šarru* meant a considerable truncation of their distinctive royal ideology that set them off from other monarchs. However, for other kings, *šarru* may have represented a semantic enrichment, particularly for those smaller rulers who could accordingly identify themselves as being made of the same stuff as the more powerful players.

16. Edel, *Korrespondenz* 20.5–7; cf. 22.vs.6′–20′.

17. Pharaoh did have a choice: the Egyptian chancery could have simply transliterated the Egyptian term *pr-ꜥ3* into Akkadian, as was done with other Egyptian words (cf. EA 71:1; 107:14; 149:30; 289:38; 294:22; 316:16, where those writing to Pharaoh transliterate Egyptian words and titles).

18. Naʿaman, "Biryawaza," 182–83.

19. We perpetuate this awareness today by reserving the Egyptian term "Pharaoh" to identify the reigning monarch of Egypt alone.

20. Schulman, "Diplomatic Marriages," 191. Lorton observes that *wr* is applied to both Egyptian vassals as well as foreign kings who had parity with Egypt: "It is clear that the texts deliberately ignore the independent status of these rulers. . . . The Egyptian usage does not agree fully with that of the diplomatic lingua franca of the age . . . , almost . . . a refusal on the part of the Egyptians, after the Hyksos period, to acknowledge in their own texts the existence of independent kings who treated on a parity basis with the Egyptian king. The difference between the Egyptian and Akkadian texts . . . should be attributed . . . to the different conceptual frameworks of the Egyptians and Asiatics. The Egyptians were geographically isolated and . . . under a unified kingship; the Mesopotamians and the inhabitants of Syria-Palestine . . . were accustomed to the existence of a plurality of kings and overlords" (*Juridical Terminology,* 62–63).

21. The terms are typically used together in epistolary introductions in conjunction with the term "brother" (EA 23:1–5 is an exception), only to be jettisoned in the rest of the letter where "brother" alone defines the relationship (EA 19:1–4; 20:1–4; 21:1–8; 27:1–3; 28:1–5; 29:1–2). *ḫatānu* defines the relationship at the end of the inventory of wedding gifts (EA 22:iv.46). A son of Ramesses II addresses the Hittite king as "my father" from "his son" (Edel, *Korrespondenz,* 9), just as the brother of the Hittite king Suppiluliuma I does the same to Pharaoh (EA 44; cf. Kühne, *Chronologie,* p. 102). Ramesses II is not averse to addressing Hittite princes as his "sons"; see his letters to the princes Kannuta, Teshub-Sarruma, and Tashmi-Sarruma (Edel, *Korrespondenz,* 14, 16, 17, respectively).

22. Wilson, "Egypt," 33. Pharaoh's daughters did marry foreigners later in the first millennium "in the humbler days of the post-imperial epoch" (Kitchen, *Third Intermediate Period*).

23. The Karnak annals of Tuthmosis III (*ARE* II sec. 447).

24. The Marriage Stela of Ramesses II (*ARE* III sec. 415f.).

25. The primary source for the peripheral Akkadian lingua franca is Old Babylonian. The raw materials for diplomacy were already forged in the Old Babylonian period, as the Mari texts make clear, adapted for a far more cosmopolitan environment in the Late Bronze Age.

26. Thompson, "Anointing," 24. Supplement Pardee's collection of data for oil-anointing ("Ugaritic Letter," 14–18) with third millennium B.C. evidence from Ebla (Biga, "Femmes," 45).

27. Debate has centered on whether or not brides were given in expectation of receiving brides in return (Pintore, *Il Matrimonio;* Liverani, *Three Amarna Essays,* 31–32; Zaccagnini, "Bronze Age Marriages," 593–95). In the period before Amarna, there is little to substantiate reciprocity in this regard. Continued work on the Old Babylonian texts from Mari, where the matrimonial experiences of Zimri-Lim and his associates are increasingly well known, reveals little expectation of reciprocity (Durand, "Les Dames," 385–435). The same lack of evidence, in spite of much documentation on royal women, seems to characterize Ebla as well (Biga, "Femmes," 41–47).

28. For perplexing but possible evidence to the contrary, see Pintore, *Il Matrimonio,* 78–79.

29. Schulman, "Diplomatic Marriages," 191.

30. Zaccagnini, "Forms of Alliance," 51, 54. Pharaoh "donned a guise forced on him from outside. He now wore the mantle of a king of kings who had to deal with monarchs of equal rank whom native mythology would never credit; he signed treaties with them, corresponded with them, sent them presents, and even married their daughters" (Redford, "Kingship," 175–76).

31. Pintore, *Il Matrimonio;* Zaccagnini, *Lo scambio.*

32. E.g., Mashuiluwa of Mira-Kuwaliya and the daughter of Suppiluliuma I.

33. Durand, "Les Dames," 385–435.

34. *u Zimri Lim mārassu liṭrudamma šarrūtam ina Karanâ līpuš* (ARM VI.26.5′–7′). Charpin and Durand ("Zimri-Lim," 335) modify Kupper's original translation, followed here, and translate this as "sa fille et qu'elle devienne Reine à Karanâ." But the noun is a masculine "kingship" and not "queenship" (as does appear in ARM X.34 *kussâm šarratam*).

35. "Once a foreigner came to reside in Egypt, learned to speak Egyptian, and adopted Egyptian dress, he might finally be accepted as one of 'the people' and was no longer the object of superior ridicule. Asiatics or Libyans or Negroes might be accepted Egyptians of high position when they had become acclimatized—might, indeed, rise to the highest position of all, that of the god-king who possessed the nation" (Wilson, "Egypt," 33).

36. Edel *Korrespondenz* 37.11′–15′. Pintore did not discuss this text (available to him as KBo VII 11), an important exception to the otherwise well-attested pattern that the develops of the future groom initiating the marital negotiations.

37. Kitchen, *Pharaoh Triumphant*, 88–89.

38. Pintore, *Il Matrimonio*, 56–62.

Chapter 14. A Social-Psychological Analysis of Amarna Diplomacy

1. Liverani, "Political Lexicon," 41.

2. For a similar approach to the analysis of contemporary regional politics, see Druckman, "Social-Psychological Factors."

3. For a discussion of applications, see Druckman and Hopmann, "Content Analysis."

4. See the discussion by Liverani, "Political Lexicon."

5. See Holmes, "Messengers of the Amarna Letters."

6. Cohen, "All in the Family."

7. For distinctions between exchange and communal systems, see Pruitt, "Flexibility in Conflict Episodes," and Stern and Druckman, "Earthquake."

8. For a discussion of these perspectives see Hopmann, "Two Paradigms of Negotiation."

9. Sharp, "MBFR as Arms Control."

10. See Fisher, "Fractionating Conflict"; see also Deutsch, Canavan, and Rubin, "The Effects of Size."

11. The distinction between these ideologies is discussed in Zaccagnini, "Aspects of Ceremonial Exchange."

12. See Pruitt, "Flexibility in Conflict Episodes."

13. Fisher and Brown, *Getting Together;* and Druckman, "The Social Psychology of Arms Control."

14. For a discussion of alternative fairness principles, see Zartman et al., "Negotiation as a Search."

15. Cohen, "All in the Family."

16. This finding is reported in Druckman and Harris, "Alternative Models."

17. Other games could be constructed. For example, the situation described in EA 26–29 can be modeled as a game of incomplete information in which players are uncertain about each other's preferences. These uncertainties can lead to misperceptions that result in nonoptimal outcomes. Modeling the interactions as a three-person game involving Tushratta, Akhenaten, and Tiye (the Queen Mother), we learn about some drawbacks to Tushratta's assumptions that (a) Pharaoh strongly desired an alliance with Mittani, and (b) Tiye was willing and able to influence her son's preferences.

18. See Druckman, Rozelle, and Baxter, *Nonverbal Communication*, 35–39.

19. Cohen, "All in the Family."

20. See the evidence presented in Jones, *Ingratiation.*

21. However, neither of Darley's two conditions for obedience to authority are met by the relations among these kings, namely, specification of goals and means and surveillance by the more powerful party. See Darley, "Constructive and Destructive Obedience."

22. For example, King, "Role Reversal Debates." For a review of these studies, see also Druckman and Hopmann, "Behavioral Aspects of Negotiations."

23. Stern and Druckman, "Earthquake."

24. Carnevale and Pruitt, "Negotiation and Mediation"; and Kressel et al., "The Settlement-Orientation."

25. See Hammond, "New Directions."

26. Cottam, *Foreign Policy Motivations.*

27. Ibid.

28. Hoffmann, "Realism and Its Discontents."

29. This point is made by Liverani, "Political Lexicon."

30. Holmes, "Messengers."

Chapter 15. Diplomatic Signaling in the Amarna Letters

1. Cohen, *The Rules of the Game,* 30.

2. Simons, *Persuasion,* 21.

3. The term "negotiation" has a more narrow denotation than "bargaining." Whereas negotiation refers to a formalized and explicit process, we may speak of a bargaining process even when the parties do not sit down at a negotiation table to exchange proposals; when communication is incomplete or indirect. Bargaining may, in fact, be tacit, involving nonverbal acts. Although most negotiation processes include elements of informal bargaining, parties may bargain with each other without ever entering into formal negotiations.

4. Berridge, *Diplomacy,* 1.

5. In international relations, the distinction between diplomacy and warfare, between persuasion and coercion, is sometimes hard to maintain. The power to hurt is essentially a kind of bargaining power, and war can be analyzed in bargaining terms. See Schelling, *Arms and Influence.* Similarly, interstate bargaining frequently includes elements of "coercive diplomacy," where force is used in combination with verbal communication to demonstrate resolve and determination to use more force if necessary. See George and Simons, *Coercive Diplomacy.*

6. George and Simons, *Coercive Diplomacy,* 50.

7. Rommetveit, "Architecture of Intersubjectivity," 93.

8. Rommetveit, *On Message Structure,* 88.

9. Remark by Raymond Cohen at the Bellagio conference.

10. Cohen, *Rules of the Game,* 32–34.

11. Cohen, "All in the Family," offers a different view, arguing that the family metaphor reflects a constitutive paradigm that affects attitudes to and the conduct of international relations.

12. Cf. Jönsson, *Superpower.*

13. Cohen, "All in the Family," 22–23.

14. Moran, xxii.

15. Keohane, "Reciprocity in International Relations." Diffuse reciprocity is simi-

lar to "generalized reciprocity," as discussed by Kevin Avruch in his contribution to this volume.

16. Ibid., 4.

17. Ibid., 4n.

18. Ibid., 23.

19. The following two examples and their interpretation were suggested to me by Raymond Westbrook in a personal communication.

20. Schelling, *The Strategy of Conflict.*

21. Ibid., 22.

22. Ibid., 67.

23. Jervis, *The Logic of Images,* 66.

24. Quoted in Seaborg, *Kennedy,* 252.

25. Cohen, "All in the Family," 13.

26. Cf. Jönsson and Aggestam, "Diplomatic Signalling."

27. Holsti, Brody, and North, "International Crisis," n. 66.

28. McNulty, "Television's Impact," 67.

29. Morgenthau, *Politics among Nations,* 546.

30. Der Derian, *On Diplomacy,* 208.

Chapter 16. The Diplomatic Service in Action: The Mittani File

1. C. Kühne, *Chronologie,* 17–48.

2. Cf. EA 11. It should be noted that the word "love" is not used by the other great powers in the Amarna correspondence. The sole use of the term occurs in EA 9: 19–38: the Babylonian king entreats his Egyptian brother, "If you love me," to discontinue relations with the Assyrians, "my vassals."

3. Egypt's failure to intervene shows that there was no treaty between Egypt and Mittani. A treaty partner was obliged to intervene in the event of murder or other illegal acts endangering the continuity of the dynasty. See, e.g., the provision on succession to the throne in the treaty between Hattusili III and Ramesses II (*ANET,* 203).

4. In my understanding, the expression "enmity(?)/hate(?) on the part of the Hatti land" may appear here. See also below, EA 24.

5. The inclusion of EA 18 in the Mittanian correspondence is still doubtful: see Moran, *Amarna,* 43. In my opinion, further research may prove its Mittanian origin.

6. See also EA 16, from Assyria. Egyptian gold was viewed in this way throughout the region.

7. On the background of the "we are one" motif, see Kalluveettil, *Declaration,* 102.

8. Wilhelm, "Mittanni Letter," 137.

9. Ibid., 138.

10. See H. Kissinger, *Diplomacy* (New York, 1994), 168.

11. See EA 11 (Babylonia), EA 16 (Assyria), EA 41 (Hatti).

12. As can be seen from EA 20, discussed above, public opinion was an important factor in the security of Tushratta's position. As we learn from the treaty concluded

between Shattiwaza, son of the (murdered) Tushratta, and Suppuliluma I of Hatti, now the "savior" of Mittani, a murderous conspiracy had already been initiated. The head of the rival Hurrian component of Mittani, Shuttarna III, turned to Assyria for help and thus took the first step toward the destructive partition of Mittani between Hatti and Assyria. For a translation of the treaty, see Beckman, *Hittite Diplomatic Texts,* 38–49.

13. See Artzi, "Good Day," 17–27, and "Mourning," 161–70.

14. See Artzi, "Middle Assyrian Kingdom," and "EA 16."

Chapter 17. Amarna Diplomacy: A Full-fledged Diplomatic System?

1. Cohen, "On Diplomacy," 247, emphasis added.

2. Ibid., 267, fn. 10.

3. Ibid., 264, emphasis added.

4. Nicolson, *Diplomatic Method,* chap. 3.

5. I base the latter conclusion on such considerations as the following: the reduced inclination of Third World states to "sever diplomatic relations" for propaganda purposes; the return of "consensus decision-making"(i.e., negotiation) to multilateral diplomacy, not least in the U.N.; and the spread of subtle new institutions like interests sections. I have discussed these questions in Berridge, *Diplomacy,* which has a list of further reading at the end of each chapter, and Berridge, *Talking to the Enemy.* For other recent accounts of diplomacy of a more or less general nature, see Anderson, *Modern Diplomacy;* Hamilton and Langhorne, *The Practice of Diplomacy;* and Dunn, *Diplomacy at the Highest Level.*

6. Wilson, *Diplomatic Privileges,* chap. 1.

7. Cohen, "On Diplomacy," 257.

8. For example, Bozeman, *Politics and Culture,* 30; Munn-Rankin, "Diplomacy in Western Asia," 104ff.

9. Meier, *The Messenger,* 30, 139; Artzi, "Middle-Assyrian Kingdom." On the assumption that the addressee is Smenkhkare, EA 41 would appear to provide a contrary case, since this message from Suppiluliuma of Hatti would have been sent at a time of "cold war" between the Egyptians and the Hittites; I am indebted to Murnane for drawing my attention to this. It is notable, however, that the point of the message was to complain of the cessation of the normal supply of Egyptian gifts and — presumably — of their bearers.

10. Munn-Rankin, "Diplomacy in Western Asia," 101.

11. Holmes, "Messengers of the Amarna Letters"; see esp. EA 3, 7, 28, 29, 126.

12. Meier, *The Messenger,* 76, 79–80, 105–6; Munn-Rankin, "Diplomacy in Western Asia," 107–8.

13. Berridge, *Diplomacy,* 2–5.

14. Cohen, "On Diplomacy," 257.

15. Ibid.

16. Ibid., 257–58.

17. Ibid., 258.

18. Moran, 131, fn. 5.

19. Liverani, "Pharaoh's Letters."

20. Cohen, "On Diplomacy," 258.

21. Edwards, *Cambridge Ancient History*, 7.

22. Cohen, "On Diplomacy," 258; see EA 1.

23. Edwards, *Cambridge Ancient History*, 29.

24. Cohen, "On Diplomacy," 258.

25. Munn-Rankin, "Diplomacy in Western Asia," 104–7; Meier, *The Messenger*, 100ff.

26. Meier, *The Messenger*, 236.

27. Munn-Rankin, "Diplomacy in Western Asia," 102.

28. Meier, *The Messenger*, 61–4.

29. Ibid., 238–39; and EA 28.

30. Munn-Rankin, "Diplomacy in Western Asia," 100.

31. Meier, *The Messenger*, 84–85.

32. Ibid., 85–89; and Bozeman, *Politics and Culture*, 35.

33. Munn-Rankin, "Diplomacy in Western Asia," 106–7.

34. Meier, *The Messenger*, chap. 2.

35. Ibid., 85.

36. Many messages appear to have been committed to memory and delivered orally; see ibid., 36–61.

37. Ibid., 168–79.

38. Wicquefort, *The Embassador and His Functions*, 53.

39. Ibid., 47.

40. Cohen, "On Diplomacy," 256.

41. Meier, *The Messenger*, 14–15.

42. Ibid., 6, 15; cf. Holmes, "Messengers of the Amarna Letters," 378, fn. 21.

43. Though linguistic talents were not a necessity since translators, as well as native escorts, were widely available, Meier, *The Messenger*, 163–65.

44. Ibid., 17–21.

45. Ibid., 3, 21, 80; and Holmes, "Messengers of the Amarna Letters," 378–81.

46. Wicquefort, *The Embassador and His Functions*, 50.

47. Nicolson, *Diplomatic Method*, 25.

48. Meier, *The Messenger*, 82–83.

49. Ibid., 203ff.

50. Nicolson, *Diplomacy*, 50–55, 162.

51. Albeit "subordinate" ones; Zaccagnini, "The Merchant," 173.

52. Butterfield, *Christianity*, 74.

53. Butterfield, "Diplomacy," 357. I am grateful to Maurice Keens-Soper for drawing this essay to my attention.

54. Ibid., 365.

55. Though Aldred suggests that Akhenaten himself, "absorbed as he must have been in his religious schemes, . . . left most of the vastly increased business of state to be carried on by his officials" (Edwards, *Cambridge Ancient History*, 52).

56. This was also a feature that handicapped the diplomacy of ancient Greece; see Adcock and Mosley, *Diplomacy in Ancient Greece*, 158.

57. Meier, *The Messenger*, 212.

58. Roux, *Ancient Iraq*, 140.

59. Munn-Rankin, "Diplomacy in Western Asia," 96.

60. Ibid., 84.

61. Bozeman, *Politics and Culture*, 31.

62. Munn-Rankin, "Diplomacy in Western Asia," 91.

63. Wight, *Systems of States*, 31–32.

64. Munn-Rankin, "Diplomacy in Western Asia," 84.

65. Ibid., 89–90.

66. Ibid., 95–96.

67. "Summitry," however, appears to have been confined to visits by minor rulers, chiefly for purposes of paying homage to the courts of their suzerain great power, ibid., 99; see also Liverani, *Prestige and Interest*, 286.

68. Munn-Rankin, "Diplomacy in Western Asia," 76f.

69. Cohen, "On Diplomacy," 252. It is one thing to maintain that the thirst for recognition stimulated diplomacy in the Amarna period; it is quite another to claim that "not the least important prerequisite for the existence of a diplomatic system is the wish for recognition and approval that can only be provided by the society of one's peers" (ibid., 9, emphasis added). This suggests the impossibility of diplomacy in the absence of such a wish. However, there are many instances that refute this, for example, between Manchu China and the Western powers and the Ottoman Empire and the Western powers.

70. Queller, *The Office of Ambassador*, 82–83.

71. The conditions for resident embassies were more propitious in the small city-states of Syria, but as vassals of one Great King or another, they were prevented from conducting separate foreign policies.

72. Moran, xxv, xxxii.

73. Meier, *Messenger*, 163–65.

74. Liverani, "Political Lexicon," 45; also, Edwards, *Cambridge Ancient History*, 99.

Chapter 18. Conclusion: The Beginnings of International Relations

1. Heisenberg, *Physics and Beyond*, vii.

2. Mauss, *The Gift*, 1.

3. Ibid., 3.

4. Introduction to ibid., ix.

5. As already noted by the contributors to Frankfort, ed., *Intellectual Adventure*.

6. Bryan's analysis remarkably confirms Van Ossenbruggen's conclusion from early in the century: gifts to men and to gods have the aim of buying peace. Quoted in Mauss, *The Gift*, 14.

7. *aḫḫūtu* (1) brotherly relationship, brotherliness (between private persons); (2) position of a brother (as legal term, *adoptio in fratrem*); group of persons of equal status; (3) brotherhood (referring to a political relationship) (*CAD*, vol. A, 186).

Bibliography

Abdul-Kader, M. "The Administration of Syria-Palestine during the New Kingdom." *Annales du Service des Antiquités de l'Egypte* 56 (1959): 105–37.

Abraham, K. "The Dowry Clause in Marriage Documents from the First Millennium B.C.E." In *La circulation des biens, des personnes et des idées dans le Proche-Orient ancien. Actes de la XXXVIIIe Rencontre Assyriologique Internationale (Paris, 8–10 juillet 1991),* ed. D. Charpin, and F. Joannès, 311–20. Paris: Editions Recherche sur les civilisations, 1992.

Adams, W. Y. *Nubia, Corridor to Africa.* Princeton: Princeton University Press, 1977.

Adcock, F., and Mosley, D. *Diplomacy in Ancient Greece.* London: Thames and Hudson, 1975.

Adler, H-P. *Das Akkadische des Königs Tusratta von Mitanni.* Reprint. Neukirchen-Vluyn: Neukirchener Verlag, 1976.

Ahituv, S. "Economic Factors in the Egyptian Conquest of Canaan." *Israel Exploration Journal* 28 (1978): 93–103.

Akkadisches Handwörterbuch. Wiesbaden: Harrassowitz 1965–81.

Albright, W. F. "The Amarna Letters from Palestine." In *The Cambridge Ancient History,* ed. I. E. S. Edwards et al., 3rd ed. Vol. 2, Pt. 2. Cambridge: Cambridge University Press, 1975.

———. "Cuneiform Material for Egyptian Prosopography, 1500–1200 BC." *Journal of Near Eastern Studies* 5 (1946): 7–25.

Aldred, C. *Akhenaten, King of Egypt.* New York: Thames and Hudson, 1988.

———. "Egypt: The Amarna Period and the End of the Eighteenth Dynasty." In *The Cambridge Ancient History,* ed. I. E. S. Edwards et al., 3rd ed. Vol. 2, Pt. 2. Cambridge: Cambridge University Press, 1975.

Allam, S. "Zur Stellung der Frau im alten Ägypten in der Zeit des Neuen Reiches." *Bibliotheca Orientalis* 26 (1969): 155–59.

———. "Ehe." *Lexikon der Ägyptologie* I, 1162–81. Wiesbaden: O. Harrassowitz, 1975.

———. "Women as Owners of Immovables in Pharaonic Egypt." In *Women's Earliest Records from Ancient Egypt and Western Asia,* ed. B. Lesko, 123–25. Atlanta: Scholar's Press, 1989.

Altman, A. "The Justification Motif in the Historical Prologues to the Treaties of Shuppiluliuma I of Hatti." *Shnaton* 2 (1977): 27–49.

———. "On the Legal Meaning of Some of the Assertions in the 'Historical Prologue' of the Kizzuwatna Treaty." In *Bar-Ilan Studies in Assyriology Dedicated to Pinhas Artzi*, 177–206. Ramat Gan: Bar-Ilan University Press, 1990.

Anchor Bible Dictionary. New York: Doubleday, 1992.

Anderson, M. S. *The Rise of Modern Diplomacy, 1450–1919*. London: Longman, 1993.

Arnaud, D. "Les ports de la 'Phénicie' à la fin de l'Age du Bronze Récent (XIV–XIII siècles) d'après les textes cuneiformes de Syrie." *Studi Micenei ed Egeo-Anatolici* 30 (1992): 179–94.

Artzi, P. "The Rise of the Middle-Assyrian Kingdom, according to el-Amarna Letters 15 & 16." In *Bar-Ilan Studies in History*, 25–42. Ramat Gan: Bar-Ilan University Press, 1978.

———. "Mourning in International Relations." *Death in Mesopotamia: Mesopotamia* 8 (1980): 161–70.

———. "The Influence of Political Marriages on the International Relations of the Amarna Age." In *La femme dans le Proche Orient antique. Compte Rendu de la XXXIIIe Rencontre Assyriologique Internationale (Paris, 7–10 Juillet 1986)*, ed. Jean-Marie Durand, 23–26. Paris: Editions Recherche sur les civilisations, 1987.

———. "The 'Good Day' Festivity of Amenhotep III." *Beer Sheva* 3 (1988): 17–27.

———, and Malamat, A. "The Great King: A Preeminent Royal Title in Cuneiform Sources and the Bible." In *The Tablet and the Scroll: Near Eastern Studies in Honor of William W. Hallo*, 28–38. Bethesda, Md.: CDL Press, 1993.

———. "EA 16." *Altorientalische Forschungen* 24 (1997): 320–36.

Baines, J. *Fecundity Figures*. Chicago: Bolchazy-Carducci, 1985.

Beckman, G. *Hittite Diplomatic Texts*. Society of Biblical Literature Writings from the Ancient World. Vol. 7. Atlanta: Scholar's Press, 1996.

Berman, L. M. In *Egypt's Dazzling Sun: Amenhotep III and His World*, ed. A. Kozloff and B. Bryan. Cleveland: Cleveland Museum of Art in cooperation with Indiana University Press, 1992.

Bezold, C. *Oriental Diplomacy*. London: Luzac and Co., 1893.

Berridge, G. R. *Talking to the Enemy: How States without "Diplomatic Relations" Communicate*. London: St. Martin's Press, 1994.

———. *Diplomacy: Theory and Practice*. New York: Prentice Hall, 1995.

Biga, M. G. "Femmes de la famille royale d'Ebla." In *La femme dans le Proche Orient antique. Compte Rendu de la XXXIIIe Rencontre Assyriologique Internationale (Paris, 7–10 Juillet 1986)*, ed. Jean-Marie Durand, 41–47. Paris: Editions Recherche sur les civilisations, 1987.

Bleiberg, E. L. *The Official Gift in Ancient Egypt*. Norman: University of Oklahoma Press, 1996.

Bozeman, A. B. *Politics and Culture in International Society: From the Ancient Near East to the Opening of the Modern Age*. 2nd ed. New Brunswick, N.J.: Rutgers University Press, 1994.

Bradbury, L. "The Tombos Inscription: A New Interpretation." *Serapis* 8 (1984-5): 1-20.

Breasted, J. H. *Ancient Records of Egypt.* Chicago: University of Chicago Press, 1906.

———. *A History of Egypt, from the Earliest Times to the Persian Conquest.* Chicago: University of Chicago Press, 1912.

Bruce, F. F. "Biblical Archeology." In *The Bible Companion,* ed. William Neil. London: Skeffington, 1959.

Bryan, B. *The Reign of Thutmose IV.* Baltimore: Johns Hopkins University Press, 1991.

———. "In Women Is Good and Bad Fortune on Earth." In *Mistress of the House, Mistress of Heaven: Women in Egyptian Art,* ed. A. Capel and G. Markoe, 25-46. New York: Hudson Hills Press in association with Cincinnati Art Museum, 1996.

Bull, H. *The Anarchical Society: A Study in International Order.* London: Macmillan, 1977.

Bush, F. W. *"A Grammar of the Hurrian Language."* Ph.D. diss., Brandeis University, 1964.

Butterfield, H. *Christianity, Diplomacy, and War.* New York: Abingdon-Cokesbury Press, 1953.

———. "Diplomacy." In *Studies in Diplomatic History: Essays in Memory of David Bayne Horn,* ed. Ragnhild Hatton and M. S. Anderson. Harlow: Longmans, 1970.

Buzan, B. "From International System to International Society: Structural Realism and Regime Theory Meet the English School." *International Organization* 47 (1993): 327-52.

Caminos, R. A. *Late Egyptian Miscellanies.* London: Oxford University Press, 1954.

Campbell, E. F. *The Chronology of the Amarna Letters.* Baltimore: Johns Hopkins Press, 1964.

Canfora, L., Liverani, M., and Zaccagnini, C., eds. *I trattati nel mondo antico: Forma, ideologia, funzione.* Rome: "L'Erma" di Bretschneider, 1990.

Carnevale, P. J., and Pruitt, D. G. "Negotiation and Mediation." *Annual Review of Psychology* 43 (1992): 531-82.

Charpin, D., and Durand, J-M. "La prise du pouvoir par Zimri-Lim." *Mari. Annales de Recherches Interdisciplinaires* 4 (1985): 293-343.

———, and Joannès, F., eds. *La circulation des biens, des personnes et des idées dans le Proche-Orient ancien. Actes de la XXXVIIIe Rencontre Assyriologique Internationale (Paris, 8-10 juillet 1991).* Paris: Editions Recherche sur les civilisations, 1992.

Charpin, D. et al. *Archives epistolaires de Mari.* Vol. 26, Pts. 1 and 2. Paris: Editions Recherche sur les civilisations, 1988.

———. "Une alliance contre L'Elam et le Rituel du Lipit Napištim." In *Contribution à l'histoire de l'Iran, Mélanges offerts à Jean Perrot,* ed. F. Vallat, 109-18. Paris: Editions Recherche sur les civilisations, 1990.

———. "Le traité entre Ibal-pi-El II d'Ešnunna et Zimri-Lim de Mari." In *Marchands, diplomates et empereurs: Études sur la civilisation mésopotamienne offertes à Paul Garelli,* ed. D. Charpin and F. Joannès, 139-66. Paris: Editions Recherche sur les civilisations, 1991.

Chicago Assyrian Dictionary. Chicago: University of Chicago Press, 1956–.

Chilton, P. *Security Metaphors: Cold War Discourse from Containment to Common House.* New York: Peter Lang, 1996.

Cioffi-Revilla, C. "Origins and Evolution of World Politics." *International Studies Quarterly* 40 (1996): 1–22.

Cohen, R. *International Politics: The Rules of the Game.* London: Longman, 1981.

———. "All in the Family: Ancient Near Eastern Diplomacy." *International Negotiation* 1 (1996): 11–28.

———. "On Diplomacy in the Ancient Near East: The Amarna Letters." *Diplomacy & Statecraft* 7 (1996): 245–70.

Cooper, J. *Reconstructing History from Ancient Inscriptions: The Lagash-Umma Border Conflict.* Sources from the Ancient Near East 2, no. 1. Malibu: Undena Publications, 1983.

Cottam, R. W. *Foreign Policy Motivations: A General Theory and a Case Study.* Pittsburgh: University of Pittsburgh Press, 1977.

Darley, J. M. "Constructive and Destructive Obedience: A Taxonomy of Principal-Agent Relationships." *Journal of Social Issues* 51 (1995): 125–54.

Der Derian, J. *On Diplomacy.* London: Basil Blackwell, 1987.

Dessler, D. "What's at Stake in the Agent-Structure Debate." *International Organization* 43 (Summer 1989): 443.

Deutsch, M., D. Canavan, and J. Z. Rubin. "The Effects of Size of Conflict and Sex of Experimenter upon Interpersonal Conflict." *Journal of Experimental Social Psychology* 7 (1971): 258–67.

Drower, M. "The Amarna Age." In *The Cambridge Ancient History,* ed. I. E. S. Edwards et al., 483–93. 3rd ed. Vol. 2, Pt. 2. Cambridge: Cambridge University Press, 1975.

Druckman, D. "Social-Psychological Factors in Regional Politics." In *Comparative Regional Systems,* ed. W. J. Feld and G. Boyd, 18–55. New York: Pergamon, 1980.

———. "The Social Psychology of Arms Control and Reciprocation." *Political Psychology* 4 (1990): 553–81.

———, R. M. Rozelle, and J. C. Baxter. *Nonverbal Communication: Survey, Theory, and Research.* Beverly Hills: Sage, 1982.

———, and Harris, R. "Alternative Models of Responsiveness in International Negotiation." *Journal of Conflict Resolution* 34 (1990): 234–51.

———, and Hopmann, P. T. "Content Analysis." In *International Negotiation: Analysis, Approaches, Issues,* ed. V. A. Kremenyuk. San Francisco: Jossey-Bass, 1991.

Dunn, D., ed. *Diplomacy at the Highest Level: The Evolution of International Summitry.* New York: St. Martins, 1996.

Dunne, T., "The Social Construction of International Society." *European Journal of International Relations* 1 (1995): 367–89.

Durand, J-M. "Les dames du palais de Mari à l'époque du royaume de haute-Mesopotamie." *Mari. Annales de Recherches Interdisciplinaires* 4 (1985): 385–435.

———, ed. *La femme dans le Proche Orient antique. Compte Rendu de la XXXIIIe*

Rencontre Assyriologique Internationale (Paris, 7–10 Juillet 1986). Paris: Editions Recherche sur les civilisations, 1987.

Edel, E. "Zur Familie des *Snj-msjj* nach einen Grabinschriften aus der Qubbet el-Hawa bei Aswan." *Zeitschrift für Ägyptische Sprache* 90 (1963): 28–31.

———. *Die ägyptisch-hethitische Korrespondenz aus Boghazköi in babylonischer und hethitischer Sprache.* Vol. 1. *Umschriften und Übersetzungen.* Abhandlungen der Rheinisch-Westfälischen Akademie der Wissenschaften 77. Opladen: Westdeutscher Verlag, 1994.

———. *Ägyptische Arzte und ägyptische Medizin am hethitischen Königshof.* Opladen: Westdeutscher Verlag, 1976.

Edgerton, W. "The Strikes in Ramses III's Twenty-Ninth Year." *Journal of Near Eastern Studies* 10 (1951): 137–45.

Edwards, I. E. S. et al. *The Cambridge Ancient History.* 3rd ed. Vol. 2, Pt. 2. Cambridge: Cambridge University Press, 1975.

Edzard, D. O. "Die Beziehungen Babyloniens und Ägyptens in der mittelbabylonischer Zeit und das Gold." *Journal of the Economic and Social History of the Orient* 3 (1960): 38–55.

———. "Die Tontafeln von Kamid el-Loz." In *Kamid el-Loz-Kumidi,* ed. D. O. Edzard et al. Bonn: R. Habelt, 1970, 55–62.

Edzard, D. O. "Der Vertrag von Ebla mit A-bar-QA." In *Literature and Literary Language at Ebla,* ed. P. Fronzaroli, 187–217. Florence: Dipartimento di Linguistica, Università di Firenze, 1992.

Eidem, J. "An Old Assyrian Treaty from Tell Leilan." In *Marchands, diplomates et empereurs: Études sur la civilisation mésopotamienne offertes à Paul Garelli,* ed. D. Charpin and F. Joannès, 185–208. Paris: Editions Recherche sur les civilisations, 1991.

Falkenstein, A. *Die neusumerischen Gerichtsurkunden.* Munich: Bayerische Akademie der Wissenschaften, Abhandlungen NF 39, 1956.

Fernandez, J., ed. *Beyond Metaphor: The Theory of Tropes in Anthropology.* Stanford: Stanford University Press, 1991.

Finlay, M. *The Bücher-Meyer Controversy.* New York, 1979.

Fisher, R. "Fractionating Conflict." In *International Conflict and Behavioral Science: The Craigville Papers,* ed. Roger Fisher, 91–109. New York: Basic Books, 1964.

———, and S. Brown. *Getting Together.* Boston: Houghton Mifflin, 1988.

Follet, R. " 'Deuxième Bureau' et information diplomatique dans L'Assyrie des Sargonides: Quelques notes." *Revista Degli Studi Orientali* 32 (1957): 61–81.

Fox, R. *Kinship and Marriage.* Baltimore: Penguin, 1967.

Frandsen, P. "Egyptian Imperialism." In *Power and Propaganda: A Symposium on Ancient Empires,* ed. M. Larsen, 167–81. Copenhagen: Akademisk Forlag, 1979.

Frankfort, H. *Kingship and the Gods.* Chicago: University of Chicago Press, 1948.

———, et al. *The Intellectual Adventure of Ancient Man.* Chicago: University of Chicago Press, 1946.

Gadd, C. J. "Assiria e Babilonia (1370–1300 A.C. circa)." In *Storia del Mondo Antico*, ed. I. E. S. Edwards et al. Vol. 2. Milano: Garzanti, 1976.

Galán, J. M. "EA 164 and the God Amun." *Journal of Near Eastern Studies* 51 (1992): 287–91.

———. "The Heritage of Thutmose III's Campaigns in the Amarna Age." In *Essays in Egyptology in Honor of Hans Goedicke*, ed. B. Bryan and D. Lorton, 91–102. San Antonio: Van Siclen, 1994.

———. *Victory and Border: Terminology Related to Egyptian Imperialism in the XVIIIth Dynasty*. Hildesheim: Gerstenberg, 1995.

Gardiner, A. H. *Egyptian Grammar—Being an Introduction to the Study of Hieroglyphs*. Oxford: Oxford University Press, 1957.

Garis Davies, Norman de. *The Tomb of Ḳen-Amūn at Thebes*. Vol. 5, *Egyptian Expedition*. New York: Metropolitan Museum of Art, 1930.

Geertz, C. *The Interpretation of Culture*. New York: Basic Books, 1973.

George, J. *Discourses of Global Politics: A Critical (Re)Introduction to International Relations*. Boulder, Colo.: Lynne Rienner Publishers, 1994.

George, A. L., and William R. Simons, eds. *The Limits of Coercive Diplomacy*. 2nd ed. Boulder, Colo.: Westview Press, 1994.

Gianto, A. *Word Order Variation in the Akkadian of Byblos*. Rome: Pontifical Biblical Institute, 1990.

Girbal, C. "Der hurritische Ausdruck für 'sowohl . . . als auch . . . .'" *Altorientalische Forschungen* 21 (1994): 376–79.

Gluckman, M., and Ely Devon. *Closed Systems and Open Minds: The Limits of Naivety in Social Anthropology*. Edinburgh: Oliver and Boyd, 1964.

Goody, J. *The Oriental, the Ancient and the Primitive: Systems of Marriage and the Family in the Pre-Industrial Societies of Eurasia*. Cambridge: Cambridge University Press, 1990.

Gordon, A. "Who Was the Southern Vizier in the Last Part of the Reign of Amenhotep III?" *Journal of Near Eastern Studies* 48 (1989): 15–23.

———. "The Tomb of the Vizier Amenhotep at Thebes." *Mitteilungen des Deutschen Archaeologischen Instituts* 39 (1983): 71–79.

Green, M. "Wenamun's Demand for Compensation." *Zeitschrift für die Ägyptische Sprache und Altertumskunde* 106 (1979): 116–20.

Grimal, N-C. *Les termes de la propagande royale égyptienne de la XIXᵉ Dynastie à la conquête d'Alexandre*. Paris: Mémoires de l'Académie d'Inscriptions et Belles Lettres, n.s. 6, 1986.

Groll, S. I. "The Egyptian Administrative System in Syria and Palestine in the 18th Dynasty." In *Fontes atque Pontes. Fs. Hellmut Brunner*, ed. M. Görg, 234–42. Wiesbaden: O. Harrassowitz, 1983.

Habachi, L. "The Administration of Nubia during the New Kingdom." *Mémoires de l'Institut d'Egypte* 59 (1969): 65–78.

Hachmann, R. "Die ägyptische Verwaltung in Syrien während der Amarnazeit." *Zeitschrift des Deutschen Palästina-Vereins* 98 (1982): 17–49.

Hagenbuchner, A. *Die Korrespondenz der Hethiter,* (I-)II. Heidelberg: C. Winter, Universitatsverlag, 1989.

Hamilton, K., and R. Langhorne. *The Practice of Diplomacy: Its Evolution, Theory, and Administration.* New York: Routledge, 1995.

Hammond, K. R. "New Directions in Research on Conflict Resolution." *Journal of Social Issues* 11 (1965): 44-66.

Harvey, S. "Monuments of Ahmose at Abydos." *Egyptian Archaeology* 4 (1995): 3-5.

Heisenberg, W. *Physics and Beyond: Encounters and Conversations.* New York: Harper Torchbooks, 1972.

Helck, W. *Zur Verwaltung des Mittleren und Neuen Reiches.* Probleme der Ägyptologie 3. Leiden: E. J. Brill, 1958.

———. *Die Beziehungen Ägyptens zu Vorderasien im 3. und 2. Jahrtausend v. Chr.* Ägyptologische Abhandlungen 5. Wiesbaden: Harrassowitz, 1971.

Herman, M. *Intelligence Power in Peace and War.* Cambridge: Cambridge University Press, 1996.

Hoch, J. E. *Semitic Words in Egyptian Texts of the New Kingdom and Third Intermediate Period.* Princeton: Princeton University Press, 1994.

Hoffmann, S. "Realism and Its Discontents." *Atlantic Monthly* (November 1985): 131-36.

Holmes, Y. L. "The Messengers of the Amarna Letters." *Journal of the American Oriental Society* 95 (1975): 376-81.

Holsti, O. R., Richard A. Brody, and Robert C. North. "The Management of International Crisis: Affect and Action in American-Soviet Relations." In *Theory and Research on the Causes of War,* ed. Dean G. Pruitt and Richard C. Snyder, 62-79. Englewood Cliffs, N.J.: Prentice-Hall, 1969.

Hopmann, P. T. "Two Paradigms of Negotiation: Bargaining and Problem Solving." *Annals of the American Academy of Political and Social Science* 542 (1995): 24-47.

Houwink ten Cate, P. "Hittite Royal Prayers." *Numen* 16 (1969): 81-98.

Jakobson, V. A. "Studies in Neo-Assyrian Law. 1. Matrimonial Law." *Alt-Orientalische Forschungen* 1 (1974): 115-19.

James, A. "System or Society." *Review of International Studies* 19 (1993): 269-88.

Janssen, J. J. "Eine Beuteliste Amenhotep II. und das Problem der Sklaverei im alten Ägypten." *Jaarbericht van het Vooraziatisch-Egyptisch Genootschap* 6 (1967): 141-47.

Jervis, R. *The Logic of Images in International Relations.* Princeton: Princeton University Press, 1970.

Joannès, F. "Le traité de vassalité d'Atamrum d'Andarig envers Zimri-Lim de Mari." In *Marchands, diplomates et empereurs: Études sur la civilisation mesopotamienne offertes à Paul Garelli,* ed. D. Charpin and F. Joannès, 167-74. Paris: Editions Recherche sur les civilisations, 1991

Jones, E. E. *Ingratiation.* New York: Appleton-Century-Crofts, 1964.

Jönsson, C. *Superpower: Comparing American and Soviet Foreign Policy.* London: Frances Pinter, 1984.

————, and K. Aggestam. "Diplomatic Signalling." In *Innovation in Diplomatic Practice*, ed. Jan Melissen. London: Macmillan, forthcoming.

Kalluveettil, P. *Declaration and Covenant*. Rome: Biblical Institute Press, 1982.

Keens-Soper, M. "Abraham de Wicquefor and Diplomatic Theory." *DSP Discussion Papers* (Leicester University) 14 (1996).

Kelsen, H. *General Theory of Law and State*, trans. A. Wedberg. New York: Russell and Russell, 1961.

Kemp, B., and S. Garfi. *A Survey of the Ancient City of El-'Amarna*. Egypt Exploration Fund, Occasional Papers 9. London, 1993.

Kemp, Barry. *Ancient Egypt: Anatomy of a Civilization*. New York: Routledge, 1989.

Kendall, T. "*Gurpiša ša aweli:* The Helmets of the Warriors at Nuzi." In *Studies on the Civilization and Culture of Nuzi and the Hurrians in Honour of Ernest R. Lacheman on His Seventy-Fifth Birthday, April 29, 1981*, ed. M. A. Morrison and D. J. Owen, 201–31. Winona Lake, Ind.: Eisenbrauns, 1981.

Kent, S. *Strategic Intelligence for American World Policy*. Princeton: Princeton University Press, 1949.

Keohane, R. H. *International Institutions and State Power*. Boulder, Colo.: Westview Press, 1989.

————. "Reciprocity in International Relations." *International Organization* 40 (1986): 1–27.

Kestemont, G. *Diplomatique et Droit International en Asie Occidentale (1600–1200 av. J.C.)*. Louvain-La-Neuve: Université Catholique de Louvain, Institut Orientaliste, 1974.

Kitchen, K. A. Review of E. F. Campbell, "The Chronology of the Amarna Letters." *Journal of Egyptian Archaeology* 5 1967: 178–80.

————. *The Third Intermediate Period in Egypt, 1100–650 B.C.E.*. Warminster: Aris and Phillips, 1973.

————. *Ramesside Inscriptions Translated and Annotated. Translations* I. Oxford: Blackwell, 1979.

————. *Ramesside Inscriptions Translated and Annotated. Translations I: Ramesses I, Sethos I, and Contemporaries*. Oxford: Blackwell, 1983.

————. *Pharaoh Triumphant*. Warminster: Aris and Phillips, 1983.

————. "The Arrival of the Libyans in Late New Kingdom Egypt." In *Libya and Egypt, c. 1300–750 B.C.E.*, ed. Anthony Leahy, 15–27. London: SOAS Centre for Near and Middle Eastern Studies, 1990.

————. *Ramesside Inscriptions Translated and Annotated. Translations II*. Oxford: Blackwell, 1996.

Korošec, V. *Hethitische Staatsverträge—ein Beitrag zu ihrer juristischen Wertung*. Leipziger rechtswissenschaftliche Studien 60. Leipzig: T. Weicher, 1931.

————. "International Relations according to Cuneiform Reports from the Tell el-Amarna and Hittite State Archives." Ljubljana: *Zbornik Znanstvenih Razprav* (Ljubljana) 23 (1950): 390–97.

Kratochwil, F. *Rules, Norms, and Decisions: On the Conditions of Practical and Legal*

Reasoning in International Relations and Domestic Affairs. Cambridge: Cambridge University Press, 1989.

Kressel, K. et al. "The Settlement-Orientation vs. the Problem-Solving Style in Custody Mediation." *Journal of Social Issues* 50 (1994): 67–84.

Kühne, C. *Die Chronologie der internationalen Korrespondenz von El-Amarna.* Neukirchen-Vluyn: Neukirchener Verlag, 1973.

Lafont, B. "Les filles du roi de Mari." In *La femme dans le Proche Orient antique. Compte Rendu de la XXXIIIe Rencontre Assyriologique Internationale (Paris, 7–10 Juillet 1986),* ed. Jean-Marie Durand, 113–23. Paris: Editions Recherche sur les civilisations, 1987.

Lakoff, G. *Women, Fire, and Dangerous Things.* Chicago: University of Chicago Press, 1987.

——, and Mark Johnson. *Metaphors We Live By.* Chicago: University of Chicago Press, 1980.

Lasswell, H. D., and Nathan Leites. *Language of Politics.* Studies in Quantitative Semantics. Cambridge: MIT Press, 1965.

Lebrun, R. "Considérations sur la femme dans la société hittite." *Hethitica* 3 (1979): 109–25.

Leclant, J. "Astarte." *Lexikon der Ägyptologie* I, 499–509. Wiesbaden: O. Harrassowitz, 1975.

Lepore, E. "Economia antica e storiografia moderna." *Ricerche storiche ed economiche in memoria di Corrado Barbagallo* I, 3–33. Naples: Edizioni scientifiche italiane, 1970.

Letellier, B. "Thoutmosis IV à Karnak." *Bulletin de la Société Française de l'Egyptologie* 122 (1991): 36–52.

Lévi-Strauss, C. *The Elementary Structures of Kinship.* Boston: Beacon Press, 1969.

Lilyquist, C. "A Gold Bowl Naming General Djehuty: A Study of Objects and Early Egyptology." *Journal of the Metropolitan Museum of Art* 23 (1988): 1–68.

——, and R. H. Brill. *Studies in Early Egyptian Glass.* New York: Metropolitan Museum of Art, 1993.

Liverani, M. "Contrasti e confluenze di concezioni politiche nell'età di el-Amarna." *Revue d'Assyriologie* 61 (1967): 1–18.

——. "Elementi 'irrazionali' nel commercio amarniano." *Oriens Antiquus* 11 (1972): 297–317.

——. "Storiografia politica hittita—I. Šunaššura, ovvero: della reciprocità." *Oriens Antiquus* 12 (1973): 267–97.

——. "Dono, tributo, commercio: ideologia dello scambio nella tarda età del bronzo." *Istituto Italiano di Numismatica. Annali* 26 (1979): 9–28.

——. *Three Amarna Essays.* Malibu: Undena Publications, 1979.

——."Pharaoh's Letters to Rib-Addi." In *Three Amarna Essays,* 3–13. Malibu: Undena Publications, 1979.

——. "Political Lexicon and Political Ideologies in the Amarna Letters." *Berytus* 31 (1983): 41–56.

———. *Antico Oriente. Storia, economia, società.* Roma: Laterza, 1988.

———. Review of *Les lettres d'el-Amarna,* ed. William L. Moran. *Rivista degli Studi Orientali* 63 (1989): 168–71.

———. *Prestige and Interest: International Relations in the Near East, circa 1600–1100 B.C.E.* Padova: Sargon, 1990.

———. "A Seasonal Pattern for the Amarna Letters." In *Lingering over Words: Studies in Ancient Near Eastern Literature in Honor of William L. Moran,* ed. T. Abusch, J. Huehnergard, and P. Steinkeller, 337–48, HSS 37. Atlanta: Scholar's Press, 1990.

———. *Guerra e diplomazia nell'Antico Oriente.* Roma: Laterza, 1994.

———. "How to Kill ʿAbdi-Ashirta: EA 101 Once Again." In *Past Links,* Israel Oriental Studies, ed. S. Izreel. Vol. 18. In press.

———. "Hattushili alle prese con la propaganda ramesside." *Orientalia* 59 (1990): 209–10.

Lorton, D. *The Juridical Terminology of International Relations in Egyptian Texts through Dynasty XVIII.* Baltimore: John Hopkins University Press, 1974.

Luard, E. *International Society.* London: Macmillan, 1990.

Mackinder, Sir H. J. *Democratic Ideals and Reality: A Study in the Politics of Reconstruction.* London: Constable, 1919.

Malinowski, B. *Argonauts of the Western Pacific.* New York: Dutton, 1922.

Manuelian, P. Der. *Studies in the Reign of Amenhotep II.* Hildesheimer Ägyptologische Beitrage 26. Hildesheim: Gerstenberg Verlag, 1987.

Marfoe, L. "Between Qadesh and Kumidi: A History of Frontier Settlement and Land Use in the Biqaʾa, Lebanon." Ph.D. diss., University of Chicago, 1978.

Martin, G. T. *Egyptian Administrative and Private-Name Seals, Principally of the Middle Kingdom and Second Intermediate Period.* Oxford: Griffith Institute, 1971.

Mauss, M. *The Gift.* New York: Norton, 1967. Originally published as "Essai sur le don." *L'année Sociologique,* II série, 1 (1923–24): 30–186.

McNulty, T. J. "Television's Impact on Executive Decisionmaking and Diplomacy." *Fletcher Forum of World Affairs* 17 (1993): 67–83.

Meier, S. *The Messenger in the Ancient Semitic World.* Harvard Semitic Monographs 45. Atlanta: Scholar's Press, 1988.

Meyer, G. "Hurija und Piphururija." *Göttinger Miszellen* 126 (1992): 87–92.

Moran, W. L. "The Ancient Near Eastern Background of the Love of God in Deuteronomy." *Catholic Biblical Quarterly* 25 (1963): 77–87.

———. "The Syrian Scribe of the Jerusalem Amarna Letters." In *Unity and Diversity: Essays in the History, Literature, and Religion of the Ancient Near East,* ed. H. Goedicke and J. J. M. Roberts, 146–66. Baltimore: Johns Hopkins University Press, 1975.

———. "Additions to the Amarna Lexicon." *Orientalia* 53 (1984): 297–302.

———. "Rib-Hadda: Job at Byblos?" In *Biblical and Related Studies Presented to Samuel Iwry,* ed. A. Kort and S. Morschauser, 173–18. Winona Lake, Ind.: Eisenbrauns, 1985.

————, ed. and trans. *The Amarna Letters*. Baltimore: Johns Hopkins University Press, 1992.

————. "Some Reflections on Amarna Politics." In *Solving Riddles and Untying Knots: Biblical, Epigraphic, and Semitic Studies in Honor of Jonas C. Greenfield*, ed. Ziony Zevit, Seymour Gitin, and M. Sokoloff, 559–72. Winona Lake, Ind.: Eisenbrauns, 1995.

Morgenthau, H. J. *Politics among Nations*. 3rd ed. New York: Alfred A. Knopf, 1966.

Morschauser, S. "The End of the s*df(3)-tr(yt)* 'Oath.'" *Journal of the American Research Center in Egypt* 25 (1988): 93–103.

Munn-Rankin, J. M. "Diplomacy in Western Asia in the Early Second Millennium B.C.E." *Iraq* 18 (1956): 68–110.

Murnane, W. J. *Ancient Egyptian Coregencies*. Chicago: Oriental Institute, 1977.

————. *The Road to Kadesh*. Studies in Ancient Oriental Civilizations 42. Chicago: Oriental Institute of the University of Chicago, 1990.

————. "Nature of the Aten: Akhenaten and His God, Problems and Proposals." *Amarna Letters* 3 (1994): 32–40.

————. *Texts from the Amarna Period in Egypt*. Society of Biblical Literature Writings from the Ancient World 5. Atlanta: Scholar's Press, 1995.

————. "'Overseer of the Northern Foreign Countries': Reflections on the Upper Administration of Egypt's Empire in Western Asia." In *Essays on Ancient Egypt in Honour of Hermann Te Velde*, ed. J. van Dijk. Groningen: Styx, 1997.

Na'aman, N. "The Political Disposition and Historical Developments of Eretz Israel according to the Amarna Letters." Ph.D. diss., Tel Aviv University, 1973.

————. "Economic Aspects of the Egyptian Occupation of Canaan." *Israel Exploration Journal*, 31 (1981): 172–85.

————. "Pharaonic Lands in the Jezreel Valley in the Late Bronze Age." In *Society and Economy in the Eastern Mediterranean*, ed. M. Heltzer and E. Lipinski, 177–85. Orientalia Lovaniensia Analecta 23. Leuven: Instituut voor Orientalistik, 1988.

————. "Biryawaza of Damascus and the date of the Kamid El-Loz Apiru Letters." In *Ugarit-Forschungen*, 179–93. Vol. 20. Neukirchen-Vluyn: Neukirchener Verlag, 1988.

————. "Praises to Pharaoh in Response to his Plans for a Campaign to Canaan." In *Lingering over Words: Studies in Ancient Near Eastern Literature in Honor of William L. Moran*, ed. T. Abusch, J. Huehnergard, and P. Steinkeller, 397–405. Harvard Semitic Studies 37. Atlanta: Scholar's Press, 1990.

Naville, E. *The Temple of Deir el Bahari* III. London: Offices of the Egypt Exploration Fund, 1898.

Nicolson, H. *The Evolution of Diplomatic Method*. London: Constable and Co., 1954.

————. *Diplomacy*. 3rd ed. London: Oxford University Press, 1963.

Niou, Emerson M. S., Peter C. Ordeshook, and Gregory F. Rose, eds. *The Balance of Power: Stability in International Systems*. New York: Cambridge University Press, 1989.

Nougayrol, J. *Le Palais Royal d'Ugarit IV— Textes Accadiens des Archives Sud archives internationales).* Paris: Imprimerie nationale, 1956.

Numelin, R. J. *The Beginnings of Diplomacy.* London: Oxford University Press, 1950.

O'Connor, D. "The Land of Irem." *Journal of Egyptian Archaeology* 73 (1987): 99–136.

———. "Early States along the Nubian Nile." In *Egypt and Africa: Nubia from Prehistory to Islam,* ed. W. V. Davies, 145–65. London: British Museum Press in association with the Egypt Exploration Society, 1991.

———, and David Silverman, eds. *Ancient Egyptian Kingship.* Probleme der Ägyptologie 9. New York: E. J. Brill, 1994.

Oppenheim, A. L. *Letters from Mesopotamia: Official Business, and Private Letters on Clay Tablets from Two Millennia.* Chicago: University of Chicago Press, 1967.

Pardee, D. "A New Ugaritic Letter." *Bibliotheca Orientalis* (1977): 3–20.

Parpola, S. *Neo-Assyrian Treaties and Loyalty Oaths.* Helsinki: Helsinki University Press, 1988.

Perelman, C., and Olbrechts-Tyteca, L. *Traité de l'argumentation. La nouvelle rhétorique.* Paris: Presses universitaires de France, 1958.

Pestman, P. W. A. *Marriage and Matrimonial Property in Ancient Egypt.* Leiden: E. J. Brill, 1961.

Pintore, F. *Il matrimonio interdinastico nel Vicino Oriente durante i Secoli XV–XIII.* Rome: Istituto per Oriente, 1978.

Polanyi, K. "The Economy as Instituted Process." In *Trade and Market in the Early Empires: Economies in History and Theories,* ed. K. Polanyi et al. Glencoe: Free Press, 1957.

Pitt-Rivers, J. A. *The Fate of Shechem and the Politics of Sex: Essays in the Anthropology of the Mediterranean.* Cambridge: Cambridge University Press, 1977.

Porter, B., and R. Moss. *Topographical Bibliography of Ancient Egyptian Hieroglyphic Texts, Reliefs, and Paintings.* Oxford: Oxford University Press, 1960–81.

Posener, G. "Mwkd." *Göttinger Miszellen* 11 (1974): 39.

Pritchard, J. ed. *Ancient Near Eastern Texts Relating to the Old Testament.* 3rd ed. Princeton: Princeton University Press, 1969.

Pruitt, D. G. "Flexibility in Conflict Episodes." *Annals of the American Academy of Political and Social Science* no. 542 (1995): 100–15.

Queller, D. E. *The Office of Ambassador in the Middle Ages.* Princeton: Princeton University Press, 1967.

Rainey, A. F. "A New English Translation of the Amarna Letters." *Archiv für Orientforschung* 42–43 (1995–1996): 109–21.

Redford, D. B. "A Gate Inscription from Karnak and Egyptian Involvement in Western Asia during the Early Eighteenth Dynasty." *Journal of the American Oriental Society* 99 (1979): 270–87.

———. *Akhenaten, The Heretic King.* Princeton: Princeton University Press, 1984.

———. *Egypt and Canaan in the New Kingdom.* BeerSheva IV. Beersheva: Ben Gurion University of the Negev Press, 1990.

———. *Egypt, Canaan, and Israel in Ancient Times*. Princeton: Princeton University Press, 1992.

———. "The Concept of Kingship during the Eighteenth Dynasty." In *Ancient Egyptian Kingship*, ed. David O'Connor and David Silverman, 157–84. Probleme der Ägyptologie 9. New York: E. J. Brill, 1995.

Renger, J. "Legal Aspects of Sealing in Ancient Mesopotamia." In *Seals and Sealing in the Ancient Near East*, ed. M. Gibson and R. Biggs, 75–88. Bibliotheca Mesopotamica 6. Malibu: Undena Publications, 1977.

———. "Probleme und Perspektiven einer Wirtschaftsgeschichte Mesopotamiens." *Saeculum* 40 (1989): 166–78.

Robins, G. "A Critical Examination of the Theory That the Right to the Throne of Ancient Egypt Passed through the Female Line in the 18th Dynasty." *Göttinger Miszellen* 62 (1983): 67–77.

———. *Women in Ancient Egypt*. London: British Museum Press, 1993.

Rommetveit, R. "On the Architecture of Intersubjectivity." In *Studies of Language, Thought and Verbal Communication*, ed. Ragnar Rommetveit and Rolv M. Blakar. New York: Academic Press, 1979.

———. *On Message Structure: A Framework for the Study of Language and Communication*. London: John Wiley, 1974.

Roux, G. *Ancient Iraq*. London: Pelican Books, 1966.

———. *Ancient Iraq*. 3rd ed. London: Penguin Books, 1992.

Sahlins, Marshall. "Exchange-Value and the Diplomacy of Primitive Trade." In *Essays in Economic Anthropology, Dedicated to the Memory of Karl Polanyi*. Proceedings of the 1965 annual spring meeting of the American Ethnological Society. Seattle: American Ethnological Society, 1965.

———. *Stone Age Economics*. Chicago: Aldine-Atherton, 1972.

Saporetti, C. *The Status of Women in the Middle Assyrian Period*, trans. Beatrice Boltze-Jordan. Sources and Monographs on the Ancient Near East 2 (1). Malibu: Undena Publications, 1979.

Sauren, H. "Le mariage selon le Code d'Eshnunna." *Revue internationale des droits de l'antiquité*. 3e. série. 33 (1986): 45–86.

Säve-Söderbergh, T. *Ägypten und Nubien*. Lund: Hakan Ohlssons Boktryckeri, 1941.

———. "The Tomb of the Prince of Teh-khet, Amenemhat." *Kush* 11 (1973): 159–74.

Schachermeyr, F. "Zur staatsrechtlichen Wertung der hethitischen Verträge." *Mitteilungen der Ägyptisch-Orientalischen Gesellschaft* 4 (1928–9): 180–86.

Schaeffer, C., ed. *Mission de Ras Shamra*. Vol. 9. *Le Palais Royal d'Ugarit* IV. Paris: Imprimerie Nationale, 1956.

Schelling, T. C. *The Strategy of Conflict*. New York: Oxford University Press, 1963.

———. *Arms and Influence*. New Haven: Yale University Press, 1966.

Schmitz, B. *Untersuchungen zur Titel s3-njśwt "Königssohn."* Bonn: Habelt, 1976.

Schulman, A. "Some Remarks on the Military Background of the Amarna Period." *Journal of the American Research Center in Egypt* 3 (1964): 51–69.

———. "Aspects of Ramesside Diplomacy: The Treaty of Year 21." *Journal of the Society for the Study of Egyptian Antiquities* 8 (1978): 112–30.

———. "Diplomatic Marriages in the Egyptian New Kingdom." *Journal of Near Eastern Studies* 38 (1979): 177–93.

———. "Hittites, Helmets, and Amarna: Akhenaten's First Hittite War." In *Akhenaten Temple Project II*, ed. D. Redford, 54–79. Toronto: Akhenaten Temple Project, 1988.

Seaborg, G. T. *Kennedy, Khrushchev, and the Test Ban.* Berkeley: University of California Press, 1981.

Sethe, K., and Helck, W., eds. *Urkunden des ägyptischen Altertums IV; Urkunden der 18. Dynastie*, 1–16. Leipzig: J.C. Hinrichs, 1906–1909, 17–22. Berlin: Akademie, 1955–1958.

Several, M. W. "Reconsidering the Egyptian Empire in Palestine." *Palestine Exploration Quarterly* 104 (1972): 123–33.

Sharp, J. M. O. "MBFR as Arms Control." *Arms Control Today* 6 (1976): 1.

Silverman, D. P. "The Nature of Egyptian Kingship." In *Ancient Egyptian Kingship*, ed. David O'Connor and David Silverman, 49–92. Probleme der Ägyptologie 9. Leiden: E. J. Brill, 1995.

Simons, H. W. *Persuasion: Understanding, Practice, and Analysis.* Reading, Mass.: Addison-Wesley, 1976.

Simons, J. J. *Handbook for the Study of Egyptian Topographical Lists Relating to Western Asia.* Leiden: E. J. Brill, 1937.

Simpson, W. K. *The Literature of Ancient Egypt: An Anthology of Stories, Instructions, and Poetry.* new ed. New Haven: Yale University Press, 1973.

———. *Heka-nefer and the Dynastic Material from Tashka and Arminna.* Pennsylvania-Yale Expedition to Egypt 1. New Haven: Peabody Museum of Natural History, Yale University, 1963.

———. "Reschef." In *Lexikon der Ägyptologie* V, 244–46. Wiesbaden: O. Harrassowitz, 1984.

Singer, I. "A Concise History of Amurru." Appendix 3 in *Amurru Akkadian: A Linguistic Study*, ed. Shlomo Izre'el. Atlanta: Scholar's Press, 1991.

Sollberger, E. "The So-Called Treaty between Ebla and 'Ashur.'" *Studi Eblaiti* 3/9–10 (1980): 129–55.

Spalinger, A. J. "Remarks on the Family of Queen Hꜥ.s-nbw and the Problem of Kingship in Dynasty XIII." *Revue d'Egyptologie* 32 (1980): 103–15.

———. "Considerations on the Hittite Treaty between Egypt and Hatti." *Studien zur altägyptischen Kultur* 9 (1981): 299–358.

———. "The Historical Implications of the Year 9 Campaign of Amenhotep II." *Journal of the Society for the Study of Egyptian Antiquities* 13 (1983): 89–101.

Spiro, M. "Collective Representations and Mental Representations in Religious Symbol Systems." In *On Symbols in Anthropology: Essays in Honor of Harry Hoijer*, ed. J. Maquet, 45–72. Malibu: Undena Publications, 1982.

Sprout, H., and Margaret Sprout, eds. *Foundations of National Power: Readings on World Politics and American Security.* Princeton: Princeton University Press, 1945.

Stadelmann, R. *Syrisch-Palästinische Gottheiten in Ägypten.* Probleme der Ägyptologie 5. Leiden: E. J. Brill, 1967.

Stager, L. "Archaeology of the Family in Ancient Israel." *Bulletin of the American Schools of Oriental Research* 260 (1985): 1–35.

Stern, P. C., and Druckman, D. "Has the 'Earthquake' of 1989 Toppled International Relations Theory?" *Peace Psychology Review* 1 (1994–1995): 109–22.

Strouhal, E. "L'Etude anthropologique et paléopathologique des restes du vizir 'Aper-El et de sa famille: premiers résultats." *Bulletin de la Société Française d'Egyptologie* 126 (1993): 24–37.

Sturtevant, E. *A Hittite Chrestomathy.* Philadelphia: Linguistic Society of America, University of Pennsylvania, 1935.

Tadmor, H. "The Decline of Empires in Western Asia ca. 1200 B.C.E." In *Symposia Celebrating the Seventy-fifth Anniversary of the American Schools of Oriental Research,* ed. F. M. Cross. Cambridge: American Schools of Oriental Research, 1979.

Théodoridès, A. "Les rélations de l'Egypte pharaonique avec ses voisins." *Revue Internationale des Droits de l'Antiquité* 22 (1975): 87–140.

Thompson, S. "The Anointing of Officials in Ancient Egypt." *Journal of Near Eastern Studies* 53 (1994): 15–25.

Turner, V. *The Forest of Symbols: Aspects of Ndembu Ritual.* Ithaca: Cornell University Press, 1967.

Vallogia, M. *Recherche sur les "messagers" (wpwtjw) dans les sources égyptiennes profanes.* Centre de Recherches d'Histoire et de Philologie de la IVème section de l'Ecole pratique des Hautes Etudes, II. Hautes Etudes Orientales 6. Geneva: Libraire Droz, 1976.

Vandersleyen, C. *L'Egypte et la vallée du Nil.* Paris: Presses universitaires de France, 1995.

Von Schuler, E. *Hethitische Dienstanweisungen für höhere Hof—und Staatsbeamte—Ein Beitrage zum antiken Recht Kleinasiens.* Archiv für Orientforschung, Beiheft 10. Osnabrück: Biblio-Verlag, 1967.

Walker, R. J. *Inside/Outside: International Relations as Political Theory.* Cambridge: Cambridge University Press, 1993.

Waltz, K. N. *Theory of International Politics.* New York: Random House, 1979.

Watson, A. *The Evolution of the International Society: A Comparative Historical Analysis.* London: Routledge, 1992.

Weinstein, J. "The Egyptian Empire in Palestine: A Reassessment." *Bulletin of the American Schools of Oriental Research* 241 (1982): 1–28.

Wendt, A. "Anarchy Is What States Make of It." *International Organization* 46 (1992): 391–425.

———. "Collective Identity Formation and the International State." *American Political Science Review* 88 (1994): 384–96.

Westbrook, R. *Studies in Biblical and Cuneiform Law.* Cahiers de la Revue Biblique 26. Paris: Gabalda, 1988.

———. *Old Babylonian Marriage Law.* Archiv für Orientforschung Beiheft 23. Horn: Ferdinand Berger, 1988.

———. "Mitgift." *Reallexikon der Assyriologie* 8 (1994): 273–83.

White, L. *The Science of Culture.* New York: Farrar, Straus and Giroux, 1949.

Wicquefort, Abraham de. *The Embassador and his Functions. To which is added, An Historical Discourse, concerning the Election of the Emperor and the Electors,* trans. J. Digby. London, 1716.

Wight, M. *Systems of States.* Leicester: Leicester University Press, 1977

———. *Power Politics.* London: Penguin, 1986.

Wilhelm, G. "Notes on the Mittanni Letter." In *Studies on the Civilization and Culture of Nuzi and the Hurrians,* ed. M. Morrison and D. Owen, 135–40. Vol. 7. Winona Lake, Ind.: Eisenbrauns, 1995.

Wilson, C. E. *Diplomatic Privileges and Immunities.* Tucson: University of Arizona Press, 1967.

Wilson, J. A. "Egypt." In *Before Philosophy: The Intellectual Adventure of Ancient Man; An Essay on Speculative Thought in the Ancient Near East,* ed. H. Frankfort et al., 31–121. Chicago: University of Chicago Press, 1946.

———. *The Burden of Egypt: An Interpretation of Ancient Egyptian Culture.* Chicago: University of Chicago Press, 1951.

Wimmer, S. "Egyptian Temples in Canaan and Sinai." *Studies in Egyptology Presented to Miriam Lichtheim,* ed. S. Israelit-Groll, 1065–1106. 2 vols. Jerusalem: Magnes Press, 1990.

Winckler, H. "Vorläufige Nachrichten über die Ausgrabungen in Boghaz-köi im Sommer 1907. 1. Die Tontafelfunde." *Mitteilungen der Deutschen Orientgesellschaft* 35 (1907): 1–59.

Winlock, H. E. *The Treasure of Three Egyptian Princesses.* New York: Metropolitan Museum of Art, 1948.

Wiseman, D. J. *The Alalakh Tablets.* London: British Institute of Archaeology at Ankara, 1953.

———. " 'Is it Peace?' "—Covenant and Diplomacy." *Vetus Testamentum* 32 (1982): 317–22.

Yurco, F. "Two Tomb-wall Painted Reliefs of Ramesses III and Sety I, and Ancient Nile Valley Population Diversity." In *Egypt in Africa,* ed. Theodore Celenko, 109–11. Indianapolis: Indiana University Press, 1996.

Zaccagnini, C. *Lo scambio dei doni nel Vicino Oriente durante i secoli XV–XIII.* Rome: Centro per le antichita e la storia dell'arte del Vicino Oriente, 1973.

———. "On Gift-Exchange in the Old Babylonian Period." In *Studi orientalistici in ricordo di Franco Pintore,* ed. O. Carruba, M. Liverani, and C. Zaccagnini, 189–253. Pavia: GJES, 1983.

———. "Patterns of Mobility among Ancient Near Eastern Craftsmen." *Journal of Near Eastern Studies* 42 (1983): 245–64.

————. "On Late Bronze Age Marriages." In *Studi in onore di Edda Bresciani*, ed. S. F. Bondi, 593–605. Pisa: Giardini, 1985.

————. "Aspects of Ceremonial Exchange in the Near East during the Late Second Millennium B.C." In *Centre and Periphery in the Ancient World*, ed. M. Rowlands, M. Larsen, and K. Kristiansen, 57–65. Cambridge: Cambridge University Press, 1987.

————. "A Note on Hittite International Relations at the Time of Tudhaliya IV." In *Studi G. Pugliese Carratelli*, ed. F. Imparati, 295–99. Firenze: Editioni Librarie Italiane Estere, 1988.

————. "Prehistory of the Achaemenid Tributary System." In *Le tribut dans l'empire perse*, ed. P. Briant and C. Herrenschmidt, 193–215. Paris: Peeters, 1989.

————. "Dono e tributo come modelli istituzionali di scambio: echi e persistenze nella documentazione amministrativa vicino-orientale del Tardo Bronzo." *Scienze dell'antichità: storia, archeologia, antropologia* 3–4 (1989–1990): 105–10.

————. "The Forms of Alliance and Subjugation in the Near East of the Late Bronze Age." In *I Trattati nel Mondo Antico: Forma, ideologia, funzione*, ed. L. Canfora et al., 37–79. Rome: "L'Erma" di Bretschneider, 1990.

————. "Ideological and Procedural Paradigms in Ancient Near Eastern Long Distance Exchanges: The Case of Enmerkar and the Lord of Aratta." *Altorientalische Forschungen* 20 (1993): 34–42.

————. "Les échanges dans l'antiquité: Paradigmes théoriques et analyse des sources." *Les échanges dans l'antiquité: le role de l'état*, ed. J. Andreau et al., 213–25. Saint-Bertrand de Comminges: Musée archéologique départemental, 1994.

————. "Lo scambio dei beni nelle relazioni internazionali del Vicino Oriente durante il Tardo Bronzo: Istituzioni, ideologie, prassi." In *Les relations internationales*, ed. E. Frézouls and A. Jacquemin, 41–68. Paris: De Boccard, 1995.

————. Review of *Il matrimonio interdinastico nel Vicino Oriente*, by Franco Pintore. *Bullettino dell'Istituto di Diritto Romano*. 3rd ser. Vol. 21 (1979): 203–21.

Zartman, I. William, Daniel Druckman, L. Jensen, Dean G. Pruitt, and H. Peyton Young. "Negotiation as a Search for Justice." *International Negotiation* 1 (1996): 79–98.

Zibelius, K. *Afrikanische Orts- und Völkernamen in hieroglyphischen und hieratischen Texte*. Wiesbaden: Dr. Ludwig Reichert Verlag, 1972.

Zivie, A-P. *Découverte à Saqqarah: Le vizir oublié*. Paris: Seuil, 1990.

Zorn, J. "The Role of the Rābiṣu in the Amarna Archive." In *Amarna in Retrospect: One Hundred Years of Amarna Studies*, ed. G. D. Young and B. Beitzel. Winona Lake, Ind.: Eisenbrauns, forthcoming.

Contributors

PINHAS ARTZI is professor emeritus of Assyriology, Bar Ilan University, Israel, where he was founding member of the Kramer Institute of Assyriology. His main fields of research are the international relations of the ancient Near East and the history and culture of the biblical period. He has written extensively, particularly on the Amarna documents.

KEVIN AVRUCH is professor of anthropology, an affiliated faculty member of the Institute for Conflict Analysis and Resolution, and a senior fellow in the Program on Peacekeeping Policy at George Mason University. He has published widely on conflict resolution and on religion, politics, and nationalism in contemporary Israel. His most recent book is *Culture and Conflict Resolution* (1998).

GEOFFREY BERRIDGE is professor of international politics and director of the Centre for the Study of Diplomacy at the University of Leicester, United Kingdom. His main interests are the history and theory of diplomacy. Among his latest books are *Talking to the Enemy: How States without "Diplomatic Relations" Communicate* (1994) and *Diplomacy: Theory and Practice* (1995). He is also general editor of the Macmillan "Studies in Diplomacy" series.

BETSY M. BRYAN is Alexander Badawy Professor of Egyptian Art and Archaeology at the Johns Hopkins University. Dr. Bryan is primarily interested in the history and art of the New Kingdom (ca. 1600–1000 B.C.E.), particularly the Eighteenth Dynasty. She has authored books and articles on the two reigns that preceded the Amarna Period, those of Thutmose IV and Amenhotep III. She also directs a field project in Luxor, Egypt, which focuses on the organization of craftsman labor as reflected in a funerary monument of the time of Amenhotep II (ca. 1430 B.C.E.).

RAYMOND COHEN is professor and chair of the Department of International Relations at the Hebrew University of Jerusalem, Israel. His main interests are international negotiation, cross-cultural communication, and diplomacy. His latest books are *Culture and Conflict in Egyptian-Israeli Relations* (1990) and *Negotiating across Cultures*, rev. ed. (1997).

STEVEN R. DAVID is professor of political science at the Johns Hopkins University, where he also serves as associate dean for academic affairs. He has written widely on security issues, particularly those relating to the developing world, and on American foreign policy. His articles have appeared in leading journals including *World Politics, International Security, Foreign Affairs,* and the *National Interest.*

DANIEL DRUCKMAN is professor of conflict resolution and coordinator of the doctoral program at the Institute for Conflict Analysis and Resolution, George Mason University. His main interests are international negotiation, nationalism, and group processes. Among his recent publications are the 1998 coedited issue of *International Negotiation* on "International Negotiation as Social Exchange" and the 1995 coedited special issue of the *Annals of the American Academy of Political and Social Science* on "Flexibility in International Negotiation and Mediation."

SERDAR GÜNER is assistant professor in the Department of International Relations, Bilkent University, Turkey. His main interests are game theory, formal modeling, and conflict resolution. His recent publications include articles on the Turkish-Syrian water dispute appearing in *Studies in Conflict and Terrorism* and in *Conflict Management and Peace Science.*

ALAN JAMES has recently retired from Keele University, United Kingdom, where he was professor of international relations. His main interests are peacekeeping, diplomacy, and international society. His latest books are *Peacekeeping in International Politics* (1990) and *Britain and the Congo Crisis, 1960–63* (1996).

CHRISTER JÖNSSON is professor of political science at Lund University, Sweden. His research interests include international negotiation and cooperation. His latest books are *International Cooperation in Response to AIDS* (1995) and *Communication and International Bargaining* (1990).

MARIO LIVERANI is professor of the history of the ancient Near East at the University of Rome, Italy. His main fields of research are international relations in the Amarna period, the historical geography of the ancient Near East, rural landscape, and urbanization. He has excavated in Syria, Turkey, and the Libyan Sahara. His latest books are *Prestige and Interest: International Relations in the Near East ca. 1600–1100 BC* (1990), *El antiguo Oriente: historia, sociedad y economia* (1995), and *Le lettere di el-Amarna* (1998).

SAMUEL A. MEIER is associate professor of Hebrew and Near Eastern languages and literatures at the Ohio State University. His research interests include royal protocol and communication in the ancient world, reflected in his books *The Messenger in the Ancient Semitic World* (1988) and *Speaking of Speaking: Marking Direct Discourse in Biblical Hebrew* (1992).

WILLIAM J. MURNANE is professor of ancient history at the University of Memphis and field director of the Karnak Great Hypostyle Hall Project in Egypt. He specializes in Egyptian history, particularly the later Eighteenth Dynasty. His publications include *Ancient Egyptian Coregencies* (1977), *The Road to Kadesh*, 2d ed. (1990), and *Texts from the Amarna Period in Egypt* (1995).

NADAV NAʿAMAN is professor of biblical history in the Department of Jewish History at Tel Aviv University, Israel. His main fields of research are biblical and ancient Near Eastern history and historiography, biblical archaeology, and geographical history. He has written recently on biblical history and historiography, the Amarna letters, and the contribution of archaeology to the historical study of early Israel.

RODOLFO RAGIONIERI is assistant professor in the Department of Political Science and Sociology of the University of Florence, Italy. His main research interests are conflict and security in the Mediterranean and the Middle East and the general theory of conflict. Among his publications are *Il Golfo delle Guerre* (1991) and *International Constraints and National Debates in the Israeli-Palestinian Peace Process* (1997).

RAYMOND WESTBROOK is professor of ancient law at the Johns Hopkins University. He has written extensively on the legal systems of the ancient Near East and of preclassical Greece and Rome. He is at present editing a reference history of ancient Near Eastern law.

CARLO ZACCAGNINI is professor of ancient Near Eastern history at the Istituto Universitario Orientale of Naples, Italy. His research interests focus on the juridical, socioeconomic, and political aspects of Mesopotamia and Syria-Palestine of the late second and first millennia. He has published extensively in major journals and publications on the ancient Near East.

Index of Terms and Proper Names

Egyptian Geographical and Personal Names

Index of Sources

Amarna Letters (EA)

Egyptian Sources

Hittite Archives

Akkadian Sources

Hebrew Bible

General Index

Information about cities, states, empires, and kingdoms is included under place names and under names of specific rulers.

Abar-SAL, kingdom of, 10
ʿAbdi-Ashirta (ʿAbdi-Ashtarti), ruler of Amurru, 116; ambition of, 63, 120; complaint against commissioners by, 136; death of, 8, 60, 121, 137; expansionism of, 8, 32; intelligence reports from and about, 91, 92, 93–94, 117; loyalty of, 38, 59, 61–62; status of, 158; tribute sent by, 129, 130
ʿAbdi-Heba, ruler of Jerusalem, 128, 130, 135–36
Abi-Milku, ruler of Tyre, 38, 90, 94, 128, 129, 136, 156, 158
Addu-nirari of Nuhašše, 39, 106
administrative responsibility, and territoriality, 20, 23
Aduna, king of Irqata, 91
Aha (Egyptian king), 82
Ahmose, son of Ebana, 71, 72
Ahmose Pennekhbet, 71, 72
Aitukama (Aitakama), ruler of Qadesh, 8, 9, 88, 91, 110, 122
Akhenaten. See Amenhotep IV (Akhenaten, Naphrureya), Pharaoh
Akhetaten (Egypt), 1
Akkadian (Babylonian) language, 9–10, 23, 37, 48, 166, 223, 235–36
Akko, Egyptian alliance with, 115, 120
Alalakh archive, 15
Alashiya (Alashia), state of: description of, 7–8; trade with, 8, 146, 148; treaty of, 41; tribute from, 149–50, 159
Albright, W. F., 120

Aleppo, Egyptian expedition to, 74
allegiance. See loyalty oaths and pledges
Amanappa (Egyptian commissioner), 88
Amarna (Egypt): bureaucratic lacunae at, 108–9; established, 102
Amarna Age: description of, xiii, 102; international law in, 28–41; international system developed in, 10–12, 15–17, 26, 42, 45–53, 225–36; length of, 234–36; polyculturalism of, 10, 12, 235
Amarna Letters (EA): correspondents of, 6–9, 46; dating of, 6, 225; discovery of (1887), 1, 15; editing and publication of, 1; literary form of, 17; root metaphors in, 157, 158–60; royal, 127–29; seasonal, 126, 129–31; types of, 1–2, 85–97, 157–58; understanding as political documents, 3–4, 15–16; understanding content of, 3, 126–27; understanding script and language of, 2–3, 9–10
ambassadors: customary law regarding, 33–34; honesty of, 218–19; pace of travel by, 22; protection of, 22–23, 33–34, 151–52; qualifications of, 217–19. See also envoys
Amenemheb (Mahu), 74
Amenemhet IV, Pharaoh, 82
Amenhotep II, Pharaoh, 75, 76–79
Amenhotep III (Mimmureya/Nimuʾwareya/Nibmureya, Nimmureya), Pharaoh, 6; foreign policy of, 83–84, 110, 151, 153, 194, 196; intelligence reports of, 86; marital alliances of, 26, 48, 79–83, 159–60, 180–83, 208; messengers detained by, 52
Amenhotep IV (Akhenaten, Naphrureya), Pharaoh, 1, 6, 18, 48; accession of, 6, 20, 128, 210, 231; capital of, at Amarna, 102;

299

Amenhotep IV (*cont.*)
    foreign policy under, 50, 71, 102, 103–7,
    110; referenced as "Good Ruler," 106;
    treatment of foreigners under, 106–7
Ammunira, ruler of Beirut, 129
Ampi, city of, 117
Amun, 106
Amurru, state of: alliance with ʿApiru, 116,
    120; alliance with Byblos, 117; description
    of, 8; expansionism of, 58, 116–17, 120–21;
    extradition by, 36; Hittite alliance with, 8,
    62, 88, 92, 111, 119, 122–23; intelligence
    reports from and about, 90, 93–94
anarchy: in Amarna period, 58–59;
    constructivist view of, 56–57; defined, 43,
    49, 55; realist assumption of, 55, 65
Anatolia (modern). *See* Arzawa, state of;
    Hatti (Hattusha), empire of
ancient history: hindsight about, 5;
    objectivity about, 5; relevance of, 5–6, 16
ancient Near East: Egyptian sphere of
    influence in, *xiv*; as international system,
    36; international system in, 4, 11, 15; map,
    xii; ontology of, 229–30; table of events,
    xiii–xvi
Ankhesenamun (Hittite prince), 82
Annals of Thutmose III, 72–73, 74, 77
anthropological analysis, 3, 154–64
Aper-El (Egyptian vizier?), 109
ʿApiru (*ḫabiru/ḫapiru*), 9, 115–16, 120, 127
Armant stela, 73
Aron, Raymond, 44
Artashumara, king of Mittani, 206
Artatama I, king of Mittani, 206; daughter
    of, 79
Arthashastra (Kautilya), 89, 90
Artzi, Pinhas, 61, 226, 231, 233
Arwad, city of, 117, 129
Arzawa, state of: conquered by Hatti, 50, 65;
    description of, 7; Egyptian alliance with,
    62, 65, 66, 86–87, 159–60
Ashkelon, Egyptian alliance with, 114
Ashur-nadin-ahhe, king of Assyria, 150
"Asiatics," non-Egyptians as, 76, 106–7, 109
Assur-uballit, king of Assyria, 7, 48, 53, 149,
    150, 159
Assyria, empire of: commercial interests of,
    22, 52; description of, 7; rise of, 20, 61, 65,
    113, 144, 150, 211; status of, 48
Astarte, cult of, 76
Atamrum, king of Andarig, 240 n. 13
Autobiography of Harkhuf, 78

Avruch, Kevin, 193, 226, 228, 232
Aziru, ruler of Amurru: complaint against
    commissioners by, 136; fear of invasion
    by, 88; Hittite alliance with, 8, 62, 92, 111,
    119, 122–23; intelligence passed to
    Egyptians by, 92–93; loyalty of, 38; oath
    of safe conduct for, 39, 41; threatened by
    Egypt, 60, 62, 89–90, 93, 127, 249 n. 19; as
    threat to Byblos, 58, 116–17; tribute sent
    by, 129–30; at war with Biryawaza, 91

Babylonia (Karaduniyash, Shanhar), empire
    of: commercial interests of, 52;
    description of, 7; Egyptian alliance with,
    65, 66, 113, 150–51; marriage alliances with
    Egypt, 80
Babylonian language. *See* Akkadian
    (Babylonian) language
balance of power: in Amarna Age, 50–51,
    53, 63, 119–20, 230–32; and equilibrium,
    44, 51; between Hellenic city-states, 51;
    between states, 56, 61–62, 224
barbarians, 9, 23, 115–16. *See also* ʿApiru
    (*ḫabiru/ḫapiru*)
bargaining: ceremonial, 147–49;
    commitments in, 199–200; defined,
    263 n. 3; limits on, 106; pace of, 22, 203–4.
    See also negotiations
barter, 27
Batruna, city of, 94, 117
Beirut, city of, 117
Bekaa Valley, 92–93, 116
Berridge, Geoffrey, 228
Biridiya, ruler of Megiddo, 9, 130
Biryawaza, ruler of Damascus (Upe), 9, 91,
    111, 116, 117, 252 n. 7 (chap. 9)
Boghazköi archive (Hittite), 11, 15, 102, 141,
    144, 146
booty (plunder and tribute): disputed
    quality and value of, 148; from Hittites,
    206; from Syrian campaigns, 74, 75, 76,
    77; from vassal states, 103, 129–31. *See also*
    deliveries (Egyptian, *inw*); gift exchange
borders: securing of, 58–59, 101; and
    territoriality, 20
Bradbury, Louise, 72
brother (Akkadian, *aḫu*), 159, 194, 257 n. 20;
    "my brother" (*aḫī*), 18
brotherhood (Akkadian, *aḫḫūtu*), ideology
    of, 47, 49, 53, 57, 63–64, 79, 144–45, 159,
    166, 193, 228, 232–33, 234–35, 257 n. 20,
    268 n. 7; critique of, 176, 229

reciprocity: balanced (*cont.*)
exchange, 24, 25–26, 154–64; lacking in
vassal relations, 25, 105; in parity treaties,
39; rules of, 47–48; in trade, 146, 176, 227
recognition, desire for, 222
Redford, D. B., 131
redistribution, 161
Reshep, cult of, 76
Retenu (southern Levant), 72
Rib-Hadda, ruler of Byblos, 158;
intelligence reports and letters from, 8–9,
38, 58, 90–96, 116, 117, 118, 121, 126, 128,
129, 132, 135, 152–53, 156–57, 214;
Pharaoh's impatience with, 96–97, 104,
121, 134
royal inscriptions, 17, 21
royalty, defined, 166
rules: of etiquette, 33; of international
society, 47–48

Sahlins, M., 160
salutations, forms of, 18, 157–59, 193,
260 n. 21
sanctions, use of, 21
Saqqara, Memphite cemetery at, 109
Sasson, J., xiii
Saul, king of Israel, 31
Schelling, Thomas, 199, 200
Schulman, A., 169
scribes, 219
secondary states-system, defined, 43,
243 n. 30
Second Intermediate Period (Egypt), 81,
101, xiii
security dilemmas, 56, 62–63, 228
semiotics, 17, 192
Shamhuna, taxation of, 130
Shamshi-Adad, king of Mari, 215
Shattiwaza, king of Mittani, 6
Shechem (Šakmu), state of, 9, 115, 119–20
Shigata, city of, 117
Shubandu, tribute sent by, 130
Shuttarna II, king of Mittani, 206, 208
Sidon, city of, 79, 116, 117
silent trade, 23, 27
silver: trade in, 146; as tribute, 75, 76, 130
Sinai desert, 112, 114
Singer, I., 117
slavery metaphor, 29
Smenkhkare, Pharaoh, 6, 265 n. 9
Smith, Adam, 161
Sobekhotep (treasurer), 79

Sobeknofru, Queen, 82
social hierarchy, 29–30, 43, 49
social-psychological analysis, 3, 174–88
social rank, parity in, 25–26
sovereignty: conception of, 166–67,
257 n. 19; and divine kingship, 106, 107;
expressed in intermarriages, 171
space (spatial theory), 20, 232
spheres of interest, 63
spies and spying. *See* espionage
states: alliances between, 56, 61–62; balance
of power between, 56, 61–62; interests of,
53; international law between, 28–30;
offensive capability of, 55, 59–60; realist
assumptions of, 55–56; self-interests (self-
help) of, 56, 63, 64; struggle for power
between, 56, 60–61; survivability of, 56,
60; uncertain intentions of, 55, 59–60
status. *See* prestige (status)
Stinnett, Caskie, 193
strategic analysis, 3
submission: metaphors of, 159; rules of,
47, 48
Suemniwet, Theban tomb of, 74–75
summitry, 267 n. 67
Ṣumur, city of: Amurru occupation of, 8,
92, 94, 95, 117, 122; restored to Egypt, 137
Suppiluliuma, king of Hatti, 7, 31, 110, 160,
162, 185, 242 n. 41
suzerainty, 31–32, 123. *See also* Egypt,
expansion of power of; vassal states
symbolic anthropology, 155–56
symbolic representation, 193–94
Syria (modern): ancient international
relations in, 10, 11. *See also* Mittani
(Hanigalbat, Nahrin), empire of; Ugarit,
state of
Syria-Palestine, vassal states in, 8–9, 21

Tadu-Hepa, Queen, 80, 83, 84, 152, 210,
215–16
Tagi, ruler of Ginti-kirmil, 130
Takhsy, conquest of, 76
Tarhundaradu, king of Arzawa, 86
taxation: and territoriality, 20; of vassal
states, 130, 131
Tehu-Tessup, 91
Tell Brak (Syria), 75
Tell el-Amarna (Egypt), 1. *See also* Amarna
(Egypt)
Tell Rimah (Syria), 75
territoriality, 20

The Library of Congress has cataloged the hardcover edition of this book as follows:

Amarna diplomacy : the beginnings of international relations / edited by Raymond
Cohen and Raymond Westbrook.

    p.   cm.

    Includes bibliographical references and index.

    ISBN 0-8018-6199-3 (alk. paper)

       1. Middle East — Foreign relations. 2. Egypt — Foreign relations. 3. Middle East —
History — To 622. 4. Egypt — History — Eighteenth dynasty, ca. 1570–1320 B.C.
5. Diplomacy — History — To 1500. 6. Tell el-Amarna tablets. I. Cohen, Raymond,
1947- II. Westbrook, Raymond.

DS62.23 .A43 2000

327′.0939′409013 21 — dc21

                                                   99-030915

ISBN 0-8018-7103-4 (pbk.)